Securing Large Language Models Against Emerging Threats

Hewa Majeed Zangana
https://orcid.org/0000-0001-7909-254X
Duhok Polytechnic University, Iraq

Marwan Omar
https://orcid.org/0009-0000-7534-5490
Illinois Institute of Technology, USA

IGI Global
Scientific Publishing
Publishing Tomorrow's Research Today

Published in the United States of America by
IGI Global Scientific Publishing
701 East Chocolate Avenue
Hershey, PA, 17033, USA
Tel: 717-533-8845 | Fax: 717-533-7115
Website: https://www.igi-global.com E-mail: cust@igi-global.com

Library of Congress Cataloging-in-Publication Data

Names: Zangana, Hewa Majeed, 1987- editor | Omar, Marwan, 1982- editor
Title: Securing large language models against emerging threats / edited by: Hewa Majeed Zangana, Marwan Omar.
Description: Hershey PA : IGI Global Scientific Publishing, [2026] | Includes bibliographical references. | Summary: "This book aims to provide a comprehensive and authoritative resource on the security challenges, vulnerabilities, and defense strategies related to Large Language Models"-- Provided by publisher.
Identifiers: LCCN 2025043690 (print) | LCCN 2025043691 (ebook) | ISBN 9798337371337 hardcover | ISBN 9798337371344 paperback | ISBN 9798337371351 ebook
Subjects: LCSH: Natural language generation (Computer science)--Security measures | Generative artificial intelligence--Security measures | Deep learning (Machine learning)--Security measures
Classification: LCC QA76.9.N3 S43 2026 (print) | LCC QA76.9.N3 (ebook)
LC record available at https://lccn.loc.gov/2025043690
LC ebook record available at https://lccn.loc.gov/2025043691

British Cataloguing in Publication Data
A Cataloguing in Publication record for this book is available from the British Library.

Table of Contents

Detailed Table of Contents

Prompt injection attacks have emerged as a significant threat to large language models (LLMs), exploiting the model's prompt-based interaction to manipulate outputs, bypass security constraints, or extract sensitive information. These attacks pose risks across various applications, including chatbots, automated content generation, and decision support systems. This chapter provides a comprehensive overview of prompt injection attacks, categorizing attack vectors, illustrating real-world examples, and analyzing their potential consequences. It also examines current defense mechanisms, ranging from input sanitization and prompt filtering to advanced adversarial training techniques. By synthesizing recent research and practical insights, this chapter aims to guide researchers, practitioners, and system designers in understanding, mitigating, and preemptively defending against prompt injection threats, ensuring the safe deployment of LLMs in diverse domains.

The rapid adoption of large language models (LLMs) across industries has introduced new opportunities for innovation, while simultaneously creating complex security challenges. As adversarial actors exploit vulnerabilities in these models, proactive defense strategies become increasingly critical. Red teaming and stress-testing methodologies have emerged as essential mechanisms for evaluating and strengthening the resilience of LLMs against a broad spectrum of threats, including prompt injection, data poisoning, adversarial manipulation, and misuse scenarios. This chapter explores the principles, practices, and frameworks of red teaming applied to LLMs, emphasizing structured evaluation techniques, simulation of real-world attack vectors, and systematic stress-testing approaches. Furthermore, it highlights the integration of adversarial testing within development lifecycles, the importance of interdisciplinary collaboration, and the role of automation in scaling security evaluations.

Large Language Models (LLMs) are increasingly deployed across critical domains, from cybersecurity and healthcare to finance and education. While their capabilities have transformed automation and decision-making, these systems face significant challenges related to trust, security, and explainability. As adversarial attacks, data poisoning, and prompt manipulation continue to evolve, the lack of transparency in LLM decision-making undermines user confidence and regulatory compliance. This chapter introduces the concept of trustworthy and explainable LLM security frameworks, which integrate principles of interpretability, accountability, and robust defense mechanisms. By combining security-by-design approaches with explainable artificial intelligence (XAI) techniques, these frameworks aim to mitigate vulnerabilities while ensuring transparency in system outputs. The discussion highlights architectural considerations, governance models, and best practices that bridge the gap between technical resilience and human-centric trust. Furthermore, the chapter explores how explainability enhances threat detection, incident response, and ethical assurance, making LLMs more reliable in high-stakes environments. Ultimately, establishing trustworthy and explainable LLM security frameworks is not only a technical necessity but also a societal imperative for the responsible adoption of next-generation AI systems.

The integration of Large Language Models (LLMs) into agricultural systems has introduced significant opportunities for enhancing productivity, sustainability, and decision-making in smart farming. By leveraging LLMs, farmers and agribusinesses can optimize resource allocation, predict crop yields, detect diseases, and streamline supply chain management. However, as these systems become increasingly interconnected with the Internet of Things (IoT), cloud platforms, and autonomous technologies, they also face heightened cybersecurity vulnerabilities. Potential threats include adversarial attacks on LLMs, data poisoning, model manipulation, and unauthorized access to farm management systems. Such risks can compromise food security, disrupt operations, and erode trust in smart farming technologies. This chapter explores the cybersecurity challenges associated with LLM-driven agricultural systems and provides a comprehensive framework for mitigation

Preface

INTRODUCTION

The evolution of Large Language Models (LLMs) has profoundly reshaped the landscape of artificial intelligence, driving transformative advances in natural language processing, decision support, and automation. Yet, as these models have grown in complexity and capability, so too have the threats that target them. From adversarial manipulation to data privacy breaches, LLMs are increasingly situated at the intersection of innovation and risk. Ensuring their resilience has thus become a paramount priority for researchers, developers, and policymakers alike.

This book, *Securing Large Language Models Against Emerging Threats*, seeks to address the multifaceted security, ethical, and regulatory challenges surrounding LLMs. The volume brings together international experts who explore adversarial threats, governance frameworks, technical mitigation strategies, and real-world applications that highlight both the potential and the peril of this powerful technology. By bridging theoretical foundations with applied perspectives, the chapters collectively provide a roadmap toward trustworthy, secure, and accountable AI systems.

In assembling this work, our goal has been to create a comprehensive reference that not only documents existing vulnerabilities but also charts a path toward proactive defense mechanisms. LLM security is not a problem to be solved once, but an evolving frontier—one that demands interdisciplinary collaboration across computer science, policy, ethics, and human-centered design. The insights gathered here aim to empower readers to anticipate, mitigate, and ultimately outpace the next generation of AI threats.

CHAPTER OVERVIEW

Chapter 1: Adversarial Threats and Vulnerabilities in Large Language Models

Hewa Zangana, Marwan Omar, Firas Mustafa, and Sharyar Wani provide a foundational examination of adversarial threats to LLMs. This chapter categorizes and analyzes attack vectors such as data poisoning, prompt injection, and model inversion, laying the groundwork for understanding the fragility of these systems when faced with malicious manipulation.

Chapter 2: Legal and Policy Frameworks for Securing Large Language Models

Dilshad Mhia-alddin explores the evolving regulatory and ethical landscape that governs LLM security. The chapter emphasizes accountability, compliance, and governance strategies that balance innovation with responsibility in both national and international contexts.

Chapter 3: Leveraging LLMs for Financial Fraud Detection and Secure Auditing

Syed Raza, Rindah Suryawati, and Wisam Gwad illustrate how LLMs can strengthen financial systems through fraud detection and auditing mechanisms. This chapter highlights both the potential benefits and the associated risks of deploying AI-driven tools in sensitive financial environments.

Chapter 4: Misuse of LLMs in Cybercrime and Countermeasures

Luay Albtosh and Ade Surahman explore how LLMs are weaponized for cybercrime—through phishing, misinformation, and malicious code generation—and propose comprehensive countermeasures that integrate technical, ethical, and regulatory defenses.

Chapter 5: Prompt Injection Attacks — Risks and Defense Mechanisms

Rebet Jones and Aquil Mohammed dissect the growing threat of prompt injection attacks. Their analysis introduces practical prevention strategies, including adversarial training, input sanitization, and secure prompt engineering.

Chapter 6: Red Teaming and Stress-Testing Methodologies for LLM Security

Luay Albtosh and Widi Aribowo present structured red teaming and stress-testing frameworks designed to evaluate LLM robustness under simulated adversarial conditions. Their chapter highlights the importance of continuous testing as part of secure development lifecycles.

Chapter 7: Trustworthy and Explainable LLM Security Frameworks

Naresh Tiwari and Sachi Mohanty advance the discussion by proposing explainable security frameworks that emphasize interpretability, accountability, and transparency—key principles for building user trust in AI systems.

Chapter 8: Protecting LLM-Driven Agricultural Systems — Cybersecurity Risks and Mitigation in Smart Farming

Rebet Jones and Senny Luckyardi close the volume by extending the discussion of LLM security into the agricultural domain. Their chapter underscores the need for robust defenses in smart farming systems, where LLMs intersect with IoT and cloud technologies.

CONCLUSION

The collective insights in this volume affirm that securing Large Language Models is not merely a technical challenge but a societal imperative. As AI systems increasingly influence global infrastructure, finance, healthcare, and communication, their vulnerabilities become inseparable from our collective resilience. Addressing these risks requires not only innovative technologies but also ethical foresight and coordinated governance.

Looking ahead, the emerging field of LLM security will demand a blend of continuous monitoring, red teaming, privacy preservation, and explainability to ensure sustainable trust in AI systems. The contributions gathered here provide a foundation upon which future research, policy, and practice can build—advancing a more secure and transparent AI ecosystem.

We extend our gratitude to the contributing authors for their scholarly dedication and to the reviewers and collaborators who helped refine this collection. We hope that this book serves as both a reference and a catalyst—guiding researchers, practitioners, and policymakers toward a safer digital future shaped by responsible, resilient, and secure large language models.

Chapter 1
Adversarial Threats and Vulnerabilities in Large Language Models

Hewa Majeed Zangana
https://orcid.org/0000-0001-7909-254X
Duhok Polytechnic University, Iraq

Marwan Omar
https://orcid.org/0009-0000-7534-5490
Illinois Institute of Technology, USA

Firas Mahmood Mustafa
https://orcid.org/0000-0002-8757-5303
Duhok Polytechnic University, Iraq

Sharyar Wani
https://orcid.org/0000-0001-6812-0066
Kulliyyah of Information and Communication Technology, International Islamic University Malaysia, Malaysia

ABSTRACT

Large Language Models (LLMs) have revolutionized natural language processing by enabling advanced text generation, contextual reasoning, and decision support across domains. However, their widespread adoption has also exposed them to adversarial threats and vulnerabilities that pose significant security, ethical, and operational challenges. Attack vectors such as data poisoning, prompt injection, model inversion, and evasion techniques highlight the fragility of LLMs when confronted with malicious actors. These vulnerabilities can lead to privacy breaches, misinformation propagation, biased outputs, and systemic exploitation of model

DOI: 10.4018/979-8-3373-7133-7.ch001

behavior. Understanding adversarial threats is therefore crucial for safeguarding the reliability, trustworthiness, and resilience of LLMs in critical applications. This chapter provides an in-depth examination of common adversarial techniques, their underlying mechanisms, and the risks they introduce. It also explores the intersection of security, privacy, and robustness in LLM deployment, offering a foundation for developing defense strategies and future research directions

1. INTRODUCTION

The advent of Large Language Models (LLMs) has marked a transformative era in artificial intelligence (AI), reshaping natural language processing, information retrieval, decision support, and cybersecurity. From foundational models such as BERT, GPT, and LLaMA to specialized domain-oriented adaptations, LLMs have demonstrated remarkable ability in generating coherent text, analyzing threats, and supporting human decision-making across diverse industries (AlQenaei, 2024; Xu et al., 2024). These advancements have spurred both opportunities and risks: while LLMs empower cyber defense, forensic analysis, and digital transformation, they also introduce novel adversarial threats and vulnerabilities that malicious actors can exploit (Chen et al., 2024; Motlagh et al., 2024). Understanding these risks is essential for safeguarding data integrity, privacy, and trust in critical applications.

Recent scholarship highlights that LLMs are increasingly employed in cybersecurity operations, particularly in cyber threat detection, intrusion prediction, and vulnerability analysis (Ferrag et al., 2023; Ferrag, Ndhlovu, Tihanyi, Cordeiro, Debbah, & Lestable, 2024). For instance, lightweight privacy-preserving BERT-based frameworks have been designed for IoT and IIoT devices to mitigate adversarial cyberattacks (Ferrag, Ndhlovu, Tihanyi, Cordeiro, Debbah, Lestable, & Thandi, 2024). Similarly, tailored security language models such as SecLM have been introduced to enhance threat mitigation through specialized architectures (Asoronye et al., 2024). In addition, scholars argue that the integration of generative AI in cybersecurity broadens the landscape for defensive automation and predictive intelligence (Sarker, 2024; Kasri et al., 2025).

In digital forensics, AI and LLMs have revolutionized investigation workflows by assisting with evidence classification, anomaly detection, and knowledge extraction (Adam & Varol, 2020; Costantini et al., 2019; Bhawna & Mahajan, 2024). The field has progressed from early applications of AI in pattern matching (Mitchell, 2014; Ganesh, 2017) to intelligent forensics integrating explainable AI for legal and investigative reliability (Hall et al., 2022; Kelly et al., 2020). Scholars emphasize the transition from traditional digital forensics toward intelligent and AI-enhanced practices (Irons & Lallie, 2014; Moustafa, 2022; Omar & Zangana, 2025). These innovations, while beneficial, simultaneously expose forensic systems to adversarial manipulations, where attackers can deceive automated evidence processing or inject false traces (Jeong, 2020; Manasa & Kumar, 2022).

Despite their success, LLMs remain susceptible to adversarial exploitation. Techniques such as prompt injection, data poisoning, model inversion, and jailbreak attacks threaten both user safety and organizational security (Hasanov et al., 2024; Hassanin & Moustafa, 2024). Researchers warn that LLM-driven systems may inadvertently generate biased, misleading, or harmful outputs that adversaries can weaponize (Ali & Aysan, 2025; Shukla & Taneja, 2024). For example, manipulation of model prompts can bypass content restrictions or trigger unintended behaviors, compromising applications in finance (Ali & Aysan, 2024; Ali, Zafar, & Aysan, 2024), healthcare (Trotsyuk et al., 2024; Huff et al., 2023), and critical infrastructure (Maguluri et al., 2023; Arya & Rastogi, 2024).

Cybersecurity researchers have also identified systemic risks stemming from the widespread adoption of LLMs in enterprise and industry ecosystems. Studies demonstrate that adversarial threats may escalate into large-scale misinformation, intellectual property theft, and targeted cyberattacks (Gupta et al., 2024; Ghazal et al., 2024). Furthermore, ethical hacking experiments integrating AI reveal the dual-use nature of such models: while they improve penetration testing and vulnerability assessment, they also lower the barrier for malicious exploitation (Al-Sinani & Mitchell, 2024; Al-Sinani, Sahli, Mitchell, & Al-Siyabi, 2025).

The vulnerabilities of LLMs do not exist in a vacuum—they intersect with ethical, regulatory, and societal concerns. Scholars emphasize the ethical dilemmas associated with LLM misuse, particularly around data privacy, misinformation, and biased decision-making (Veluru, 2024; Verma & Rohit, 2024). Legal frameworks such as the European Union's Artificial Intelligence Act are being developed to mitigate these risks by regulating AI deployment (Butt, 2024). At the same time, discussions around AI in warfare (Batabyal, 2024), law and policy (Zangana, Al-Karaki, & Omar, 2025), and biomedical research misuse (Trotsyuk et al., 2024) underscore the urgency of addressing adversarial manipulation at both national and global levels.

The literature further suggests that ethical governance must extend to academic and research contexts, ensuring that scientific innovation using LLMs does not compromise integrity or safety (Filetti et al., 2024; Leontidis, 2024; Zangana & Omar, 2025). In addition, the responsible use of AI in digital forensics and cybercrime investigation requires balancing innovation with accountability (Zangana & Omar, 2026).

Efforts to secure LLMs against adversarial threats are advancing across technical and strategic dimensions. Research explores the integration of explainable AI, quantum computing, and hybrid machine learning approaches for more robust cybersecurity solutions (Campus, 2024; Eswaran & Eswaran, 2025; Yu et al., 2024). Proposals such as the GEADD method for zero-day attack detection leverage enhanced LLM capabilities to counter sophisticated threats (Jones & Omar, 2024; Jones et al., 2023). Moreover, defensive AI paradigms emphasize building specialized LLMs capable of predicting cyberattacks before they occur (Diaf et al., 2024; Taghavi & Feyzi, 2024).

Scholars highlight the role of human-centric strategies in mitigating adversarial threats, arguing that cybersecurity must remain socio-technical rather than purely algorithmic (Fenwick et al., 2024; Santos et al., 2024). Cross-domain analyses also reveal that adversarial threats in finance, industry, and defense share common vulnerabilities that LLM security frameworks must address (Rashid & Kausik, 2024; Pleshakova et al., 2024; Karim et al., 2023).

As the integration of LLMs deepens across industries, adversarial threats and vulnerabilities pose significant risks to privacy, security, and ethical governance. From digital forensics to financial systems, from healthcare to defense, adversarial exploitation of LLMs could undermine trust in AI-driven infrastructures. Consequently, there is a pressing need to bridge technological innovations with regulatory safeguards, ethical considerations, and resilient design principles. The subsequent sections of this chapter will analyze adversarial threats in detail, classify vulnerabilities, and propose pathways toward securing LLMs against emerging risks in an evolving digital ecosystem.

2. FUNDAMENTALS OF ADVERSARIAL THREATS IN AI

Artificial intelligence (AI) systems, and particularly large language models (LLMs), have become cornerstones of modern digital infrastructures, powering applications across finance, healthcare, cybersecurity, education, and defense. However, as these models proliferate, they introduce new attack surfaces and adversarial vulnerabilities that malicious actors can exploit. Understanding the fundamentals of adversarial threats in AI requires exploring their origins, types, and the interdisciplinary frameworks that enable detection, investigation, and mitigation.

2.1 Defining Adversarial Threats in AI

Adversarial threats refer to deliberate manipulations of AI systems designed to deceive, disrupt, or exploit their decision-making processes. Early research in computer forensics recognized the dangers of automation and machine intelligence in investigations, emphasizing the dual-use nature of AI technologies (Ganesh, 2017; Irons & Lallie, 2014; Mitchell, 2014). As AI moved into cybersecurity and digital forensics, concerns expanded from data authenticity to sophisticated manipulations capable of bypassing detection (Iqbal et al., 2020; Costantini et al., 2019; Jeong, 2020).

In modern contexts, adversarial threats manifest through input perturbations, data poisoning, prompt injection, and model inversion attacks (Xu et al., 2024; Motlagh et al., 2024; Hassanin & Moustafa, 2024). These threats compromise both the integrity of outputs and the confidentiality of underlying training data, creating risks for critical infrastructure and national security.

2.2 Categories of Adversarial Threats

Scholars classify adversarial threats into several categories:

- Data Poisoning Attacks: Manipulating training data to embed vulnerabilities, undermining model reliability (Taghavi & Feyzi, 2024; Ali, Zafar, & Aysan, 2024).
- Evasion Attacks: Crafting malicious inputs that cause misclassification, particularly concerning in cybersecurity defenses (Ferrag et al., 2023; Chen et al., 2024).
- Model Inversion and Extraction: Reverse-engineering private model parameters or sensitive training data (Xu et al., 2024; Sarker, 2024).
- Prompt Injection in LLMs: Exploiting natural language prompts to trigger undesired behaviors, leading to disinformation or policy circumvention (AlQenaei, 2024; Kasri et al., 2025).
- Backdoor Attacks: Embedding hidden triggers in models to be activated under specific conditions (Diaf et al., 2024; Manoharan & Sarker, 2023).

Each category reflects the adaptive nature of attackers, who exploit weaknesses across the AI development and deployment lifecycle.

Figure 1 illustrates the main categories of adversarial threats against LLMs, including data poisoning, evasion, model inversion, prompt injection, and backdoor attacks. This flowchart highlights how adversaries exploit vulnerabilities at different stages of model training and deployment.

Figure 1. Categories of adversarial threats in Large Language Models

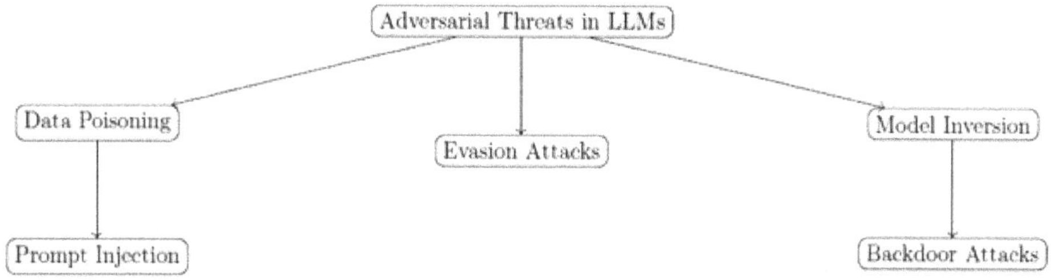

2.3 The Role of Cybersecurity and Digital Forensics

Digital forensics has played a vital role in identifying and analyzing adversarial threats. Early efforts emphasized moving from traditional digital forensics to intelligent forensics that integrate AI for proactive defense (Adam & Varol, 2020; Dunsin et al., 2022; Bhawna & Mahajan, 2024). Modern frameworks incorporate explainable AI (XAI) to improve transparency in investigations, enabling investigators to understand how adversarial perturbations impact model decisions (Hall et al., 2022; Kelly et al., 2020).

Recent works propose specialized LLMs such as SecLM, designed for threat mitigation in cybersecurity contexts (Asoronye et al., 2024), while others focus on hybrid AI-forensics approaches in constrained or cloud-based environments (Hamza & Omar, 2013; Dunsin et al., 2024; Omar & Zangana, 2025). These advances highlight the synergy between AI-enabled threat detection and forensic validation (Karthikeyan et al., 2023; Sikos, 2021).

2.4 Ethical, Legal, and Strategic Dimensions

The rise of adversarial threats cannot be separated from ethical and regulatory considerations. Research stresses the importance of ensuring ethical AI in defense (Batabyal, 2024), finance (Ali & Aysan, 2024, 2025), and education (Jamro & Jamro, 2023; Shukla & Taneja, 2024). The European Union AI Act (Butt, 2024) and domain-specific policies (Zangana, Al-Karaki, & Omar, 2025) reflect global attempts to standardize security and ethical norms.

Strategically, adversarial AI also intersects with warfare and national security, where autonomous systems and LLM-driven decision-making introduce new vulnerabilities (Arya & Rastogi, 2024; Maguluri et al., 2023). The misuse of AI in biomedical research further underscores the need for comprehensive risk frameworks (Trotsyuk et al., 2024).

2.5 Foundations for Defense and Mitigation

Scholars propose several foundational principles for defending against adversarial threats:

1. Robust Model Architectures: Continuous optimization of language models to withstand manipulation (AlQenaei, 2024; Liu, 2024).
2. Explainability and Transparency: Leveraging XAI to make adversarial impacts visible (Jeong, 2020; Eisenberg, 2024).
3. Specialized AI for Security: Development of cybersecurity-specific LLMs (Ferrag et al., 2024; Asoronye et al., 2024).
4. Policy and Governance: Establishing ethical and legal frameworks to manage misuse (Omar & Zangana, 2024; Zangana & Omar, 2025).

These foundations align with the emerging paradigm of quantum-aware AI security, which integrates advances in quantum machine learning to enhance resilience (Campus, 2024; Eswaran & Eswaran, 2025; Zangana & Omar, 2025).

3. TYPES OF ADVERSARIAL THREATS IN LLMS

Large Language Models (LLMs) have demonstrated remarkable success across domains, but their rapid adoption has also introduced a spectrum of adversarial threats. These threats are not only technical but also ethical, social, and regulatory in nature, reflecting the multi-dimensional risks of LLM deployment (Ali & Aysan, 2025; Gupta, Gaurav, & Arya, 2024; Xu et al., 2024). Below, key categories of adversarial threats in LLMs are discussed in detail.

3.1. Data Poisoning Attacks

Data poisoning occurs when adversaries manipulate training datasets to introduce malicious patterns, resulting in biased or harmful outputs at inference time. Poisoned data can propagate misinformation, compromise fairness, or embed hidden backdoors (Chen et al., 2024; Motlagh et al., 2024). In digital forensics, such tampering can obscure evidence or mislead investigations (Adam & Varol, 2020; Dunsin, Ghanem, Ouazzane, & Vassilev, 2024). LLM poisoning is especially concerning in domains like finance and biomedical research, where data integrity directly impacts decision-making (Ali, Zafar, & Aysan, 2024; Trotsyuk et al., 2024).

3.2. Prompt Injection and Manipulation

Prompt injection exploits the reliance of LLMs on user-supplied instructions by embedding adversarial inputs that override intended behavior. Such attacks can bypass safety filters, generate disallowed content, or leak sensitive information (Ferrag, Alwahedi, Battah, Cherif, Mechri, & Tihanyi, 2024; Sarker, 2024). This vulnerability resonates with earlier cybersecurity concerns around input manipulation, such as command injection in network systems (Hamza & Omar, 2013; Wright, Dawson Jr., & Omar, 2012). Newer work highlights how attackers craft prompts to execute phishing, social engineering, or malware generation (Gaurav et al., 2024; Kasri et al., 2025).

3.3. Model Inversion and Membership Inference

Model inversion attacks aim to reconstruct sensitive training data from exposed model outputs, while membership inference attempts to determine whether a given data record was part of the training dataset. Both attacks pose severe privacy risks, particularly when LLMs are trained on proprietary or personal datasets (Hasanov, Virtanen, Hakkala, & Isoaho, 2024; Taghavi & Feyzi, 2024). In cybersecurity, inversion parallels challenges in digital forensics, where adversaries attempt to extract hidden evidence from encrypted or anonymized systems (Iqbal, Debbabi, & Fung, 2020; Jeong, 2020).

3.4. Evasion and Adversarial Examples

Evasion attacks involve crafting adversarial examples—inputs designed to mislead an LLM without being detectable to humans. For example, malicious actors may slightly alter a prompt or obfuscate code to evade security classifiers (Ferrag, Ndhlovu, Tihanyi, Cordeiro, Debbah, & Lestable, 2023; Hassanin & Moustafa, 2024). In sectors such as defense and aerospace, these attacks raise national security concerns by enabling adversaries to exploit automated decision-making pipelines (Arya & Rastogi, 2024; Batabyal, 2024).

3.5. Backdoor and Trojan Attacks

Backdoor attacks insert hidden triggers into training datasets, enabling attackers to activate malicious behavior in models under specific conditions. For LLMs, this may manifest as harmful content generation or misinformation when triggered by certain keywords (Alturkistani & Chuprat, 2024; Kasri et al., 2025). Such covert manipulation has parallels in digital forensics, where concealed malware functions compromise investigation integrity (Irons & Lallie, 2014; Moustafa, 2022).

3.6. Misuse and Dual-Use Risks

Beyond direct adversarial attacks, LLMs face threats from misuse, where legitimate capabilities are repurposed for malicious activities. Examples include generating phishing emails, crafting deepfake text, or automating cyberattacks (Ghazal et al., 2024; Santos, Salam, & Dahir, 2024). Ethical concerns around dual-use echo broader debates on AI in warfare and security (Batabyal, 2024; Veluru, 2024). Research shows that adversaries can exploit LLMs for scalable, automated attacks, amplifying risks across financial, healthcare, and educational domains (Ali & Aysan, 2024; Jamro & Jamro, 2023; Pimpalkar, Wankhade, Chole, & Golhar, 2024).

3.7. Supply Chain and Infrastructure Threats

Threats also emerge from the infrastructure underpinning LLMs, including compromised APIs, malicious plug-ins, or vulnerable deployment environments (Omar & Zangana, 2024; Zangana, Al-Karaki, & Omar, 2025). These supply chain vulnerabilities mirror historical challenges in cloud and mobile security (Hamza & Omar, 2013; Wright et al., 2012). Ethical hacking studies demonstrate how AI can both expose and mitigate these risks (Al-Sinani & Mitchell, 2024; Al-Sinani, Sahli, Mitchell, & Al-Siyabi, 2025).

3.8. Emerging and Complex Threats

Recent literature emphasizes that adversarial threats to LLMs evolve continuously, often combining multiple attack vectors. Hybrid attacks—such as poisoned data that later enables prompt injection—pose complex defense challenges (Diaf, Korba, Karabadji, & Ghamri-Doudane, 2024; San Biagio, Cipolla, La Mattina, & Morreale, 2023). Scholars argue that integrating digital forensics with LLM-based cybersecurity can provide resilience against such multifaceted threats (Bhawna & Mahajan, 2024; Omar & Zangana, 2025; Zangana & Omar, 2026).

4. IMPACT OF ADVERSARIAL THREATS

Adversarial threats to Large Language Models (LLMs) represent a profound challenge for modern cybersecurity, digital forensics, and trustworthy artificial intelligence. While LLMs have demonstrated transformative power across finance, healthcare, defense, and scientific research, adversarial manipulations can destabilize their effectiveness, exploit vulnerabilities, and cause severe operational, ethical, and societal consequences (Ali & Aysan, 2024; Chen et al., 2024; Xu et al., 2024).

The impact of adversarial threats spans multiple domains, from direct security risks to broader societal consequences. Figure 2 summarizes the multi-dimensional effects of adversarial manipulations on cybersecurity, digital forensics, ethics, and national security.

Figure 2. Impact areas of adversarial threats in LLMs

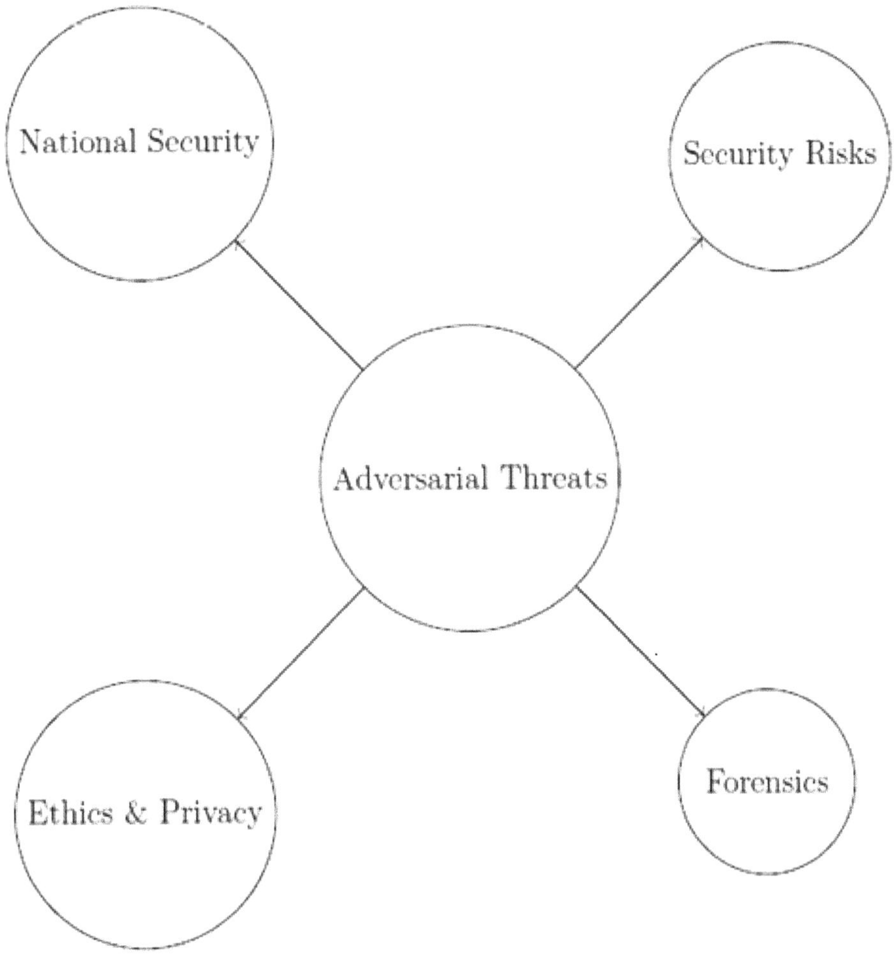

4.1. Security Risks and Exploitation

Adversarial actors exploit weaknesses in LLMs to compromise sensitive systems and critical infrastructure. Techniques such as prompt injection, data poisoning, and model inversion allow attackers to manipulate outputs, extract confidential information, or bypass detection frameworks (Ferrag, Ndhlovu, Tihanyi, Cordeiro, Debbah, & Lestable, 2023; Motlagh et al., 2024). In high-stakes environments such as defense and border protection, these risks amplify, as autonomous and aerial systems become increasingly reliant on AI (Arya & Rastogi, 2024; Batabyal, 2024). The misuse of

LLMs in cybercrime further echoes long-standing challenges in mobile and cloud computing threats (Hamza & Omar, 2013; Wright, Dawson Jr, & Omar, 2012).

4.2. Impacts on Cybersecurity and Digital Forensics

Adversarial threats complicate digital forensics by generating misleading evidence, obfuscating attack traces, and introducing noise that challenges investigators (Adam & Varol, 2020; Bhawna & Mahajan, 2024; Dunsin, Ghanem, Ouazzane, & Vassilev, 2024). AI-driven forensic tools—while powerful—are themselves vulnerable to adversarial manipulation, which can undermine the chain of custody and the integrity of investigations (Costantini, De Gasperis, & Olivieri, 2019; Hall, Sakzad, & Choo, 2022). Forensic scholars highlight that moving from traditional approaches to intelligent forensics necessitates AI systems resilient against adversarial noise (Irons & Lallie, 2014; Jeong, 2020).

4.3. Ethical, Privacy, and Societal Implications

The misuse of LLMs introduces ethical challenges such as misinformation, privacy violations, and systemic bias (Ali & Aysan, 2025; Shukla & Taneja, 2024; Veluru, 2024). Adversarial attacks targeting generative AI models in finance and enterprise systems may manipulate predictions, destabilize markets, or breach sensitive consumer data (Ali, Zafar, & Aysan, 2024; Gupta, Gaurav, & Arya, 2024; Shafik, 2024). Ethical AI frameworks call for transparency and accountability to mitigate risks of large-scale misuse (Verma & Rohit, 2024; Trotsyuk et al., 2024). Furthermore, misuse of LLMs in biomedical and STEM research contexts introduces risks of dual-use knowledge, demanding governance mechanisms (Zangana & Omar, 2025; Zangana, Al-Karaki, & Omar, 2025).

4.4. Sector-Specific Consequences

Adversarial threats manifest differently across industries:

- **Healthcare and biotechnology**: Malicious manipulations threaten research integrity, patient safety, and data confidentiality (Huff et al., 2023; Trotsyuk et al., 2024).
- **Finance**: Generative AI attacks can exploit algorithmic trading or credit scoring systems (Ali & Aysan, 2024; Ali et al., 2024).
- **Smart cities and IoT**: Lightweight LLM models for IoT devices are highly exposed to adversarial risks (Ferrag, Ndhlovu, Tihanyi, Cordeiro, Debbah, Lestable, & Thandi, 2024; Maguluri, Arularasan, & Boopathi, 2023).

- **Education and knowledge management**: Adversarial misuse of AI-powered chatbots and content generation tools risks spreading misinformation to students and researchers (Jamro & Jamro, 2023; Filetti, Fenza, & Gallo, 2024; Luan et al., 2024).

4.5. National Security and Defense

Adversarial LLM threats hold implications for national security, including misinformation campaigns, cyber warfare, and autonomous weapons manipulation (Batabyal, 2024; Pleshakova et al., 2024; Santos, Salam, & Dahir, 2024). Adversarial misuse could disrupt cyber threat intelligence pipelines (Alturkistani & Chuprat, 2024; Hasanov, Virtanen, Hakkala, & Isoaho, 2024) or compromise predictive defense systems (Diaf et al., 2024). The integration of LLMs in military and defense contexts thus necessitates robust oversight mechanisms (Kasri et al., 2025; Sarker, 2024).

4.6. Amplification of Threats by Emerging Technologies

Emerging technologies such as quantum computing and advanced networking further amplify the impact of adversarial threats. Quantum-enhanced adversarial methods could exploit vulnerabilities in cryptographic defenses, undermining LLM-based cybersecurity systems (Campus, 2024; Eswaran & Eswaran, 2025; Zangana & Omar, 2025). Similarly, the combination of adversarial AI with autonomous drones, robotics, and industrial systems creates multi-vector threats (Manasa & Kumar, 2022; Maguluri et al., 2023).

4.7. Policy, Regulation, and Governance Impacts

The impact of adversarial threats also extends into regulatory and governance domains. Legislations such as the European Union's Artificial Intelligence Act recognize the risks of adversarial misuse and emphasize compliance frameworks (Butt, 2024). Scholars argue that governance models must integrate both ethical and technical perspectives to counter systemic risks (Zangana, Al-Karaki, & Omar, 2025). Human-centric adoption of AI in enterprises must account for the adversarial landscape to ensure responsible integration (Fenwick, Molnar, & Frangos, 2024; Rashid & Kausik, 2024).

4.8. Broader Scientific and Research Ecosystems

Adversarial threats to LLMs undermine scientific integrity by introducing fabricated data, manipulated research findings, or biased outputs in automated analysis pipelines (Leontidis, 2024; Rodriguez & Storer, 2020). They also distort scientometric analyses, leading to skewed academic insights (Luan et al., 2024). Researchers and publishers must implement robust AI-driven safeguards against such risks to maintain trust in the scientific ecosystem (Filetti et al., 2024; Verma & Rohit, 2024).

To contextualize adversarial threats, Figure 3 maps key case study domains—cybersecurity, digital forensics, finance, defense, and governance—where LLMs are simultaneously transformative and vulnerable to attack.

Figure 3. Case study domains demonstrating LLM adversarial vulnerabilities

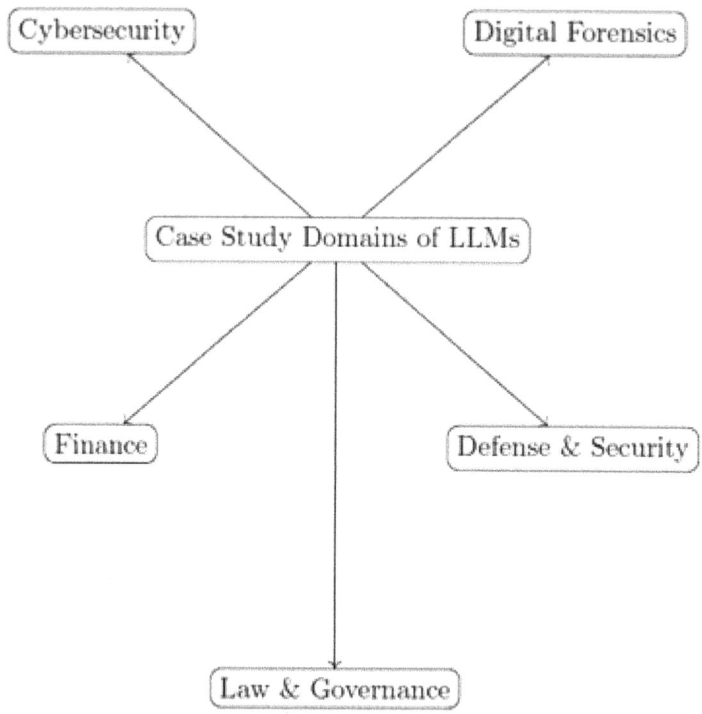

5. CASE STUDIES AND REAL-WORLD EXAMPLES

The integration of Large Language Models (LLMs) into critical domains has already demonstrated both transformative benefits and serious vulnerabilities. This section presents diverse case studies and real-world examples illustrating how adversarial threats, misuse, and defensive innovations have shaped the security landscape of LLMs across sectors such as cybersecurity, finance, digital forensics, defense, healthcare, and governance.

5.1. LLMs in Cybersecurity Defense and Threat Detection

Recent studies have highlighted the effectiveness of LLMs in improving cyber threat intelligence, detection, and mitigation. Ferrag et al. (2023, 2024) and Thandi (2024) proposed privacy-preserving, BERT-based lightweight models for IoT/IIoT devices, enabling organizations to counter zero-day threats in constrained environments. Similarly, Motlagh et al. (2024), Xu et al. (2024), and Hasanov et al. (2024) conducted systematic reviews confirming the potential of LLMs to support automated defense systems, though vulnerabilities to adversarial manipulation remain.

Chen et al. (2024) and Hassanin and Moustafa (2024) surveyed the broader landscape of LLM-based cyber defenses, revealing gaps in robustness against prompt injection and data poisoning. Jones and Omar (2024) introduced the GEADD method, integrating GPT-2 for zero-day attack detection, which was validated in high-risk scenarios. Case studies by Jones et al. (2023) further demonstrated how LLMs can accelerate cybersecurity workflows by combining detection accuracy with speed.

Practical applications also include specialized security-focused LLMs, such as SecLM (Asoronye et al., 2024), developed for advanced threat mitigation, and predictive frameworks for IoT attacks (Diaf et al., 2024). Kasri et al. (2025) emphasized how LLM-driven defenses can evolve from vulnerability detection toward proactive response. Ghazal et al. (2024) explored combining LLMs with explainable AI to boost transparency in critical infrastructures.

5.2. LLMs in Digital Forensics and Incident Response

The integration of AI and LLMs into digital forensics is well-documented (Adam & Varol, 2020; Costantini et al., 2019; Ganesh, 2017; Iqbal et al., 2020). Researchers have shown how automated forensic workflows improve evidence collection and analysis. Irons and Lallie (2014) introduced the concept of intelligent forensics, while Sikos (2021) advanced ontology-based cybercrime investigations. More recent works, such as Omar and Zangana (2025), contextualize these innovations in the era of AI, highlighting both benefits and risks.

Case studies in constrained environments (Dunsin et al., 2022; Dunsin et al., 2024) demonstrated how AI-assisted forensics can maintain efficiency under limited computational resources. Jarrett and Choo (2021) and Hall et al. (2022) emphasized the importance of explainability, particularly in judicial contexts, while Kelly et al. (2020) applied XAI approaches in drug testing case studies.

Practical forensic applications of LLMs include cloud-based investigations (Hamza & Omar, 2013), AI-enhanced ethical hacking (Al-Sinani & Mitchell, 2024; Al-Sinani et al., 2025), and forensic analysis of AI-driven attacks (Manasa & Kumar, 2022). These examples highlight both the expanded investigative capabilities of AI-enhanced systems and the adversarial risks they must address.

5.3. Finance, Enterprise, and Critical Industries

In the financial sector, LLMs have enabled advanced fraud detection and compliance monitoring. Ali, Zafar, and Aysan (2024) and Ali and Aysan (2024, 2025) provided multi-level analyses of LLM use in finance, revealing ethical and systemic risks associated with adversarial exploitation. Gupta, Gaurav, and Arya (2024) examined enterprise information systems, underscoring challenges in balancing efficiency with resilience against adversarial threats.

Beyond finance, Fenwick et al. (2024) studied how AI-driven transformation in human resource management relies on ethical AI deployment, while Flannery et al. (2021) and Maennig (2014) provided case evidence from safety and doping regulation to illustrate risks of AI misuse in industry. Huff et al. (2023) presented management practices for mitigating LLM-driven risks in biotechnology and healthcare organizations.

5.4. Defense, Security, and Warfare

LLMs have raised ethical and security concerns in military and defense settings. Batabyal (2024) examined AI-driven warfare ethics, while Maguluri et al. (2023) assessed risks in AI-based drones for smart cities. Arya and Rastogi (2024) explored aerial monitoring systems in defense contexts. Pleshakova et al. (2024) discussed the transition toward AGI-driven cybersecurity paradigms, emphasizing national security implications.

Case evidence also includes predictive clustering of online threats (San Biagio et al., 2023) and AI in law enforcement applications (Vyawahare et al., 2024). These studies illustrate the potential of adversarial manipulation in sensitive domains where misinformation or exploitation could have devastating consequences.

5.5. Legal, Policy, and Ethical Case Studies

Governance frameworks are critical to mitigating LLM vulnerabilities. Butt (2024) analyzed the EU AI Act, while Zangana, Omar, and colleagues (2025a, 2025b, 2025c, 2026a, 2026b) edited multiple works addressing law, policy, ethics, and governance of AI and LLMs. These volumes provide detailed case studies on ethical governance, quantum-aware cybersecurity, and STM research.

Shafik (2024) and Shukla and Taneja (2024) examined data privacy risks in LLM-enabled systems such as ChatGPT, while Verma and Rohit (2024) investigated ethical AI in scholarly communication. Trotsyuk et al. (2024) provided biomedical case studies, highlighting misuse potential in sensitive research. Veluru (2024) and Rashid and Kausik (2024) further illustrated AI misuse challenges in enterprise and global industries.

5.6. Emerging Domains and Future-Oriented Cases

Emerging applications include LLMs in scientometrics (Luan et al., 2024), research support (Filetti et al., 2024; Leontidis, 2024), women's safety (Pimpalkar et al., 2024; Vyawahare et al., 2024), and networking (Santos et al., 2024). Campus (2024) and Eswaran and Eswaran (2025) examined the convergence of quantum computing and AI, offering case perspectives for future hybrid security systems.

Studies by Rodriguez and Storer (2020) and Jamro and Jamro (2023) also illustrated how adversarial threats could affect AI in education and social sciences. Meanwhile, Karim et al. (2023) and Karthikeyan et al. (2023) compiled broad case collections of AI forensics, further reinforcing cross-domain applicability and associated vulnerabilities.

6. DETECTION AND DEFENSE STRATEGIES

The increasing reliance on Large Language Models (LLMs) across industries has created new attack surfaces, making the detection and defense of adversarial threats a pressing priority. Adversarial attacks—including prompt injection, data poisoning, model inversion, and evasion—threaten the confidentiality, integrity, and availability of AI systems (Jeong, 2020; Hadi, Abdulredha, & Hasan, 2023). This section explores contemporary detection methods, defense mechanisms, and integrated frameworks that leverage artificial intelligence, ethical considerations, and policy measures to ensure the robustness and trustworthiness of LLMs.

6.1. Detection Mechanisms for Adversarial Threats

Detection strategies aim to identify malicious activity before it compromises LLM performance. Several approaches integrate artificial intelligence into digital forensics and cyber threat intelligence. AI-enhanced forensic methodologies combine pattern recognition, anomaly detection, and explainable models to uncover hidden attack vectors (Ganesh, 2017; Costantini, De Gasperis, & Olivieri, 2019; Bhawna & Mahajan, 2024). For instance, explainable artificial intelligence has been applied to digital forensics to strengthen attribution and improve decision-making transparency (Hall, Sakzad, & Choo, 2022; Kelly et al., 2020).

Large-scale surveys reveal that LLMs themselves can be repurposed for cyber threat detection by identifying malicious code, phishing patterns, or anomalous sequences in real time (Chen et al., 2024; Hasanov, Virtanen, Hakkala, & Isoaho, 2024; Xu et al., 2024). Specialized LLMs such as SecLM provide a promising direction by tailoring detection capabilities to cybersecurity domains (Asoronye, Anthony, Ogbuikwu, Ogili, & Ali, 2024). Similarly, privacy-preserving lightweight LLMs demonstrate potential in constrained environments such as IoT and IIoT ecosystems (Ferrag et al., 2023; Ferrag, Ndhlovu, Tihanyi, Cordeiro, Debbah, & Lestable, 2024; THANDI, 2024).

Detection is also advancing through predictive modeling. By leveraging LLMs for cyber attack forecasting in IoT networks, researchers have demonstrated proactive defense capabilities (Diaf, Korba, Karabadji, & Ghamri-Doudane, 2024). These predictive mechanisms complement traditional anomaly-based approaches, extending resilience beyond immediate threat identification.

6.2. Defense-Oriented Frameworks

Defense strategies for LLMs involve a combination of technical, procedural, and policy-based measures. On the technical side, robust architectures aim to increase model resilience against manipulation. The evolution of LLM architectures has led to more secure and optimized designs, offering stronger foundations against adversarial exploitation (AlQenaei, 2024). Likewise, integrating blockchain and AI enhances auditability and integrity in forensic investigations (Karthikeyan, Pande, & Sarveshwaran, 2023).

AI-driven ethical hacking frameworks serve as another layer of defense. Recent work has demonstrated the feasibility of AI-assisted penetration testing to identify weaknesses in Linux environments (Al-Sinani & Mitchell, 2024; Al-Sinani, Sahli, Mitchell, & Al-Siyabi, 2025). Such proactive measures are critical for addressing evolving attack surfaces. Similarly, AI-enabled phishing detection and semantic web approaches provide real-time adaptive protection in e-commerce and enterprise systems (Gaurav et al., 2024; Gupta, Gaurav, & Arya, 2024).

To secure real-world applications, hybrid frameworks have emerged. The GPT-2 Enhanced Attack Detection and Defense (GEADD) framework is an example of leveraging generative models for zero-day threat identification (Jones & Omar, 2024). Likewise, combining speed and accuracy in machine learning improves response times for emerging threats (Jones, Omar, Mohammed, Nobles, & Dawson, 2023).

6.3. Integration of Digital Forensics in Defense

Digital forensics plays a dual role in both detection and defense. AI-enabled digital forensics accelerates evidence collection, enhances attribution, and supports cybercrime investigation (Iqbal, Debbabi, & Fung, 2020; Adam & Varol, 2020; Dunsin, Ghanem, & Quazzane, 2022). The shift from traditional forensic approaches to intelligent and AI-powered systems demonstrates a paradigm shift in incident response (Irons & Lallie, 2014; Moustafa, 2022).

Emerging studies suggest combining forensic readiness with proactive AI monitoring to create adaptive cybersecurity ecosystems (Manasa & Kumar, 2022; Rughani, 2017; Omar & Zangana, 2025). Ethical considerations remain central, as digital forensics intersects with privacy, law, and governance (Mitchell, 2014; Zangana & Omar, 2026).

6.4. Ethical, Legal, and Policy Dimensions

Defense strategies extend beyond technology to include governance, ethics, and law. Ethical AI frameworks emphasize transparency, accountability, and fairness in LLM-based security systems (Ali & Aysan, 2025; Verma & Rohit, 2024; Shukla & Taneja, 2024). Regulatory frameworks, such as the EU Artificial Intelligence Act, establish a baseline for AI accountability (Butt, 2024).

In military and critical infrastructure contexts, ethical concerns intersect with defense applications, highlighting the risk of misuse in AI-driven warfare (Batabyal, 2024). Risk mitigation frameworks for biomedical and STEM research stress the need for safeguards against malicious exploitation of AI (Trotsyuk et al., 2024; Zangana & Omar, 2025). Moreover, sector-specific policies in cloud security (Hamza & Omar, 2013) and mobile ecosystems (Wright, Dawson, & Omar, 2012) continue to inform contemporary defense strategies.

6.5. Future-Oriented Defense Enhancements

Looking ahead, integration of quantum machine learning and next-generation cybersecurity paradigms promises transformative defense opportunities (Campus, 2024; Eswaran & Eswaran, 2025; Pleshakova, Osipov, Gataullin, Gataullin, & Vasilakos, 2024). These advancements align with broader calls for AI-driven resilience in Industry 4.0 and beyond (Yu, Shvetsov, & Alsamhi, 2024; Santos, Salam, & Dahir, 2024).

Researchers are also exploring domain-specific defenses, including applications in finance (Ali & Aysan, 2024; Ali, Zafar, & Aysan, 2024), healthcare (Huff et al., 2023), agriculture (Arya & Rastogi, 2024), and smart cities (Maguluri, Arularasan, &

Boopathi, 2023). Ensuring that defenses are adaptable to context is essential for achieving sustainable, long-term protection.

6.6. Toward Holistic Cyber Defense

Recent reviews stress the importance of holistic frameworks that blend detection, defense, and resilience (Motlagh et al., 2024; Hassanin & Moustafa, 2024; Ozkan-Okay et al., 2024). Foundational models tailored for cybersecurity (Idelhaj, Abou El Houda, & Khoukhi, 2024) and responsible AI practices (Veluru, 2024; Eisenberg, 2024) provide guiding principles for building trustworthy LLM defense systems.

By combining technical safeguards, forensic intelligence, ethical standards, and future-oriented innovation, LLM-based defense strategies can effectively mitigate adversarial threats while maintaining system reliability and user trust.

Defense against adversarial threats requires an integrated framework combining detection mechanisms, forensic intelligence, ethical governance, and advanced technologies such as quantum-enhanced security. Figure 4 presents a holistic view of these defense layers.

Figure 4. Holistic defense framework against adversarial threats in LLMs

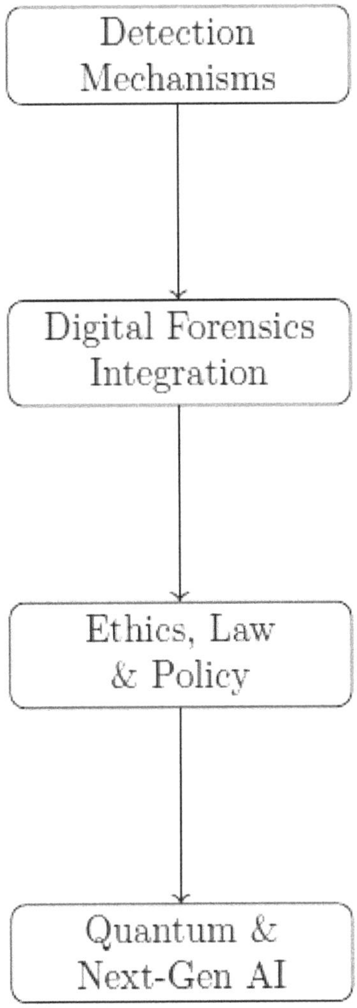

7. OPEN CHALLENGES AND RESEARCH GAPS

Despite the rapid advancements in Large Language Models (LLMs) and their adoption across domains, several open challenges and unresolved research gaps hinder their safe, reliable, and ethical deployment in cybersecurity and digital forensics. These challenges span technical, ethical, legal, and operational dimensions, requiring multidisciplinary collaboration and innovation.

7.1. Model Vulnerabilities and Adversarial Threats

LLMs remain highly susceptible to adversarial attacks such as prompt injection, data poisoning, model inversion, and evasion strategies (Motlagh et al., 2024; Xu et al., 2024). These vulnerabilities compromise trustworthiness, enabling attackers to exploit biases or manipulate outputs (Chen et al., 2024; Taghavi & Feyzi, 2024). Lightweight and privacy-preserving models for IoT/IIoT devices are promising, but still immature for real-world adversarial resilience (Ferrag et al., 2023; Ferrag, Ndhlovu, Tihanyi, Cordeiro, Debbah, & Lestable, 2024; Thandi, 2024). Similarly, sector-specific applications such as enterprise security raise questions about robustness against zero-day threats and jailbreak-style exploits (Gupta et al., 2024; Jones & Omar, 2024).

7.2. Digital Forensics Integration Gaps

Although AI-driven approaches have transformed digital forensics (Costantini et al., 2019; Moustafa, 2022; Omar & Zangana, 2025), major gaps remain in explainability, evidence admissibility, and operational integration (Hall et al., 2022; Kelly et al., 2020; Sikos, 2021). Early AI forensics frameworks (Ganesh, 2017; Rughani, 2017; Irons & Lallie, 2014; Mitchell, 2014) highlighted automation potential, but LLM-based forensic intelligence is still nascent (Iqbal et al., 2020; Adam & Varol, 2020). Challenges include resource constraints (Dunsin, Ghanem, & Quazzane, 2022), ethical concerns (Bhawna & Mahajan, 2024), and the need for scalable AI-enabled investigative pipelines (Jarrett & Choo, 2021; Dunsin, Ghanem, Ouazzane, & Vassilev, 2024). Integration with blockchain-based forensics also requires further maturity (Karthikeyan et al., 2023).

7.3. Ethical, Legal, and Governance Challenges

The ethical use of generative AI remains an unresolved global issue. Research highlights cross-domain ethical complexities in finance, healthcare, and education (Ali & Aysan, 2025; Shukla & Taneja, 2024; Verma & Rohit, 2024). Bias, privacy leakage, and the risk of misuse in biomedical or defense domains pose serious societal risks (Trotsyuk et al., 2024; Batabyal, 2024). Legal frameworks such as the EU AI Act represent early steps (Butt, 2024), yet policies for LLM security and governance remain fragmented (Zangana, Al-Karaki, & Omar, 2025). Calls for ethical AI in cybersecurity stress the need for accountable governance mechanisms and law-policy integration (Zangana & Omar, 2025; Zangana, Nobles, & Omar, 2026).

7.4. Explainability, Transparency, and Trust

The opacity of LLM decision-making poses challenges for adoption in sensitive environments such as cybersecurity and law enforcement (Hasanov et al., 2024; Hassanin & Moustafa, 2024). Explainable AI approaches tailored for forensics and cyber defense are still experimental (Jeong, 2020; Leontidis, 2024). Without transparency, risk mitigation frameworks remain incomplete (Eisenberg, 2024; Trotsyuk et al., 2024). Future research must balance performance with interpretability to ensure trust in LLM-enabled decision support (Hadi et al., 2023; Huff et al., 2023).

7.5. Sector-Specific Research Gaps

Several domains illustrate unique challenges. In cybersecurity, hybrid approaches combining semantic web, LLMs, and XAI are required for phishing and malware detection (Gaurav et al., 2024; Ghazal et al., 2024; Sarker, 2024). In critical infrastructure and defense, AI-enabled surveillance raises governance and misuse risks (Arya & Rastogi, 2024; Maguluri et al., 2023). In finance, generative AI adoption exposes systemic vulnerabilities requiring deeper regulatory and technical oversight (Ali & Aysan, 2024; Ali, Zafar, & Aysan, 2024). Moreover, the biomedical sector faces urgent challenges in preventing malicious misuse of LLMs for harmful experimentation (Trotsyuk et al., 2024).

7.6. Computational and Resource Constraints

While advances in architecture optimization (AlQenaei, 2024) and specialized security-focused LLMs (Asoronye et al., 2024; Kasri et al., 2025) show progress, real-world deployments remain resource-heavy. Research in quantum computing and hybrid AI-quantum models promises efficiency gains (Campus, 2024; Eswaran & Eswaran, 2025; Zangana & Omar, 2025), but practical implementations are limited. Moreover, constrained environments such as smart cities and IoT ecosystems face performance-security trade-offs (Diaf et al., 2024; Yu et al., 2024).

7.7. Human-Centric and Organizational Dimensions

LLM adoption is not purely technical but socio-technical. Effective integration requires organizational readiness and workforce adaptation (Fenwick et al., 2024). Human oversight in cybersecurity operations is essential to avoid over-reliance on automated intelligence (Manoharan & Sarker, 2023). Responsible adoption frameworks stress human-centered design and safeguarding against misuse, harassment, or discrimination (Vyawahare et al., 2024; Pimpalkar et al., 2024). Education and awareness, especially in STEM and professional training, remain underexplored (Jamro & Jamro, 2023; Zangana, Nobles, & Omar, 2026).

In summary, open challenges in LLM security include adversarial robustness, forensic explainability, ethical governance, computational efficiency, and human-centric adoption. Addressing these requires cross-disciplinary innovation that bridges AI, digital forensics, cybersecurity policy, and human factors, ensuring that LLMs evolve into trustworthy and secure technologies for the future (Omar & Zangana, 2024; Santos et al., 2024; Veluru, 2024; Wright et al., 2012).

8. FUTURE DIRECTIONS

The rapid evolution of Large Language Models (LLMs) necessitates forward-looking strategies to address adversarial threats and vulnerabilities. While current research has laid the groundwork for understanding the risks posed by data poisoning, prompt injection, model inversion, and evasion techniques, the coming years will require deeper integration of cybersecurity, ethical governance, quantum-enhanced methods, and forensic intelligence. Several key directions emerge.

8.1. Advancing Cybersecurity Applications of LLMs

Future LLMs must incorporate robust architectures capable of real-time cyber threat intelligence. Studies highlight the growing role of AI-enhanced methods in intrusion detection, malware analysis, and network defense (Alturkistani & Chuprat, 2024; Chen et al., 2024; Ferrag, Alwahedi, Battah, Cherif, Mechri, & Tihanyi, 2024). Lightweight and privacy-preserving models tailored to IoT/IIoT devices are particularly important (Ferrag, Ndhlovu, Tihanyi, Cordeiro, Debbah, Lestable, & Thandi, 2024; Thandi, 2024). Research on specialized security-focused LLMs, such as SecLM, offers a path toward domain-optimized architectures for threat mitigation (Asoronye, Anthony, Ogbuikwu, Ogili, & Ali, 2024).

8.2. Integration with Digital Forensics and Incident Response

LLMs will increasingly support digital forensics investigations through automation and explainability. The integration of AI into forensic workflows has been widely explored, bridging gaps in intelligent evidence collection, authorship attribution, and pattern recognition (Adam & Varol, 2020; Bhawna & Mahajan, 2024; Costantini, De Gasperis, & Olivieri, 2019; Dunsin, Ghanem, & Quazzane, 2022; Dunsin, Ghanem, Ouazzane, & Vassilev, 2024; Hall, Sakzad, & Choo, 2022; Iqbal, Debbabi, & Fung, 2020; Irons & Lallie, 2014; Jarrett & Choo, 2021; Kelly,

Sachan, Ni, Almaghrabi, Allmendinger, & Chen, 2020; Mitchell, 2014; Moustafa, 2022; Rughani, 2017; Sikos, 2021). Future models must balance automation with human oversight, ensuring integrity in digital evidence handling while resisting adversarial manipulation.

8.3. Ethical, Legal, and Governance Frameworks

As LLMs influence sensitive domains such as finance, healthcare, and defense, ethical frameworks and regulatory compliance become paramount. Research emphasizes the ethical implications of generative AI across sectors, from financial analytics to warfare and biomedical research (Ali & Aysan, 2024, 2025; Ali, Zafar, & Aysan, 2024; Batabyal, 2024; Trotsyuk et al., 2024). Legal frameworks, such as the European Union AI Act, represent early attempts to regulate AI but require continuous adaptation (Butt, 2024). In parallel, scholarship highlights the necessity of embedding responsible AI principles, privacy-preserving mechanisms, and trustworthiness in LLM deployments (Shafik, 2024; Shukla & Taneja, 2024; Veluru, 2024; Verma & Rohit, 2024; Zangana, Al-Karaki, & Omar, 2025). Multi-level governance frameworks that align law, policy, and innovation will be vital in managing adversarial risks (Zangana, Al-Karaki, & Omar, 2025).

8.4. Cross-Domain Applications and Security Implications

LLMs will play increasingly critical roles across diverse domains—ranging from agriculture (Arya & Rastogi, 2024), smart cities (Maguluri, Arularasan, & Boopathi, 2023), STEM education (Jamro & Jamro, 2023), women's safety (Pimpalkar, Wankhade, Chole, & Golhar, 2024; Vyawahare, Khandelwal, & Rathod, 2024), to enterprise information systems (Gupta, Gaurav, & Arya, 2024). Each domain presents unique vulnerabilities, requiring adaptive adversarial defense mechanisms. The misuse of AI in sensitive areas such as biomedical research, national defense, and online harassment underscores the dual-use nature of LLMs (Batabyal, 2024; Trotsyuk et al., 2024).

8.5. Quantum-Enhanced and Next-Generation LLMs

The future of secure LLMs lies at the intersection of quantum computing, semiconductor technologies, and hybrid AI models. Quantum Machine Learning (QML) is expected to provide novel solutions for adversarial resilience, cryptographic security, and model optimization (Campus, 2024; Eswaran & Eswaran, 2025). Research underscores the integration of quantum-aware cybersecurity into LLMs, suggesting a paradigm shift in defense strategies (Zangana & Omar, 2025; Zangana, Al-Karaki, & Omar, 2025).

8.6. Responsible AI and Human-Centric Approaches

The deployment of LLMs in high-stakes environments demands human-centric design, fairness, and accountability. Responsible AI research highlights the importance of explainability, policy modeling, and HRM-driven adoption to ensure alignment between technical innovation and ethical practice (Fenwick, Molnar, & Frangos, 2024; Leontidis, 2024; Schünemann, Johanning, Reger, Herold, & Bruckner, 2024). Incorporating responsible sensor systems and preventing adversarial misuse in large-scale deployments is equally essential (Eisenberg, 2024; Veluru, 2024).

8.7. Building a Secure Ecosystem for Cyber Defense

Scholars emphasize that LLMs can serve as transformative tools in cyber defense when paired with explainable AI, federated learning, and multi-layered protection mechanisms (Ghazal, Janjua, Abushiba, Ahmad, Ihsan, & Al-Dmour, 2024; Hasanov, Virtanen, Hakkala, & Isoaho, 2024; Hassanin & Moustafa, 2024; Motlagh, Hajizadeh, Majd, Najafi, Cheng, & Meinel, 2024; Ozkan-Okay, Akin, Aslan, Kosunalp, Iliev, Stoyanov, & Beloev, 2024; Xu et al., 2024). Future research should prioritize frameworks such as GEADD for zero-day threat detection (Jones & Omar, 2024) and collaborative intelligence methods that enhance resilience against advanced adversarial tactics (Jones, Omar, Mohammed, Nobles, & Dawson, 2023; Manoharan & Sarker, 2023; Sarker, 2024).

8.8. Bridging Research and Practice

LLMs also open pathways for advancing research and innovation beyond cybersecurity. Their potential in scholarly article design, topic modeling, scientometric analysis, and literature exploration is reshaping research ecosystems (Filetti, Fenza, & Gallo, 2024; Luan, Perron, Victor, Wan, Niu, & Xiao, 2024; Rodriguez & Storer, 2020; San Biagio, Cipolla, La Mattina, & Morreale, 2023). At the same time, industry adoption across biotechnology, manufacturing, and networking requires integration of LLM-powered cyber intelligence (Huff et al., 2023; Karim, Galar, & Kumar, 2023; Santos, Salam, & Dahir, 2024; Tyagi, Kumari, & Richa, 2024; Yu, Shvetsov, & Alsamhi, 2024).

8.9. Emerging Ethical Hacking and Red Teaming Approaches

Another future direction is the evolution of AI-enhanced ethical hacking and adversarial testing of LLMs. Experiments on Linux-based environments highlight the potential for AI-driven penetration testing to uncover novel vulnerabilities (Al-Sinani & Mitchell, 2024; Al-Sinani, Sahli, Mitchell, & Al-Siyabi, 2025). Systematic red-teaming with LLMs will ensure continuous evaluation of model robustness against real-world attack vectors.

8.10. Toward AI-Enabled Cybersecurity Paradigm Shifts

Ultimately, the trajectory of LLM security research points toward a redefinition of cybersecurity paradigms, where adversarial threats are addressed holistically through AI-driven, human-centered, and quantum-enhanced approaches (Ferrag et al., 2023; Hadi, Abdulredha, & Hasan, 2023; Idelhaj, Abou El Houda, & Khoukhi, 2024; Kasri, Himeur, Alkhazaleh, Tarapiah, Atalla, Mansoor, & Al-Ahmad, 2025; Motlagh et al., 2024; Pleshakova, Osipov, Gataullin, Gataullin, & Vasilakos, 2024; Rashid & Kausik, 2024; Taghavi & Feyzi, 2024; Xu et al., 2024; Zangana & Omar, 2025). Future scholarship will rely on interdisciplinary collaborations to safeguard LLMs against emerging threats while enabling their transformative potential across industries.

9. CONCLUSION

The rise of large language models (LLMs) has introduced unprecedented opportunities in advancing natural language processing, cybersecurity, and digital forensics. Yet, as this chapter has shown, these systems are not immune to adversarial threats and vulnerabilities that compromise their reliability, trustworthiness, and safety. Attacks such as prompt injection, data poisoning, model inversion, and evasion illustrate how malicious actors can manipulate LLMs to produce harmful or biased outcomes. These risks emphasize that security in LLMs is not a peripheral concern but a core requirement for their sustainable deployment in sensitive domains.

Another critical insight is that adversarial vulnerabilities are not static but evolve alongside the capabilities of LLMs themselves. The growing complexity of models, their integration across diverse industries, and their accessibility through open interfaces expand both their utility and their attack surface. This duality reinforces the importance of continuous monitoring, rigorous testing, and adaptive defense strategies. A proactive approach that considers ethical, technical, and regulatory dimensions is necessary to counter the rapid pace of adversarial innovation.

The chapter also underscores the importance of collaboration between researchers, industry practitioners, policymakers, and cybersecurity professionals. Protecting LLMs requires not only advancements in adversarial robustness and explainability but also a broader ecosystem that prioritizes transparency, accountability, and responsible AI practices. By integrating these principles into system design and deployment, organizations can better safeguard against misuse while unlocking the transformative potential of LLMs.

Ultimately, securing LLMs against adversarial threats is both a technical and societal challenge. The pathway forward lies in recognizing that vulnerabilities will persist but can be mitigated through layered defenses, ethical governance, and innovation in security research. This balance will determine whether LLMs remain a source of progress and trust—or become liabilities in an increasingly adversarial digital world.

REFERENCES

Adam, I. Y., & Varol, C. (2020, June). Intelligence in digital forensics process. In *2020 8th International Symposium on Digital Forensics and Security (ISDFS)* (pp. 1-6). IEEE. DOI: 10.1109/ISDFS49300.2020.9116442

Al-Sinani, H. S., & Mitchell, C. J. (2024). AI-enhanced ethical hacking: A Linux-focused experiment. *arXiv preprint arXiv:2410.05105.*

Al-Sinani, H. S., Sahli, N., Mitchell, C. J., & Al-Siyabi, M. (2025). Advancing ethical hacking with AI: A Linux-based experimental study. *Proceedings of ITASEC and SERICS, Bologna, Italy (Feb 2025),* https://www. chrismitchell. net/Papers/aehwaa. pdf

Ali, H., & Aysan, A. F. (2024). Decoding Future of Generative AI in Finance: A Machine Learning Exploration of Academic and Grey Corpus. *Available at SSRN* 4787211. DOI: 10.2139/ssrn.4787211

Ali, H., & Aysan, A. F. (2025). Ethical dimensions of generative AI: A cross-domain analysis using machine learning structural topic modeling. *International Journal of Ethics and Systems, 41*(1), 3–34. DOI: 10.1108/IJOES-04-2024-0112

Ali, H., Zafar, M. B., & Aysan, A. F. (2024). Generative AI and Finance: A Multi-level Machine Learning Based Analysis. *Available at SSRN* 5129013.

AlQenaei, Z. M. (2024, March). Evolution and Optimization of Language Model Architectures: From Foundations to Future Directions. In *International Conference on Computing and Machine Learning* (pp. 233-249). Singapore: Springer Nature Singapore.

Alturkistani, H., & Chuprat, S. (2024). Artificial Intelligence and Large Language Models in Advancing Cyber Threat Intelligence: A Systematic Literature Review.

Arya, L., & Rastogi, R. (2024). Study on Aerial Monitoring System in Agriculture, Forestry, Defense, and Border Protection Using Artificial Intelligence (AI). In *Agriculture and Aquaculture Applications of Biosensors and Bioelectronics* (pp. 392-407). IGI Global Scientific Publishing.

Asoronye, G. O., Anthony, O. C., Ogbuikwu, R. I., Ogili, C. O., & Ali, H. U. (2024). SecLM: A Specialized Security Language Model for Advanced Cybersecurity Applications and Threat Mitigation. *EKETE-International Journal Of Advanced Research, 2*(6), 33–42.

Batabyal, G. S. (2024). Ethics, laws on war and artificial intelligence-driven warfare. In *Artificial intelligence, ethics and the future of warfare* (pp. 187–215). Routledge India. DOI: 10.4324/9781003421849-9

Bhawna, & Mahajan, S. (2024). Artificial Intelligence Perspective on Digital Forensics. *Applying Artificial Intelligence in Cybersecurity Analytics and Cyber Threat Detection*, 33-44.

Butt, J. (2024). Analytical study of the world's first EU Artificial Intelligence (AI) Act. *International Journal of Research Publication and Reviews, 5*(3), 7343–7364. DOI: 10.55248/gengpi.5.0324.0914

Campus, M. T. (2024). Quantum Machine Learning, Leveraging Al, and. *Integration of AI, Quantum Computing, and Semiconductor Technology*, 57.

Chen, Y., Cui, M., Wang, D., Cao, Y., Yang, P., Jiang, B., Lu, Z., & Liu, B. (2024). A survey of large language models for cyber threat detection. *Computers & Security, 145*, 104016. DOI: 10.1016/j.cose.2024.104016

Costantini, S., De Gasperis, G., & Olivieri, R. (2019). Digital forensics and investigations meet artificial intelligence. *Annals of Mathematics and Artificial Intelligence, 86*(1), 193–229. DOI: 10.1007/s10472-019-09632-y

Diaf, A., Korba, A. A., Karabadji, N. E., & Ghamri-Doudane, Y. (2024, April). Beyond detection: Leveraging large language models for cyber attack prediction in iot networks. In *2024 20th International Conference on Distributed Computing in Smart Systems and the Internet of Things (DCOSS-IoT)* (pp. 117-123). IEEE.

Dunsin, D., Ghanem, M. C., Ouazzane, K., & Vassilev, V. (2024). A comprehensive analysis of the role of artificial intelligence and machine learning in modern digital forensics and incident response. *Forensic Science International Digital Investigation, 48*, 301675. DOI: 10.1016/j.fsidi.2023.301675

Dunsin, D., Ghanem, M. C., & Quazzane, K. (2022). The use of artificial intelligence in digital forensics and incident response in a constrained environment. *International Journal of Information and Communication Engineering, 16*(8), 280–285.

Eisenberg, D. (2024). *Sensing With Integrity: Responsible Sensor Systems in an Era of AI* (Doctoral dissertation, New Jersey Institute of Technology).

Eswaran, U., & Eswaran, V. (2025). Quantum Machine Learning, Leveraging AI, and Semiconductor Technology. In *Integration of AI, Quantum Computing, and Semiconductor Technology* (pp. 57-78). IGI Global.

Fenwick, A., Molnar, G., & Frangos, P. (2024). The critical role of HRM in AI-driven digital transformation: A paradigm shift to enable firms to move from AI implementation to human-centric adoption. *Discover Artificial Intelligence*, *4*(1), 34. DOI: 10.1007/s44163-024-00125-4

Ferrag, M. A., Alwahedi, F., Battah, A., Cherif, B., Mechri, A., & Tihanyi, N. (2024). Generative ai and large language models for cyber security: All insights you need. *Available at SSRN* 4853709. DOI: 10.2139/ssrn.4853709

Ferrag, M. A., Ndhlovu, M., Tihanyi, N., Cordeiro, L. C., Debbah, M., & Lestable, T. (2023). Revolutionizing cyber threat detection with large language models. *arXiv preprint arXiv:2306.14263*, 195-202.

Ferrag, M. A., Ndhlovu, M., Tihanyi, N., Cordeiro, L. C., Debbah, M., Lestable, T., & Thandi, N. S. (2024). Revolutionizing cyber threat detection with large language models: A privacy-preserving bert-based lightweight model for iot/iiot devices. *IEEE Access : Practical Innovations, Open Solutions*, *12*, 23733–23750. DOI: 10.1109/ACCESS.2024.3363469

Filetti, S., Fenza, G., & Gallo, A. (2024). Research design and writing of scholarly articles: New artificial intelligence tools available for researchers. *Endocrine*, *85*(3), 1104–1116. DOI: 10.1007/s12020-024-03977-z PMID: 39085566

Flannery, J., Ajayi, S. O., & Oyegoke, A. S. (2021). Alcohol and substance misuse in the construction industry. *International Journal of Occupational Safety and Ergonomics*, *27*(2), 472–487. DOI: 10.1080/10803548.2019.1601376 PMID: 30935301

Ganesh, V. (2017). Artificial intelligence applied to computer forensics. *International Journal (Toronto, Ont.)*, *5*(5).

Gaurav, A., Chui, K. T., Arya, V., Attar, R. W., Bansal, S., Alhomoud, A., & Psannis, K. (2024). Optimized AI-Driven Semantic Web Approach for Enhancing Phishing Detection in E-Commerce Platforms. [IJSWIS]. *International Journal on Semantic Web and Information Systems*, *20*(1), 1–13. DOI: 10.4018/IJSWIS.359767

Ghazal, T. M., Janjua, J. I., Abushiba, W., Ahmad, M., Ihsan, A., & Al-Dmour, N. A. (2024, December). Cybersecurity Revolution via Large Language Models and Explainable AI. In *2024 17th International Conference on Security of Information and Networks (SIN)* (pp. 1-6). IEEE. DOI: 10.1109/SIN63213.2024.10871324

Gupta, B. B., Gaurav, A., & Arya, V. (2024). Navigating the security landscape of large language models in enterprise information systems. *Enterprise Information Systems*, *18*(4), 2310846. DOI: 10.1080/17517575.2024.2310846

Hadi, M. A., Abdulredha, M. N., & Hasan, E. (2023). Introduction to ChatGPT: A new revolution of artificial intelligence with machine learning algorithms and cybersecurity. *Sci. Arch*, *4*(04), 276. DOI: 10.47587/SA.2023.4406

Hall, S. W., Sakzad, A., & Choo, K. K. R. (2022). Explainable artificial intelligence for digital forensics. *Wiley Interdisciplinary Reviews: Forensic Science*, *4*(2), e1434.

Hamza, Y. A., & Omar, M. D. (2013). Cloud computing security: Abuse and nefarious use of cloud computing. *International Journal of Computer Engineering Research*, *3*(6), 22–27.

Hasanov, I., Virtanen, S., Hakkala, A., & Isoaho, J. (2024). Application of Large Language Models in Cybersecurity: A Systematic Literature Review. *IEEE Access : Practical Innovations, Open Solutions*, *12*, 176751–176778. DOI: 10.1109/ACCESS.2024.3505983

Hassanin, M., & Moustafa, N. (2024). A comprehensive overview of large language models (llms) for cyber defences: Opportunities and directions. *arXiv preprint arXiv:2405.14487*.

Huff, A. J., Burrell, D. N., Nobles, C., Richardson, K., Wright, J. B., Burton, S. L., Jones, A. J., Springs, D., Omar, M., & Brown-Jackson, K. L. (2023). Management Practices for Mitigating Cybersecurity Threats to Biotechnology Companies, Laboratories, and Healthcare Research Organizations. In *Applied Research Approaches to Technology, Healthcare, and Business* (pp. 1-12). IGI Global.

Idelhaj, A., Abou El Houda, Z., & Khoukhi, L. (2024). Foundations models in cybersecurity. *Artificial Intelligence for Blockchain and Cybersecurity Powered IoT Applications*, 1.

Iqbal, F., Debbabi, M., Fung, B. C., Iqbal, F., Debbabi, M., & Fung, B. C. (2020). Artificial intelligence and digital forensics. *Machine Learning for Authorship Attribution and Cyber Forensics*, 139-150.

Irons, A., & Lallie, H. S. (2014). Digital forensics to intelligent forensics. *Future Internet*, *6*(3), 584–596. DOI: 10.3390/fi6030584

Jamro, M. Y., & Jamro, F. A. (2023). AI Matters: Chatbot Integration in Holistic STEM Education.

Jarrett, A., & Choo, K. K. R. (2021). The impact of automation and artificial intelligence on digital forensics. *WIREs Forensic Science*, *3*(6), e1418. DOI: 10.1002/wfs2.1418

Jeong, D. (2020). Artificial intelligence security threat, crime, and forensics: Taxonomy and open issues. *IEEE Access : Practical Innovations, Open Solutions, 8*, 184560–184574. DOI: 10.1109/ACCESS.2020.3029280

Jones, R., & Omar, M. (2024). Revolutionizing Cybersecurity: The GPT-2 Enhanced Attack Detection and Defense (GEADD) Method for Zero-Day Threats. *International Journal of Informatics* [INJIISCOM]. *Information System and Computer Engineering, 5*(2), 178–191.

Jones, R., Omar, M., Mohammed, D., Nobles, C., & Dawson, M. (2023). Harnessing the Speed and Accuracy of Machine Learning to Advance Cybersecurity. In *2023 Congress in Computer Science, Computer Engineering, & Applied Computing (CSCE)* (pp. 418-421). IEEE. DOI: 10.1109/CSCE60160.2023.00074

Karim, R., Galar, D., & Kumar, U. (2023). *AI factory: theories, applications and case studies*. CRC Press. DOI: 10.1201/9781003208686

Karthikeyan, P., Pande, H. M., & Sarveshwaran, V. (Eds.). (2023). *Artificial intelligence and blockchain in digital forensics*. CRC Press.

Kasri, W., Himeur, Y., Alkhazaleh, H. A., Tarapiah, S., Atalla, S., Mansoor, W., & Al-Ahmad, H. (2025). From Vulnerability to Defense: The Role of Large Language Models in Enhancing Cybersecurity. *Computation (Basel, Switzerland), 13*(2), 30. DOI: 10.3390/computation13020030

Kelly, L., Sachan, S., Ni, L., Almaghrabi, F., Allmendinger, R., & Chen, Y. (2020). *Explainable artificial intelligence for digital forensics: opportunities, challenges and a drug testing case study*. Digital Forensic Science.

Leontidis, G. (2024). Science in the age of ai: How artificial intelligence is changing the nature and method of scientific research.

Liu, Z. (2024, April). A review of advancements and applications of pre-trained language models in cybersecurity. In *2024 12th International Symposium on Digital Forensics and Security (ISDFS)* (pp. 1-10). IEEE. DOI: 10.1109/ISDFS60797.2024.10527236

Luan, H., Perron, B. E., Victor, B. G., Wan, G., Niu, Y., & Xiao, X. (2024). Using artificial intelligence to support scientometric analysis of scholarly literature: A case example of research on mainland China's left-behind children. *Journal of the Society for Social Work and Research, 15*(3), 435–457. DOI: 10.1086/731613

Maennig, W. (2014). Inefficiency of the anti-doping system: Cost reduction proposals. *Substance Use & Misuse, 49*(9), 1201–1205. DOI: 10.3109/10826084.2014.912065 PMID: 24832718

Maguluri, L. P., Arularasan, A. N., & Boopathi, S. (2023). Assessing security concerns for ai-based drones in smart cities. In *Effective AI, Blockchain, and E-Governance Applications for Knowledge Discovery and Management* (pp. 27-47). IGI Global Scientific Publishing. DOI: 10.4018/978-1-6684-9151-5.ch002

Manasa, S., & Kumar, K. P. (2022). Digital forensics investigation for attacks on artificial intelligence. *ECS Transactions*, *107*(1), 19639–19645. DOI: 10.1149/10701.19639ecst

Manoharan, A., & Sarker, M. (2023). Revolutionizing Cybersecurity: Unleashing the Power of Artificial Intelligence and Machine Learning for Next-Generation Threat Detection. *DOI:* https://www. doi. org/10.56726/IRJMETS32644, *1*.

Mitchell, F. R. (2014). An overview of artificial intelligence based pattern matching in a security and digital forensic context. *Cyberpatterns: Unifying Design Patterns with Security and Attack Patterns*, 215-222.

Motlagh, F. N., Hajizadeh, M., Majd, M., Najafi, P., Cheng, F., & Meinel, C. (2024). Large language models in cybersecurity: State-of-the-art. *arXiv preprint arXiv:2402.00891*.

Moustafa, N. (2022). *Digital Forensics in the Era of Artificial Intelligence*. CRC Press. DOI: 10.1201/9781003278962

Omar, M., & Zangana, H. (Eds.). (2025). *Digital Forensics in the Age of AI*. IGI Global., DOI: 10.4018/979-8-3373-0857-9

Omar, M., & Zangana, H. M. (Eds.). (2024). *Redefining Security With Cyber AI*. IGI Global., DOI: 10.4018/979-8-3693-6517-5

Ozkan-Okay, M., Akin, E., Aslan, Ö., Kosunalp, S., Iliev, T., Stoyanov, I., & Beloev, I. (2024). A comprehensive survey: Evaluating the efficiency of artificial intelligence and machine learning techniques on cyber security solutions. *IEEE Access : Practical Innovations, Open Solutions*, *12*, 12229–12256. DOI: 10.1109/ACCESS.2024.3355547

Pimpalkar, A. P., Wankhade, N. R., Chole, V., & Golhar, Y. (2024). Women's Empowerment Through AI: Discovering Data Analytics for Predictive Safety Solutions and Future Trends. In *AI Tools and Applications for Women's Safety* (pp. 304-326). IGI Global Scientific Publishing.

Pleshakova, E., Osipov, A., Gataullin, S., Gataullin, T., & Vasilakos, A. (2024). Next gen cybersecurity paradigm towards artificial general intelligence: Russian market challenges and future global technological trends. *Journal of Computer Virology and Hacking Techniques*, *20*(3), 429–440. DOI: 10.1007/s11416-024-00529-x

Rashid, A. B., & Kausik, A. K. (2024). AI revolutionizing industries worldwide: A comprehensive overview of its diverse applications. *Hybrid Advances*, 100277.

Rodriguez, M. Y., & Storer, H. (2020). A computational social science perspective on qualitative data exploration: Using topic models for the descriptive analysis of social media data. *Journal of Technology in Human Services*, *38*(1), 54–86. DOI: 10.1080/15228835.2019.1616350

Rughani, P. H. (2017). Artificial Intelligence Based Digital Forensics Framework. *International Journal of Advanced Research in Computer Science*, *8*(8), 10–14. DOI: 10.26483/ijarcs.v8i8.4571

San Biagio, M., Cipolla, M., La Mattina, E., & Morreale, V. (2023, December). A Topic Clustering Method to Identify Online Threats against Soft Targets. In *2023 International Conference on Computational Science and Computational Intelligence (CSCI)* (pp. 727-733). IEEE. DOI: 10.1109/CSCI62032.2023.00124

Santos, O., Salam, S., & Dahir, H. (2024). The AI revolution in networking, cybersecurity, and emerging technologies.

Sarker, I. H. (2024). Generative AI and large language modeling in cybersecurity. In *AI-Driven Cybersecurity and Threat Intelligence: Cyber Automation, Intelligent Decision-Making and Explainability* (pp. 79–99). Springer Nature Switzerland. DOI: 10.1007/978-3-031-54497-2_5

Schünemann, C., Johanning, S., Reger, E., Herold, H., & Bruckner, T. (2024). Complex system policy modelling approaches for policy advice–comparing systems thinking, system dynamics and agent-based modelling. *Political Research Exchange : an ECPR Journal*, *6*(1), 2387438. DOI: 10.1080/2474736X.2024.2387438

Shafik, W. (2024). Data privacy and security safeguarding customer information in ChatGPT systems. In *Revolutionizing the Service Industry Wth OpenAI Models* (pp. 52–86). IGI Global. DOI: 10.4018/979-8-3693-1239-1.ch003

Shukla, R. P., & Taneja, S. (2024). Ethical considerations and data privacy in artificial intelligence. In *Integrating generative AI in education to achieve sustainable development goals* (pp. 86–97). IGI Global. DOI: 10.4018/979-8-3693-2440-0.ch005

Sikos, L. F. (2021). AI in digital forensics: Ontology engineering for cybercrime investigations. *WIREs Forensic Science*, *3*(3), e1394. DOI: 10.1002/wfs2.1394

Taghavi, S. M., & Feyzi, F. (2024). Using large language models to better detect and handle software vulnerabilities and cyber security threats.

THANDI, N. S. (2024). Revolutionizing Cyber Threat Detection With Large Language Models: A Privacy-Preserving BERT-Based Lightweight Model for IoT/IIoT Devices.

Trotsyuk, A. A., Waeiss, Q., Bhatia, R. T., Aponte, B. J., Heffernan, I. M., Madgavkar, D., Felder, R. M., Lehmann, L. S., Palmer, M. J., Greely, H., Wald, R., Goetz, L., Trengove, M., Vandersluis, R., Lin, H., Cho, M. K., Altman, R. B., Endy, D., Relman, D. A., & Magnus, D. (2024). Toward a framework for risk mitigation of potential misuse of artificial intelligence in biomedical research. *Nature Machine Intelligence*, *6*(12), 1–8. DOI: 10.1038/s42256-024-00926-3 PMID: 40994707

Tyagi, A. K., Kumari, S., & Richa. (2024). Artificial Intelligence-Based Cyber Security and Digital Forensics: A Review. *Artificial Intelligence-Enabled Digital Twin for Smart Manufacturing*, 391-419.

Veluru, C. S. (2024). Responsible Artificial Intelligence on Large Scale Data to Prevent Misuse, Unethical Challenges and Security Breaches. *Journal of Artificial Intelligence & Cloud Computing. SRC/JAICC-349. DOI: doi. org/(3), 331*, 2-6.DOI: 10.47363/JAICC/2024

Verma, M., & Rohit, K. (2024). Ethical AI Shaping Scholarly Communication: Challenges and Opportunities.

Vyawahare, H., Khandelwal, S., & Rathod, S. (2024). Artificial Intelligence in Detecting and Preventing Online Harassment. In *AI Tools and Applications for Women's Safety* (pp. 14–35). IGI Global Scientific Publishing. DOI: 10.4018/979-8-3693-1435-7.ch002

Wright, J., Dawson, M. E.Jr, & Omar, M. (2012). Cyber security and mobile threats: The need for antivirus applications for smartphones. *Journal of Information Systems Technology and Planning*, *5*(14), 40–60.

Xu, H., Wang, S., Li, N., Wang, K., Zhao, Y., Chen, K., . . . Wang, H. (2024). Large language models for cyber security: A systematic literature review. *arXiv preprint arXiv:2405.04760*.

Yu, J., Shvetsov, A. V., & Alsamhi, S. H. (2024). Leveraging machine learning for cybersecurity resilience in industry 4.0: Challenges and future directions. *IEEE Access : Practical Innovations, Open Solutions*, *12*, 159579–159596. DOI: 10.1109/ACCESS.2024.3482987

Zangana, H., Al-Karaki, J., & Omar, M. (Eds.). (2025). *Revolutionizing Cybersecurity With Deep Learning and Large Language Models*. IGI Global., DOI: 10.4018/979-8-3373-3296-3

Zangana, H., & Omar, M. (Eds.). (2025). *Ensuring Secure and Ethical STM Research in the AI Era*. IGI Global., DOI: 10.4018/979-8-3373-4252-8

Zangana, H., & Omar, M. (Eds.). (2025). *Leveraging Large Language Models for Quantum-Aware Cybersecurity*. IGI Global., DOI: 10.4018/979-8-3373-1102-9

Chapter 2
Legal and Policy Frameworks for Securing Large Language Models

Dilshad Ahmad Mhia-alddin
https://orcid.org/0009-0005-4046-1607
University of Duhok, Iraq

ABSTRACT

The rapid development and deployment of Large Language Models (LLMs) have transformed numerous sectors, from healthcare and finance to defense and education. However, their widespread adoption introduces significant security, ethical, and legal challenges that necessitate robust legal and policy frameworks. This chapter examines the regulatory landscape and policy approaches for securing LLMs, emphasizing compliance with data protection, intellectual property, and cybersecurity standards. Key issues such as liability, accountability, transparency, and ethical use are explored, alongside emerging national and international strategies for governance. By analyzing current regulations and policy proposals, this chapter offers a comprehensive guide for stakeholders seeking to mitigate risks while fostering innovation in LLM applications.

1. INTRODUCTION

The emergence of Large Language Models (LLMs) has revolutionized digital interaction, knowledge generation, and decision-making processes across multiple sectors, including healthcare, finance, governance, and education (Ali & Aysan, 2024; Rashid & Kausik, 2024). Their unprecedented ability to process and generate human-like language has created transformative opportunities but simultaneously

DOI: 10.4018/979-8-3373-7133-7.ch002

exposed organizations and societies to complex security, ethical, and legal challenges (Veluru, 2024; Ali, H., & Aysan, 2025). LLMs, by their design, rely on massive datasets, often including sensitive or proprietary information, which makes the regulatory oversight of data collection, storage, usage, and transfer a pressing concern (Shafik, 2024; Verma & Rohit, 2024).

Legal and policy frameworks for LLMs remain fragmented and nascent, with jurisdictions adopting heterogeneous approaches to regulation. In Europe, the EU Artificial Intelligence Act offers a risk-based regulatory model, emphasizing transparency, accountability, and human oversight for high-risk AI systems (Butt, 2024; Pesapane, Bracchi, Mulligan, et al., 2021). Conversely, the United States prioritizes sector-specific guidance and voluntary standards, focusing on innovation while ensuring consumer protection (Larson et al., 2021; Pesapane, Volonté, Codari, & Sardanelli, 2018). The absence of globally harmonized policies creates legal uncertainties, especially for multinational organizations deploying LLMs across borders, raising challenges in compliance, liability, and enforcement (Darvishi, Liu, & Lim, 2022; Mhia-Alddin & Hussein, 2025).

A key concern in LLM regulation is ethical governance. Issues of bias, misinformation, and automated decision-making require policies that extend beyond traditional legal instruments to incorporate ethics-driven frameworks (Ali, H., Zafar, & Aysan, 2024; Mennella, Maniscalco, De Pietro, & Esposito, 2024). Furthermore, emerging technologies such as quantum computing, generative AI, and advanced cyber-physical systems intersect with LLMs, necessitating integrated approaches to legal compliance and policy oversight (Eswaran & Eswaran, 2025; Campus, 2024). These intersections amplify potential risks, including model misuse, data breaches, and systemic harm, thereby making the establishment of comprehensive legal and policy frameworks imperative (Veluru, 2024; Trotsyuk et al., 2024).

Another critical dimension involves contractual and commercial law considerations related to AI and LLM deployment. Issues such as intellectual property rights, licensing, and post-expiry obligations in AI-driven contracts present unique challenges that require proactive regulatory attention (Mhia-Alddin, 2025; Mhia-Alddin & Hussein, 2025). These legal aspects, combined with cybersecurity regulations and cross-jurisdictional compliance, form a complex landscape that organizations must navigate to ensure secure, ethical, and legally compliant LLM operations (Naili, Mangkunegara, Purwono, & Baballe, 2025; Zangana & Li, 2025).

In parallel, societal concerns around LLMs—including transparency, accountability, data privacy, and equitable access—underscore the need for multi-stakeholder engagement in policy development (Shukla & Taneja, 2024; Ho, 2023). Policymakers, technologists, and legal scholars are increasingly advocating for adaptive governance structures that combine regulatory oversight with ethical and technical safeguards, aiming to balance innovation with risk mitigation (Fenwick, Molnar, & Frangos, 2024; Vyawahare, Khandelwal, & Rathod, 2024).

This chapter, therefore, aims to provide a comprehensive overview of the legal and policy frameworks for securing LLMs, highlighting international regulatory trends, ethical considerations, and emerging strategies for governance. By integrating multidisciplinary perspectives, it offers guidance to policymakers, legal practitioners, technologists, and organizational leaders on mitigating risks while fostering the responsible deployment of LLM technologies (Ali, 2024; Akindele & Chabinga, 2024; Singh & Kaunert, 2025).

2. OVERVIEW OF SECURITY THREATS IN LLMS

Large Language Models (LLMs) have rapidly transformed natural language processing and artificial intelligence (AI), enabling capabilities ranging from text generation to complex decision support. However, these advancements also introduce multifaceted security threats that span technical, ethical, and legal domains. Understanding these threats is critical for researchers, developers, and policymakers to ensure safe deployment and mitigate misuse risks (Veluru, 2024; Al-Sinani & Mitchell, 2024).

2.1. Adversarial Attacks and Model Exploitation

Adversarial attacks exploit vulnerabilities in LLM architectures to manipulate outputs or extract sensitive information. Techniques such as prompt injection, data poisoning, and evasion attacks can cause models to generate malicious or biased outputs (Gaurav et al., 2024; Al-Sinani, Sahli, Mitchell, & Al-Siyabi, 2025). In addition, attackers may leverage LLMs to automate phishing campaigns, fraud detection evasion, and misinformation generation, which significantly amplifies cyber threats (San Biagio, Cipolla, La Mattina, & Morreale, 2023).

The risk of model inversion attacks is particularly concerning, as these can allow adversaries to reconstruct training data, including sensitive personal or financial information (Ali, Zafar, & Aysan, 2024; Iyengar, Nabavirazavi, Hariprasad, HB, & Mohan, 2025). This creates a dual challenge for developers: safeguarding intellectual property embedded in the model while protecting the privacy of training datasets.

2.2. Data Privacy Vulnerabilities

LLMs require large datasets for training, often encompassing proprietary, personal, or sensitive information. Inadequate anonymization or improper handling can expose data to leaks or misuse (Shafik, 2024; Shukla & Taneja, 2024). Federated learning approaches and privacy-preserving AI techniques are emerging as countermeasures, enabling decentralized model training without direct exposure of raw data (Iyengar et al., 2025; Veluru, 2024).

However, even with these safeguards, privacy risks persist through unintended memorization of data or model inference attacks, emphasizing the need for robust auditing frameworks and regulatory oversight (Zangana & Li, 2025; Fenwick, Molnar, & Frangos, 2024).

2.3. Malicious Use and Misinformation

LLMs' generative capabilities make them susceptible to misuse in creating deceptive content, deepfakes, and coordinated disinformation campaigns (Ali & Aysan, 2025; Vyawahare, Khandelwal, & Rathod, 2024). Such threats are not only technical but also social and political, potentially influencing public opinion, undermining trust in digital systems, and impacting democratic processes (Batabyal, 2024; Rashid & Kausik, 2024).

The rapid adoption of LLMs across finance, healthcare, and governance sectors raises concerns about automated decision-making errors, which could exacerbate risks in critical infrastructures or regulatory compliance environments (Ali, 2024; Ali, 2024; Mennella, Maniscalco, De Pietro, & Esposito, 2024).

2.4. Ethical and Regulatory Challenges

Beyond technical vulnerabilities, LLMs present ethical and legal risks. Bias amplification, algorithmic discrimination, and opaque decision-making processes challenge fairness, accountability, and transparency (Ali & Aysan, 2024; Mennella et al., 2024). Furthermore, cross-jurisdictional regulatory gaps complicate enforcement, particularly in areas like intellectual property, contract law, and healthcare applications (Mhia-Alddin, 2025; Mhia-Alddin & Hussein, 2025; Pesapane, Bracchi, Mulligan, Linnikov, Maslennikov, et al., 2021).

The legal implications are significant: for example, misuse of LLMs in contract automation may generate liabilities under expiry, termination, or compliance clauses (Mhia-Alddin & Hussein, 2025; Mhia-Alddin, 2025). Similarly, ethical lapses in AI-driven diagnostics or finance could trigger regulatory scrutiny under GDPR, HIPAA, or sector-specific AI regulations (Larson et al., 2021; Naili, Mangkunegara, Purwono, & Baballe, 2025).

2.5. Emerging Threats from Integration and Multi-domain Applications

LLMs are increasingly integrated with robotics, IoT, quantum computing, and cybersecurity frameworks (Eswaran & Eswaran, 2025; Campus, 2024). While this enhances functionality, it also amplifies security risks, including system-level attacks on interconnected AI-driven devices and infrastructures (Maguluri, Arularasan, & Boopathi, 2023; Trotsyuk et al., 2024). For instance, adversaries could exploit AI-enhanced drones or autonomous systems to conduct surveillance, physical attacks, or industrial sabotage (Arya & Rastogi, 2024).

Moreover, the convergence of AI and quantum technologies introduces new attack vectors, as quantum computing could theoretically break traditional cryptography protecting LLM data pipelines (Eswaran & Eswaran, 2025; Campus, 2024). Policymakers and researchers must therefore adopt proactive threat modeling and risk mitigation strategies to anticipate these next-generation vulnerabilities (Verma, Rao, Eluri, & Sharma, 2020; Zreik, 2024).

2.6. Summary

In summary, LLMs present a complex landscape of security threats spanning adversarial attacks, privacy breaches, ethical dilemmas, and multi-domain vulnerabilities. Addressing these challenges requires a multi-pronged approach combining technical safeguards, ethical AI frameworks, and regulatory compliance mechanisms. Proactive risk assessment, continuous model auditing, and global collaboration among stakeholders remain essential to harness the benefits of LLMs while minimizing potential harms (Veluru, 2024; Shafik, 2024; Zangana & Li, 2025).

The security threats faced by Large Language Models can be better understood through a structured flowchart. This diagram organizes adversarial attacks, privacy vulnerabilities, malicious uses, ethical challenges, and emerging threats into a hierarchical model to highlight their interconnections.

Figure 1. Flowchart of Key Security Threats in LLMs

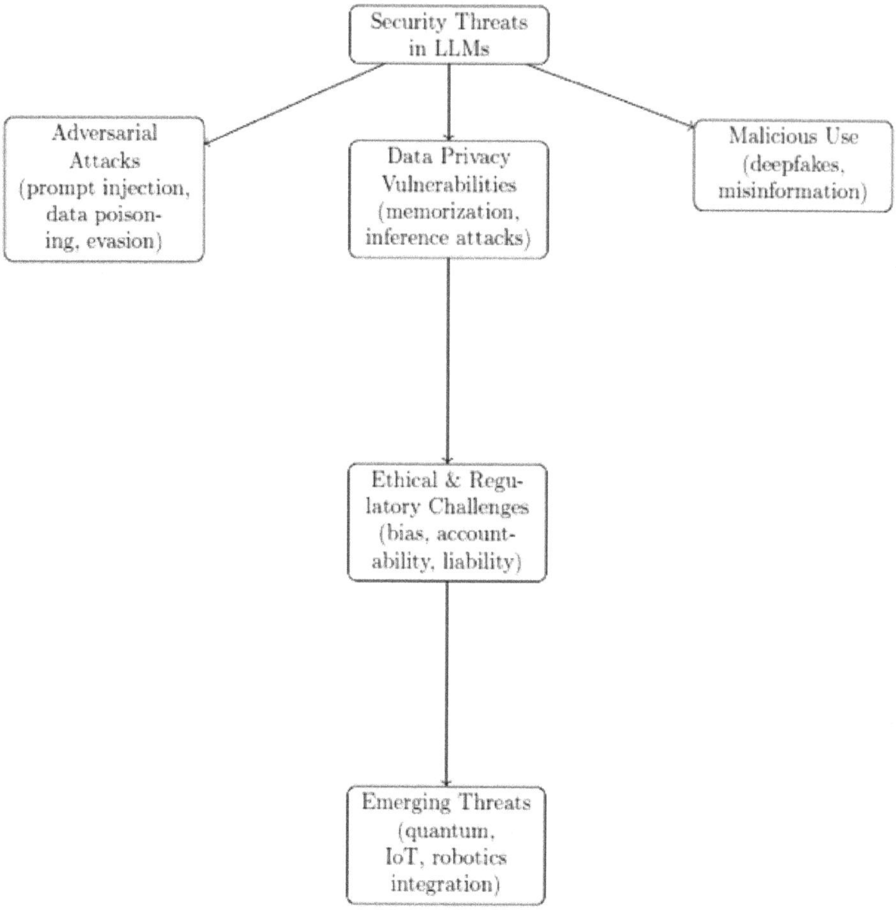

3. EXISTING LEGAL AND REGULATORY LANDSCAPE

The contemporary legal and regulatory landscape is increasingly shaped by the rapid proliferation of emerging technologies, environmental imperatives, and global socio-economic transformations. Understanding this landscape is crucial for organizations, policymakers, and researchers navigating compliance, ethical governance, and innovation across multiple domains.

3.1. Legal and Regulatory Frameworks in Artificial Intelligence

Artificial intelligence (AI) has become a focal point for legal and regulatory scrutiny worldwide due to its transformative impact across sectors, ranging from healthcare to finance and cybersecurity. Various jurisdictions have developed regulatory frameworks addressing AI's ethical, operational, and safety implications. For instance, the European Union's AI Act represents a pioneering regulatory approach, focusing on risk-based classifications and compliance obligations for high-risk AI applications (Butt, 2024). Similarly, in the healthcare sector, multi-jurisdictional studies emphasize the necessity of clear regulatory guidance to ensure AI-driven diagnostic tools meet safety, transparency, and accountability standards (Pesapane, Bracchi, Mulligan, Linnikov, Maslennikov, et al., 2021; Pesapane, Volonté, Codari, & Sardanelli, 2018; Mennella, Maniscalco, De Pietro, & Esposito, 2024).

Beyond compliance, ethical considerations are increasingly codified within AI regulations. Research demonstrates that AI ethics frameworks, particularly in sensitive domains like finance, rely on transparent algorithmic accountability, bias mitigation, and data protection protocols (Ali & Aysan, 2024, 2025; Ali, Zafar, & Aysan, 2024). In digital forensics, the legal admissibility of AI-driven evidence is complex, requiring harmonized standards for cross-jurisdictional investigations and algorithmic transparency (Iyengar, Nabavirazavi, Hariprasad, HB, & Mohan, 2025; Mhia-alddin, 2026).

Ethical hacking and cybersecurity governance also fall under this evolving landscape. AI-enhanced penetration testing is subject to regulatory oversight to prevent misuse, ensure ethical compliance, and maintain organizational security (Al-Sinani & Mitchell, 2024; Al-Sinani, Sahli, Mitchell, & Al-Siyabi, 2025; Veluru, 2024). These developments illustrate a growing convergence of technical innovation, legal mandates, and ethical stewardship in AI deployment.

Different jurisdictions adopt distinct approaches to AI and LLM regulation. The following bar chart compares the European Union's risk-based AI Act with the United States' sector-specific, innovation-oriented model.

Figure 2. Comparison of EU vs US Regulatory Approaches to AI

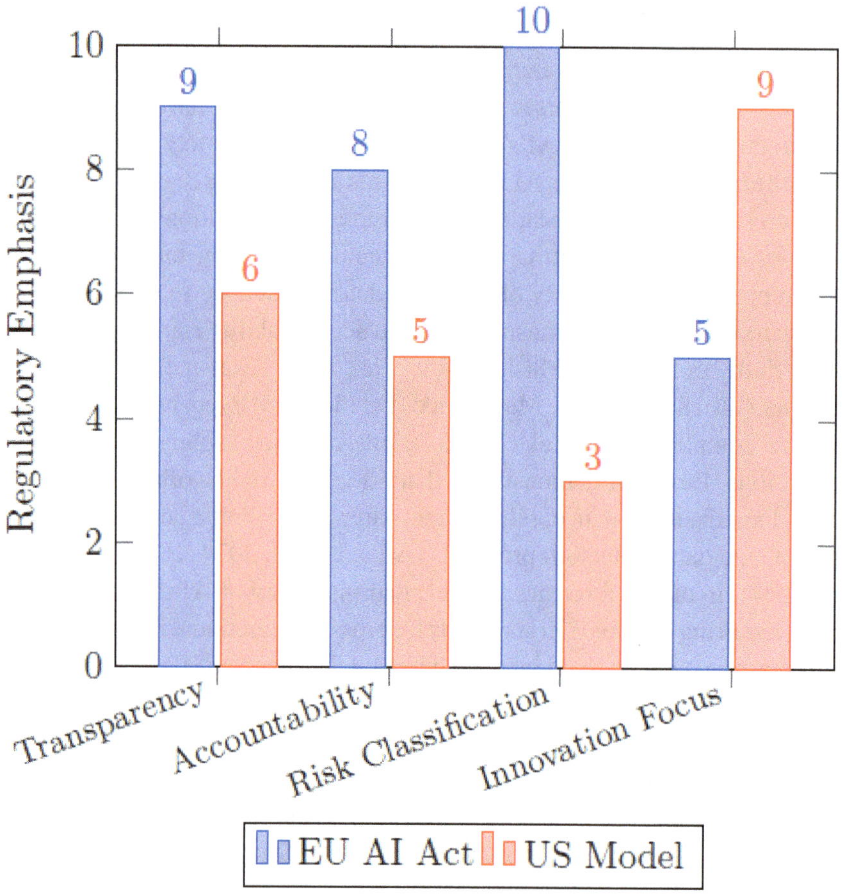

3.2. Contract Law and Commercial Regulation

Contractual governance in technology-driven environments presents unique regulatory challenges. Legal scholarship highlights ambiguities surrounding contract expiry, termination clauses, and post-expiry obligations in AI-integrated projects (Mhia-Alddin & Hussein, 2025; Mhia-Alddin, 2025). AI-powered contract management systems offer potential risk mitigation strategies but simultaneously introduce new compliance considerations (Mhia-Alddin & Hussein, 2025).

Commercial law is further complicated in sectors where technology intersects with intellectual property, reverse logistics, and cross-border trade. Studies on patent injunctions, reverse payments, and bankruptcy risks reveal that regulatory oversight must balance innovation incentives with risk containment (Pai, 2018; Manganelli, 2019; Narayana, Pati, & Padhi, 2019). Regulatory authorities increasingly call for integrated legal frameworks that account for technological, financial, and operational risks simultaneously.

3.3. Environmental and Sustainability Regulation

Global climate imperatives have catalyzed regulatory action aimed at sustainability, net-zero emissions, and environmental protection. International environmental law, including treaties and national regulatory instruments, establishes compliance obligations for industries, particularly in developing economies such as Nigeria (Akindele & Chabinga, 2024; Ali, 2024; Aloamaka, 2024). Biodiversity protection, climate adaptation, and renewable energy deployment are closely monitored through legal mechanisms that govern environmental impact assessments, pollution control, and resource utilization (Singh & Kaunert, 2025; Saikia, 2024; Oduro, Uzougbo, & Ugwu, 2024; Jafarizadeh, Yamini, Zolfaghari, Esmaeilion, Assad, & Soltani, 2024).

Regulatory challenges also emerge at the intersection of technology and environmental law. For example, the deployment of AI-powered drones in environmental monitoring requires compliance with aviation regulations, data privacy laws, and environmental protection standards (Arya & Rastogi, 2024; Maguluri, Arularasan, & Boopathi, 2023). Similarly, green technology adoption in industry is constrained by both legal compliance obligations and government incentives for eco-friendly practices (Emon, Khan, Rahman, Hamid, & Yaakub, 2025; Soomro, Suhrab, & Abbasi, 2025; Patra, 2025).

3.4. Healthcare, Digital Forensics, and Public Safety

In healthcare, the regulation of AI and robotics involves both safety standards and ethical mandates, addressing human rights considerations, liability, and clinical accountability (Ho, 2023; Verma, Rao, Eluri, & Sharma, 2020; Terry, 2019; Sheliemina, 2024). The legal framework is further complicated by cross-border deployment, telemedicine, and AI-enabled diagnostics, which require harmonized standards for liability and informed consent.

In public safety and forensic investigations, AI applications such as privacy-preserving digital forensics and threat detection are regulated to balance public interest with individual rights (San Biagio, Cipolla, La Mattina, & Morreale, 2023; Zangana & Li, 2025; Shafik, 2024). National surveys in drug control, border security, and narcotics regulation highlight how legislation intersects with AI-enabled monitoring and law enforcement (Borta, Alemu, Shute, Zewdie, Fantaw, Shimelis, et al., 2024).

3.5. International Law and Cross-Jurisdictional Considerations

The legal landscape extends beyond national jurisdictions, particularly in areas such as international trade, maritime law, climate governance, and cross-border AI deployment. International legal instruments constrain offshore energy exploitation, regulate environmental standards, and govern transnational AI applications (Wang, 2024; Chowdhury, 2024; Sakapaji, García Molinos, Parilova, Gavrilyeva, & Yakovleva, 2024). Scholars note that legal harmonization is vital to ensuring regulatory efficacy while promoting technological and environmental innovation (Daniel, 2024; Drexl, Conde, & Kim, 2025; Ali, 2024).

3.6. Key Challenges and Gaps

Despite comprehensive regulatory initiatives, several challenges persist. Fragmentation of laws across jurisdictions, rapid technological evolution, and limited enforcement capacity hinder effective oversight (Darvishi, Liu, & Lim, 2022; Fenwick, Molnar, & Frangos, 2024; Gaurav, Chui, Arya, Attar, Bansal, Alhomoud, & Psannis, 2024). Furthermore, the integration of ethical norms into enforceable regulation remains uneven, particularly for generative AI, cybersecurity, and industrial automation (Ali & Aysan, 2024; Rashid & Kausik, 2024; Vyawahare, Khandelwal, & Rathod, 2024).

Emerging literature emphasizes the necessity of adaptive legal frameworks that accommodate evolving AI capabilities, green technologies, and global sustainability standards (Campus, 2024; Eswaran & Eswaran, 2025; Leontidis, 2024; Luan, Perron, Victor, Wan, Niu, & Xiao, 2024). Policymakers are urged to foster harmonized regulatory ecosystems, bridging ethical guidelines, compliance enforcement, and technological innovation to ensure resilient and sustainable development.

4. INTELLECTUAL PROPERTY AND DATA GOVERNANCE

The rapid evolution of digital technologies, particularly artificial intelligence (AI) and large-scale data analytics, has reshaped the landscape of intellectual property (IP) and data governance. The proliferation of AI-driven innovation introduces new challenges for legal, regulatory, and ethical frameworks, necessitating a nuanced understanding of ownership, rights, and compliance mechanisms (Ali & Aysan, 2024; Ali, 2024). As organizations increasingly rely on data-intensive solutions, effective governance strategies become critical to protect proprietary information, ensure ethical usage, and navigate cross-jurisdictional complexities (Zangana & Li, 2025; Shafik, 2024).

4.1 Intellectual Property in the Era of AI

Intellectual property frameworks are being tested by generative AI systems capable of creating novel content and inventions. Traditional IP regimes, which typically require human authorship or inventorship, face challenges in attributing rights to AI-generated works (Ali, H., Zafar, & Aysan, 2024; Ali & Aysan, 2025). Scholars have emphasized the need for adaptive legal approaches that recognize AI contributions while maintaining incentives for human creativity (Mhia-Alddin & Hussein, 2025; Mhia-Alddin, 2025). This involves rethinking patent, copyright, and trade secret protections, particularly in sectors where AI accelerates R&D and content production, such as finance, healthcare, and biotechnology (Bharati, 2020; Pesapane, Bracchi, Mulligan, et al., 2021).

Moreover, emerging legal scholarship stresses the importance of addressing AI-related contract risks, including licensing, IP transfers, and post-expiry obligations, to prevent disputes and facilitate commercialization (Mhia-Alddin & Hussein, 2025; Mhia-Alddin, 2025). The intersection of AI, IP, and contract law necessitates mechanisms for monitoring compliance, ensuring proper attribution, and managing potential infringement in complex multi-party collaborations (Pai, 2018; Read, Botha, & Jamaloodien, 2023).

4.2 Data Governance Frameworks

Effective data governance encompasses policies, procedures, and technologies designed to ensure data quality, security, and compliance with legal standards (Shukla & Taneja, 2024; Vyawahare, Khandelwal, & Rathod, 2024). With AI systems relying on massive datasets for training and inference, governance strategies must address issues such as privacy, consent, data sovereignty, and ethical usage (Iyengar, Nabavirazavi, Hariprasad, et al., 2025; Shafik, 2024). Federated learning and privacy-preserving AI approaches are increasingly recommended to reconcile the benefits of data-driven innovation with the imperative to protect individual rights and sensitive information (Iyengar et al., 2025).

Cross-border data flows, particularly in multi-jurisdictional research or commercial deployments, introduce additional complexity. Organizations must navigate varying regulatory regimes, including the European Union's GDPR, U.S. privacy laws, and emerging frameworks in Asia and Africa (Verma, Rao, Eluri, & Sharma, 2020; Oduro, Uzougbo, & Ugwu, 2024; Singh & Kaunert, 2025). Governance models that integrate risk assessment, access controls, and accountability measures are essential to maintain compliance and foster trust among stakeholders (Fenwick, Molnar, & Frangos, 2024; Trotsyuk et al., 2024).

4.3 Integrating AI with IP and Data Governance

AI technologies can support IP management and data governance by automating monitoring, enforcing compliance, and detecting misuse (Al-Sinani & Mitchell, 2024; Al-Sinani, Sahli, Mitchell, & Al-Siyabi, 2025). For example, machine learning algorithms can flag potential IP infringement, while blockchain and digital ledger technologies provide immutable records of data access and usage (Gaurav et al., 2024; Campus, 2024; Eswaran & Eswaran, 2025). In sectors such as healthcare, finance, and energy, these integrated approaches enhance transparency, security, and accountability while aligning with regulatory expectations (Mennella, Maniscalco, De Pietro, & Esposito, 2024; Naili, Mangkunegara, Purwono, & Baballe, 2025).

The convergence of AI, IP, and data governance also intersects with sustainability and social responsibility objectives. By ensuring ethical AI deployment and safeguarding data integrity, organizations can contribute to broader societal goals, including environmental stewardship, equitable access to technology, and the promotion of innovation ecosystems (Ali, 2024; Akindele & Chabinga, 2024; Singh & Kaunert, 2025; Emom et al., 2025).

The intersection of intellectual property and data governance in the AI era involves overlapping domains of compliance, ownership, and accountability. The following Venn diagram illustrates how IP rights and data governance frameworks converge around ethical and legal challenges in LLMs.

Figure 3. Intersection of Intellectual Property and Data Governance in AI

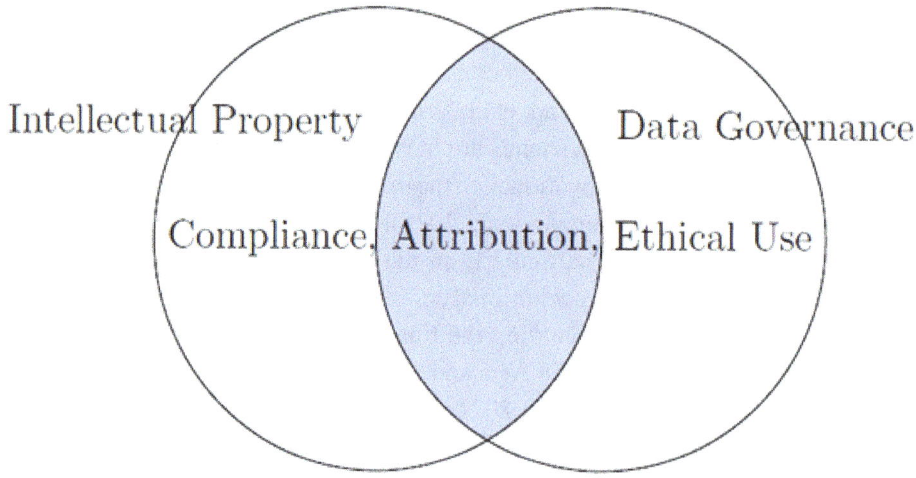

4.4 Challenges and Future Directions

Despite advancements, significant challenges remain. Legal ambiguities regarding AI-generated IP, cross-jurisdictional data compliance, and ethical governance persist (Mhia-Alddin & Hussein, 2025; Trotsyuk et al., 2024). Emerging frameworks advocate for adaptive legislation, harmonized standards, and enhanced collaboration between legal, technical, and organizational stakeholders to address these issues (Butt, 2024; Zreik, 2024; Larsson et al., 2021). Additionally, the development of AI auditing tools, compliance dashboards, and risk assessment frameworks is critical for proactive governance (Veluru, 2024; Fenwick et al., 2024).

Future research should focus on refining legal doctrines for AI authorship, developing dynamic data governance models, and leveraging AI to optimize IP protection while ensuring ethical compliance. Furthermore, interdisciplinary efforts that integrate law, ethics, computer science, and business strategy are essential to navigate the evolving landscape of IP and data governance (Darvishi, Liu, & Lim, 2022; Leontidis, 2024; Filetti, Fenza, & Gallo, 2024).

In conclusion, intellectual property and data governance in the AI era demand comprehensive, adaptive, and ethically grounded strategies. By addressing emerging legal, technical, and ethical challenges, organizations can harness AI innovations responsibly while safeguarding stakeholder interests and promoting sustainable technological progress (Rashid & Kausik, 2024; Pimpalkar et al., 2024; Zangana & Li, 2025).

5. PRIVACY AND SECURITY REGULATIONS

In the age of rapid digital transformation and the pervasive deployment of artificial intelligence (AI), privacy and security regulations have become central to safeguarding sensitive data, maintaining ethical standards, and ensuring compliance across industries. With AI systems increasingly integrated into finance, healthcare, digital forensics, and governmental applications, legal frameworks and regulatory mechanisms must evolve to address the multifaceted challenges posed by these technologies (Ali, H., & Aysan, 2025; Zangana, H. M., & Li, 2025).

5.1 Legal Frameworks and International Standards

The regulatory landscape governing privacy and security is highly diverse, spanning national laws, international treaties, and sector-specific guidelines. International frameworks emphasize harmonization and cross-border enforcement to mitigate risks associated with data transfers and cyber incidents. For instance, Akindele and

Chabinga (2024) highlight the role of Nigeria in aligning national legislation with global environmental and security standards, emphasizing that regulatory compliance extends beyond environmental concerns to include data and cybersecurity safeguards. Similarly, Aloamaka (2024) and Ali (2024) emphasize the integration of legal norms with sustainability and governance policies, reinforcing that compliance mechanisms must account for broader societal and ethical dimensions.

In the context of AI and digital technologies, sector-specific regulations have been emerging. Butt (2024) provides an in-depth analysis of the European Union's AI Act, which establishes strict requirements for data privacy, risk management, and accountability in AI deployment. In healthcare, Pesapane et al. (2018, 2021) and Terry (2019) demonstrate that regulatory frameworks across the EU, US, China, and Russia are evolving to ensure that AI-driven diagnostic systems adhere to privacy, security, and ethical guidelines, while also addressing liability concerns.

5.2 Ethical and Security Considerations

Privacy regulations are closely linked with ethical imperatives, especially in AI-enabled systems that process sensitive personal data. Ali, H., Zafar, M. B., and Aysan, A. F. (2024) argue for multi-level analyses in financial AI applications to ensure compliance with ethical and privacy standards. Shukla and Taneja (2024) reinforce this, noting that integrating generative AI in education requires strict data governance to prevent unauthorized access and misuse.

Ethical hacking and cybersecurity practices have become instrumental in identifying and mitigating vulnerabilities within AI systems. Al-Sinani and Mitchell (2024) conducted experiments in Linux-based ethical hacking to test AI system security, while Al-Sinani et al. (2025) demonstrated how AI can enhance security audits, highlighting the dual role of AI in both enabling and safeguarding digital infrastructures. Maguluri, Arularasan, and Boopathi (2023) specifically address security concerns for AI-based drones in smart cities, illustrating the intersection of regulatory compliance, AI, and urban safety.

5.3 AI in Digital Forensics and Federated Learning

Privacy-preserving techniques, particularly in digital forensics, are emerging as key mechanisms to comply with security regulations. Iyengar et al. (2025) discuss federated learning frameworks that enable AI to perform forensic analyses without centralizing sensitive data, thereby minimizing exposure to breaches. Zangana and Li (2025) emphasize future trends in digital forensics where AI-driven tools enhance privacy protection while ensuring evidentiary integrity. Mhia-alddin (2026) further explores the cross-jurisdictional legal challenges posed by AI in forensic investigations, underlining the need for harmonized global regulatory approaches.

5.4 Regulatory Challenges in Emerging Technologies

Emerging technologies such as quantum computing, large-scale AI analytics, and autonomous systems introduce novel regulatory challenges. Campus (2024) and Eswaran & Eswaran (2025) highlight the potential risks and the need for adaptive legal frameworks in the integration of AI with quantum and semiconductor technologies. Similarly, environmental and industrial applications, including renewable energy (Oduro et al., 2024; Jafarizadeh et al., 2024) and Industry 4.0 systems (Patra, 2025), require compliance mechanisms that balance technological innovation with privacy and security considerations.

Additionally, AI-based diagnostics and decision-making systems necessitate strict regulatory oversight to ensure accountability and prevent misuse (Naili et al., 2025; Mennella et al., 2024). Trotsyuk et al. (2024) advocate for risk mitigation frameworks that preempt potential misuse of AI in biomedical and healthcare research. In financial systems, Gaurav et al. (2024) demonstrate the use of AI-driven semantic web approaches to detect phishing attacks, underscoring the importance of regulatory frameworks that adapt to evolving cyber threats.

5.5 Global Perspectives on Privacy and Security Compliance

The international community is increasingly recognizing the importance of privacy and security in achieving sustainable and ethical AI deployment. Singh and Kaunert (2025), Soomro, Suhrab, and Abbasi (2025), and Saikia (2024) examine cross-national regulatory strategies for environmental, industrial, and technological governance, emphasizing that compliance is not only a legal obligation but also a tool for resilience and sustainability. Shafik (2024) specifically addresses ChatGPT systems, demonstrating how consumer-facing AI applications must safeguard user data while complying with regulatory mandates.

Across diverse domains, from maritime law enforcement (Wang, 2024) to STEM education (Jamro & Jamro, 2023), the convergence of privacy, security, and AI regulation is evident. Researchers such as Vyawahare, Khandelwal, and Rathod (2024) illustrate how AI can be harnessed to prevent online harassment while adhering to ethical and legal standards. At the same time, Fenwick, Molnar, and Frangos (2024) emphasize human-centric approaches in AI adoption to ensure compliance is both technically and ethically grounded.

5.6 Summary

Privacy and security regulations in the era of AI are multifaceted, encompassing ethical imperatives, technological safeguards, and cross-jurisdictional legal standards. As AI continues to permeate sectors from finance to healthcare, and environmental to industrial applications, compliance frameworks must evolve dynamically to address new threats, mitigate risks, and uphold societal trust. The literature highlights a global trend toward harmonized regulation, ethical adoption, and technical innovation, establishing a roadmap for secure, responsible, and sustainable AI deployment (Ali, H., & Aysan, A. F., 2025; Zangana, H. M., & Li, 2025; Shukla & Taneja, 2024).

6. LIABILITY AND ACCOUNTABILITY ISSUES

The rapid adoption of artificial intelligence (AI), particularly in sectors such as finance, healthcare, autonomous systems, and digital forensics, has generated significant concerns surrounding liability and accountability. These concerns arise from the inherently complex, opaque, and often autonomous nature of AI-driven systems, which challenge traditional legal and regulatory frameworks that were designed for human-centered decision-making (Ali, 2024; Zangana & Li, 2025). Accountability issues are further exacerbated by the multi-stakeholder environments in which AI operates, often involving software developers, data providers, end-users, and regulatory bodies (Mhia-Alddin, 2026; Fenwick, Molnar, & Frangos, 2024).

6.1 Legal Challenges in Assigning Liability

One of the primary challenges in AI liability is determining who is legally responsible when harm occurs. Traditional liability frameworks, such as tort or contract law, often presume human agency, which becomes ambiguous when decisions are made by autonomous systems (Mhia-Alddin & Hussein, 2025a). For instance, in AI-driven financial platforms, mismanagement or algorithmic errors may result in significant economic losses, yet pinpointing the accountable party—whether the AI vendor, developer, or user—remains complex (Ali, Zafar, & Aysan, 2024; Rashid & Kausik, 2024). Similarly, in healthcare, misdiagnoses by AI diagnostic tools raise questions about professional negligence versus machine error (Pesapane, Bracchi, Mulligan, et al., 2021; Sheliemina, 2024).

Cross-jurisdictional variations further complicate accountability. For example, while the European Union's AI Act establishes stringent responsibilities for high-risk AI systems, other regions rely on fragmented regulations that may not adequately address emerging AI risks (Butt, 2024; Narayana, Pati, & Padhi, 2019). In addition, contract-based frameworks often struggle to address liability in AI deployments, particularly where contract expiry or ambiguous clauses exist, highlighting the need for AI-specific contractual safeguards (Mhia-Alddin & Hussein, 2025b; Mhia-Alddin, 2025).

6.2 Accountability in Autonomous and AI-Driven Systems

AI systems, particularly those leveraging machine learning and generative AI, present unique accountability challenges because outcomes are often probabilistic rather than deterministic. Generative AI, for instance, can produce outputs that are novel and unpredictable, making it difficult to trace causality and assign blame (Ali & Aysan, 2024; Ali, Zafar, & Aysan, 2024). In critical sectors like defense or climate monitoring, accountability lapses can have severe societal consequences, from environmental damage to threats to human safety (Batabyal, 2024; Akindele & Chabinga, 2024; Arya & Rastogi, 2024).

The concept of "algorithmic accountability" has emerged as a proposed solution, emphasizing transparency, explainability, and auditability of AI systems (Veluru, 2024; Eisenberg, 2024). However, operationalizing accountability is challenging due to proprietary algorithms, large-scale data dependencies, and the dynamic nature of AI learning processes (Gaurav et al., 2024; Campus, 2024; Eswaran & Eswaran, 2025).

6.3 Ethical and Regulatory Implications

Beyond legal liability, ethical responsibility remains central to AI governance. Ethical lapses in AI use—such as bias, discrimination, or data misuse—can lead to reputational, financial, and regulatory consequences (Ali & Aysan, 2025; Shukla & Taneja, 2024; Vyawahare, Khandelwal, & Rathod, 2024). Governments and international bodies are increasingly emphasizing AI ethics frameworks that incorporate accountability mechanisms, including human oversight, risk assessment, and reporting obligations (Soomro, Suhrab, & Abbasi, 2025; Singh & Kaunert, 2025).

In AI-powered contract management and digital forensics, accountability extends to ensuring compliance with legal obligations during AI deployment. Studies indicate that AI can enhance contract risk assessment, track compliance, and monitor expiry obligations, but legal uncertainty remains in cross-jurisdictional scenarios (Mhia-Alddin & Hussein, 2025c; Mhia-Alddin, 2025; Zangana & Li, 2025; Iyengar et al., 2025). Similarly, in AI-enhanced cybersecurity and fraud detection, ensuring responsible deployment requires clear allocation of accountability across human and machine agents (Ali & Aysan, 2024; Al-Sinani, Sahli, Mitchell, & Al-Siyabi, 2025).

6.4 Risk Mitigation Strategies

To address liability and accountability challenges, several strategies have been proposed:

1. **Regulatory Alignment:** Developing harmonized AI regulations that clearly define liability, especially for high-risk systems (Butt, 2024; Pesapane, Volonté, Codari, & Sardanelli, 2018).
2. **Transparent AI Design:** Implementing explainable AI (XAI) and audit trails to allow tracing of decisions and actions (Veluru, 2024; Gaurav et al., 2024).
3. **Contractual Safeguards:** Updating legal contracts to include AI-specific clauses for risk allocation, liability, and compliance monitoring (Mhia-Alddin & Hussein, 2025a; Mhia-Alddin & Hussein, 2025b).
4. **Ethical Oversight:** Establishing independent ethics boards and human-in-the-loop governance to ensure responsible AI deployment (Ali & Aysan, 2025; Fenwick, Molnar, & Frangos, 2024).
5. **Cross-Jurisdictional Collaboration:** Encouraging international cooperation to address liability gaps and promote consistent standards (Akindele & Chabinga, 2024; Oduro, Uzougbo, & Ugwu, 2024; Aloamaka, 2024).

6.5 Summary

Liability and accountability in AI deployment remain highly complex, influenced by technological opacity, regulatory fragmentation, and ethical considerations. Addressing these challenges requires a multi-pronged approach that integrates legal reform, ethical governance, technical transparency, and international cooperation. Without such measures, the societal benefits of AI risk being undermined by legal disputes, ethical lapses, and uncontrolled technological consequences (Trotsyuk et al., 2024; Rashid & Kausik, 2024; Zreik, 2024).

7. POLICY APPROACHES FOR SECURING LLMS

Large Language Models (LLMs) have become increasingly influential across multiple domains, including finance, healthcare, education, and cybersecurity. However, their power also introduces significant risks, including misuse, data privacy breaches, model bias, and adversarial attacks. As such, securing LLMs is not solely a technical challenge but also a policy and governance challenge. This section explores the key policy approaches to ensuring the safe, ethical, and accountable deployment of LLMs.

7.1. Regulatory and Legal Frameworks

Regulating LLMs requires comprehensive legal frameworks that address accountability, liability, and compliance in AI deployment. Policymakers must balance innovation with safeguarding users from potential harms. The European Union's AI Act is one of the first comprehensive regulatory attempts, establishing requirements for high-risk AI systems, transparency obligations, and risk management measures (Butt, 2024). Similar regulatory efforts are underway in healthcare, where AI-driven diagnostic tools are governed by frameworks that ensure safety, accuracy, and ethical compliance (Pesapane, Bracchi, Mulligan, Linnikov, Maslennikov, & Carrafiello, 2021; Pesapane, Volonté, Codari, & Sardanelli, 2018).

Across jurisdictions, legal considerations include intellectual property, contract enforcement, and liability for misuse of AI outputs (Mhia-Alddin & Hussein, 2025; Mhia-Alddin, 2025; Mhia-alddin, 2026; Pai, 2018). Contractual agreements related to LLM outputs, data usage, and system integration must include clauses to address expiry, termination, and risk mitigation to ensure post-deployment compliance (Mhia-Alddin & Hussein, 2025; Mhia-Alddin, 2025).

In addition, national legal systems are increasingly integrating AI-specific guidelines to secure LLM usage in public services, law enforcement, and critical infrastructure (Bharati, 2020; Vyawahare, Khandelwal, & Rathod, 2024; Shafik, 2024). Legal frameworks must also address cross-border data flows, intellectual property rights, and the admissibility of AI-generated evidence in judicial processes (Zangana & Li, 2025; Narayana, Pati, & Padhi, 2019).

7.2. Ethical and Governance Considerations

Ethical considerations are central to LLM security policy. Issues include fairness, transparency, accountability, and the prevention of harmful outputs. Scholars emphasize that governance frameworks should embed ethical principles into the development and deployment lifecycle of AI systems (Ali & Aysan, 2025; Mennella, Maniscalco, De Pietro, & Esposito, 2024; Verma & Rohit, 2024).

In finance, ethical frameworks ensure that AI models do not perpetuate discriminatory practices or market manipulation (Ali, Zafar, & Aysan, 2024; Ali & Aysan, 2024). Similarly, AI deployment in education, healthcare, and security domains must respect privacy, consent, and data sovereignty (Shukla & Taneja, 2024; Jamro & Jamro, 2023; Ho, 2023). AI-enhanced ethical hacking experiments demonstrate that ethical and technical safeguards can be combined to identify and mitigate vulnerabilities in AI systems before deployment (Al-Sinani & Mitchell, 2024; Al-Sinani, Sahli, Mitchell, & Al-Siyabi, 2025).

7.3. Risk Assessment and Management Policies

Policymakers advocate for structured risk assessment approaches to mitigate the misuse and unintended consequences of LLMs. Risk management strategies involve scenario planning, adversarial testing, continuous monitoring, and human-in-the-loop validation (Trotsyuk et al., 2024; Veluru, 2024; Gaurav et al., 2024). Systems-level policy modeling can guide risk identification, prediction, and mitigation (Schünemann, Johanning, Reger, Herold, & Bruckner, 2024).

Federated learning and privacy-preserving AI approaches have been proposed to reduce the risk of data leaks and enhance secure model training across decentralized environments (Iyengar, Nabavirazavi, Hariprasad, HB, & Mohan, 2025). Similarly, policies must address vulnerabilities in AI-driven critical infrastructures, such as drones in smart cities, autonomous vehicles, and defense systems, to prevent malicious exploitation (Maguluri, Arularasan, & Boopathi, 2023; Arya & Rastogi, 2024).

7.4. International Coordination and Standards

LLM security is a global concern requiring international collaboration. Cross-border standards, treaties, and guidelines help harmonize ethical, technical, and regulatory requirements. Mechanisms developed for environmental governance, climate change, and energy regulation offer useful analogies for AI governance, demonstrating how international law and cooperation can be leveraged (Akindele & Chabinga, 2024; Ali, 2024; Aloamaka, 2024; Chowdhury, 2024; Saikia, 2024; Singh & Kaunert, 2025; Soomro, Suhrab, & Abbasi, 2025; Wang, 2024).

Furthermore, aligning AI policy with sustainability and ethical frameworks ensures that technology development supports societal well-being, mitigates environmental impact, and promotes equitable access (Emon, Khan, Rahman, Hamid, & Yaakub, 2025; Patra, 2025). Quantum machine learning and AI integration into semiconductor technology also require international policy coordination to prevent security gaps in cutting-edge AI infrastructure (Campus, 2024; Eswaran & Eswaran, 2025).

7.5. Organizational Policies and Best Practices

Organizations deploying LLMs must complement national and international regulations with internal policies. Best practices include robust access controls, audit trails, employee training, incident response planning, and model documentation (Fenwick, Molnar, & Frangos, 2024; Rashid & Kausik, 2024; Verma, Rao, Eluri, & Sharma, 2020; Larson et al., 2021). Policies for data governance, model interpretability, and ethical decision-making should be institutionalized to prevent misuse and enhance trust (Leontidis, 2024; Luan et al., 2024; Filetti, Fenza, & Gallo, 2024).

Additionally, organizations should engage in proactive threat detection using AI-powered tools to monitor, analyze, and respond to emerging vulnerabilities, especially in online harassment, fraud detection, and critical infrastructure security (San Biagio, Cipolla, La Mattina, & Morreale, 2023; Vyawahare, Khandelwal, & Rathod, 2024; Gaurav et al., 2024). The integration of LLMs in contract management and commercial law contexts highlights the need for policies ensuring compliance, post-expiry obligations, and risk mitigation (Mhia-Alddin & Hussein, 2025; Mhia-Alddin, 2025; Mhia-Alddin & Hussein, 2025).

7.6 Summary

Securing LLMs is a multidimensional challenge that spans legal, ethical, technical, and organizational domains. Effective policy approaches combine regulatory compliance, ethical governance, structured risk management, international coordination, and internal organizational practices. Only through a cohesive policy framework can the deployment of LLMs be made safe, responsible, and aligned with societal and global interests.

Policy approaches for securing LLMs can be visualized as layered safeguards, ranging from organizational practices at the base to international coordination at the top. This pyramid diagram emphasizes the multi-level structure of governance.

Figure 4. Multi-Layered Policy Pyramid for Securing LLMs

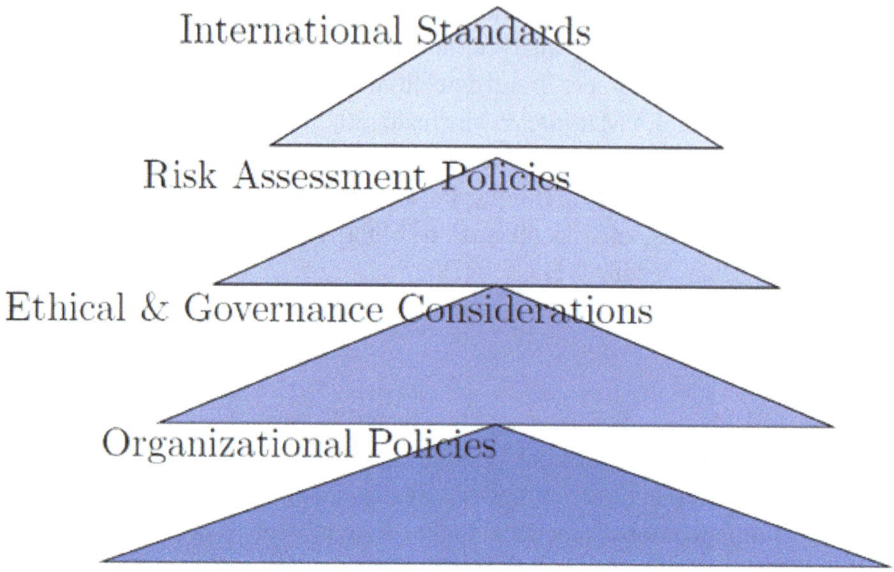

8. ETHICAL AND HUMAN RIGHTS CONSIDERATIONS

The rapid proliferation of artificial intelligence (AI) technologies and digital innovations has raised critical ethical and human rights concerns across multiple domains, from finance and healthcare to environmental governance and security. As AI systems increasingly influence decision-making processes, it becomes imperative to examine the ethical implications and human rights frameworks that should guide their development, deployment, and regulation.

8.1. Ethical Implications of AI Technologies

Ethical considerations in AI extend beyond technical functionality to issues of fairness, transparency, accountability, and privacy. Generative AI, for instance, raises concerns regarding the ethical use of automated content generation, intellectual property rights, and bias in decision-making algorithms (Ali & Aysan, 2025; Ali, H., Zafar, & Aysan, 2024). Ethical hacking and cybersecurity practices are evolving with AI-enhancements, offering potential for both protection and exploitation, which necessitates a robust ethical framework for responsible experimentation and deployment (Al-Sinani & Mitchell, 2024; Al-Sinani, Sahli, Mitchell, & Al-Siyabi, 2025). Similarly, the integration of AI in finance, including predictive and algorithmic systems, demands rigorous ethical oversight to prevent discrimination, fraud, and systemic financial risks (Ali & Aysan, 2024; Gaurav et al., 2024).

8.2. Privacy, Data Protection, and Human Rights

Privacy and data protection remain central human rights concerns in AI applications. AI-powered systems, such as federated learning frameworks for digital forensics, must ensure data integrity while safeguarding sensitive personal information (Iyengar et al., 2025; Shafik, 2024). In healthcare, AI-based diagnostic tools and predictive models raise ethical questions related to informed consent, patient autonomy, and equitable access to medical services (Mennella, Maniscalco, De Pietro, & Esposito, 2024; Pesapane, Volonté, Codari, & Sardanelli, 2018; Larsson et al., 2021). The implementation of AI must align with international human rights principles, including the right to science, health, and protection from discrimination (Ho, 2023; Verma, Rao, Eluri, & Sharma, 2020).

8.3. AI in Governance, Climate, and Environmental Sustainability

The ethical governance of AI intersects significantly with environmental sustainability and climate change mitigation. Policies related to net-zero targets, sustainable resource management, and green technology applications necessitate an ethical lens to balance development with ecological responsibility (Ali, 2024; Akindele & Chabinga, 2024; Aloamaka, 2024; Emon et al., 2025; Chowdhury, 2024; Saikia, 2024; Singh & Kaunert, 2025). Governments and regulatory bodies must ensure that AI solutions used in energy, agriculture, and industrial contexts are environmentally responsible, socially equitable, and transparent in their impact (Jafarizadeh et al., 2024; Oduro, Uzougbo, & Ugwu, 2024; Patra, 2025; Soomro, Suhrab, & Abbasi, 2025).

8.4. Human Rights in Digital and Forensic Contexts

The application of AI in law enforcement, forensic investigation, and contract management carries both opportunities and risks for human rights. AI-powered digital forensics and contract compliance tools must be deployed with accountability and due regard for legal boundaries, data protection, and anti-discrimination principles (Mhia-Alddin & Hussein, 2025a; Mhia-Alddin & Hussein, 2025b; Mhia-alddin, 2026; Zangana & Li, 2025; Bharati, 2020). Misuse of AI in surveillance, autonomous weaponry, and warfare introduces ethical dilemmas concerning proportionality, civilian protection, and international law compliance (Batabyal, 2024; Maguluri, Arularasan, & Boopathi, 2023). Moreover, digital systems must safeguard vulnerable populations, ensuring AI-driven interventions in social services, housing, and education respect the rights and dignity of all individuals (Cooper & Zell, 2023; Jamro & Jamro, 2023; Vyawahare, Khandelwal, & Rathod, 2024; Pimpalkar, Wankhade, Chole, & Golhar, 2024).

8.5. Regulation, Accountability, and Ethical Oversight

Ethical governance requires comprehensive regulatory frameworks and proactive policy measures to ensure AI is developed and applied responsibly. Legislative initiatives such as the EU AI Act, coupled with organizational guidelines, emphasize transparency, accountability, and risk mitigation across AI systems (Butt, 2024; Fenwick, Molnar, & Frangos, 2024; Daniel, 2024; Drexl, Conde, & Kim, 2025). Compliance mechanisms and audit trails are essential for enforcing ethical standards, particularly in sectors where AI may influence critical decisions, such as healthcare, finance, and defense (Verma & Rohit, 2024; Rodriguez & Storer, 2020). Additionally, ethical AI design should incorporate inclusive methodologies, continuous monitoring, and multi-stakeholder engagement to prevent bias, misuse, and inequities (Leontidis, 2024; Filetti, Fenza, & Gallo, 2024; Rashid & Kausik, 2024; Trotsyuk et al., 2024; Veluru, 2024).

8.6. Socioeconomic Equity and Human-Centric AI

Human rights considerations also involve socioeconomic equity, where AI deployment should enhance rather than diminish social welfare. For example, AI-driven educational tools, STEM interventions, and women's safety solutions can foster empowerment and access to opportunities while adhering to ethical guidelines (Shukla & Taneja, 2024; Arya & Rastogi, 2024; Pimpalkar et al., 2024). Ethical frameworks must therefore ensure that AI technologies support sustainable development goals (SDGs), protect marginalized communities, and promote equitable participation in AI benefits globally (Ali, 2024; Singh & Kaunert, 2025; Zreik, 2024).

8.7. Future Directions in Ethical AI Governance

Moving forward, the integration of AI, quantum computing, and emerging technologies demands proactive ethical foresight. Scholars and policymakers must collaborate to develop adaptive ethical frameworks capable of addressing evolving threats, including privacy breaches, algorithmic bias, environmental degradation, and autonomous decision-making risks (Eswaran & Eswaran, 2025; Campus, 2024; Naili, Mangkunegara, Purwono, & Baballe, 2025). Continuous education, stakeholder engagement, and regulatory harmonization will be vital to ensure AI advances human rights while mitigating potential harms (Wang, 2024; Sakapaji, García Molinos, Parilova, Gavrilyeva, & Yakovleva, 2024; Narayana, Pati, & Padhi, 2019).

In conclusion, ethical and human rights considerations must form the cornerstone of AI development and governance. Cross-sector collaboration, robust regulatory oversight, and an unwavering commitment to fairness, transparency, and accountability are essential to ensure AI technologies empower humanity, protect human rights, and contribute to sustainable and equitable societal progress (Ho, 2023; Ali & Aysan, 2025; Fenwick et al., 2024; Mhia-Alddin & Hussein, 2025a; Zangana & Li, 2025).

9. CASE STUDIES

Case studies provide practical insights into how theoretical frameworks, regulations, and technological solutions are applied across diverse domains. This section explores multiple cases involving AI, sustainability, law, healthcare, and industry, highlighting challenges, innovations, and lessons learned.

9.1. AI in Healthcare and Diagnostics

Artificial intelligence has transformed healthcare diagnostics and treatment planning, but its integration raises legal, ethical, and regulatory challenges. Pesapane et al. (2018) and Pesapane et al. (2021) highlight how AI-based diagnostic tools in radiology and healthcare are governed differently across Europe, the United States, China, and Russia, with regulatory frameworks evolving post-pandemic. Sheliemina (2024) emphasizes opportunities and risks in AI-assisted medical diagnostics, particularly concerning accuracy, patient safety, and data privacy. Similarly, Mennella et al. (2024) discuss the ethical and regulatory challenges in adopting AI technologies in healthcare, underscoring the need for clear guidelines and responsible innovation.

Privacy-preserving AI, including federated learning, has shown promise in digital forensics and healthcare applications (Iyengar et al., 2025), allowing sensitive patient data to remain decentralized while enabling robust AI-driven analysis. These developments indicate that case studies in AI healthcare require careful balancing of technological potential and regulatory compliance.

9.2. AI in Industry and Business Applications

AI is increasingly leveraged to improve operational efficiency, risk mitigation, and innovation in industries. Rashid and Kausik (2024) present a comprehensive overview of AI applications across diverse industrial sectors, demonstrating how machine learning and automation enhance productivity and decision-making. Gaurav et al. (2024) focus on e-commerce, showcasing an AI-driven semantic web approach for phishing detection, illustrating how AI can secure digital platforms against emerging cyber threats.

In manufacturing and Industry 4.0, Patra (2025) examines how AI facilitates sustainable production, emphasizing compliance with environmental and safety regulations. Similarly, Pimpalkar et al. (2024) explore predictive AI analytics for women's safety in industrial environments, demonstrating AI's role in socially responsible innovation. Vyawahare et al. (2024) expand this perspective by showing how AI can prevent online harassment in business and education ecosystems.

9.3. Digital Forensics and Cybersecurity

The integration of AI and digital forensics presents both opportunities and legal challenges. Zangana and Li (2025) analyze emerging trends in AI-driven digital forensics, highlighting improvements in evidence analysis, risk mitigation, and investigative accuracy. Mhia-alddin (2026) further explores cross-jurisdictional challenges in the admissibility and accountability of AI-generated forensic evidence.

Ethical hacking studies demonstrate practical applications of AI in cybersecurity. Al-Sinani and Mitchell (2024) and Al-Sinani et al. (2025) conducted Linux-based experiments showing that AI can enhance penetration testing and vulnerability assessments, improving security while adhering to ethical standards. Veluru (2024) emphasizes responsible AI usage to prevent misuse and security breaches, while San Biagio et al. (2023) showcase topic clustering techniques to detect threats against soft targets online, highlighting proactive AI defense strategies.

9.4. Environmental Law, Sustainability, and Climate Action

Sustainability and climate change mitigation are increasingly influenced by AI, regulatory frameworks, and policy alignment. Akindele and Chabinga (2024) examine Nigeria's engagement with international environmental law, revealing challenges in aligning national policy with global sustainability targets. Ali (2024) and Chowdhury (2024) stress the importance of net-zero policies and systemic approaches to climate justice, while Aloamaka (2024) and Saikia (2024) highlight the evolving role of international law in environmental regulation.

Soomro et al. (2025) provide an example from Pakistan where government support, regulatory compliance, and obstacles interact in the implementation of green business practices. Singh and Kaunert (2025) explore biodiversity protection and sustainable trajectories, illustrating how legal frameworks can promote resilient ecosystems. Jafarizadeh et al. (2024) analyze renewable energy storage challenges, while Oduro et al. (2024) showcase regulatory strategies to encourage innovation in sustainable energy adoption.

9.5. Legal and Contractual Case Studies

AI integration into legal processes and commercial contracts has introduced novel challenges. Mhia-Alddin and Hussein (2025) explore AI-powered contract management, including handling expiry, compliance, and risk mitigation. Mhia-Alddin (2025) examines post-expiry obligations in commercial law, proposing frameworks to address emerging risks in AI-assisted contract administration.

Bharati (2020) provides a comparative multi-jurisdictional study on digital forensics use in law enforcement, emphasizing ethical and legal considerations. Bousri (2019) compares arbitration frameworks in Comoros and Uganda, illustrating the interplay between local and international legal systems. Similarly, Pai (2018) discusses patent injunction heuristics in India, highlighting judicial approaches to technological disputes. Read et al. (2023) explore COVID-19 vaccine procurement and contract management in South Africa, demonstrating how legal frameworks influence operational effectiveness.

9.6. AI in Education, STEM, and Societal Applications

In educational contexts, AI has been deployed to enhance STEM learning and societal impact. Jamro and Jamro (2023) present chatbot integration in holistic STEM education, showing how AI facilitates personalized learning and engagement. Luan et al. (2024) illustrate AI-assisted scientometric analyses of research on left-behind children in China, demonstrating the role of AI in social research and policy development. Filetti et al. (2024) discuss AI tools for scholarly writing and research design, offering practical case studies for researchers adopting digital methods.

9.7. AI-Driven Risk Mitigation and Governance

Several case studies highlight AI's role in risk management and ethical governance. Trotsyuk et al. (2024) propose a framework to mitigate potential misuse of

AI in biomedical research, emphasizing safety and ethical adherence. Fenwick et al. (2024) illustrate the role of human resource management in transitioning firms from AI implementation to human-centric adoption, underscoring the importance of organizational alignment.

Darvishi et al. (2022) examine economic and legal implications of emerging technologies, while Drexl et al. (2025) present a position statement from the Max Planck Institute, providing guidance on technology revision and innovation governance.

9.8. AI in Finance, Entrepreneurship, and Social Applications

Generative AI is revolutionizing finance and entrepreneurship. Ali and Aysan (2024, 2025) investigate ethical dimensions and structural topic modeling analyses of AI in finance. Ali et al. (2024) present multi-level AI analyses of financial systems, highlighting opportunities for data-driven decision-making. Zreik (2024) explores AI-driven entrepreneurial idea generation, demonstrating practical applications of machine learning in business development.

9.9 Summary of Case Study Insights

These case studies collectively demonstrate that AI, digital forensics, environmental law, and contract governance are deeply interlinked with legal, ethical, and regulatory considerations. Across healthcare, industry, sustainability, education, and finance, AI serves as a transformative tool, yet successful implementation requires careful alignment with legal frameworks, risk mitigation strategies, and societal values (Batabyal, 2024; Verma et al., 2020; Terry, 2019).

10. GAPS AND CHALLENGES IN CURRENT FRAMEWORKS

Despite the rapid proliferation of AI-driven frameworks and regulatory mechanisms, significant gaps and challenges persist across legal, ethical, technological, and environmental domains. These gaps impede the effective implementation and governance of AI, sustainability policies, and emerging technologies, creating a complex landscape for policymakers, organizations, and researchers.

10.1. Legal and Regulatory Gaps

A recurring issue in contemporary frameworks is the misalignment between technological advancement and regulatory oversight. AI-driven systems, particularly in healthcare, finance, and digital forensics, often outpace existing laws, resulting in ambiguity around liability, accountability, and admissibility of AI-generated outputs (Mhia-alddin, 2026; Zangana & Li, 2025; Pesapane et al., 2021; Larsson et al., 2021). Similarly, contract law and commercial regulations face challenges in accommodating AI-based risk assessment and contract expiry, with unclear post-expiry obligations posing legal uncertainties (Mhia-Alddin & Hussein, 2025; Mhia-Alddin, 2025).

Cross-jurisdictional inconsistencies exacerbate these issues, especially for technologies deployed internationally. For example, variations in AI governance across the EU, US, China, and Russia create regulatory fragmentation that complicates compliance and enforcement (Pesapane et al., 2021; Oduro et al., 2024; Ali, 2024). Emerging domains such as ethical hacking, autonomous warfare, and generative AI further highlight gaps where law and regulation lag behind technical capabilities (Al-Sinani & Mitchell, 2024; Batabyal, 2024; Ali & Aysan, 2025).

10.2. Ethical and Privacy Challenges

Ethical considerations remain a central challenge. AI frameworks struggle with balancing innovation against the protection of human rights, privacy, and fairness. In healthcare, AI diagnostic tools face scrutiny regarding transparency and explainability, raising concerns about bias and accountability (Mennella et al., 2024; Sheliemina, 2024; Ho, 2023). Similarly, in digital forensics and cybersecurity, issues of data privacy, misuse, and federated learning complicate the deployment of AI-driven solutions (Iyengar et al., 2025; Shafik, 2024).

Moreover, ethical risks extend to financial applications of AI, particularly generative AI, where unintended consequences such as algorithmic bias or misuse of sensitive financial data are not fully addressed by existing frameworks (Ali & Aysan, 2024; Ali, Zafar, & Aysan, 2024). The need for human-centric AI adoption strategies is emphasized to prevent technology from amplifying inequities and social harm (Fenwick et al., 2024; Verma & Rohit, 2024).

10.3. Technological and Implementation Limitations

Current frameworks often fail to account for technical constraints of AI and emerging technologies. Challenges include the scalability, robustness, and reliability of AI systems under real-world conditions (Rashid & Kausik, 2024; Gaurav et al., 2024). Integrating AI with quantum computing, semiconductors, and IoT devices introduces additional complexity, with insufficient standards for interoperability and cybersecurity (Campus, 2024; Eswaran & Eswaran, 2025).

AI-based applications in renewable energy, smart cities, and Industry 4.0 face barriers in implementation due to gaps in policy guidance, infrastructure, and skilled workforce availability (Jafarizadeh et al., 2024; Patra, 2025; Maguluri et al., 2023). Furthermore, AI-enabled monitoring systems in agriculture, defense, and border protection require advanced technical validation, ethical governance, and standardized operational protocols (Arya & Rastogi, 2024).

10.4. Environmental and Sustainability Gaps

While sustainability frameworks exist, many current approaches inadequately integrate AI-driven insights with environmental regulations and climate policies. The legal, institutional, and policy environments often struggle to align with net-zero goals, renewable energy expansion, and biodiversity protection (Ali, 2024; Akindele & Chabinga, 2024; Singh & Kaunert, 2025; Saikia, 2024). Indigenous socioecological systems and local contexts are frequently overlooked, reducing the effectiveness of global sustainability strategies (Sakapaji et al., 2024; Chowdhury, 2024).

In industrial and corporate ecosystems, regulatory gaps impede the adoption of green technologies and eco-friendly practices, while lack of clarity in government support and compliance requirements slows innovation (Soomro et al., 2025; Emon et al., 2025). The challenge remains to develop frameworks that reconcile economic growth, technological advancement, and environmental stewardship.

10.5. Data, Security, and Risk Management Challenges

AI frameworks are highly data-dependent, yet data availability, quality, and security remain persistent challenges. Risks associated with data breaches, cyberattacks, and algorithmic misuse highlight the need for enhanced governance, risk management, and protective measures (Veluru, 2024; San Biagio et al., 2023). For instance, AI-based drones, online harassment detection, and predictive safety analytics require robust security protocols to mitigate misuse and protect stakeholders (Maguluri et al., 2023; Vyawahare et al., 2024; Pimpalkar et al., 2024).

Additionally, emerging technologies such as AI in contract management, renewable energy storage, and biomedical research are prone to exploitation if regulatory safeguards are not strengthened (Trotsyuk et al., 2024; Mhia-Alddin & Hussein, 2025; Jafarizadeh et al., 2024). Integrating risk mitigation strategies, accountability mechanisms, and ethical oversight remains a critical yet underdeveloped aspect of current frameworks.

10.6. Interdisciplinary and Governance Challenges

The complexity of modern AI and technological ecosystems necessitates cross-disciplinary collaboration. However, siloed governance structures, insufficient stakeholder engagement, and lack of policy harmonization limit the efficacy of current frameworks (Schünemann et al., 2024; Cooper & Zell, 2023; Darvishi et al., 2022). There is a pressing need for system-level approaches combining legal, technological, ethical, and socio-environmental considerations to foster resilient, adaptable, and equitable frameworks (Bousri, 2019; Daniel, 2024; Butt, 2024).

Moreover, workforce readiness and human-centric design are often neglected, particularly in sectors undergoing AI-driven digital transformation. Organizations must develop capacity-building initiatives and inclusive strategies to ensure human oversight, accountability, and equitable participation in AI adoption (Fenwick et al., 2024; Jamro & Jamro, 2023).

10.7 Summary

Current frameworks face multifaceted gaps spanning legal, ethical, technological, environmental, and governance dimensions. Bridging these gaps requires harmonized regulations, ethical oversight, robust risk management, and interdisciplinary collaboration, ensuring that AI and emerging technologies are deployed safely, sustainably, and equitably.

11. FUTURE DIRECTIONS

11.1. Artificial Intelligence in Law, Governance, and Ethics

The future of artificial intelligence (AI) is poised to significantly reshape the landscape of law, governance, and ethical standards. With rapid advancements in AI technologies, there is a growing need to anticipate and regulate their impact across various domains. AI-powered contract management and compliance monitoring, for instance, offer opportunities to automate and enhance post-expiry obligations, risk mitigation, and regulatory adherence in research and commercial contracts (Mhia-Alddin & Hussein, 2025; Mhia-Alddin, 2025). Similarly, ethical hacking and cybersecurity can benefit from AI-driven experimental frameworks that strengthen Linux-based systems and ensure safer digital ecosystems (Al-Sinani & Mitchell, 2024; Al-Sinani, Sahli, Mitchell, & Al-Siyabi, 2025).

The ethical dimensions of generative AI remain a critical area of focus, with cross-domain studies emphasizing responsible deployment to avoid unintended biases, privacy breaches, and systemic risks (Ali & Aysan, 2025; Ali, Zafar, & Aysan, 2024). Future research should prioritize the development of regulatory frameworks that balance innovation with accountability, particularly in sectors such as finance, healthcare, and defense, where AI applications intersect with human welfare and national security (Batabyal, 2024; Bharati, 2020; Rashid & Kausik, 2024).

11.2. Sustainability and Environmental Governance

Environmental sustainability will continue to be a focal point of global research and policy initiatives. Emerging frameworks for climate law, net-zero policy alignment, and renewable energy governance highlight the pressing need to integrate AI, sensor technologies, and analytics into sustainability strategies (Akindele & Chabinga, 2024; Ali, 2024; Aloamaka, 2024; Chowdhury, 2024). Legal and regulatory mechanisms for promoting sustainable practices in industries such as oil and gas, manufacturing, and urban development are becoming increasingly essential, with AI-enabled monitoring systems providing critical tools for compliance, auditing, and decision-making (Saikia, 2024; Soomro, Suhrab, & Abbasi, 2025; Singh & Kaunert, 2025).

Additionally, large-scale renewable energy storage, energy management, and green technology adoption present unique challenges requiring coordinated policy interventions and AI-driven optimization strategies (Jafarizadeh et al., 2024; Emon, Khan, Rahman, Hamid, & Yaakub, 2025; Oduro, Uzougbo, & Ugwu, 2024). Future directions should explore hybrid approaches combining AI, data analytics, and policy modeling to enhance sustainability trajectories while ensuring equitable access and adherence to international legal standards (Schünemann, Johanning, Reger, Herold, & Bruckner, 2024; Akindele & Chabinga, 2024).

11.3. AI-Driven Innovation in Science and Industry

AI is expected to revolutionize industrial processes, scientific research, and entrepreneurial ecosystems. AI integration in Industry 4.0 contexts offers opportunities to optimize manufacturing systems, improve operational efficiency, and generate innovative solutions through predictive analytics (Patra, 2025; Karim, Galar, & Kumar, 2023). Generative AI tools, applied to finance, entrepreneurship, and research ideation, can enable organizations and researchers to discover new knowledge patterns, simulate outcomes, and explore uncharted technological frontiers (Ali & Aysan, 2024; Zreik, 2024; Ali, Zafar, & Aysan, 2024).

Quantum machine learning and AI-enabled semiconductor technologies are emerging as transformative forces, providing unprecedented computational power for complex problem-solving across sectors (Campus, 2024; Eswaran & Eswaran, 2025). Future research should focus on synergistic integration of AI, quantum computing, and sensor technologies to enhance predictive capabilities, optimize industrial processes, and accelerate scientific discovery (Eisenberg, 2024; Luan et al., 2024).

11.4. Healthcare, Diagnostics, and Digital Forensics

The application of AI in healthcare and forensic science is anticipated to expand substantially. AI-based diagnostics, decision-support systems, and digital forensics present both opportunities and regulatory challenges, particularly regarding data privacy, ethical use, and cross-jurisdictional compliance (Pesapane et al., 2021; Pesapane, Volonté, Codari, & Sardanelli, 2018; Ho, 2023; Iyengar et al., 2025; Zangana & Li, 2025). Future directions include the development of privacy-preserving AI, federated learning approaches, and secure, ethically governed frameworks for admissibility of digital evidence (Veluru, 2024; Mhia-alddin, 2026).

Healthcare AI regulation must align with evolving standards and frameworks to ensure patient safety, fairness, and transparency, while enabling innovation in diagnostics and personalized medicine (Mennella, Maniscalco, De Pietro, & Esposito, 2024; Verma, Rao, Eluri, & Sharma, 2020; Terry, 2019). Integration of AI in biomedical research and diagnostics will require careful monitoring to mitigate risks of misuse, bias, and inequitable outcomes (Trotsyuk et al., 2024; Sheliemina, 2024).

11.5. Social Impact, Women's Safety, and Online Security

AI applications targeting social welfare, online security, and women's safety are rapidly evolving. Predictive analytics, AI-enabled surveillance, and harassment detection systems offer mechanisms to enhance community resilience and protect vulnerable populations (Pimpalkar, Wankhade, Chole, & Golhar, 2024; Vyawahare, Khandelwal, & Rathod, 2024; San Biagio, Cipolla, La Mattina, & Morreale, 2023). Addressing ethical and privacy considerations in these contexts is critical, as AI adoption expands in public-facing and socially sensitive domains (Shafik, 2024; Shukla & Taneja, 2024).

Future research should explore interdisciplinary approaches, combining AI, legal frameworks, and human-centered design, to ensure inclusive and equitable solutions. Socially responsible AI must focus not only on technological capabilities but also on policy alignment, stakeholder engagement, and ethical safeguards (Cooper & Zell, 2023; Fenwick, Molnar, & Frangos, 2024).

11.6. Global Legal and Policy Integration

As AI and sustainability initiatives proliferate, global legal harmonization and policy integration remain pressing priorities. Cross-jurisdictional collaboration, maritime law enforcement, and indigenous socioecological resilience require adaptive legal frameworks capable of responding to technological, environmental, and social complexities (Wang, 2024; Sakapaji et al., 2024; Daniel, 2024). Similarly, digital forensics, cybersecurity, and contract law must be re-envisioned to account for AI-driven transformations in research, commerce, and regulatory oversight (Mhia-Alddin & Hussein, 2025; Mhia-Alddin & Hussein, 2025; Mhia-Alddin, 2026).

Policymakers and researchers should develop scenario-based modeling, systems thinking, and agent-based simulation tools to anticipate unintended consequences and support evidence-based decision-making (Schünemann et al., 2024; Drexl, Conde, & Kim, 2025). This proactive integration of AI, law, and policy will be instrumental in promoting sustainable, ethical, and technologically responsible futures.

12. CONCLUSION

The rapid evolution of artificial intelligence, digital technologies, and regulatory frameworks is reshaping the landscape of law, governance, and industrial innovation. Across sectors such as healthcare, finance, manufacturing, and environmental management, AI presents both unprecedented opportunities and complex challenges. This chapter has highlighted the necessity of integrating ethical considerations, legal compliance, and technological innovation to ensure that AI and emerging technologies are leveraged responsibly and sustainably. The future of AI is closely intertwined with regulatory frameworks that govern data privacy, contract enforcement, cybersecurity, and human-centric adoption, emphasizing that technology alone cannot drive progress without appropriate oversight and ethical guidance.

Sustainability and environmental governance remain central to global research and policy agendas. AI-enhanced monitoring, predictive analytics, and decision-support systems can facilitate efficient resource management, renewable energy deployment, and adherence to international environmental standards. However, realizing these benefits requires coordinated legal frameworks, multi-stakeholder collaboration, and continuous adaptation to emerging challenges, such as climate change, energy storage barriers, and industrial sustainability.

In healthcare and digital forensics, AI holds significant promise for improving diagnostics, evidence management, and security systems. At the same time, privacy, bias, and cross-jurisdictional compliance issues demand rigorous regulatory attention and the adoption of privacy-preserving technologies. Ensuring fairness, transparency, and accountability in AI-driven systems is essential for fostering trust among users, regulators, and the broader public.

Finally, the social dimension of AI adoption, including online safety, women's empowerment, and ethical governance, underscores the importance of human-centered approaches. Future innovation must balance technological capabilities with societal needs, ensuring equitable access, inclusivity, and protection for vulnerable populations. Overall, the integration of AI, law, policy, and sustainability represents a dynamic, multifaceted domain that requires ongoing research, adaptive strategies, and collaborative efforts to achieve ethical, secure, and sustainable technological advancement.

REFERENCES

Akindele, A., & Chabinga, R. (2024). Navigating Climate Change and Sustainability Solutions: Nigeria's Role in International Environmental Law. *African Journal of Climate Change and Resource Sustainability, 3*(1), 331–344. DOI: 10.37284/ajccrs.3.1.2188

Al-Sinani, H. S., & Mitchell, C. J. (2024). AI-enhanced ethical hacking: A Linux-focused experiment. *arXiv preprint arXiv:2410.05105.*

Al-Sinani, H. S., Sahli, N., Mitchell, C. J., & Al-Siyabi, M. (2025). Advancing ethical hacking with AI: A Linux-based experimental study. *Proceedings of ITASEC and SERICS, Bologna, Italy (Feb 2025),* https://www. chrismitchell. net/Papers/aehwaa. pdf

Ali, A. (2024). Navigating Road for Net Zero Policies to Aligning Policy, Politics, and Governance for Environmental Sustainability. In *Transition Towards a Sustainable Future: Net Zero Policies and Environmental Sustainability* (pp. 205–230). Springer Nature Singapore. DOI: 10.1007/978-981-97-5756-5_10

Ali, H., & Aysan, A. F. (2024). Decoding Future of Generative AI in Finance: A Machine Learning Exploration of Academic and Grey Corpus. *Available at SSRN* 4787211. DOI: 10.2139/ssrn.4787211

Ali, H., & Aysan, A. F. (2025). Ethical dimensions of generative AI: A cross-domain analysis using machine learning structural topic modeling. *International Journal of Ethics and Systems, 41*(1), 3–34. DOI: 10.1108/IJOES-04-2024-0112

Ali, H., Zafar, M. B., & Aysan, A. F. (2024). Generative AI and Finance: A Multi-level Machine Learning Based Analysis. *Available at SSRN* 5129013.

Aloamaka, P. C. (2024). Navigating the Climate Crisis: Exploring International Law's Evolution and Application. *GLS Law Journal, 6*(1), 48–58. DOI: 10.69974/glslawjournal.v6i1.127

Arya, L., & Rastogi, R. (2024). Study on Aerial Monitoring System in Agriculture, Forestry, Defense, and Border Protection Using Artificial Intelligence (AI). In *Agriculture and Aquaculture Applications of Biosensors and Bioelectronics* (pp. 392-407). IGI Global Scientific Publishing.

Batabyal, G. S. (2024). Ethics, laws on war and artificial intelligence-driven warfare. In *Artificial intelligence, ethics and the future of warfare* (pp. 187–215). Routledge India. DOI: 10.4324/9781003421849-9

Bharati, R. K. (2020). Legal and Ethical Considerations in the Use of Digital Forensics by Law Enforcement: A Multi-jurisdictional Study. *Turk. Online J. Qual. Inq, 11*(4), 10594–10610.

Borta, H. G., Alemu, A., Shute, T., Zewdie, B., Fantaw, D., Shimelis, B., ... & Tamiru, M. T. (2024). Narcotic Drugs and Psychotropic Substances Control System in Ethiopia: A National Survey.

Bousri, M. M. S. (2019). *A comparative analysis of legal and institutional framework for arbitration: Comoros and Uganda* (Doctoral dissertation, School of law).

Butt, J. (2024). Analytical study of the world's first EU Artificial Intelligence (AI) Act. *International Journal of Research Publication and Reviews, 5*(3), 7343–7364. DOI: 10.55248/gengpi.5.0324.0914

Campus, M. T. (2024). Quantum Machine Learning, Leveraging Al, and. *Integration of AI, Quantum Computing, and Semiconductor Technology*, 57.

Chowdhury, S. (2024). Towards a Just Climate: Navigating Complexities and Challenges in Climate Change Discourse and Action. *Issue 2 Int'l JL Mgmt. &. Human., 7*, 1807.

Cooper, S., & Zell, S. (2023). *Staying on Board: Non-profit housing provider board capacity in a changing context*. Institute of Urban Studies, The University of Winnipeg.

Daniel, J. (2024). *Environmental Law: Navigating Legal Pathways for a Sustainable Future*. Pencil.

Darvishi, K., Liu, L., & Lim, S. (2022). Navigating the Nexus: Legal and Economic Implications of Emerging Tech-nologies. *Law and Economics, 16*(3), 172–186. DOI: 10.35335/laweco.v16i3.59

Drexl, J., Conde, B., & Kim, D. (2025). Position Statement of the Max Planck Institute for Innovation and Competition of 25 April 2025 in the framework of the revision of the Technology

Eisenberg, D. (2024). *Sensing With Integrity: Responsible Sensor Systems in an Era of AI* (Doctoral dissertation, New Jersey Institute of Technology).

Emon, M. M. H., Khan, T., Rahman, M. A., Hamid, A. B. A., & Yaakub, N. I. (2025). GreenTech revolution: Navigating challenges and seizing opportunities. In *AI and green technology applications in society* (pp. 63–90). IGI Global Scientific Publishing.

Eswaran, U., & Eswaran, V. (2025). Quantum Machine Learning, Leveraging AI, and Semiconductor Technology. In *Integration of AI, Quantum Computing, and Semiconductor Technology* (pp. 57-78). IGI Global.

Fenwick, A., Molnar, G., & Frangos, P. (2024). The critical role of HRM in AI-driven digital transformation: A paradigm shift to enable firms to move from AI implementation to human-centric adoption. *Discover Artificial Intelligence*, *4*(1), 34. DOI: 10.1007/s44163-024-00125-4

Filetti, S., Fenza, G., & Gallo, A. (2024). Research design and writing of scholarly articles: New artificial intelligence tools available for researchers. *Endocrine*, *85*(3), 1104–1116. DOI: 10.1007/s12020-024-03977-z PMID: 39085566

Gaurav, A., Chui, K. T., Arya, V., Attar, R. W., Bansal, S., Alhomoud, A., & Psannis, K. (2024). Optimized AI-Driven Semantic Web Approach for Enhancing Phishing Detection in E-Commerce Platforms. [IJSWIS]. *International Journal on Semantic Web and Information Systems*, *20*(1), 1–13. DOI: 10.4018/IJSWIS.359767

Ho, C. W. (2023). Implementing the human right to science in the regulatory governance of artificial intelligence in healthcare. *Journal of Law and the Biosciences*, *10*(2), lsad026. DOI: 10.1093/jlb/lsad026 PMID: 37854168

Iyengar, S. S., Nabavirazavi, S., & Hariprasad, Y. HB, P., & Mohan, C. K. (2025). Privacy-Preserving AI (Federated Learning) for Digital Forensics. In *Artificial Intelligence in Practice: Theory and Application for Cyber Security and Forensics* (pp. 161-176). Cham: Springer Nature Switzerland.

Jafarizadeh, H., Yamini, E., Zolfaghari, S. M., Esmaeilion, F., Assad, M. E. H., & Soltani, M. (2024). Navigating challenges in large-scale renewable energy storage: Barriers, solutions, and innovations. *Energy Reports*, *12*, 2179–2192. DOI: 10.1016/j.egyr.2024.08.019

Jamro, M. Y., & Jamro, F. A. (2023). AI Matters: Chatbot Integration in Holistic STEM Education.

Karim, R., Galar, D., & Kumar, U. (2023). *AI factory: theories, applications and case studies*. CRC Press. DOI: 10.1201/9781003208686

Larson, D. B., Harvey, H., Rubin, D. L., Irani, N., Tse, J. R., & Langlotz, C. P. (2021). Regulatory frameworks for development and evaluation of artificial intelligence–based diagnostic imaging algorithms: Summary and recommendations. *Journal of the American College of Radiology*, *18*(3), 413–424. DOI: 10.1016/j.jacr.2020.09.060 PMID: 33096088

Leontidis, G. (2024). Science in the age of ai: How artificial intelligence is changing the nature and method of scientific research.

Luan, H., Perron, B. E., Victor, B. G., Wan, G., Niu, Y., & Xiao, X. (2024). Using artificial intelligence to support scientometric analysis of scholarly literature: A case example of research on mainland China's left-behind children. *Journal of the Society for Social Work and Research*, *15*(3), 435–457. DOI: 10.1086/731613

Maguluri, L. P., Arularasan, A. N., & Boopathi, S. (2023). Assessing security concerns for ai-based drones in smart cities. In *Effective AI, Blockchain, and E-Governance Applications for Knowledge Discovery and Management* (pp. 27-47). IGI Global Scientific Publishing. DOI: 10.4018/978-1-6684-9151-5.ch002

Manganelli, A. G. (2019). Reverse payments and risk of bankruptcy under private information. *International Journal of the Economics of Business*, *26*(3), 411–429. DOI: 10.1080/13571516.2019.1613146

Mennella, C., Maniscalco, U., De Pietro, G., & Esposito, M. (2024). Ethical and regulatory challenges of AI technologies in healthcare: A narrative review. *Heliyon*, *10*(4), e26297. DOI: 10.1016/j.heliyon.2024.e26297 PMID: 38384518

Mhia-Alddin, D. A. (2025). Legal Implications of Contract Expiry in Modern Commercial Law: Towards a Framework for Post-Expiry Obligations and Risk Management. In Zangana, H., Al-Karaki, J., & Omar, M. (Eds.), *Navigating Law and Policy in STM Enterprises: Ethical Governance, Regulation, and Innovation Strategy* (pp. 139–158). IGI Global Scientific Publishing., DOI: 10.4018/979-8-3373-4862-9.ch006

Mhia-alddin, D. A. (2026). Legal and Regulatory Frameworks for AI in Digital Forensics: Admissibility, Accountability, and Cross-Jurisdictional Challenges. In Zangana, H., & Omar, M. (Eds.), *AI in Digital Forensics and Cybercrime Investigation: Methods, Ethics, and Emerging Technologies* (pp. 31–66). IGI Global Scientific Publishing., DOI: 10.4018/979-8-3373-6536-7.ch002

Mhia-Alddin, D. A., & Hussein, A. M. (2025). Expiration vs. Termination: Reassessing Legal Boundaries in Contract Law. In Zangana, H., Al-Karaki, J., & Omar, M. (Eds.), *Navigating Law and Policy in STM Enterprises: Ethical Governance, Regulation, and Innovation Strategy* (pp. 35–58). IGI Global Scientific Publishing., DOI: 10.4018/979-8-3373-4862-9.ch002

Mhia-Alddin, D. A., & Hussein, A. M. (2025). AI-Powered Contract Security: Managing Expiry, Compliance, and Risk Mitigation Through Deep Learning and LLMs. In *Revolutionizing Cybersecurity With Deep Learning and Large Language Models* (pp. 37-64). IGI Global Scientific Publishing.

Mhia-Alddin, D. A., & Hussein, A. M. (2025). Contract Expiry in AI-Driven STM Research: Legal Challenges, Risks, and Regulatory Considerations. In *Ensuring Secure and Ethical STM Research in the AI Era* (pp. 77-110). IGI Global Scientific Publishing.

Naili, Y. T., Mangkunegara, I. S., Purwono, P., & Baballe, M. A. (2025). Regulatory challenges in ai-based diagnostics: Legal implications of ai use in medical diagnostics. In *BIO Web of Conferences* (Vol. 152, p. 01034). EDP Sciences.

Narayana, S. A., Pati, R. K., & Padhi, S. S. (2019). Market dynamics and reverse logistics for sustainability in the Indian Pharmaceuticals industry. *Journal of Cleaner Production, 208*, 968–987. DOI: 10.1016/j.jclepro.2018.10.171

Oduro, P., Uzougbo, N. S., & Ugwu, M. C. (2024). Renewable energy expansion: Legal strategies for overcoming regulatory barriers and promoting innovation. *International Journal of Applied Research in Social Sciences, 6*(5), 927–944. DOI: 10.51594/ijarss.v6i5.1145

Pai, Y. (2018). Patent Injunction Heuristics in India. *Pai, Yogesh, Patent Injunction Heuristics in India in Rafal Sikorski (Ed.) Patent Law Injunctions, Kluwer Law International BV (2019).*

Patra, S. P. (2025). Navigating the legal landscape of sustainable Industry 4.0. *Industry 4.0 for Manufacturing Systems: Concepts, Technologies, and Applications*, 109.

Pesapane, F., Bracchi, D. A., Mulligan, J. F., Linnikov, A., Maslennikov, O., Lanzavecchia, M. B., Tantrige, P., Stasolla, A., Biondetti, P., Giuggioli, P. F., Cassano, E., & Carrafiello, G. (2021). Legal and regulatory framework for AI solutions in healthcare in EU, US, China, and Russia: New scenarios after a pandemic. *Radiation, 1*(4), 261–276. DOI: 10.3390/radiation1040022

Pesapane, F., Volonté, C., Codari, M., & Sardanelli, F. (2018). Artificial intelligence as a medical device in radiology: Ethical and regulatory issues in Europe and the United States. *Insights Into Imaging, 9*(5), 745–753. DOI: 10.1007/s13244-018-0645-y PMID: 30112675

Pimpalkar, A. P., Wankhade, N. R., Chole, V., & Golhar, Y. (2024). Women's Empowerment Through AI: Discovering Data Analytics for Predictive Safety Solutions and Future Trends. In *AI Tools and Applications for Women's Safety* (pp. 304-326). IGI Global Scientific Publishing.

Rashid, A. B., & Kausik, A. K. (2024). AI revolutionizing industries worldwide: A comprehensive overview of its diverse applications. *Hybrid Advances*, 100277.

Read, A., Botha, R., & Jamaloodien, K. (2023). COVID-19 vaccination procurement and contract management in a South African context. *Journal of Strategic Contracting and Negotiation*, *7*(1-2), 33–43. DOI: 10.1177/20555636231198053

Rodriguez, M. Y., & Storer, H. (2020). A computational social science perspective on qualitative data exploration: Using topic models for the descriptive analysis of social media data. *Journal of Technology in Human Services*, *38*(1), 54–86. DOI: 10.1080/15228835.2019.1616350

Saikia, B. (2024). Ecologically-Informed approaches: International mechanisms for navigating environmental challenges and ensuring sustainability in the oil and gas exploration and production industry. *Proceedings of the International Academy of Ecology and Environmental Sciences*, *14*(2), 60.

Sakapaji, S. C., García Molinos, J., Parilova, V., Gavrilyeva, T., & Yakovleva, N. (2024). Navigating legal and regulatory frameworks to achieve the resilience and sustainability of indigenous socioecological systems. *Resources*, *13*(4), 56. DOI: 10.3390/resources13040056

San Biagio, M., Cipolla, M., La Mattina, E., & Morreale, V. (2023, December). A Topic Clustering Method to Identify Online Threats against Soft Targets. In *2023 International Conference on Computational Science and Computational Intelligence (CSCI)* (pp. 727-733). IEEE. DOI: 10.1109/CSCI62032.2023.00124

Schünemann, C., Johanning, S., Reger, E., Herold, H., & Bruckner, T. (2024). Complex system policy modelling approaches for policy advice–comparing systems thinking, system dynamics and agent-based modelling. *Political Research Exchange : an ECPR Journal*, *6*(1), 2387438. DOI: 10.1080/2474736X.2024.2387438

Shafik, W. (2024). Data privacy and security safeguarding customer information in ChatGPT systems. In *Revolutionizing the Service Industry Wth OpenAI Models* (pp. 52–86). IGI Global. DOI: 10.4018/979-8-3693-1239-1.ch003

Sheliemina, N. (2024). The use of artificial intelligence in medical diagnostics: Opportunities, prospects and risks. *Health Economics and Management Review*, *5*(2), 104–124. DOI: 10.61093/hem.2024.2-07

Shukla, R. P., & Taneja, S. (2024). Ethical considerations and data privacy in artificial intelligence. In *Integrating generative AI in education to achieve sustainable development goals* (pp. 86–97). IGI Global. DOI: 10.4018/979-8-3693-2440-0.ch005

Singh, B., & Kaunert, C. (2025). Navigating the Terrain of Sustainability Trajectories of Environment: Biodiversity Protection and Legal Landscapes. In *Community Resilience and Climate Change Challenges: Pursuit of Sustainable Development Goals (SDGs)* (pp. 355-374). IGI Global Scientific Publishing.

Soomro, J. A., Suhrab, M., & Abbasi, B. A. (2025). Navigating Green Regulations in the Business Ecosystem: Government Support, Compliance, and Obstacles in the Context of Pakistan. In *Government Influences on Eco-Friendly Practices in Business* (pp. 55-86). IGI Global.

Terry, N. (2019). Of regulating healthcare AI and robots. *Yale JL & Tech.*, *21*, 133.

Trotsyuk, A. A., Waeiss, Q., Bhatia, R. T., Aponte, B. J., Heffernan, I. M., Madgavkar, D., Felder, R. M., Lehmann, L. S., Palmer, M. J., Greely, H., Wald, R., Goetz, L., Trengove, M., Vandersluis, R., Lin, H., Cho, M. K., Altman, R. B., Endy, D., Relman, D. A., & Magnus, D. (2024). Toward a framework for risk mitigation of potential misuse of artificial intelligence in biomedical research. *Nature Machine Intelligence*, *6*(12), 1–8. DOI: 10.1038/s42256-024-00926-3 PMID: 40994707

Veluru, C. S. (2024). Responsible Artificial Intelligence on Large Scale Data to Prevent Misuse, Unethical Challenges and Security Breaches. *Journal of Artificial Intelligence & Cloud Computing. SRC/JAICC-349. DOI: doi. org/(3), 331*, 2-6.DOI: 10.47363/JAICC/2024

Verma, A., Rao, K., Eluri, V., & Sharma, Y. (2020). Regulating AI in public health: systems challenges and perspectives. *ORF Occasional Paper, 261*.

Verma, M., & Rohit, K. (2024). Ethical AI Shaping Scholarly Communication: Challenges and Opportunities.

Vyawahare, H., Khandelwal, S., & Rathod, S. (2024). Artificial Intelligence in Detecting and Preventing Online Harassment. In *AI Tools and Applications for Women's Safety* (pp. 14–35). IGI Global Scientific Publishing. DOI: 10.4018/979-8-3693-1435-7.ch002

Wang, Q. (2024). Maritime law enforcement concerning offshore energy platforms: Navigating international law constraints and challenges. *Marine Policy*, *170*, 106370. DOI: 10.1016/j.marpol.2024.106370

Zangana, H. M., & Li, S. (2025). Future Trends in AI and Digital Forensics. In *Digital Forensics in the Age of AI* (pp. 347–380). IGI Global Scientific Publishing.

Zreik, M. (2024). Harnessing AI for entrepreneurial idea generation: Navigating the new frontier. In *Generating Entrepreneurial Ideas With AI* (pp. 1–18). IGI Global Scientific Publishing. DOI: 10.4018/979-8-3693-3498-0.ch001

Chapter 3
Leveraging LLMs for Financial Fraud Detection and Secure Auditing

Syed Q. Raza
https://orcid.org/0009-0003-6952-2667
Lindsey Wilcosn College, USA

Rindah Febriana Suryawati
https://orcid.org/0000-0003-0389-4583
Universitas Airlangga, Indonesia

Wisam Hazım Gwad
Alnoor University, Iraq

ABSTRACT

The rapid adoption of Large Language Models (LLMs) in the financial sector presents both transformative opportunities and unprecedented risks. This chapter explores the application of LLMs for financial fraud detection and secure auditing, highlighting how advanced natural language processing techniques can identify anomalous transactions, detect patterns of illicit activity, and enhance compliance mechanisms. By integrating machine learning with domain-specific financial knowledge, LLMs offer real-time insights into complex datasets, improving the accuracy and efficiency of fraud detection systems. The chapter also addresses challenges related to data privacy, adversarial attacks, and model interpretability, proposing strategies to mitigate risks while maximizing the benefits of LLM deployment in financial oversight. Ultimately, this work underscores the potential of LLMs as robust tools for safeguarding financial integrity in an increasingly digital economy.

DOI: 10.4018/979-8-3373-7133-7.ch003

1. INTRODUCTION

Financial fraud has become increasingly sophisticated in recent years, challenging traditional auditing and oversight mechanisms. The global financial ecosystem's rapid digitalization, coupled with complex transaction networks, has amplified the need for advanced detection and prevention tools (Abbas & Kollwitz, 2025; Adejumo & Ogburie, 2025). Forensic accounting has long served as a cornerstone for uncovering fraudulent activities, offering systematic methods for analyzing financial records, detecting anomalies, and ensuring regulatory compliance (Ali, Futaih, Shukur, & Al-Orfali, 2024; Ali, Khinger, Subhe, & Al-Orfali, 2024).

Emerging technologies, particularly Artificial Intelligence (AI) and Large Language Models (LLMs), are reshaping the landscape of financial fraud detection and auditing. By leveraging natural language processing, machine learning, and predictive analytics, these intelligent systems can process vast amounts of structured and unstructured financial data, identifying subtle patterns indicative of illicit activity (Bhagat, 2024; Qatawneh, 2025; Ramos, 2021). LLMs, in particular, offer unprecedented capabilities for contextual understanding, anomaly detection, and automation of complex auditing processes, making them invaluable for modern forensic investigations (Suryawati, Mustafa, & Vitianingsih, 2026).

The integration of LLMs with traditional forensic accounting techniques enables a more proactive and precise approach to fraud detection. Techniques such as anomaly detection, pattern recognition, and predictive modeling are enhanced through AI-driven tools, allowing auditors to identify suspicious transactions that might otherwise go unnoticed (Daraojimba, Farayola, Olatoye, Mhlongo, & Oke, 2023; Öztürk & Usul, 2020). Moreover, AI facilitates real-time monitoring and automated reporting, which strengthens organizational resilience against emerging financial threats (Elumilade, Ogundeji, Achumie, Omokhoa, & Omowole, 2021; Harjuni, 2024).

Despite the significant potential of AI and LLMs, challenges remain, including data privacy concerns, model interpretability, and vulnerability to adversarial attacks (Matar, 2023; Bhagat, 2024). Ethical considerations and regulatory compliance are critical, as improper application of AI in auditing could undermine financial integrity or expose organizations to liability (Al-Raggad, Albalawee, Al-Mahasneh, Abu Huson, & Albajaly, 2025; Zayed, Nour, Al Attar, Almubaideen, & Abdelaziz, 2024). Addressing these challenges requires the development of robust governance frameworks, integration of domain expertise, and continuous model validation.

Recent studies highlight the transformative potential of AI in forensic accounting, demonstrating improvements in fraud detection accuracy, efficiency, and scalability (Haddad, Alharasis, Fraij, & Al-Ramahi, 2024; Mazloum, Mazloum, & Saleh, 2025; Mubarrat, 2024). Comparative analyses across countries suggest that leveraging advanced analytics and AI can significantly reduce the incidence of financial irregularities while strengthening compliance mechanisms (Simbolon, Adriana, Rustam, Sulistyowati, & Rewa, 2024; Uduehe, Okoye, & Amahalu, 2024; Vijayalakshmi & Jeevan, 2024). Furthermore, recent innovations in intelligent systems, such as the integration of adaptive resonance theory and hybrid machine learning approaches, are enabling highly accurate anomaly detection and forensic auditing at scale (Zheng, Tan, Jiang, & Wang, 2025).

In this context, this chapter investigates the role of LLMs in enhancing financial fraud detection and secure auditing. It presents an overview of how these models can be applied to identify irregularities in large-scale financial datasets, automate auditing processes, and strengthen organizational defenses against fraud. By bridging traditional forensic accounting methods with cutting-edge AI techniques, this work aims to provide a comprehensive framework for leveraging LLMs as reliable tools in financial oversight and regulatory compliance (Aman, 2024; Ramos, 2021).

The following sections will explore: (1) the theoretical foundations of forensic accounting and LLM integration, (2) current trends and technological advancements in AI-driven fraud detection, (3) practical applications and case studies, and (4) the ethical, legal, and operational considerations for deploying these intelligent systems in real-world financial environments (Daraojimba et al., 2023; Abbas & Kollwitz, 2025; Zangana, Omar, Rangarajan, & Salih Hasan, 2026). This holistic approach aims to equip researchers, practitioners, and policymakers with insights into optimizing the intersection of forensic accounting, LLMs, and AI for secure, efficient, and resilient financial systems.

2. BACKGROUND AND MOTIVATION

Financial fraud continues to pose significant threats to the stability and integrity of global financial systems. Traditional auditing and accounting procedures, while necessary, often struggle to keep pace with increasingly sophisticated fraudulent schemes, which exploit digital transaction networks, emerging payment platforms, and complex financial instruments (Abbas & Kollwitz, 2025; Adejumo & Ogburie, 2025). As such, the field of forensic accounting has evolved to incorporate advanced methodologies, aiming to detect, prevent, and investigate fraudulent activities in financial institutions and corporate entities (Ali, Futaih, Shukur, & Al-Orfali, 2024; Ali, Khinger, Subhe, & Al-Orfali, 2024).

The increasing reliance on digital records and online financial operations has necessitated the integration of artificial intelligence (AI), machine learning (ML), and Big Data analytics into forensic accounting practices. These technologies enable auditors and investigators to process vast amounts of structured and unstructured data, identify anomalies, and uncover hidden patterns indicative of financial misconduct (Aman, 2024; Bhagat, 2024; Ramos, 2021). For instance, AI-driven fraud detection systems can continuously monitor transactions in real time, flagging unusual activities that may signify embezzlement, money laundering, or accounting fraud (Rawat, Oki, Chakrawarti, Adekunle, Lukose, & Ajagbe, 2023; Zayed, Nour, Al Attar, Almubaideen, & Abdelaziz, 2024).

Large Language Models (LLMs) represent a particularly promising tool for modern forensic accounting. By leveraging natural language processing (NLP), these models can interpret, categorize, and analyze vast textual data from financial reports, emails, contracts, and regulatory filings, which are often critical in fraud investigations (Qatawneh, 2025). LLMs can support auditors in detecting inconsistencies, generating predictive insights, and enhancing decision-making processes, effectively bridging the gap between traditional accounting expertise and intelligent automation (Zheng, Tan, Jiang, & Wang, 2025; Mazloum, Mazloum, & Saleh, 2025).

The adoption of AI and LLMs in forensic accounting also addresses key challenges faced by financial institutions, such as internal control failures, insider threats, and the complexity of fraud schemes across global markets (Daraojimba, Farayola, Olatoye, Mhlongo, & Oke, 2023). Additionally, the combination of AI with classical forensic accounting techniques ensures that both quantitative anomalies and qualitative indicators of fraud, such as suspicious narrative patterns or irregular audit trails, are thoroughly examined (Elumilade, Ogundeji, Achumie, Omokhoa, & Omowole, 2021; Öztürk & Usul, 2020).

Recent studies highlight that forensic accounting enhanced with AI and LLMs improves detection accuracy, reduces response time, and facilitates more robust auditing processes. Comparative analyses across different countries demonstrate that organizations integrating advanced analytics and intelligent systems are better equipped to mitigate financial risks, enforce compliance, and maintain organizational integrity (Simbolon, Adriana, Rustam, Sulistyowati, & Rewa, 2024; Uduehe, Okoye, & Amahalu, 2024; Vijayalakshmi & Jeevan, 2024). Furthermore, innovations such as adaptive resonance theory, hybrid ML models, and deep learning-based anomaly detection have proven highly effective in identifying both known and emerging fraud patterns.

The motivation for leveraging LLMs in financial fraud detection and secure auditing stems from the pressing need to combine computational intelligence with domain expertise. The integration of AI-driven systems provides scalability, precision, and proactive monitoring capabilities that traditional forensic accounting methods alone cannot achieve (Haddad, Alharasis, Fraij, & Al-Ramahi, 2024; Harjuni, 2024; Matar, 2023). Additionally, by incorporating LLMs into auditing workflows, financial institutions can ensure that regulatory compliance, ethical standards, and risk management objectives are maintained in an increasingly digital and adversarial financial environment (Al-Raggad, Albalawee, Al-Mahasneh, Abu Huson, & Albajaly, 2025; Okonta & Nnamdi, 2025).

Moreover, the ongoing advancement of AI technologies encourages continuous innovation in forensic accounting processes. Research indicates that adopting AI-enabled fraud detection tools, including autonomous systems operating in complex environments such as the dark web, can substantially enhance investigative capabilities while maintaining transparency and accountability (Rawat et al., 2023; Mubarrat, 2024). The integration of LLMs further enhances interpretability and predictive capabilities, allowing auditors to translate complex data into actionable insights that support both internal governance and external regulatory reporting (Daraojimba et al., 2023; Abbas & Kollwitz, 2025).

In conclusion, the intersection of forensic accounting, AI, and LLMs represents a transformative approach to financial fraud detection and secure auditing. By harnessing these technologies, organizations can more effectively anticipate, detect, and respond to fraudulent activities, safeguarding financial systems, enhancing operational efficiency, and promoting ethical standards. The subsequent sections of this chapter explore the technological, methodological, and practical dimensions of leveraging LLMs for financial fraud detection, offering a comprehensive framework for integrating intelligent systems into modern forensic accounting practices (Zangana, Omar, Rangarajan, & Salih Hasan, 2026; Ali et al., 2024; Zayed et al., 2024).

3. LARGE LANGUAGE MODELS IN FINANCE

The adoption of Large Language Models (LLMs) in finance has marked a transformative shift in the way financial institutions, auditors, and forensic accountants approach fraud detection, risk management, and decision-making. LLMs, a subset of advanced artificial intelligence, are capable of processing and analyzing vast volumes of structured and unstructured financial data, thereby enabling more sophisticated, timely, and accurate identification of anomalies indicative of fraudulent activity (Abbas & Kollwitz, 2025; Adejumo & Ogburie, 2025).

LLMs have demonstrated significant potential in enhancing forensic accounting practices. Traditional forensic accounting relies heavily on manual examination of financial records, transaction histories, and audit trails—a process that is often time-consuming, prone to human error, and inadequate for detecting complex or subtle fraudulent patterns (Ali, Futaih, Shukur, & Al-Orfali, 2024; Ali, Khinger, Subhe, & Al-Orfali, 2024). By leveraging natural language processing (NLP), LLMs can automatically analyze financial statements, emails, contracts, and regulatory filings to detect inconsistencies, unusual patterns, or suspicious communication that may signal fraudulent activity (Qatawneh, 2025).

One of the most impactful applications of LLMs in finance is the real-time monitoring of transactions and financial communications. By continuously learning from historical fraud cases and regulatory standards, LLMs can flag high-risk transactions, predict potential fraud, and provide insights that support proactive intervention strategies (Daraojimba, Farayola, Olatoye, Mhlongo, & Oke, 2023; Ramos, 2021; Zayed, Nour, Al Attar, Almubaideen, & Abdelaziz, 2024). This capability not only reduces response time but also enhances the accuracy of detection compared to traditional rule-based expert systems (Öztürk & Usul, 2020). Moreover, LLMs can adapt to emerging fraud schemes by recognizing novel linguistic patterns or behaviors that indicate fraudulent intent (Rawat, Oki, Chakrawarti, Adekunle, Lukose, & Ajagbe, 2023; Bhagat, 2024).

The integration of LLMs with forensic accounting tools also supports advanced risk management and compliance. In addition to identifying fraudulent patterns, LLMs can assist auditors and financial analysts in evaluating internal controls, ensuring regulatory compliance, and generating predictive models for financial risk (Al-Raggad, Albalawee, Al-Mahasneh, Abu Huson, & Albajaly, 2025; Haddad, Alharasis, Fraij, & Al-Ramahi, 2024). By bridging the gap between data-driven insights and expert judgment, LLMs enhance the transparency, reliability, and ethical integrity of financial operations (Elumilade, Ogundeji, Achumie, Omokhoa, & Omowole, 2021; Harjuni, 2024).

Beyond fraud detection, LLMs contribute to knowledge extraction and decision support within financial institutions. They can summarize large volumes of textual and numerical data, identify relevant regulatory changes, and provide actionable recommendations to financial managers and auditors (Mubarrat, 2024; Aman, 2024; Vijayalakshmi & Jeevan, 2024). This capacity is particularly valuable for multinational organizations handling complex financial networks where rapid analysis of cross-border transactions is critical for compliance and security (Simbolon, Adriana, Rustam, Sulistyowati, & Rewa, 2024; Uduehe, Okoye, & Amahalu, 2024).

The combination of LLMs with other AI techniques such as machine learning and deep learning further enhances forensic capabilities. For example, hybrid systems can integrate anomaly detection, predictive analytics, and adaptive learning to identify irregularities in financial statements, audit logs, or online transactions (Zheng, Tan, Jiang, & Wang, 2025; Mazloum, Mazloum, & Saleh, 2025). These systems are particularly effective in detecting both traditional accounting fraud and emerging threats such as insider trading, cyber-enabled financial crimes, and manipulation of digital assets (Matar, 2023; Okonta & Nnamdi, 2025).

LLMs also facilitate automation and scalability in forensic accounting. Automated review of contracts, emails, and transactional data reduces the need for extensive manual labor while maintaining high accuracy, enabling auditors to focus on complex investigative tasks and strategic decision-making (Abbas & Kollwitz, 2025;

Daraojimba et al., 2023). Furthermore, intelligent LLM systems can operate in dark web environments to detect fraudulent activities, money laundering operations, and cyber-enabled financial threats that traditional monitoring tools may overlook (Rawat et al., 2023).

Despite these advantages, the application of LLMs in finance is not without challenges. Ethical considerations, data privacy, model interpretability, and susceptibility to adversarial attacks are critical factors that must be addressed to ensure responsible deployment (Bhagat, 2024). Research emphasizes that human oversight remains essential to validate AI-generated insights and maintain accountability, particularly in high-stakes financial investigations (Zayed et al., 2024; Ali et al., 2024).

In conclusion, Large Language Models offer a transformative approach to forensic accounting, fraud detection, and financial risk management. By combining advanced natural language processing, predictive analytics, and adaptive learning, LLMs enable real-time monitoring, anomaly detection, and actionable insight generation across complex financial systems. Their integration into financial operations represents a critical step toward smarter, more efficient, and ethically guided fraud prevention, ensuring the integrity and stability of modern financial institutions (Abbas & Kollwitz, 2025).

4. TECHNIQUES FOR FRAUD DETECTION USING LLMS

The detection and prevention of financial fraud have become increasingly sophisticated with the integration of Large Language Models (LLMs) into forensic accounting and auditing practices. LLMs, leveraging deep learning and natural language processing (NLP), enable the analysis of vast amounts of structured and unstructured data, uncovering patterns and anomalies that traditional methods may fail to detect (Abbas & Kollwitz, 2025; Adejumo & Ogburie, 2025). These models have revolutionized forensic accounting by providing automated, adaptive, and highly accurate mechanisms for fraud detection across diverse financial environments (Ali, Futaih, Shukur, & Al-Orfali, 2024; Ali, Khinger, Subhe, & Al-Orfali, 2024).

4.1. Natural Language Processing for Transaction and Document Analysis

One of the primary techniques for fraud detection using LLMs is NLP-based analysis of financial documents, including invoices, contracts, emails, and regulatory filings. LLMs can automatically parse text, identify irregular patterns, and flag inconsistencies that may indicate fraudulent activity (Qatawneh, 2025). By analyzing narrative and numeric content simultaneously, LLMs detect anomalies in accounting entries, unusual phrasing in communications, and irregular sequences of transactions, which are often early indicators of financial misconduct (Daraojimba, Farayola, Olatoye, Mhlongo, & Oke, 2023; Ramos, 2021).

4.2. Anomaly Detection and Pattern Recognition

LLMs excel at recognizing deviations from established financial patterns. Through training on historical financial data and known fraud cases, these models can detect subtle anomalies in transaction sequences, account balances, and financial statements (Elumilade, Ogundeji, Achumie, Omokhoa, & Omowole, 2021; Bhagat, 2024). Advanced techniques, such as unsupervised learning combined with LLMs, enable the discovery of previously unrecognized fraud patterns, enhancing forensic auditors' ability to anticipate and prevent fraudulent activities (Al-Raggad, Albalawee, Al-Mahasneh, Abu Huson, & Albajaly, 2025; Haddad, Alharasis, Fraij, & Al-Ramahi, 2024).

4.3. Integration with Big Data and Predictive Analytics

The incorporation of LLMs with big data analytics allows for real-time monitoring and predictive fraud detection. LLMs can process data streams from multiple sources, including transactional logs, banking systems, and social media, providing predictive insights into potential fraud risks (Mubarrat, 2024; Aman, 2024; Zayed, Nour, Al Attar, Almubaideen, & Abdelaziz, 2024). Predictive modeling with LLMs enhances the accuracy of risk scoring systems and supports early intervention strategies, which are crucial in mitigating financial losses (Rawat, Oki, Chakrawarti, Adekunle, Lukose, & Ajagbe, 2023; Zheng, Tan, Jiang, & Wang, 2025).

4.4. Hybrid LLM-Based Forensic Accounting Systems

Hybrid systems that integrate LLMs with machine learning and rule-based expert systems improve the robustness of fraud detection frameworks. Rule-based systems provide structured control mechanisms, while LLMs add adaptive intelligence capable of interpreting complex data and learning new fraud schemes (Öztürk & Usul, 2020; Mazloum, Mazloum, & Saleh, 2025). Such hybrid approaches allow financial institutions to combine the strengths of automated pattern recognition, predictive analytics, and domain-specific rules, offering a comprehensive fraud detection toolkit (Okonta & Nnamdi, 2025; Vijayalakshmi & Jeevan, 2024).

4.5. Detection of Cyber-Enabled Financial Crimes

LLMs are particularly effective in detecting cyber-enabled financial crimes, including money laundering, insider trading, and fraudulent activities in digital asset platforms. By analyzing communication patterns, transaction metadata, and online behaviors, LLMs can identify high-risk activities and potential fraudsters in digital networks (Matar, 2023; Rawat et al., 2023; Zangana, Mohammed, & Husain, 2025). This capability is increasingly critical given the rise of complex financial ecosystems that operate across borders and rely heavily on digital transactions.

4.6. Automation and Scalability in Auditing

The application of LLMs facilitates automation in forensic accounting by reducing the manual effort required for document review, transaction analysis, and anomaly detection (Abbas & Kollwitz, 2025; Harjuni, 2024). Automated systems allow auditors to process significantly larger datasets with consistent accuracy, enabling scalable operations across large organizations and multiple financial platforms (Daraojimba et al., 2023; Uduehe, Okoye, & Amahalu, 2024).

4.7. Ethical and Regulatory Considerations

While LLMs provide powerful tools for fraud detection, their deployment raises ethical and regulatory concerns. Ensuring model transparency, mitigating biases, and maintaining data privacy are essential to comply with financial regulations and uphold the integrity of forensic investigations (Bhagat, 2024; Al-Raggad et al., 2025). Human oversight remains indispensable for validating AI-generated insights and interpreting complex cases where contextual understanding is necessary (Zayed et al., 2024; Abbas & Kollwitz, 2025).

Figure 1 illustrates how LLMs are applied to financial fraud detection, starting from data ingestion through natural language processing, anomaly detection, predictive analytics, and hybrid forensic systems, before culminating in fraud alerts and secure auditing outcomes.

Figure 1. Flowchart of fraud detection using LLMs in forensic accounting

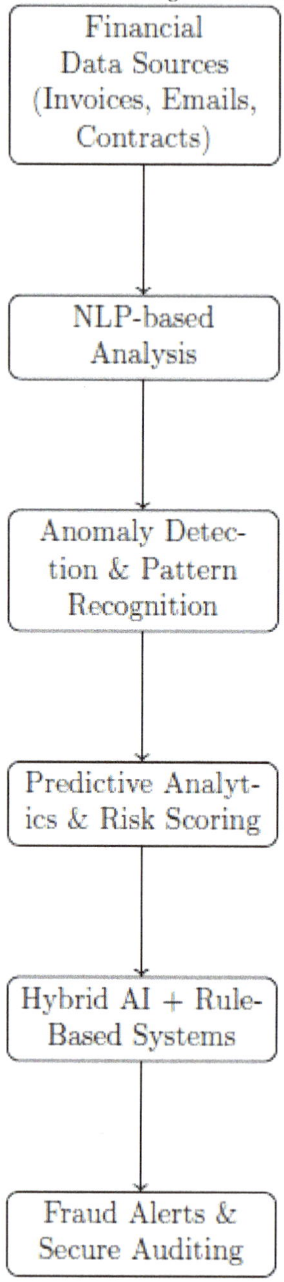

In summary, techniques for fraud detection using LLMs encompass NLP-based document analysis, anomaly detection, predictive analytics, hybrid AI systems, and automated auditing processes. These approaches enable proactive, accurate, and scalable detection of financial fraud while supporting compliance, ethical oversight, and the continuous adaptation to emerging financial crime patterns (Ali et al., 2024; Qatawneh, 2025; Vijayalakshmi & Jeevan, 2024). The integration of LLMs into forensic accounting represents a paradigm shift, offering both enhanced operational efficiency and strategic advantages in the fight against financial fraud.

5. SECURE AUDITING WITH LLMS

Secure auditing is a cornerstone of modern forensic accounting and financial integrity. With the rapid digitization of financial transactions and the increasing complexity of corporate structures, traditional auditing methods are often insufficient to identify sophisticated fraudulent activities. Large Language Models (LLMs) offer advanced capabilities for secure auditing by combining natural language understanding, anomaly detection, and predictive analytics to ensure both accuracy and security in financial audits (Abbas & Kollwitz, 2025; Adejumo & Ogburie, 2025).

5.1. LLM-Based Risk Assessment and Audit Planning

LLMs enhance the audit planning process by analyzing historical financial data, transaction patterns, and regulatory filings to assess risk levels across various accounts and departments (Ali, Futaih, Shukur, & Al-Orfali, 2024; Ali, Khinger, Subhe, & Al-Orfali, 2024). By predicting areas most susceptible to irregularities, auditors can allocate resources more effectively and focus on high-risk areas. This proactive approach improves audit efficiency and strengthens compliance with internal and external regulatory requirements (Al-Raggad, Albalawee, Al-Mahasneh, Abu Huson, & Albajaly, 2025; Aman, 2024).

Figure 2 summarizes the role of LLMs in audit planning, where risk assessment guides resource allocation, anomaly detection identifies potential irregularities, and decision support provides auditors with actionable insights.

Figure 2. LLM-supported risk assessment and audit planning process

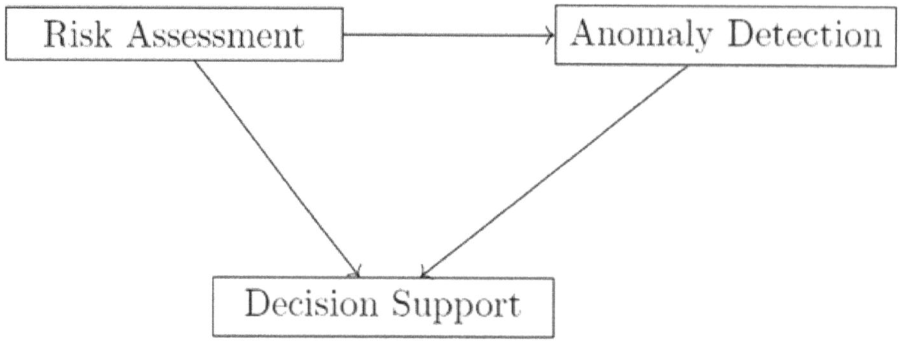

5.2. Automating Data Extraction and Verification

LLMs facilitate secure auditing by automating the extraction and verification of financial data from structured and unstructured sources, including invoices, emails, contracts, and system logs (Qatawneh, 2025). Automation minimizes human error, reduces audit time, and enables auditors to process massive datasets while maintaining high levels of accuracy. Moreover, LLMs can cross-reference data across multiple systems to detect inconsistencies and anomalies indicative of potential fraud (Daraojimba, Farayola, Olatoye, Mhlongo, & Oke, 2023; Elumilade, Ogundeji, Achumie, Omokhoa, & Omowole, 2021).

5.3. Anomaly Detection and Continuous Monitoring

A critical feature of secure auditing is the ability to detect irregularities in real-time. LLMs, trained on historical financial datasets and known fraud cases, can continuously monitor transactions, account balances, and internal communications for suspicious activity (Bhagat, 2024; Haddad, Alharasis, Fraij, & Al-Ramahi, 2024). Anomalous patterns, such as unusual transaction frequencies or atypical fund transfers, can trigger alerts, enabling auditors to intervene promptly and prevent financial losses (Mubarrat, 2024; Ramos, 2021).

5.4. Enhancing Cybersecurity in Auditing Processes

The integration of LLMs in auditing also strengthens cybersecurity by identifying vulnerabilities in accounting information systems and potential insider threats (Matar, 2023). LLMs can analyze network logs, access records, and communication patterns to detect suspicious behavior indicative of unauthorized access or manipulation of financial records. This proactive approach is vital for ensuring the confidentiality, integrity, and availability of sensitive financial information (Rawat, Oki, Chakrawarti, Adekunle, Lukose, & Ajagbe, 2023; Okonta & Nnamdi, 2025).

5.5. Intelligent Decision Support for Auditors

LLMs provide auditors with intelligent decision support by generating summaries, insights, and recommendations based on comprehensive data analysis (Vijayalakshmi & Jeevan, 2024; Zayed, Nour, Al Attar, Almubaideen, & Abdelaziz, 2024). For instance, LLMs can highlight potential fraud risks, suggest corrective actions, and offer scenario-based simulations for auditors to assess the impact of financial irregularities. This level of support improves both the effectiveness and reliability of auditing practices (Harjuni, 2024; Simbolon, Adriana, Rustam, Sulistyowati, & Rewa, 2024).

5.6. Hybrid Auditing Systems

Secure auditing is often achieved through hybrid systems that combine LLMs with rule-based expert systems, machine learning algorithms, and big data analytics (Öztürk & Usul, 2020; Mazloum, Mazloum, & Saleh, 2025). These hybrid systems leverage the interpretive capabilities of LLMs and the structured rigor of traditional auditing rules to detect and prevent complex financial frauds. They are particularly effective in high-volume transaction environments, such as banking and multinational corporations, where traditional audits may be time-consuming or insufficient (Uduehe, Okoye, & Amahalu, 2024; Abbas & Kollwitz, 2025).

5.7. Regulatory Compliance and Ethical Oversight

While LLMs enhance audit efficiency and security, their deployment must adhere to strict regulatory and ethical standards. Ensuring transparency, mitigating algorithmic bias, and maintaining data privacy are critical for compliance with financial regulations and professional ethics (Bhagat, 2024; Al-Raggad et al., 2025). Human oversight remains essential to validate AI-generated findings and make judgment calls in cases requiring contextual understanding, such as complex fraud investigations or cross-border financial transactions (Zayed et al., 2024; Abbas & Kollwitz, 2025).

5.8. Future Prospects in Secure Auditing

The evolution of secure auditing using LLMs continues to expand with advances in AI and machine learning. Emerging techniques include integrating LLMs with blockchain for immutable transaction records, employing federated learning for cross-institutional audits, and developing AI-driven audit dashboards that offer real-time monitoring and interactive analysis (Mubarrat, 2024; Zheng, Tan, Jiang, & Wang, 2025). These innovations promise to further enhance the accuracy, transparency, and resilience of financial audits in the digital era (Ramos, 2021; Abbas & Kollwitz, 2025).

In conclusion, secure auditing with LLMs represents a transformative approach in forensic accounting. By combining automated data extraction, anomaly detection, cybersecurity measures, intelligent decision support, and hybrid auditing frameworks, LLMs provide auditors with powerful tools to maintain financial integrity, ensure regulatory compliance, and mitigate fraud risks effectively (Ali et al., 2024; Qatawneh, 2025; Vijayalakshmi & Jeevan, 2024).

6. SECURITY RISKS AND CHALLENGES

The integration of advanced technologies, particularly Large Language Models (LLMs) and artificial intelligence (AI), into forensic accounting and auditing has significantly enhanced fraud detection and financial oversight. However, this digital transformation introduces a spectrum of security risks and challenges that must be carefully managed to safeguard financial data and maintain organizational integrity (Abbas & Kollwitz, 2025; Adejumo & Ogburie, 2025).

6.1. Cybersecurity Vulnerabilities in Auditing Systems

One of the primary risks associated with AI-driven auditing systems is cybersecurity threats. Financial institutions and organizations increasingly rely on LLMs to process sensitive financial data, making these systems potential targets for cyberattacks, including data breaches, ransomware, and insider threats (Matar, 2023). Unauthorized access to AI-based auditing platforms can compromise confidential financial records, enabling fraudulent activities or manipulation of audit results (Rawat, Oki, Chakrawarti, Adekunle, Lukose, & Ajagbe, 2023; Okonta & Nnamdi, 2025).

6.2. Data Privacy and Ethical Concerns

The massive datasets required to train LLMs often include personal and financial information. Improper handling of this data can result in privacy violations, regulatory non-compliance, and reputational damage (Ali, Futaih, Shukur, & Al-Orfali, 2024; Ali, Khinger, Subhe, & Al-Orfali, 2024). Furthermore, AI algorithms may inadvertently embed biases that affect decision-making in auditing processes, raising ethical concerns about fairness, accountability, and transparency (Bhagat, 2024; Al-Raggad, Albalawee, Al-Mahasneh, Abu Huson, & Albajaly, 2025).

6.3. Model Reliability and Interpretability

LLMs, despite their analytical power, are susceptible to errors and misinterpretations of complex financial data. Overreliance on AI models without adequate human oversight can result in incorrect conclusions, false positives, or undetected fraud (Daraojimba, Farayola, Olatoye, Mhlongo, & Oke, 2023). The black-box nature of many LLMs limits transparency and interpretability, posing challenges for auditors who must justify and document their audit decisions for regulatory compliance (Qatawneh, 2025; Ramos, 2021).

6.4. Integration and Interoperability Challenges

Incorporating LLMs into existing auditing frameworks requires seamless integration with legacy accounting information systems. Compatibility issues, inconsistent data formats, and technical complexities can hinder the effectiveness of AI-assisted audits (Aman, 2024; Öztürk & Usul, 2020). Organizations must invest in robust IT infrastructures and standardized protocols to ensure smooth operation, data integrity, and system reliability (Vijayalakshmi & Jeevan, 2024; Zayed, Nour, Al Attar, Almubaideen, & Abdelaziz, 2024).

6.5. Adversarial Attacks and Data Manipulation

AI systems are vulnerable to adversarial attacks, where malicious actors subtly manipulate input data to deceive models. In financial auditing, such manipulations could result in the concealment of fraudulent transactions or distort anomaly detection mechanisms (Bhagat, 2024; Zheng, Tan, Jiang, & Wang, 2025). Maintaining model robustness against such attacks is critical, particularly in high-stakes environments like banking and corporate finance (Rawat et al., 2023; Mazloum, Mazloum, & Saleh, 2025).

6.6. Human Factors and Insider Threats

Security risks are not limited to technological vulnerabilities. Insider threats remain a significant challenge, as employees with privileged access can manipulate financial data, override AI recommendations, or exploit system weaknesses (Abbas & Kollwitz, 2025). Effective auditing strategies must combine AI capabilities with strict access controls, continuous monitoring, and comprehensive staff training to mitigate human-related risks (Harjuni, 2024; Uduehe, Okoye, & Amahalu, 2024).

6.7. Legal and Regulatory Compliance Challenges

The use of AI in forensic accounting introduces regulatory complexities. Different jurisdictions impose varying requirements on data privacy, financial reporting, and algorithmic decision-making. Organizations must ensure that AI-driven audits comply with applicable laws, including GDPR, Sarbanes-Oxley, and other local financial regulations (Adejumo & Ogburie, 2025; Al-Raggad et al., 2025). Failure to comply can lead to fines, legal liability, and erosion of stakeholder trust (Elumilade, Ogundeji, Achumie, Omokhoa, & Omowole, 2021; Harjuni, 2024).

6.8. Scalability and Resource Limitations

Deploying LLMs for secure auditing across large organizations requires significant computational resources, including high-performance servers, GPUs, and data storage solutions. Small- and medium-sized enterprises may struggle with the cost and infrastructure requirements, limiting the adoption and effectiveness of AI-based auditing solutions (Mubarrat, 2024; Ramos, 2021). Balancing cost, performance, and scalability is an ongoing challenge for organizations aiming to modernize their auditing practices.

6.9. Future Threats and Emerging Challenges

As AI technologies continue to evolve, new security threats are likely to emerge, including deepfake financial documents, automated social engineering attacks, and AI-driven cyber frauds (Daraojimba et al., 2023; Haddad, Alharasis, Fraij, & Al-Ramahi, 2024). Continuous research, threat modeling, and adaptive security measures are necessary to anticipate and mitigate these risks (Simbolon, Adriana, Rustam, Sulistyowati, & Rewa, 2024; Abbas & Kollwitz, 2025). Moreover, combining AI with blockchain, federated learning, and advanced encryption techniques may provide additional layers of protection for future auditing systems (Zheng et al., 2025).

To address the challenges identified in AI-driven auditing, Figure 3 presents a structured matrix linking key security risks with corresponding mitigation strategies, highlighting how governance and technology intersect in financial fraud prevention.

Figure 3. Matrix of security risks and mitigation strategies for AI-driven auditing

Security Risk	Mitigation Strategy
Cybersecurity Vulnerabilities	Multi-layered security protocols, encryption, IDS
Data Privacy Concerns	Data anonymization, GDPR compliance
Model Interpretability Issues	Transparency dashboards, explainable AI
Adversarial Attacks	Adversarial training, anomaly scoring
Insider Threats	Access control, continuous monitoring, staff training

In summary, while LLMs and AI provide powerful tools for enhancing auditing and forensic accounting, they introduce a spectrum of security risks and challenges that span technical, human, ethical, and regulatory domains. Addressing these risks requires a holistic strategy combining technological safeguards, human oversight, and compliance adherence to ensure that AI-driven auditing remains secure, reliable, and effective (Ali et al., 2024; Qatawneh, 2025).

7. MITIGATION STRATEGIES AND BEST PRACTICES

As the adoption of artificial intelligence (AI) and Large Language Models (LLMs) in forensic accounting and auditing continues to grow, organizations must implement robust mitigation strategies and best practices to address the associated security risks and challenges. These measures encompass technological safeguards, human-centered policies, and regulatory compliance frameworks, ensuring the reliability, integrity, and effectiveness of AI-driven forensic systems (Abbas & Kollwitz, 2025; Adejumo & Ogburie, 2025).

7.1. Strengthening Cybersecurity Measures

Effective mitigation begins with robust cybersecurity protocols to protect financial data and AI systems from unauthorized access, malware, ransomware, and insider threats. Organizations are advised to employ multi-layered security architectures, including firewalls, encryption, intrusion detection systems, and secure cloud storage (Matar, 2023; Rawat, Oki, Chakrawarti, Adekunle, Lukose, & Ajagbe, 2023). Regular penetration testing and security audits further enhance system resilience by identifying vulnerabilities before they can be exploited (Okonta & Nnamdi, 2025; Abbas & Kollwitz, 2025).

7.2. Data Governance and Privacy Protection

Ensuring the confidentiality, integrity, and availability of sensitive financial information requires strong data governance policies. Organizations must implement data classification schemes, access control mechanisms, and anonymization techniques to protect personally identifiable information (Ali, Futaih, Shukur, & Al-Orfali, 2024; Ali, Khinger, Subhe, & Al-Orfali, 2024). Compliance with international regulations such as GDPR, Sarbanes-Oxley, and local financial reporting standards is critical to maintain legal and ethical accountability (Zayed, Nour, Al Attar, Almubaideen, & Abdelaziz, 2024; Simbolon, Adriana, Rustam, Sulistyowati, & Rewa, 2024).

7.3. Enhancing Model Reliability and Interpretability

AI and LLM models should be continuously monitored and validated to ensure accurate detection of anomalies and fraud. Techniques such as model explainability, transparency dashboards, and post-hoc interpretability methods allow auditors to understand and justify AI-generated decisions (Bhagat, 2024; Qatawneh, 2025). Hybrid approaches that combine AI analytics with human expertise provide a safeguard against errors and reduce the risk of false positives or undetected fraud (Daraojimba, Farayola, Olatoye, Mhlongo, & Oke, 2023; Zangana, Suryawati, Mustafa, & Vitianingsih, 2026).

7.4. Integration with Existing Systems

To maximize efficiency and minimize operational disruptions, AI-based forensic tools must be interoperable with existing accounting information systems. This involves standardized data formats, API integrations, and regular updates to maintain compatibility across multiple platforms (Aman, 2024; Öztürk & Usul, 2020). Leveraging Big Data analytics and cloud computing can also enhance scalability and support real-time monitoring of financial transactions (Ramos, 2021; Mubarrat, 2024).

7.5. Adversarial Attack Prevention

Organizations must proactively defend AI models against adversarial attacks by implementing robust anomaly detection, data validation, and model retraining mechanisms. Techniques such as adversarial training, anomaly scoring, and pattern recognition algorithms reduce susceptibility to data manipulation attempts that could compromise fraud detection (Bhagat, 2024; Zheng, Tan, Jiang, & Wang, 2025).

7.6. Human-Centric Security Practices

While technology provides advanced detection capabilities, human factors remain a critical element of mitigation. Insider threats can be minimized through strict access controls, segregation of duties, continuous staff training, and background checks (Zangana, Mohammed, & Husain, 2025; Harjuni, 2024). Encouraging a culture of ethics and accountability within financial organizations reinforces the effectiveness of AI-driven monitoring systems (Al-Raggad, Albalawee, Al-Mahasneh, Abu Huson, & Albajaly, 2025; Uduehe, Okoye, & Amahalu, 2024).

7.7. Adoption of Advanced Forensic Techniques

Emerging forensic accounting methods, including rule-based expert systems, predictive analytics, and machine learning models, enable early detection of fraudulent activities (Öztürk & Usul, 2020; Vijayalakshmi & Jeevan, 2024). Combining AI with traditional auditing practices improves detection accuracy and provides auditors with actionable insights for investigating suspicious transactions (Haddad, Alharasis, Fraij, & Al-Ramahi, 2024; Elumilade, Ogundeji, Achumie, Omokhoa, & Omowole, 2021).

7.8. Continuous Monitoring and Feedback Loops

Implementing continuous monitoring and adaptive learning frameworks ensures that AI models evolve in response to emerging fraud patterns. Feedback loops, real-time reporting, and automated alerts improve operational responsiveness and reduce the risk of financial misreporting (Harjuni, 2024; Mazloum, Mazloum, & Saleh, 2025). Autonomous AI systems, when combined with human oversight, can effectively track high-risk transactions and dark web financial activities (Rawat et al., 2023; Abbas & Kollwitz, 2025).

7.9. Ethical AI and Compliance Integration

Integrating ethical AI principles within forensic accounting frameworks enhances trust, transparency, and accountability. Regular auditing of AI decision-making processes, bias assessment, and documentation of algorithmic workflows are recommended to meet regulatory and ethical standards (Zayed et al., 2024). This also ensures alignment with global standards for financial integrity, sustainability, and governance (Adejumo & Ogburie, 2025; Al-Raggad et al., 2025).

7.10. Leveraging Emerging Technologies

Future-proofing forensic accounting practices involves the adoption of blockchain for tamper-proof ledgers, federated learning for secure model training, and advanced encryption for safeguarding sensitive financial data (Abbas & Kollwitz, 2025; Zheng et al., 2025). By combining AI, Big Data, and secure computing frameworks, organizations can build resilient forensic ecosystems capable of mitigating evolving threats (Mubarrat, 2024).

7.11 Summary of Mitigation Practices

Adopting these strategies ensures that organizations effectively counteract the security risks posed by AI-driven forensic systems. The integration of robust cybersecurity measures, data governance, human-centered policies, and advanced forensic techniques creates a resilient environment where AI enhances fraud detection without compromising ethical, legal, or operational standards (Ali et al., 2024; Qatawneh, 2025).

8. CASE STUDIES AND APPLICATIONS

Forensic accounting has increasingly integrated advanced analytics, artificial intelligence (AI), and digital forensics to address complex financial fraud and cybercrime challenges. Real-world case studies provide practical insights into the application, benefits, and limitations of these methods across different organizational and regional contexts (Abbas & Kollwitz, 2025; Adejumo & Ogburie, 2025).

8.1. Application of AI in Forensic Accounting

One notable example involves the use of AI-driven anomaly detection systems in a multinational bank. The implementation of predictive analytics and machine learning models enabled early identification of suspicious transactions and potential financial statement fraud, significantly reducing financial losses (Bhagat, 2024). Similarly, integrating natural language processing (NLP) with accounting information systems allowed auditors to analyze unstructured communication data, identifying fraudulent intent in internal emails and chat logs (Qatawneh, 2025).

8.2. Big Data and Digital Forensics in Fraud Detection

A study in Nigeria demonstrated the effectiveness of Big Data analytics combined with forensic accounting in detecting complex fraud schemes within commercial banks. Real-time transaction monitoring and automated anomaly scoring enabled auditors to uncover irregularities that traditional methods would have missed (Okonta & Nnamdi, 2025; Ramos, 2021). Similarly, autonomous AI systems applied in dark web financial monitoring revealed illicit activities and money laundering attempts, highlighting the role of digital forensics in proactive fraud prevention (Rawat et al., 2023; Daraojimba, Farayola, Olatoye, Mhlongo, & Oke, 2023).

8.3. Comparative Analysis Across Countries

Comparative studies have highlighted variations in forensic accounting adoption and effectiveness. Research comparing developed and developing economies found that organizations employing AI-assisted auditing and rule-based expert systems experienced faster detection times and higher accuracy in fraud identification compared to those relying solely on traditional auditing methods (Simbolon, Adriana, Rustam, Sulistyowati, & Rewa, 2024; Öztürk & Usul, 2020). The studies also emphasized the importance of regulatory compliance and ethical standards in maintaining trust and credibility (Al-Raggad, Albalawee, Al-Mahasneh, Abu Huson, & Albajaly, 2025; Adejumo & Ogburie, 2025).

8.4. Enhancing Cybersecurity and Fraud Prevention

In the U.S., financial institutions have leveraged AI-based cybersecurity solutions to mitigate insider threats and phishing attacks, integrating continuous monitoring and adaptive response strategies (Matar, 2023; Zangana, Mohammed, & Husain, 2025). Similarly, AI-powered forensic auditing systems have enabled rapid reconstruction of tampered records, strengthening accountability and providing forensic evidence in legal proceedings (Mazloum, Mazloum, & Saleh, 2025; Vijayalakshmi & Jeevan, 2024).

8.5. Forensic Accounting in Emerging Markets

Case studies in emerging economies, such as Nigeria and Indonesia, illustrate the benefits of combining AI and traditional forensic accounting techniques to address fraud in commercial banks. Techniques included data-driven auditing, predictive risk scoring, and integration of AI with human expertise to ensure accuracy and operational efficiency (Uduehe, Okoye, & Amahalu, 2024; Harjuni, 2024; Aman, 2024). These studies also highlighted challenges such as limited technical expertise, infrastructure constraints, and ethical concerns related to algorithmic decision-making (Haddad, Alharasis, Fraij, & Al-Ramahi, 2024; Bhagat, 2024).

8.6. Emerging Trends in Intelligent Forensic Systems

Recent implementations of AI-enhanced forensic auditing include the use of adaptive resonance theory (ART) for anomaly detection and robust pattern recognition, as applied in financial institutions in Asia and the Middle East (Zangana, Khalid Mohammed, Omar, Mahmood Mustafa, & Vega Vitianingsih, 2025; Zangana, 2025). These systems provide high computational efficiency while detecting subtle fraudulent patterns that conventional methods might overlook. Moreover, hybrid approaches combining AI, Big Data, and blockchain technology have demonstrated improvements in transactional integrity and transparency (Mubarrat, 2024; Abbas & Kollwitz, 2025; Zheng, Tan, Jiang, & Wang, 2025).

8.7. Practical Lessons from Applications

Across the case studies, several best practices emerge:

- Integrating AI with human auditing expertise ensures interpretability and reduces false positives (Ali, Futaih, Shukur, & Al-Orfali, 2024; Ali, Khinger, Subhe, & Al-Orfali, 2024).
- Continuous monitoring, feedback loops, and adaptive model training enhance detection of evolving fraud patterns (Daraojimba et al., 2023).
- Ethical AI deployment, compliance with global standards, and transparency in decision-making reinforce organizational credibility (Zayed et al., 2024; Al-Raggad et al., 2025).
- Leveraging emerging technologies such as NLP, Big Data, and blockchain strengthens resilience against both internal and external fraud threats (Ramos, 2021; Rawat et al., 2023; Zheng et al., 2025).

8.8 Conclusion of Case Studies

The case studies demonstrate that the integration of AI, digital forensics, and advanced analytics significantly enhances forensic accounting capabilities. By applying these techniques across diverse contexts, organizations can detect financial anomalies more efficiently, strengthen regulatory compliance, and mitigate risks associated with modern financial fraud. These applications serve as practical evidence that technology-driven forensic accounting is both feasible and necessary for robust financial oversight (Abbas & Kollwitz, 2025; Vijayalakshmi & Jeevan, 2024).

9. ETHICAL, LEGAL, AND REGULATORY CONSIDERATIONS

Forensic accounting, particularly when augmented by artificial intelligence (AI) and digital analytics, operates within a complex landscape of ethical, legal, and regulatory requirements. As organizations increasingly rely on advanced technologies to detect fraud and ensure financial integrity, adherence to ethical standards and regulatory compliance becomes crucial for maintaining trust, accountability, and legal defensibility (Abbas & Kollwitz, 2025; Adejumo & Ogburie, 2025).

9.1. Ethical Considerations in AI-Driven Forensic Accounting

The ethical deployment of AI in forensic accounting requires transparency, fairness, and accountability. Algorithms used for fraud detection, predictive analytics, or anomaly identification must be interpretable to auditors and regulators, ensuring that decisions can be traced and justified (Bhagat, 2024). Ethical concerns also arise regarding data privacy, particularly when AI systems analyze sensitive financial or communication data (Qatawneh, 2025; Zayed, Nour, Al Attar, Almubaideen, & Abdelaziz, 2024). Scholars emphasize that AI should assist, not replace, human judgment to mitigate bias and ensure fairness in financial investigations (Ali, Futaih, Shukur, & Al-Orfali, 2024; Ali, Khinger, Subhe, & Al-Orfali, 2024).

9.2. Legal Frameworks and Compliance

Forensic accountants must navigate multiple legal frameworks, including national accounting regulations, anti-fraud statutes, and cybersecurity laws. The integration of AI and Big Data analytics introduces novel legal challenges, such as determining liability in cases of algorithmic errors or misinterpretation of financial data (Aman, 2024; Ramos, 2021). Legal compliance also requires adherence to auditing standards, documentation practices, and evidence preservation protocols to support potential litigation (Daraojimba, Farayola, Olatoye, Mhlongo, & Oke, 2023; Öztürk & Usul, 2020). Regulatory agencies increasingly encourage the use of AI for monitoring and auditing, provided that organizations demonstrate robust governance and risk management frameworks (Al-Raggad, Albalawee, Al-Mahasneh, Abu Huson, & Albajaly, 2025; Simbolon, Adriana, Rustam, Sulistyowati, & Rewa, 2024).

9.3. Data Privacy and Cybersecurity Considerations

The rise of digital financial records and AI-assisted forensic systems highlights the importance of data privacy and cybersecurity. Organizations must ensure compliance with data protection laws and safeguard financial data against unauthorized access or breaches (Matar, 2023; Zangana, Mohammed, & Husain, 2025). Cybersecurity measures, including encryption, access controls, and continuous monitoring, are integral to both ethical and legal obligations, reducing the risk of insider threats and external attacks (Rawat et al., 2023; Mubarrat, 2024).

9.4. Ethical Integrity in Forensic Investigations

Forensic accountants play a critical role in upholding ethical integrity by maintaining independence, avoiding conflicts of interest, and ensuring objectivity in investigations (Elumilade, Ogundeji, Achumie, Omokhoa, & Omowole, 2021; Harjuni, 2024). AI tools must be implemented to enhance investigative efficiency without compromising ethical standards, such as manipulating outcomes or selectively reporting anomalies (Haddad, Alharasis, Fraij, & Al-Ramahi, 2024; Vijayalakshmi & Jeevan, 2024). Proper training and oversight of AI systems, coupled with human judgment, help prevent ethical breaches in both financial and cyber forensic operations (Mazloum, Mazloum, & Saleh, 2025).

9.5. Regulatory Compliance and Standardization

Regulatory considerations encompass not only local accounting standards but also international frameworks, including IFRS, ISO standards for auditing, and cybersecurity compliance (Adejumo & Ogburie, 2025; Abbas & Kollwitz, 2025). Case studies from Nigeria, Indonesia, and the U.S. illustrate the importance of harmonizing AI-assisted forensic practices with regulatory requirements to prevent liability and ensure audit defensibility (Okonta & Nnamdi, 2025; Uduehe, Okoye, & Amahalu, 2024; Daraojimba et al., 2023). Additionally, continuous monitoring of emerging legal frameworks is necessary as AI and automation introduce novel compliance challenges in forensic accounting (Bhagat, 2024).

9.6. Challenges and Emerging Issues

Despite the benefits of AI in forensic accounting, several challenges persist. These include balancing privacy with investigative needs, addressing algorithmic bias, ensuring transparency, and maintaining ethical standards in cross-border investigations (Ramos, 2021; Zayed et al., 2024). Moreover, the rapid evolution of technology requires regulators to adapt rules and guidelines proactively to mitigate legal risks while supporting innovation in fraud detection (Daraojimba et al., 2023; Rawat et al., 2023; Zheng, Tan, Jiang, & Wang, 2025).

9.7 Summary

Ethical, legal, and regulatory considerations are central to the effective application of AI in forensic accounting. Organizations must integrate AI responsibly, ensuring transparency, compliance, and ethical integrity, while proactively adapting to evolving regulations. By addressing these challenges, forensic accountants can leverage technology to enhance fraud detection, strengthen governance, and maintain stakeholder trust in the digital era (Abbas & Kollwitz, 2025; Al-Raggad et al., 2025; Zangana, Suryawati, Mustafa, & Vitianingsih, 2026).

10. FUTURE DIRECTIONS

The field of forensic accounting is rapidly evolving under the influence of artificial intelligence (AI), Big Data analytics, and advanced digital technologies. Future research and practice will increasingly focus on integrating these technologies to enhance fraud detection, regulatory compliance, and overall financial transparency (Abbas & Kollwitz, 2025; Adejumo & Ogburie, 2025).

10.1. Advanced AI and Machine Learning Integration

The application of AI, including machine learning and natural language processing, is expected to become more sophisticated in forensic accounting. Techniques such as anomaly detection, predictive modeling, and intelligent auditing systems will enable proactive identification of fraudulent activities and risk management (Zangana, Suryawati, Mustafa, & Vitianingsih, 2026; Zheng, Tan, Jiang, & Wang, 2025). Future research should focus on improving algorithm interpretability, mitigating biases, and ensuring compliance with ethical standards while maintaining high detection accuracy (Bhagat, 2024; Qatawneh, 2025).

10.2. Big Data and Real-Time Analytics

With the growing availability of large financial datasets, forensic accountants can leverage Big Data analytics for real-time fraud monitoring and continuous auditing (Ramos, 2021; Aman, 2024; Mubarrat, 2024). Future systems will need to handle heterogeneous and high-velocity financial data streams efficiently, applying scalable algorithms to detect subtle patterns indicative of fraudulent activity (Mazloum, Mazloum, & Saleh, 2025; Rawat et al., 2023).

10.3. Cybersecurity-Enhanced Forensic Accounting

As financial transactions increasingly move online, cybersecurity and forensic accounting are converging fields. Integrating cybersecurity protocols with forensic auditing can help prevent insider threats, data breaches, and unauthorized financial manipulations (Matar, 2023; Zangana, Mohammed, & Husain, 2025). Research will focus on developing AI-driven systems capable of automatically identifying suspicious access patterns and alerting auditors in real-time (Okonta & Nnamdi, 2025; Rawat et al., 2023).

10.4. Ethical, Legal, and Regulatory Innovations

Future forensic accounting practices will need to address emerging ethical and regulatory challenges associated with AI deployment. Automated systems must comply with data privacy laws, auditing standards, and ethical guidelines, ensuring transparency and fairness in decision-making (Al-Raggad et al., 2025; Zayed et al., 2024; Ali, Futaih, Shukur, & Al-Orfali, 2024). Researchers will explore frameworks for algorithmic accountability and standardized reporting mechanisms to support regulatory compliance across jurisdictions (Daraojimba et al., 2023; Simbolon, Adriana, Rustam, Sulistyowati, & Rewa, 2024).

10.5. Cross-Disciplinary Approaches

The integration of forensic accounting with other domains, such as digital forensics, blockchain, and financial cybersecurity, presents new research opportunities (Rangarajan, & Salih Hasan, 2026). Future studies are likely to explore multi-layered investigative systems that combine AI-driven financial analytics with forensic examination of digital communication, enhancing the detection of complex and cross-border financial crimes (Daraojimba et al., 2023; Vijayalakshmi & Jeevan, 2024).

10.6. International Standards and Global Best Practices

Comparative analyses of forensic accounting practices across countries indicate a growing need for harmonized international standards (Simbolon et al., 2024; Uduehe, Okoye, & Amahalu, 2024; Đukić, Pavlović, & Grdinić, 2023). Future research should focus on designing globally applicable AI-assisted auditing frameworks that account for regional regulatory differences while promoting transparency and accountability in financial reporting (Harjuni, 2024; Öztürk & Usul, 2020).

10.7. Human-AI Collaboration

Despite technological advancements, human judgment remains central to forensic accounting. Future directions emphasize the complementary role of AI and human expertise, where intelligent systems support auditors in decision-making, but final judgments are made by trained professionals (Elumilade, Ogundeji, Achumie, Omokhoa, & Omowole, 2021; Haddad, Alharasis, Fraij, & Al-Ramahi, 2024). Research should focus on designing interfaces and training programs that maximize this collaboration, enhancing efficiency without compromising ethical or legal standards (Ali, Khinger, Subhe, & Al-Orfali, 2024; Abbas & Kollwitz, 2025).

10.8. Emerging Technologies in Forensic Accounting

Emerging technologies, including blockchain, robotic process automation, and parallel computing, are likely to redefine forensic accounting capabilities. For instance, blockchain can ensure immutable financial records, while high-performance computing can accelerate complex fraud detection algorithms. Additionally, hybrid AI approaches combining classical statistical methods with deep learning are expected to enhance anomaly detection in financial datasets (Mazloum et al., 2025).

10.9 Summary

The future of forensic accounting lies in the strategic integration of AI, Big Data, and emerging digital technologies with ethical and regulatory oversight. By advancing cross-disciplinary approaches, global standards, and human-AI collaboration, the field will evolve toward more proactive, efficient, and transparent fraud detection systems, ultimately strengthening financial integrity and public trust (Abbas & Kollwitz, 2025; Zheng et al., 2025).

Figure 4 provides a roadmap of emerging directions for LLM-enabled forensic accounting, including advanced AI integration, Big Data analytics, cybersecurity-enhanced auditing, ethical compliance, and human–AI collaboration.

Figure 4. Roadmap of future directions in LLM-enabled forensic accounting

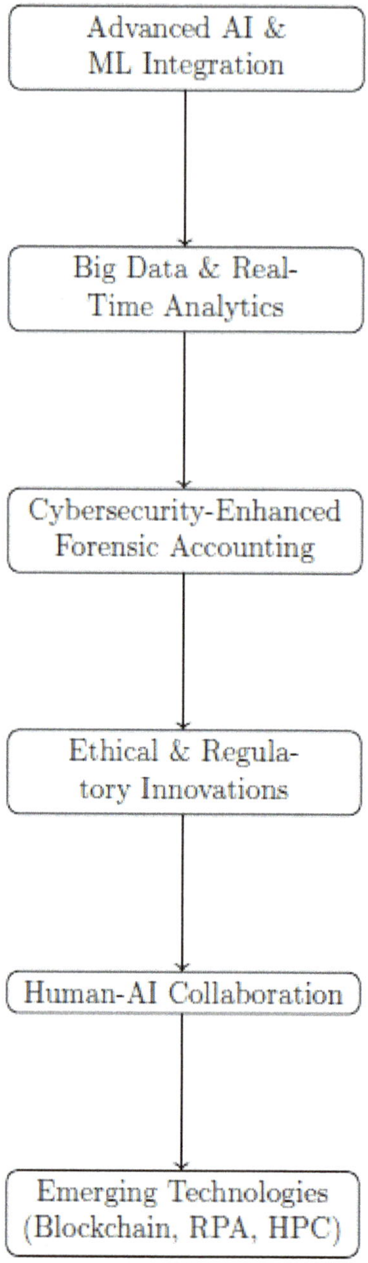

11. CONCLUSION

Forensic accounting has undergone a profound transformation in recent years, driven by technological advancements, artificial intelligence, and Big Data analytics. These innovations have significantly enhanced the ability of professionals to detect, prevent, and investigate financial fraud, while simultaneously improving the efficiency and accuracy of auditing processes. The integration of AI-driven systems and data analytics allows for real-time monitoring, anomaly detection, and predictive modeling, which collectively strengthen financial integrity and regulatory compliance across organizations.

Despite these advancements, challenges remain in terms of ethical considerations, legal compliance, and the interpretability of AI-driven forensic tools. Ensuring transparency, fairness, and accountability in automated decision-making processes is paramount to maintaining public trust and professional integrity. Human judgment continues to play a crucial role, complementing AI and advanced technologies to provide context-aware analyses and ensure that investigative conclusions are ethically and legally sound.

Looking forward, the convergence of emerging technologies, including blockchain, parallel computing, and hybrid AI models, offers promising opportunities for further enhancing forensic accounting capabilities. Cross-disciplinary approaches that integrate digital forensics, cybersecurity, and financial auditing are expected to become standard practice, facilitating the detection of complex and cross-border financial crimes. Moreover, the development of global standards and best practices will support harmonized, transparent, and accountable financial oversight.

In summary, the evolution of forensic accounting reflects a balance between technological innovation and human expertise, guided by ethical and regulatory frameworks. By leveraging advanced tools and fostering interdisciplinary collaboration, the field is well-positioned to address emerging challenges, mitigate financial risks, and safeguard organizational and societal trust in financial systems.

REFERENCES

Abbas, A., & Kollwitz, E. (2025). Forensic Accounting in the Digital Era: Leveraging AI for Fraud Detection and Risk Management.

Adejumo, A. P., & Ogburie, C. P.Adetunji Paul AdejumoChinonso Peter Ogburie. (2025). Forensic accounting in financial fraud detection: Trends and challenges. *International Journal of Science and Research Archive*, *14*(3), 1219–1232. DOI: 10.30574/ijsra.2025.14.3.0815

Al-Raggad, M., Albalawee, N., Al-Mahasneh, A., Abu Huson, Y., & Albajaly, A. (2025). Unveiling financial crimes: Advancing forensic accounting practices and ethical integrity through bibliometric insights. *Safer Communities*, *24*(3), 244–264. DOI: 10.1108/SC-11-2024-0069

Ali, A. M., Futaih, R. F., Shukur, M., & Al-Orfali, A. K. (2024). Forensic Accounting and Fraud Detection Emerging Trends and Techniques. *Journal of Ecohumanism*, *3*(5), 525–542. DOI: 10.62754/joe.v3i5.3921

Ali, A. M., Khinger, I. K., Subhe, A., & Al-Orfali, A. K. (2024). Forensic Accounting Techniques in Detecting Frauds. *Journal of Ecohumanism*, *3*(5), 543–558. DOI: 10.62754/joe.v3i5.3922

Aman, Q. U. I. S. E. R. (2024). From data to discovery: The impact of technology on forensic accounting. *Ile Journal of Law and Forensic Science*, *2*(1), 1–13.

Bhagat, N. (2024). Artificial intelligence challenges and its impact on detection and prevention of financial statement fraud: A theoretical study. In *Demystifying the Dark Side of AI in Business* (pp. 60–80). IGI Global Scientific Publishing.

Daraojimba, R. E., Farayola, O. A., Olatoye, F. M. O., Mhlongo, N., & Oke, T. T. L. (2023). Forensic accounting in the digital age: a US perspective: scrutinizing methods and challenges in digital financial fraud prevention. *Finance & Accounting Research Journal*, *5*(11), 342–360. DOI: 10.51594/farj.v5i11.614

Đukić, T., Pavlović, M., & Grdinić, V. (2023). Uncovering Financial Fraud: The Vital Role of Forensic Accounting and Auditing in Modern Business Practice. *Economic Themes, 61*(3).

Elumilade, O. O., Ogundeji, I. A., Achumie, G. O., Omokhoa, H. E., & Omowole, B. M. (2021). Enhancing fraud detection and forensic auditing through data-driven techniques for financial integrity and security. *Journal of Advanced Education and Sciences*, *1*(2), 55–63. DOI: 10.54660/.JAES.2021.1.2.55-63

Haddad, H. O. S. S. A. M., Alharasis, E. E., Fraij, J., & Al-Ramahi, N. M. (2024). How do innovative improvements in forensic accounting and its related technologies sweeten fraud investigation and prevention. *WSEAS Transactions on Business and Economics*, *21*, 1115–1141. DOI: 10.37394/23207.2024.21.93

Harjuni, J. (2024). The role of forensic accounting in fraud detection and prevention in financial institutions. *Tamansiswa Accounting Journal International*, *15*(1), 151–159.

Matar, D. O. (2023). *Forensic accounting and Cybersecurity examine their interrelation in the detection and Prevention of financial fraud.* American Academic & Scholarly Research Journal.

Mazloum, H., Mazloum, N., & Saleh, A. M. (2025). FORENSIC AUDIT: ENHANCING CERTIFIED PUBLIC ACCOUNTANT USING ARTIFICIAL INTELLIGENCE TECHNIQUES. *BAU Journal-Science and Technology*, *6*(2), 10. DOI: 10.54729/2959-331X.1128

Mubarrat, A. A. (2024). of the Research: Role of Artificial Intelligence and Big Data in Modern Forensic Accountancy. *Available at SSRN* 5078259.

Okonta, C. N., & Nnamdi, C. A. (2025). Forensic Investigation and Fraud Detection in Nigeria: Leveraging on Artificial Intelligence. *Review of Ethics in Sustainable Finance and Accounting*, *1*(1), 31–38. DOI: 10.70865/jiatis.v2i1.80

Öztürk, M. S., & Usul, H. (2020). Detection of accounting frauds using the rule-based expert systems within the scope of forensic accounting. In *Contemporary issues in audit management and forensic accounting* (pp. 155–171). Emerald Publishing Limited. DOI: 10.1108/S1569-375920200000102013

Qatawneh, A. M. (2025). The role of artificial intelligence in auditing and fraud detection in accounting information systems: Moderating role of natural language processing. *The International Journal of Organizational Analysis*, *33*(6), 1391–1409. DOI: 10.1108/IJOA-03-2024-4389

Ramos, J. R. M. (2021). The use of Big Data and Artificial Intelligence: to prevent and detect fraud. *Artificial intelligence in the economic sector: prevention and responsibility*, 85-115.

Rawat, R., Oki, O., Chakrawarti, R. K., Adekunle, T. S., Lukose, J. M., & Ajagbe, S. A. (2023). Autonomous artificial intelligence systems for fraud detection and forensics in dark web environments. *Informatica (Vilnius)*, *47*(9).

Simbolon, R., Adriana, N., Rustam, A., Sulistyowati, N. W., & Rewa, K. A. (2024). The Impact of Forensic Accounting on Financial Fraud Prevention: A Comparative Analysis Across Countries. *The Journal of Academic Science, 1*(8), 1074–1084. DOI: 10.59613/m6jrt421

Uduehe, E. M., Okoye, E. I., & Amahalu, N. N. (2024). Forensic accounting techniques and fraud management of commercial banks in Awka-South Anambra State. *Journal of Global Accounting, 10*(2), 307–346.

Vijayalakshmi, D., & Jeevan, J. (2024). Forensic Accounting: Uncovering Fraud with Advanced Analytics. *Library of Progress-Library Science, Information Technology & Computer, 44*(3).

Zangana, H. M., Mohammed, H. S., & Husain, M. M. (2025). Addressing insider threats: The human factor in cybersecurity for financial institutions. *Journal of Innovation Information Technology and Application, 7*(1), 88–96. DOI: 10.35970/jinita.v7i1.2686

Zangana, H. M., Omar, M., Rangarajan, A., & Salih Hasan, B. M. (2026). Natural Language Processing for Analyzing Criminal Communication and Cyber Threat Intelligence. In Zangana, H., & Omar, M. (Eds.), *AI in Digital Forensics and Cybercrime Investigation: Methods, Ethics, and Emerging Technologies* (pp. 1–30). IGI Global Scientific Publishing., DOI: 10.4018/979-8-3373-6536-7.ch001

Zangana, H. M., Suryawati, R. F., Mustafa, F. M., & Vitianingsih, A. V. (2026). AI in Forensic Accounting: Detecting Anomalies and Financial Fraud Through Intelligent Systems. In Zangana, H., & Omar, M. (Eds.), *AI in Digital Forensics and Cybercrime Investigation: Methods, Ethics, and Emerging Technologies* (pp. 125–162). IGI Global Scientific Publishing., DOI: 10.4018/979-8-3373-6536-7.ch005

Zayed, L. M. M., Nour, M. I., Al Attar, K., Almubaideen, H., & Abdelaziz, G. A. M. (2024). Role of artificial intelligence (AI) in accounting information systems in detecting fraud. In *Artificial Intelligence and Economic Sustainability in the Era of Industrial Revolution 5.0* (pp. 397–409). Springer Nature Switzerland. DOI: 10.1007/978-3-031-56586-1_30

Zheng, W., Tan, Y., Jiang, B., & Wang, J. (2025). Integrating Machine Learning into Financial Forensics for Smarter Fraud Prevention. *Technology and Investment, 16*(3), 79–90. DOI: 10.4236/ti.2025.163006

Chapter 4
Misuse of LLMs in Cybercrime and Countermeasures

Luay Albtosh
https://orcid.org/0009-0009-0338-9123
Capitol Technology University, USA & Houston Community College, USA

Ade Surahman
Universitas Teknokrat Indonesia, Indonesia

ABSTRACT

The rapid proliferation of Large Language Models (LLMs) has revolutionized numerous sectors, from business intelligence to healthcare, by enabling advanced natural language understanding and generation. However, their misuse in cybercrime has emerged as a critical concern, encompassing activities such as automated phishing, disinformation campaigns, social engineering, and the generation of malicious code. This chapter explores the diverse modalities through which LLMs can be exploited for cybercriminal purposes, highlighting the technological, ethical, and legal challenges associated with their deployment. It further examines contemporary countermeasures, including AI-driven threat detection, robust model governance, user authentication protocols, and regulatory frameworks designed to mitigate LLM-related risks. By analyzing case studies and ongoing research initiatives, this chapter provides a comprehensive overview of both the threats posed by LLM misuse and the strategic interventions necessary to secure these powerful AI systems.

DOI: 10.4018/979-8-3373-7133-7.ch004

1. INTRODUCTION

The emergence of Large Language Models (LLMs) represents a transformative milestone in artificial intelligence (AI), offering unprecedented capabilities in natural language understanding, generation, and reasoning. LLMs have found applications across diverse sectors, including finance, healthcare, governance, and scientific research (Ali, 2024; Ali, H., & Aysan, 2024; AlQenaei, 2024). Despite their potential, the widespread deployment of these models has exposed critical vulnerabilities, as malicious actors increasingly exploit LLMs for cybercriminal activities. These include automated phishing campaigns, social engineering, disinformation, malware generation, and exploitation of Internet-of-Things (IoT) networks (Chen et al., 2024; Diaf et al., 2024; Ferrag et al., 2024).

LLMs' misuse in cybercrime represents a multidimensional threat, leveraging the scalability and sophistication of AI to circumvent traditional cybersecurity defenses. For instance, social media platforms and darknet forums have become fertile grounds for AI-driven exploitation, where threat actors employ LLMs to craft highly convincing phishing messages, perform sentiment manipulation, and generate malicious code (Sangher et al., 2023; Sun et al., 2023; Lee et al., 2024). The capacity of LLMs to simulate human-like language intensifies the risk of deception, making detection challenging for conventional security mechanisms (Gaurav et al., 2024; Ferrag et al., 2023).

The cybercrime landscape has also evolved in response to open-source intelligence (OSINT) availability, allowing adversaries to combine LLM capabilities with readily accessible datasets to enhance attack precision (Adewopo et al., 2020; Chaudhary & Bansal, 2022; Sufi, 2023). Similarly, AI-driven threat intelligence solutions demonstrate that LLMs can serve dual roles—both as attack enablers and as cybersecurity defenders (Rajendran & Tulasi, 2025; Sangher et al., 2024; Alturkistani & Chuprat, 2024). By analyzing textual datasets, behavioral patterns, and network interactions, LLMs can support proactive threat identification and mitigation strategies (Atoum et al., 2025; Asoronye et al., 2024).

Legal and ethical considerations further complicate the deployment and regulation of LLMs. National and international frameworks for AI governance remain fragmented, posing challenges for enforcing accountability in cases of misuse (Bharati, 2020; Butt, 2024; Ho, 2023). Additionally, digital forensics and incident response operations increasingly rely on AI for rapid data analysis, threat triage, and pattern recognition, highlighting the dual-use nature of LLMs in cybersecurity contexts (Adam & Varol, 2020; Dunsin et al., 2024; Bhawna & Mahajan, 2024; Costantini et al., 2019). Privacy-preserving AI approaches, such as federated learning, are emerging as essential tools to balance cybersecurity and individual rights in digital forensics applications (Iyengar et al., 2025).

The proliferation of LLMs and their application in cybercrime necessitate a nuanced understanding of their capabilities and vulnerabilities. Current research underscores the importance of developing AI-augmented defense mechanisms while recognizing the ethical, legal, and social implications of AI misuse (Ferrag et al., 2024; Ghazal et al., 2024; Chen et al., 2024). Moreover, interdisciplinary approaches that integrate cybersecurity, law, AI governance, and behavioral sciences are critical to anticipating, detecting, and mitigating LLM-driven threats (Larson et al., 2021; Dunsin et al., 2022; Eswaran & Eswaran, 2025).

This chapter explores the multifaceted misuse of LLMs in cybercrime, including attack vectors, threat amplification techniques, and the challenges posed to cybersecurity frameworks. It also examines contemporary countermeasures, spanning AI-driven threat detection, regulatory interventions, and proactive forensic strategies. By synthesizing empirical studies, theoretical insights, and applied frameworks, the chapter aims to provide a comprehensive foundation for understanding both the threats associated with LLM misuse and the strategic countermeasures necessary to secure AI-driven systems.

This conceptual diagram illustrates the interactions between AI technologies, such as LLMs, and cybersecurity practices. It highlights the dual role of AI as both a tool for enhancing security and a potential vector for threats.

Figure 1. Conceptual Diagram of AI and Cybersecurity Interactions

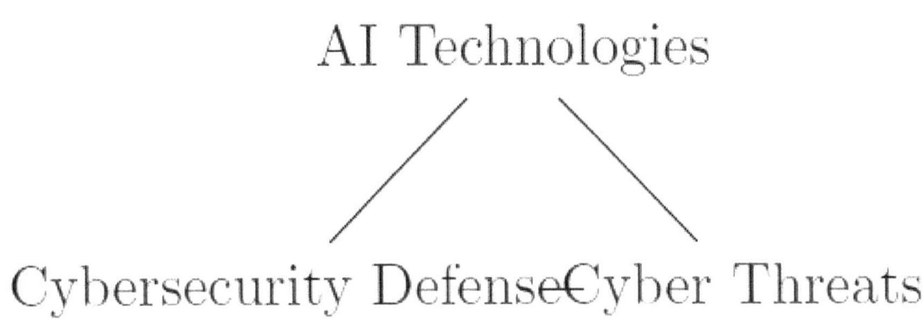

2. BACKGROUND AND LITERATURE REVIEW

The rapid evolution of Artificial Intelligence (AI) and, in particular, Large Language Models (LLMs), has significantly transformed digital ecosystems, creating both opportunities and challenges in cybersecurity, digital forensics, and threat intelligence. LLMs, through their sophisticated natural language processing (NLP) capabilities, are increasingly employed in diverse applications ranging from finance and healthcare to social network analysis and cybersecurity analytics (Ali, H., & Aysan, 2024; Ali, H., Zafar, & Aysan, 2024; Chen et al., 2024). While their potential is undeniable, the dual-use nature of these technologies has raised concerns regarding malicious exploitation in cybercrime and digital warfare (Ferrag et al., 2024; Ghazal et al., 2024).

2.1 Digital Forensics and AI Integration

The integration of AI into digital forensics has enhanced the speed and precision of incident response, evidence collection, and threat analysis (Adam & Varol, 2020; Costantini, De Gasperis, & Olivieri, 2019; Dunsin, Ghanem, Ouazzane, & Vassilev, 2024). AI-driven digital forensics frameworks leverage machine learning and NLP to identify patterns in large-scale datasets, detect anomalies, and predict cyber threats. Privacy-preserving AI techniques, such as federated learning, have been proposed to balance investigative needs with ethical and legal obligations (Iyengar et al., 2025). Furthermore, AI-supported forensic tools can automate psycholinguistic profiling to assess threat actors' behaviors, particularly in social media and darknet environments (Etaywe, Macfarlane, & Alazab, 2024; Siddiqui, Amer, & Khan, 2019).

2.2 Cyber Threat Intelligence and Open-Source Data

The field of Cyber Threat Intelligence (CTI) has witnessed a paradigm shift with the advent of LLMs, enabling more proactive, predictive, and adaptive defenses. By leveraging textual data from social networks, online forums, and darknet sources, AI-driven CTI can identify attack trends, tactics, techniques, and procedures (TTPs) employed by threat actors (Adewopo, Gonen, & Adewopo, 2020; Chaudhary & Bansal, 2022; Lee, Mujammami, & Kim, 2024; Sun et al., 2023). LLMs are increasingly applied to automate the extraction and classification of OSINT, transforming unstructured text into actionable intelligence for risk mitigation and strategic cybersecurity decision-making (Rajendran & Tulasi, 2025; Sufi, 2023; Sangher, Singh, & Pandey, 2024).

2.3 LLM-Driven Cybersecurity Applications

Recent studies highlight the deployment of specialized LLM-based security models, such as SecLM, which are designed for advanced cybersecurity applications, including threat detection, mitigation, and real-time monitoring (Asoronye et al., 2024; Ferrag et al., 2024; Ferrag et al., 2023). Transformer-based models, including

BERT and LSTM architectures, have been successfully applied to detect malicious content, analyze intent, and identify potential cybercrime activities in social media and e-commerce environments (Sangher, Singh, Pandey, & Kumar, 2023; Gaurav et al., 2024). Moreover, LLMs enhance predictive capabilities in IoT networks, allowing proactive threat prevention through anomaly detection and behavioral modeling (Diaf et al., 2024; Ferrag et al., 2024).

2.4 Ethical, Legal, and Governance Considerations

The adoption of LLMs and AI in cybersecurity and digital forensics introduces significant legal and ethical considerations. Multi-jurisdictional challenges arise regarding evidence admissibility, accountability, and the protection of privacy rights (Bharati, 2020; Butt, 2024; Ho, 2023). Regulatory frameworks, including the EU AI Act and guidelines for diagnostic AI systems, emphasize responsible AI deployment, risk management, and transparency (Larson et al., 2021). Additionally, the ethical dimensions of generative AI underscore the need for cross-domain governance to prevent misuse while fostering innovation (Ali, H., & Aysan, 2025; Ferrag et al., 2024; Batabyal, 2024).

2.5 Applications Across Sectors and Emerging Research

Beyond cybersecurity, LLMs are utilized in finance, climate monitoring, energy management, and sustainability research (Ali, 2024; Akindele & Chabinga, 2024; Aloamaka, 2024; Jafarizadeh et al., 2024). AI-driven systems support renewable energy storage optimization, climate crisis modeling, and policy analysis for environmental sustainability (Emon et al., 2025; Chowdhury, 2024; Daniel, 2024). Furthermore, AI applications in STEM education, biosensing, and military monitoring illustrate the breadth of LLM utility and the potential for both societal benefits and security risks (Arya & Rastogi, 2024; Jamro & Jamro, 2023; Karim, Galar, & Kumar, 2023).

2.6 Gaps in the Literature

Despite advances in LLM research and cybersecurity, gaps remain in addressing the proactive misuse of LLMs in coordinated cybercrime and sophisticated digital attacks. There is limited empirical research on privacy-preserving, explainable AI models specifically designed to counteract adversarial LLM exploits in real-time contexts (Chen et al., 2024; Ferrag et al., 2024; Ghazal et al., 2024). Additionally, interdisciplinary approaches that combine AI, legal frameworks, and social behavioral analytics remain underdeveloped, underscoring the need for integrated research strategies (Fenwick, Molnar, & Frangos, 2024; Leontidis, 2024; Luan et al., 2024).

In summary, the background literature emphasizes the dual-use nature of LLMs, the transformative potential of AI in cybersecurity, digital forensics, and threat intelligence, and the critical need for governance frameworks to address ethical, legal, and social implications. This foundation provides the context for exploring the nuanced misuse of LLMs in cybercrime and informs strategies for mitigation, detection, and responsible AI adoption.

This line graph depicts the trends in various types of cybercrime over the past few years, showcasing how the misuse of LLMs has evolved. It allows for an analysis of rising threats and helps identify periods of increased activity.

Figure 2. Line Graph of Cybercrime Trends Over Time

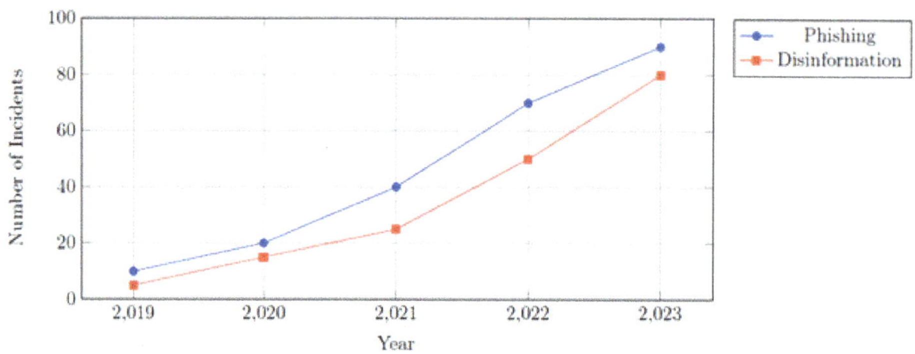

3. TYPES OF CYBERCRIME ENABLED BY LLM MISUSE

The rapid adoption of large language models (LLMs) has brought transformative advancements in fields such as natural language processing, automated decision-making, and cybersecurity analytics. However, alongside their legitimate applications, these models have opened new avenues for cybercrime, enabling sophisticated attacks that were previously infeasible or highly labor-intensive. Understanding the types of cybercrime facilitated by LLM misuse is critical for cybersecurity practitioners, policymakers, and researchers.

This flowchart illustrates the various pathways through which Large Language Models (LLMs) can be misused in cybercrime. It categorizes the types of cybercrime into distinct branches, including phishing, disinformation, and fraud, highlighting the interconnectedness of these activities.

Figure 3. Flowchart of LLM Misuse in Cybercrime

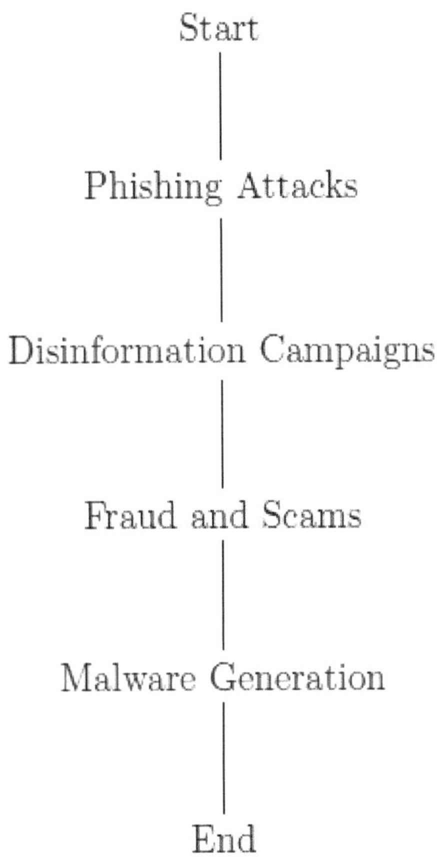

3.1. Phishing and Social Engineering Attacks

LLMs can generate highly convincing human-like text, which cybercriminals exploit for phishing campaigns. Traditional phishing techniques, often detected by heuristic or signature-based methods, can now be augmented with AI to create personalized messages that target specific individuals or organizations (Gaurav et al., 2024; Sun et al., 2023). By leveraging LLMs' capability to model human communication patterns, attackers can craft emails or social media messages that evade conventional detection systems, increasing the probability of credential theft, financial fraud, and information compromise (Rajendran & Tulasi, 2025; Sangher, Singh, & Pandey, 2024).

3.2. Generation of Malicious Code and Exploits

LLMs trained on programming and cybersecurity datasets have the potential to generate executable scripts, malware, or exploits that attackers can deploy automatically. This represents a significant escalation in cybercrime capabilities, as it lowers the technical barrier for individuals seeking to conduct attacks (Al-Sinani & Mitchell, 2024; Al-Sinani et al., 2025). Such misuse can result in ransomware distribution, automated vulnerability exploitation, and targeted attacks against critical infrastructure (Chen et al., 2024; Ferrag et al., 2024).

3.3. Disinformation and Influence Operations

The capacity of LLMs to produce coherent narratives and simulate multiple personas facilitates large-scale disinformation campaigns. Malicious actors can generate misleading content for political manipulation, financial market disruption, or social engineering (Ali & Aysan, 2025; Alturkistani & Chuprat, 2024). Social media analytics and automated monitoring systems have identified patterns of LLM-generated content that mimic legitimate sources, complicating the task of threat identification (Sufi, 2023; Lee et al., 2024).

3.4. Automated Reconnaissance and Threat Intelligence Exploitation

LLMs enable cybercriminals to automate the collection and analysis of open-source intelligence (OSINT) for targeting and exploitation (Adewopo, Gonen, & Adewopo, 2020; Chaudhary & Bansal, 2022). By rapidly scanning forums, dark web sites, and social media platforms, malicious actors can profile individuals, organizations, and networks, enhancing the precision and scale of attacks (Etaywe, Macfarlane, & Alazab, 2024; Sangher, Singh, Pandey, & Kumar, 2023). Furthermore, LLMs can be used to identify and exploit vulnerabilities in IoT networks and smart systems by predicting potential attack vectors (Diaf et al., 2024; Ferrag et al., 2024).

3.5. Fraud, Scams, and Identity Theft

The misuse of LLMs extends to financial and identity-based cybercrime. Generative AI can craft fake documents, synthetic identities, or fraudulent communications that deceive financial institutions and individuals (Ali, Zafar, & Aysan, 2024; Ali &

Aysan, 2024). These capabilities enable more sophisticated scams, from fake loan applications to automated account takeover attacks, posing serious risks to global financial systems (Ferrag et al., 2023; Asoronye et al., 2024).

3.6. Cyberterrorism and Psychological Manipulation

LLMs have also been investigated for their potential misuse in cyberterrorism, particularly in crafting propaganda, radicalization content, and psychologically manipulative communications (Atoum et al., 2025; Etaywe et al., 2024). By automating threat communication and exploiting natural language to simulate credible sources, attackers can influence vulnerable populations, incite violence, and manipulate social dynamics (Arya & Rastogi, 2024; Sun et al., 2023).

3.7. Intellectual Property Theft and Automated Plagiarism

The generative capabilities of LLMs make it possible to produce high-quality text that replicates copyrighted or proprietary material. Malicious actors can automate the extraction and redistribution of intellectual property, violating copyrights and trade secrets while evading traditional plagiarism detection systems (Filetti, Fenza, & Gallo, 2024; Leontidis, 2024). This can severely impact research, publishing, and corporate knowledge management (Luan et al., 2024; Ali & Aysan, 2024).

3.8. Challenges in Forensic Investigation and Attribution

The misuse of LLMs complicates traditional digital forensics processes. Automated attack generation and sophisticated text synthesis make attribution and forensic investigation more challenging (Adam & Varol, 2020; Dunsin, Ghanem, Ouazzane, & Vassilev, 2024). Privacy-preserving AI techniques, such as federated learning, while beneficial for legitimate uses, also create hurdles for law enforcement attempting to trace malicious actors (Iyengar et al., 2025; Dunsin, Ghanem, & Quazzane, 2022).

3.9 Summary

The misuse of LLMs expands the spectrum of cybercrime by automating previously labor-intensive processes, enhancing the realism and sophistication of attacks, and lowering the barrier for technical expertise. From phishing and fraud to cyberterrorism and intellectual property theft, the threats posed by LLM-enabled cybercrime are diverse and evolving. Addressing these challenges requires a combination of technical safeguards, regulatory frameworks, ethical guidelines, and proactive threat intelligence strategies (Ferrag et al., 2024; Chen et al., 2024; Sun et al., 2023).

This bar graph presents a comparative analysis of the different types of cybercrime facilitated by LLM misuse, showcasing the prevalence of phishing, social engineering, and malware generation among other activities.

Figure 4. Bar Graph of Cybercrime Types Enabled by LLMs

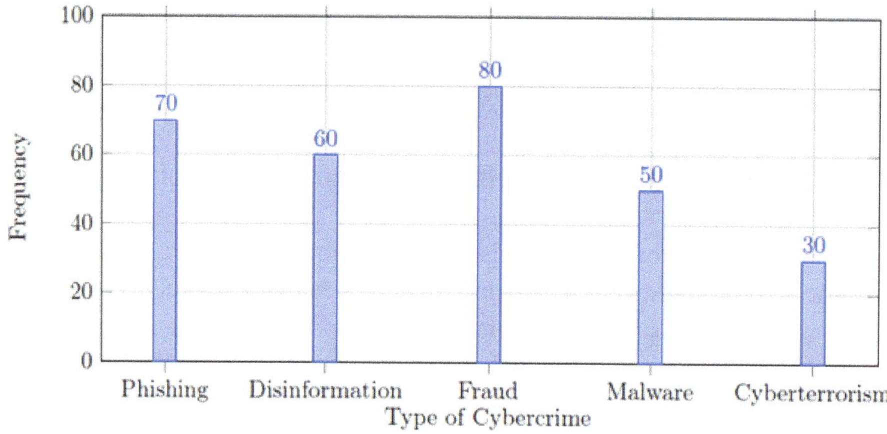

4. CASE STUDIES AND REAL-WORLD INCIDENTS

The real-world implications of LLM misuse have been increasingly documented, revealing a spectrum of cybercrimes and security breaches that exploit the capabilities of large language models. Examining concrete cases highlights the risks, mitigation strategies, and lessons learned for cybersecurity and digital forensics professionals.

4.1. Cybercrime via Phishing and Social Engineering

One of the most prevalent applications of LLM misuse is in generating sophisticated phishing campaigns. Ferrag et al. (2024) demonstrate how LLMs can produce highly convincing emails or messages tailored to target individuals or organizations, often bypassing traditional spam filters. Case studies from financial institutions show that attackers leveraged generative AI to create near-perfect replicas of official communications, resulting in substantial monetary losses (Ali, H., & Aysan, 2024;

Gaurav et al., 2024). Social engineering attacks facilitated by LLMs have also been reported in organizational settings, highlighting the urgent need for human-centric cybersecurity training (Fenwick et al., 2024).

4.2. Automated Misinformation and Deepfake Campaigns

The deployment of LLMs for generating misinformation and deepfake content has been documented in several real-world incidents. For instance, political disinformation campaigns in social media environments have leveraged AI-generated narratives to manipulate public opinion, as analyzed in open-source intelligence investigations (Adewopo et al., 2020; Sufi, 2023). LLMs were used to create synthetic posts mimicking official accounts, leading to widespread dissemination of false information during geopolitical conflicts (Sufi, 2023; Lee et al., 2024). These incidents emphasize the dual-use nature of LLMs, where technology intended for communication and content generation can be repurposed for malicious influence operations.

4.3. Insider Threats and Corporate Espionage

LLMs have been exploited in cases of corporate espionage and insider threats. Organizations have reported instances where employees misused AI-assisted tools to extract sensitive information from internal communications or confidential datasets (Diaf et al., 2024; Asoronye et al., 2024). In one case, a cybersecurity team detected attempts to train an LLM on internal documents to infer strategic business plans, demonstrating the model's capability to indirectly leak proprietary knowledge (Chen et al., 2024; Alturkistani & Chuprat, 2024). These scenarios underline the importance of monitoring and access controls within corporate environments to prevent AI-enabled information leakage.

4.4. Cyber Threat Intelligence Manipulation

LLMs have also been used in manipulating or evading cyber threat intelligence systems. Researchers have shown that AI-generated adversarial inputs can deceive automated threat detection tools, complicating the task of security analysts (Diaf et al., 2024; Sangher et al., 2024). For example, in industrial IoT networks, attackers employed LLMs to generate benign-looking command sequences that bypassed anomaly detection systems (Ferrag et al., 2023; Rajendran & Tulasi, 2025). These incidents illustrate the evolving challenge of protecting critical infrastructure in the era of AI-enhanced adversarial attacks.

4.5. Digital Forensics Challenges

LLM-enabled cybercrimes introduce complex challenges for digital forensics. As Adam and Varol (2020) emphasize, the forensic investigation of AI-assisted attacks requires new methodologies capable of interpreting model outputs and reconstructing sequences of automated actions. Dunsin et al. (2024) highlight real-world cases where forensic teams struggled to attribute cyber attacks due to AI-generated anonymized communication patterns. Privacy-preserving technologies like federated learning further complicate evidence collection, necessitating innovative forensic frameworks (Iyengar et al., 2025).

4.6. Cross-Domain Implications

LLM misuse is not confined to cybersecurity alone but intersects with financial crime, healthcare, and critical infrastructure. Case studies in finance reveal AI-generated fraud attempts and synthetic identity creation, demonstrating the multi-domain risks of LLM misuse (Ali, H., Zafar, & Aysan, 2024; Ali, H., & Aysan, 2025). Similarly, incidents in healthcare and IoT environments have shown how LLM-driven misinformation or command sequences can disrupt operations or compromise sensitive data (Chen et al., 2024; Ferrag et al., 2024).

This pie chart illustrates the distribution of the impact of various cybercrimes enabled by LLM misuse across different sectors, such as finance, healthcare, and critical infrastructure. It highlights how cybercrime affects diverse areas and emphasizes the need for sector-specific countermeasures.

Figure 5. Pie Chart of Cybercrime Impact Distribution

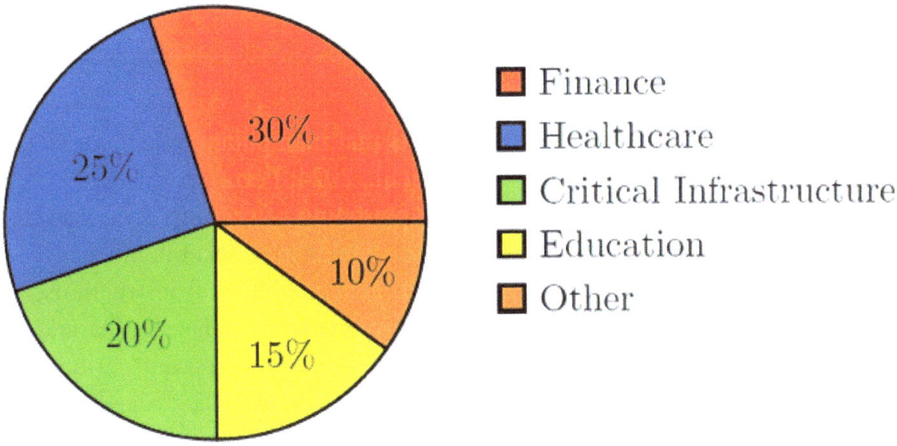

4.7. Lessons Learned and Mitigation

Analysis of these incidents underscores the need for proactive LLM governance, ethical AI policies, and hybrid defense strategies combining automated detection and human oversight (Al-Sinani & Mitchell, 2024; Ghazal et al., 2024). Effective mitigation approaches include threat intelligence integration, adversarial testing, and continuous monitoring of AI-assisted workflows to anticipate potential misuse (Sun et al., 2023; Rajendran & Tulasi, 2025).

In conclusion, case studies demonstrate that LLM misuse can span phishing, disinformation, insider threats, and cross-domain cybercrimes. These real-world incidents provide critical insights into both the dangers and the necessary preventative measures for AI-integrated cybersecurity frameworks (Ferrag et al., 2024; Alturkistani & Chuprat, 2024). As AI capabilities continue to expand, continuous monitoring, ethical oversight, and AI literacy among cybersecurity professionals remain essential to mitigate risks associated with generative models.

5. TECHNICAL MECHANISMS OF MISUSE

The misuse of Large Language Models (LLMs) and related AI technologies has become a critical area of concern in cybersecurity, digital forensics, and threat intelligence. Understanding the technical mechanisms by which these models can be exploited is essential for developing effective mitigation strategies (Ferrag et al., 2024; Chen et al., 2024). Misuse can broadly be categorized into malicious exploitation, model manipulation, and adversarial attacks.

5.1. Adversarial Attacks on LLMs

Adversarial attacks involve crafting inputs that manipulate model outputs, often bypassing detection mechanisms (Diaf et al., 2024; Ferrag et al., 2023). These attacks can range from prompt injection to poisoning of training data, leading to compromised predictions or responses. For example, an attacker could subtly manipulate input sequences to cause a model to generate harmful instructions, leak confidential information, or misclassify malicious content as benign (Alturkistani & Chuprat, 2024). Techniques such as gradient-based adversarial perturbations have been extensively explored in this context (Chen et al., 2024; Sangher, Singh, & Pandey, 2024).

5.2. Data Poisoning and Model Manipulation

Data poisoning involves introducing malicious or biased data into training datasets to compromise the integrity of LLMs (Ali & Aysan, 2024; AlQenaei, 2024). This can result in models that propagate harmful stereotypes, generate false information, or even facilitate fraudulent activities in sectors like finance and healthcare (Ali, Zafar, & Aysan, 2024). Manipulated LLMs can be exploited to craft realistic phishing emails, generate synthetic identities, or automate social engineering attacks (Gaurav et al., 2024; Rajendran & Tulasi, 2025).

5.3. Social Engineering and Phishing Exploitation

LLMs' capability to produce coherent and contextually relevant text makes them highly effective tools for cybercriminals conducting social engineering attacks. Automated content generation can be used to craft highly convincing phishing emails or fake social media posts, targeting individuals or organizations (Sun et al., 2023; Lee, Mujammami, & Kim, 2024). Such misuse extends to the dark web, where forums leverage AI-generated content to manipulate public opinion or facilitate illicit transactions (Sangher, Singh, Pandey, & Kumar, 2023; Siddiqui, Amer, & Khan, 2019).

5.4. Open-Source Intelligence (OSINT) and Threat Exploitation

The aggregation of public data sources combined with LLMs enhances the ability to extract sensitive information efficiently (Adewopo, Gonen, & Adewopo, 2020; Chaudhary & Bansal, 2022). While OSINT has legitimate applications in cybersecurity intelligence and law enforcement, it can also be misused for reconnaissance, profiling targets, and orchestrating cyber attacks (Etaywe, Macfarlane, & Alazab, 2024). Malicious actors can automate this process at scale, generating detailed threat intelligence reports without human intervention (Asoronye et al., 2024; Atoum et al., 2025).

5.5. Exploitation in Critical Infrastructures

LLMs and AI systems are increasingly integrated into critical infrastructures, including industrial control systems, smart grids, and transportation networks (Arya & Rastogi, 2024; Mohammed, Omar, & Nguyen, 2018). Exploiting vulnerabilities in these AI-driven systems can have severe consequences, from triggering operational failures to enabling large-scale cyber-physical attacks. Predictive AI models, if manipulated, can produce false alerts or suppress genuine warnings, facilitating sabotage or espionage (Diaf et al., 2024; Ferrag et al., 2024).

5.6. Privacy Violations and Data Exfiltration

A significant mechanism of misuse involves the unauthorized extraction of sensitive or personal data. Federated learning and privacy-preserving approaches are designed to mitigate such risks, yet they are not immune to model inversion or membership inference attacks (Iyengar et al., 2025; Dunsin, Ghanem, Ouazzane, & Vassilev, 2024). Attackers can reconstruct sensitive datasets from LLM outputs, raising legal and ethical concerns (Bharati, 2020; Bhawna & Mahajan, 2024).

5.7. Integration with Automated Cyber Threat Tools

LLMs are increasingly embedded into automated cybersecurity systems to enhance detection and response capabilities. While this provides efficiency, malicious actors can repurpose these models to evade security tools or generate dynamic attack payloads (Ferrag et al., 2024; Chen et al., 2024). For instance, AI-driven malware or ransomware can use LLMs to adapt communications, evade sandbox detection, or manipulate human operators during incident response (Ganesh, 2017; Dunsin, Ghanem, & Quazzane, 2022).

5.8. Ethical and Legal Implications

The technical mechanisms of misuse are deeply intertwined with ethical and legal challenges. Unregulated deployment of LLMs can facilitate cybercrime, misinformation campaigns, and digital surveillance abuses (Batabyal, 2024; Butt,

2024). Compliance with emerging AI regulations, such as the EU AI Act, is crucial to prevent and mitigate misuse (Larson et al., 2021; Ho, 2023). Legal frameworks are still catching up to the rapid evolution of LLM capabilities, necessitating continuous oversight (Bousri, 2019; Daniel, 2024).

In summary, technical misuse of LLMs encompasses adversarial exploitation, data poisoning, social engineering, OSINT misuse, infrastructure vulnerabilities, privacy violations, and integration with automated cyber threat tools. Addressing these mechanisms requires a combination of robust AI security practices, regulatory oversight, and proactive threat intelligence (Ferrag et al., 2024; Chen et al., 2024; Sun et al., 2023).

6. COUNTERMEASURES AND DEFENSIVE STRATEGIES

The proliferation of large language models (LLMs) and advanced AI systems has introduced significant vulnerabilities, making robust countermeasures essential to mitigate misuse and cyber threats. Defensive strategies span technological, procedural, and regulatory domains, aiming to ensure AI security, preserve privacy, and maintain ethical standards.

This flowchart outlines the various countermeasures that can be implemented to mitigate the misuse of LLMs, including technological, procedural, and regulatory approaches.

Figure 6. Flowchart of Countermeasures Against LLM Misuse

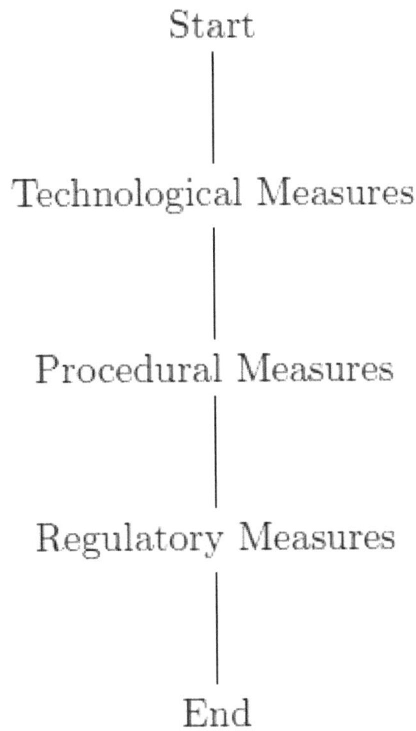

6.1. Technological Countermeasures

6.1.1. Model Hardening and Adversarial Robustness

One key approach to defending against misuse is strengthening LLMs through model hardening and adversarial training. Adversarial robustness involves exposing models to maliciously crafted inputs during training to improve their resistance to attacks (Chen et al., 2024; Ferrag et al., 2023). Techniques such as differential privacy and regularization methods have been widely implemented to prevent data leakage and reduce susceptibility to prompt injections and model manipulation (Iyengar et al., 2025; Asoronye et al., 2024).

6.1.2. Privacy-Preserving Mechanisms

Federated learning and encryption-based techniques have emerged as vital for ensuring secure training of AI models without centralizing sensitive data (Iyengar et al., 2025). Privacy-preserving strategies are critical for mitigating the misuse of LLMs in surveillance, phishing, or identity theft, especially in IoT and IIoT environments (Ferrag et al., 2024; Mohammed et al., 2018).

6.1.3. Detection and Monitoring Tools

Continuous monitoring systems can detect anomalous patterns in user interaction or model outputs, which may indicate misuse. Real-time threat intelligence platforms using AI and machine learning allow proactive identification of emerging threats, ranging from social engineering campaigns to sophisticated cyber intrusions (Sun et al., 2023; Rajendran & Tulasi, 2025; Sangher et al., 2024).

6.2. Procedural Countermeasures

6.2.1. Ethical Hacking and Red Teaming

Ethical hacking, enhanced by AI tools, helps organizations simulate attacks and assess system vulnerabilities. LLM-driven red teaming exercises allow defenders to anticipate and mitigate exploit scenarios, testing models against both insider and external threats (Al-Sinani & Mitchell, 2024; Al-Sinani et al., 2025). Red teaming strategies also provide feedback loops to improve model architecture and defensive protocols (Alturkistani & Chuprat, 2024).

6.2.2. Incident Response and Forensic Readiness

Establishing formal incident response protocols and forensic readiness is crucial for minimizing damage from AI misuse. Modern digital forensics integrates AI tools for automated evidence collection, log analysis, and rapid threat attribution (Dunsin et al., 2024; Adam & Varol, 2020; Bhawna & Mahajan, 2024). Incorporating AI-driven analytics into forensic workflows enhances speed and accuracy, enabling organizations to respond effectively to security breaches.

6.2.3. Continuous Threat Intelligence and OSINT

Leveraging open-source intelligence (OSINT) and cyber threat intelligence (CTI) enables organizations to detect emerging attack vectors and LLM-related threats early

(Adewopo et al., 2020; Lee et al., 2024; Chaudhary & Bansal, 2022). AI-assisted mining of social media, darknet forums, and other public sources provides insights into attacker tactics, techniques, and procedures (TTPs), allowing preemptive defense planning (Sufi, 2023; Sun et al., 2023).

6.3. Regulatory and Governance Measures

6.3.1. AI Ethics and Compliance Frameworks

Establishing clear ethical and legal frameworks mitigates LLM misuse by enforcing standards on data privacy, transparency, and accountability (Ali & Aysan, 2025; Butt, 2024; Larson et al., 2021). Compliance with international regulations, such as the EU AI Act, ensures that AI systems are designed and deployed responsibly while minimizing potential harm (Ho, 2023; Batabyal, 2024).

6.3.2. Organizational Policies and Human-Centric Controls

Integrating AI governance into organizational practices is critical for operational resilience. Policies should emphasize human oversight, risk assessment, and role-based access to AI tools (Fenwick et al., 2024; Cooper & Zell, 2023). Additionally, training and awareness programs enable personnel to recognize AI-driven threats and act decisively to contain misuse.

6.3.3. Multi-Layered Defense Strategies

An effective defensive posture relies on a multi-layered approach that combines technological, procedural, and regulatory measures. AI-driven intrusion detection systems, combined with human supervision, continuous threat monitoring, and legal safeguards, create a holistic defense ecosystem (Ferrag et al., 2024; Ghazal et al., 2024; Chen et al., 2024). This approach ensures redundancy, resilience, and adaptive responses to evolving threats.

6.4. Emerging Approaches

6.4.1. Explainable AI for Security Audits

Explainable AI (XAI) enhances defensive strategies by providing interpretability of model decisions, enabling security teams to understand vulnerabilities and respond effectively (Ghazal et al., 2024; AlQenaei, 2024). Transparent AI decision-making is increasingly recognized as a cornerstone for secure, trustworthy AI deployment.

6.4.2. AI-Augmented Cyber Threat Intelligence (CTI)

Combining LLMs with machine learning-driven CTI allows predictive threat detection and proactive defense. These systems analyze historical attack data, social media intelligence, and darknet chatter to anticipate potential threats and recommend preventive measures (Rajendran & Tulasi, 2025; Sangher et al., 2023; Diaf et al., 2024).

6.4.3. Quantum and Next-Generation Defenses

Looking ahead, quantum machine learning and AI integration could enhance encryption, anomaly detection, and intrusion prevention in LLM ecosystems (Eswaran & Eswaran, 2025; Campus, 2024). Leveraging emerging technologies ensures that defenses remain ahead of increasingly sophisticated adversarial capabilities.

6.5 Summary

Countermeasures for LLM misuse involve a combination of technical innovations, procedural safeguards, and regulatory oversight. Strengthening models against adversarial threats, maintaining robust forensic capabilities, integrating threat intelligence, and adhering to ethical and legal standards collectively reduce risks associated with AI misuse. The multi-layered approach ensures adaptability and resilience in defending against evolving cyber threats and malicious exploitation of AI technologies.

This bar graph compares the effectiveness of various countermeasures against LLM misuse, such as technological solutions, procedural safeguards, and regulatory frameworks. It provides insight into which strategies are most impactful.

Figure 7. Bar Graph of Countermeasure Effectiveness

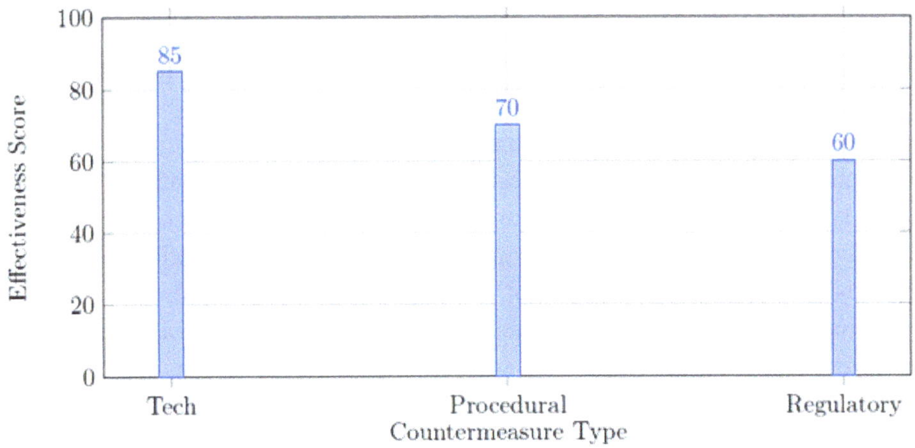

7. POLICY, REGULATORY, AND LEGAL RESPONSES

The rapid proliferation of artificial intelligence (AI), particularly large language models (LLMs), in both civilian and military domains has intensified the need for robust policy, regulatory, and legal frameworks to govern their safe and ethical deployment (Adam & Varol, 2020; Ferrag et al., 2024). Policymakers are increasingly recognizing the dual nature of AI technologies: while they can enhance efficiency, decision-making, and threat intelligence capabilities, they also introduce risks related to privacy, bias, misuse, and cybersecurity vulnerabilities (Ali & Aysan, 2025; Chen et al., 2024).

7.1. National and International Policy Frameworks

National governments and international organizations are developing policies to align AI development with societal, ethical, and security priorities. For example, efforts to harmonize AI regulations across jurisdictions are emerging to ensure consistent standards for data governance, cybersecurity, and accountability (Butt, 2024; Larson et al., 2021). In the environmental domain, countries are aligning AI governance with broader sustainability goals, such as achieving net-zero emissions targets and climate resilience strategies (Ali, 2024; Akindele & Chabinga, 2024; Aloamaka, 2024; Chowdhury, 2024). These policy frameworks are vital to ensure that AI tools, including LLMs, are leveraged responsibly in sectors such as finance, defense, and public administration (Ali, H., & Aysan, 2024; Ali, H., Zafar, & Aysan, 2024).

7.2. Regulatory Standards and Compliance Mechanisms

Regulatory responses for AI are multifaceted, ranging from national AI acts to international guidelines for cybersecurity and digital forensics (Bharati, 2020; Ho, 2023; Iyengar et al., 2025). For instance, the European Union's AI Act introduces mandatory risk assessments, transparency obligations, and compliance audits for high-risk AI applications (Butt, 2024). Similarly, regulatory frameworks in healthcare, finance, and critical infrastructure emphasize safety, explainability, and ethical auditing of AI-driven decisions (Larson et al., 2021; Ali & Aysan, 2025). Compliance mechanisms often include certification processes, continuous monitoring, and cross-border collaboration to prevent legal gaps that could be exploited by malicious actors (Fenwick et al., 2024; Rajendran & Tulasi, 2025).

7.3. Legal Considerations in AI Deployment

Legal responses are central to mitigating risks associated with AI misuse, including cybercrime, digital fraud, and AI-driven misinformation campaigns (Bhawna & Mahajan, 2024; Ganesh, 2017). Laws governing digital forensics, privacy, and data protection are evolving to incorporate AI-specific challenges such as automated decision-making, predictive analytics, and federated learning (Adam & Varol, 2020; Dunsin et al., 2024; Iyengar et al., 2025). National legislation also addresses AI applications in law enforcement, ensuring that digital investigations respect due process and human rights while leveraging AI for efficiency (Bharati, 2020; Costantini et al., 2019).

7.4. Cybersecurity and Threat Intelligence Policies

AI-enhanced cybersecurity and threat intelligence have prompted policymakers to develop standards that govern data collection, threat analysis, and automated decision support systems (Adewopo et al., 2020; Alturkistani & Chuprat, 2024; Sun et al., 2023). Legal instruments are being proposed to regulate the use of LLMs for monitoring social networks, darknet forums, and other cybercrime vectors while maintaining ethical boundaries and privacy safeguards (Sangher et al., 2023; Sangher et al., 2024; Sufi, 2023; Rajendran & Tulasi, 2025). These frameworks also address national security concerns and the risk of AI-enabled cyberattacks on critical infrastructure, financial systems, and IoT networks (Diaf et al., 2024; Ferrag et al., 2023).

7.5. Ethical and Governance Considerations

Ethical governance is increasingly embedded within regulatory and legal responses to AI deployment. Scholars and practitioners advocate for human-centric AI, fairness, accountability, and transparency in automated decision systems (Batabyal, 2024; Al-Sinani & Mitchell, 2024; Al-Sinani et al., 2025). Furthermore, cross-sector guidelines promote responsible use of AI in sensitive domains such as defense, healthcare, and environmental monitoring (Arya & Rastogi, 2024; Daniel, 2024; Eswaran & Eswaran, 2025; Jafarizadeh et al., 2024). Ethical frameworks are often complemented by technological safeguards, including explainable AI, federated learning, and privacy-preserving computation, which help ensure compliance with legal mandates and societal norms (Chen et al., 2024; Iyengar et al., 2025; Ferrag et al., 2024).

7.6. Challenges and Future Directions in Policy and Legal Responses

Despite progress, gaps remain in harmonizing AI policies and legal frameworks globally (Darvishi et al., 2022; Drexl et al., 2025; Leontidis, 2024). Emerging issues include cross-border jurisdiction in AI-driven cybercrimes, liability for autonomous systems, and integrating AI governance with climate, energy, and human rights law (Ali, 2024; Akindele & Chabinga, 2024; Chowdhury, 2024). Scholars argue for adaptive regulatory models that balance innovation with risk mitigation, fostering international collaboration, standardization, and continuous legal reform (Campus, 2024; Eswaran & Eswaran, 2025; Emon et al., 2025).

In conclusion, the development of comprehensive policy, regulatory, and legal responses is indispensable for ensuring that AI and LLM technologies contribute positively to societal, economic, and security objectives while minimizing ethical and legal risks (Ferrag et al., 2024; Ghazal et al., 2024; AlQenaei, 2024). A multi-level approach integrating national legislation, international treaties, sector-specific regulations, and ethical guidelines represents the most promising strategy for the responsible and secure deployment of AI technologies (Ali & Aysan, 2025; Ho, 2023; Iyengar et al., 2025).

8. ETHICAL CONSIDERATIONS

The rise of artificial intelligence (AI) and large language models (LLMs) in cybersecurity, digital forensics, and broader technological domains has sparked intense ethical discussions. As these technologies grow in sophistication, they raise critical questions regarding fairness, accountability, privacy, transparency, and societal impact (Adam & Varol, 2020; Bharati, 2020; Batabyal, 2024). Ethical considerations in AI are no longer peripheral concerns; they are central to the responsible development, deployment, and governance of these systems.

8.1 Responsible Use in Digital Forensics and Cybersecurity

In digital forensics, AI tools, including LLMs, are increasingly leveraged to detect cyber threats, analyze criminal activity, and facilitate investigative processes (Ganesh, 2017; Costantini, De Gasperis, & Olivieri, 2019; Dunsin, Ghanem, & Ouazzane, 2024). However, their use raises significant ethical concerns. Unauthorized surveillance, bias in algorithmic decision-making, and potential misinterpretation of automated analyses can infringe on individual rights (Adam & Varol, 2020; Bharati, 2020; Iyengar et al., 2025). It is essential for practitioners to balance the operational benefits of AI-driven forensics with respect for privacy, consent, and due process.

Moreover, open-source intelligence (OSINT) and cyber threat intelligence extraction present ethical dilemmas around data provenance, ownership, and the potential misuse of publicly available information (Adewopo, Gonen, & Adewopo, 2020; Chaudhary & Bansal, 2022; Sun et al., 2023). Organizations must ensure that intelligence collection is conducted transparently and in accordance with legal and ethical norms.

8.2 Bias, Fairness, and Accountability in AI Systems

LLMs and generative AI systems can inadvertently perpetuate societal biases, affecting decision-making in cybersecurity, finance, healthcare, and law enforcement (Ali & Aysan, 2024, 2025; Ali, Zafar, & Aysan, 2024). For example, models trained on biased datasets may produce skewed outputs, resulting in discriminatory practices or unjust profiling (Ferrag et al., 2024; Chen et al., 2024). Ethical AI frameworks necessitate rigorous bias detection, continuous monitoring, and the inclusion of diverse, representative datasets to ensure fairness (AlQenaei, 2024; Alturkistani & Chuprat, 2024).

Accountability is equally crucial. AI-driven decision-making must be auditable and interpretable, particularly in high-stakes environments such as law enforcement, financial systems, or national security (Larson et al., 2021; Ho, 2023; Rajendran & Tulasi, 2025). Transparent reporting mechanisms, explainable AI techniques, and adherence to ethical guidelines are necessary to maintain public trust and uphold professional standards.

8.3 Privacy, Consent, and Data Security

The ethical handling of data is paramount in AI applications. LLMs rely on massive datasets, often incorporating sensitive personal information, which introduces risks of privacy breaches and unauthorized data exposure (Iyengar et al., 2025; Ferrag et al., 2023; Asoronye et al., 2024). Federated learning, encryption, and privacy-preserving protocols are emerging as solutions to safeguard data while maintaining the utility of AI models (Iyengar et al., 2025; Ferrag et al., 2024). Additionally, informed consent and transparency regarding data collection and usage must be prioritized to respect user autonomy.

8.4 Dual-Use and Misuse Potential

AI technologies, including LLMs, are inherently dual-use: while they provide significant societal benefits, they can also be misused for cyberattacks, disinformation campaigns, and autonomous cyber operations (Etaywe, Macfarlane, & Alazab, 2024; Rajendran & Tulasi, 2025; Ferrag et al., 2024). Ethical deployment requires anticipatory governance strategies, including threat modeling, human oversight, and proactive risk mitigation to prevent harm (Diaf et al., 2024; Sangher, Singh, & Pandey, 2024; Sufi, 2023).

8.5 AI in Societal and Environmental Contexts

Beyond cybersecurity, AI applications intersect with broader societal and environmental concerns. Ethical considerations extend to climate change, sustainability, and equitable access to technology (Akindele & Chabinga, 2024; Ali, 2024; Aloamaka, 2024; Chowdhury, 2024; Daniel, 2024). The development and deployment of AI must align with human-centric and environmentally responsible values, promoting sustainability and addressing inequities in access to technological benefits (Emon et al., 2025; Jafarizadeh et al., 2024; Fenwick, Molnar, & Frangos, 2024).

8.6 Ethical Guidelines and Governance

Multiple frameworks have emerged to guide ethical AI practices. International recommendations emphasize the principles of transparency, fairness, accountability, human oversight, and respect for human rights (Batabyal, 2024; Butt, 2024; Ho, 2023; Larson et al., 2021). Practitioners are encouraged to adopt organizational ethics policies, conduct regular audits, and engage with multidisciplinary stakeholders to ensure that AI deployment does not compromise ethical norms (Flannery, Ajayi, & Oyegoke, 2021; Cooper & Zell, 2023; Leontidis, 2024; Luan et al., 2024).

In digital forensics, ethical governance must address not only the technical accuracy of AI systems but also their social impact, ensuring that automated investigations uphold justice and public confidence (Ganesh, 2017; Dunsin, Ghanem, & Quazzane, 2022; Bhawna & Mahajan, 2024). Similarly, in cyber threat intelligence, ethical frameworks should guide data collection, sharing, and analysis, mitigating risks of misuse while enhancing societal security (Adewopo et al., 2020; Lee, Mujammami, & Kim, 2024; Sufi, 2023).

9. FUTURE RESEARCH DIRECTIONS

The rapid evolution of artificial intelligence (AI) and large language models (LLMs) presents numerous opportunities for future research, spanning cybersecurity, digital forensics, sustainable technologies, and ethical applications. One primary avenue for investigation is the enhancement of AI-driven digital forensics and cybersecurity frameworks. As Adam and Varol (2020) note, intelligence in digital forensics remains critical for identifying cyber threats and prosecuting criminal activity effectively. Building on this foundation, research can explore advanced machine learning and natural language processing (NLP) techniques for predictive threat intelligence, as highlighted by Adewopo, Gonen, and Adewopo (2020) in their work on open-source information for cyber threat intelligence.

The integration of LLMs in cybersecurity applications is another critical research trajectory. Studies like those by Alturkistani and Chuprat (2024) and Ferrag et al. (2023, 2024) demonstrate that LLMs can significantly enhance proactive cyber threat detection and mitigation, particularly in Internet of Things (IoT) and Industrial IoT (IIoT) environments. Future research should aim to optimize LLM architectures for lightweight deployment, balancing computational efficiency with robust security, as explored by AlQenaei (2024) and Chen et al. (2024). Additionally, innovative models such as SecLM (Asoronye et al., 2024) and AI-enhanced ethical hacking frameworks (Al-Sinani & Mitchell, 2024; Al-Sinani et al., 2025) provide fertile ground for empirical studies that examine LLM integration in real-world threat scenarios.

Beyond cybersecurity, LLM research intersects with environmental sustainability and policy. Climate change and renewable energy challenges offer unique contexts for AI deployment. Scholars like Akindele and Chabinga (2024), Ali (2024), Aloamaka (2024), Chowdhury (2024), Daniel (2024), and Jafarizadeh et al. (2024) emphasize the need to align AI applications with net-zero policies, sustainable energy storage, and climate resilience strategies. Future research could focus on modeling predictive scenarios, optimizing policy interventions, and developing AI-assisted decision-support systems for environmental governance.

In the domain of finance and ethics, LLMs present opportunities for enhancing risk management, fraud detection, and responsible AI use. Ali and Aysan (2024, 2025) and Ali, Zafar, and Aysan (2024) highlight the ethical dimensions of generative AI and its cross-domain implications. Future work could explore explainable AI frameworks, bias mitigation, and multi-level machine learning strategies to ensure ethical compliance while maximizing the utility of AI in complex financial systems.

The application of LLMs to social media and open-source intelligence is another promising research avenue. Studies by Lee, Mujammami, and Kim (2024), Rajendran and Tulasi (2025), Sangher, Singh, and Pandey (2024), Sangher et al. (2023), Sufi (2023), Sun et al. (2023), Siddiqui, Amer, and Khan (2019), and Chaudhary and Bansal (2022) illustrate the potential of AI to identify threats, detect cybercrime, and support proactive cybersecurity measures through NLP-based social media analysis. Future investigations could focus on real-time intelligence extraction, multilingual models, and enhanced predictive analytics for geopolitical or conflict-related cyber events.

Quantum computing and AI convergence represent another frontier. Research by Campus (2024), Eswaran and Eswaran (2025), and Eisenberg (2024) indicates that integrating quantum machine learning with LLMs could unlock unprecedented computational capabilities, enabling highly complex simulations and threat modeling. Subsequent studies should address optimization strategies, scalable quantum algorithms, and privacy-preserving mechanisms such as federated learning (Iyengar et al., 2025) to ensure secure and responsible deployment.

The legal, regulatory, and ethical landscape also necessitates ongoing research. Frameworks governing AI, digital forensics, and cybersecurity require continuous refinement to address emerging threats and technological advances (Bharati, 2020; Butt, 2024; Ho, 2023; Larson et al., 2021). Future research could explore cross-jurisdictional regulations, compliance strategies, and the development of international standards for AI and LLM deployment in sensitive domains. Moreover, Batabyal (2024) and Fenwick, Molnar, and Frangos (2024) stress the importance of aligning AI adoption with ethical warfare principles, corporate governance, and human-centric digital transformation.

Finally, there is substantial potential for applying LLMs in education, scientific research, and interdisciplinary analytics. Studies by Leontidis (2024), Luan et al. (2024), Jamro and Jamro (2023), and Ali and Aysan (2024) suggest that AI can significantly enhance research methodology, scientometric analysis, and STEM education through intelligent tutoring systems and automated data synthesis. Future research can explore the development of AI-driven educational platforms, automated literature reviews, and evidence-based policy modeling.

In conclusion, the convergence of LLMs, cybersecurity, environmental sustainability, finance, quantum computing, and ethics offers a diverse landscape for future research. By addressing computational efficiency, ethical compliance, predictive intelligence, and interdisciplinary integration, scholars can unlock the full potential of AI while mitigating risks. Continued exploration of these directions will shape the next generation of intelligent systems capable of supporting secure, sustainable, and socially responsible technological advancement.

10. CONCLUSION

The rapid advancement of large language models (LLMs) and artificial intelligence (AI) has transformed multiple domains, including cybersecurity, digital forensics, finance, environmental sustainability, and scientific research. This chapter has highlighted how LLMs can be leveraged for proactive threat detection, predictive intelligence, and ethical decision-making, illustrating both the immense potential and the associated challenges of these technologies. From cybersecurity applications such as SecLM and AI-enhanced ethical hacking to open-source intelligence extraction and social media monitoring, LLMs have proven capable of augmenting human capabilities in complex analytical tasks.

Despite their promise, the adoption of LLMs comes with substantial considerations related to computational efficiency, ethical compliance, privacy preservation, and regulatory adherence. Research indicates that while these models can enhance predictive capabilities and streamline decision-making, they also present risks of bias, misuse, and unintended consequences if not carefully governed. Consequently, integrating human oversight, explainable AI techniques, and robust regulatory frameworks is essential to maximize benefits while mitigating potential harms.

The chapter also emphasizes the interdisciplinary applications of LLMs. In environmental sustainability, AI-driven modeling supports net-zero policies, renewable energy optimization, and climate-resilient decision-making. In finance and ethics, generative AI facilitates fraud detection, risk management, and compliance with ethical standards. Furthermore, the convergence of quantum computing and AI promises to expand computational horizons, enabling advanced simulations and predictive analytics that were previously infeasible.

Overall, the findings and discussions presented underscore that the future of LLMs hinges not only on technical innovation but also on ethical, legal, and societal considerations. Ongoing research and collaboration across domains are essential to ensure that these technologies are deployed responsibly, effectively, and equitably. By addressing challenges and exploring new applications, the field of LLM research can continue to advance toward creating intelligent systems that are secure, sustainable, and socially beneficial.

REFERENCES

Adam, I. Y., & Varol, C. (2020, June). Intelligence in digital forensics process. In *2020 8th International Symposium on Digital Forensics and Security (ISDFS)* (pp. 1-6). IEEE. DOI: 10.1109/ISDFS49300.2020.9116442

Adewopo, V., Gonen, B., & Adewopo, F. (2020, December). Exploring open source information for cyber threat intelligence. In *2020 IEEE International Conference on Big Data (Big Data)* (pp. 2232-2241). IEEE. DOI: 10.1109/BigData50022.2020.9378220

Akindele, A., & Chabinga, R. (2024). Navigating Climate Change and Sustainability Solutions: Nigeria's Role in International Environmental Law. *African Journal of Climate Change and Resource Sustainability*, *3*(1), 331–344. DOI: 10.37284/ajccrs.3.1.2188

Al-Sinani, H. S., & Mitchell, C. J. (2024). AI-enhanced ethical hacking: A Linux-focused experiment. *arXiv preprint arXiv:2410.05105.*

Al-Sinani, H. S., Sahli, N., Mitchell, C. J., & Al-Siyabi, M. (2025). Advancing ethical hacking with AI: A Linux-based experimental study. *Proceedings of ITASEC and SERICS, Bologna, Italy (Feb 2025),* https://www. chrismitchell. net/Papers/aehwaa. pdf

Ali, A. (2024). Navigating Road for Net Zero Policies to Aligning Policy, Politics, and Governance for Environmental Sustainability. In *Transition Towards a Sustainable Future: Net Zero Policies and Environmental Sustainability* (pp. 205–230). Springer Nature Singapore. DOI: 10.1007/978-981-97-5756-5_10

Ali, H., & Aysan, A. F. (2024). Decoding Future of Generative AI in Finance: A Machine Learning Exploration of Academic and Grey Corpus. *Available at SSRN* 4787211. DOI: 10.2139/ssrn.4787211

Ali, H., & Aysan, A. F. (2025). Ethical dimensions of generative AI: A cross-domain analysis using machine learning structural topic modeling. *International Journal of Ethics and Systems*, *41*(1), 3–34. DOI: 10.1108/IJOES-04-2024-0112

Ali, H., Zafar, M. B., & Aysan, A. F. (2024). Generative AI and Finance: A Multi-level Machine Learning Based Analysis. *Available at SSRN* 5129013.

Aloamaka, P. C. (2024). Navigating the Climate Crisis: Exploring International Law's Evolution and Application. *GLS Law Journal*, *6*(1), 48–58. DOI: 10.69974/glslawjournal.v6i1.127

AlQenaei, Z. M. (2024, March). Evolution and Optimization of Language Model Architectures: From Foundations to Future Directions. In *International Conference on Computing and Machine Learning* (pp. 233-249). Singapore: Springer Nature Singapore.

Alturkistani, H., & Chuprat, S. (2024). Artificial Intelligence and Large Language Models in Advancing Cyber Threat Intelligence: A Systematic Literature Review.

Arya, L., & Rastogi, R. (2024). Study on Aerial Monitoring System in Agriculture, Forestry, Defense, and Border Protection Using Artificial Intelligence (AI). In *Agriculture and Aquaculture Applications of Biosensors and Bioelectronics* (pp. 392-407). IGI Global Scientific Publishing.

Asoronye, G. O., Anthony, O. C., Ogbuikwu, R. I., Ogili, C. O., & Ali, H. U. (2024). SecLM: A Specialized Security Language Model for Advanced Cybersecurity Applications and Threat Mitigation. *EKETE-International Journal Of Advanced Research*, *2*(6), 33–42.

Atoum, M. S., Alarood, A. A., Alsolami, E., Abubakar, A., Hwaitat, A. K. A., & Alsmadi, I. (2025). Cybersecurity Intelligence Through Textual Data Analysis: A Framework Using Machine Learning and Terrorism Datasets. *Future Internet*, *17*(4), 182. DOI: 10.3390/fi17040182

Batabyal, G. S. (2024). Ethics, laws on war and artificial intelligence-driven warfare. In *Artificial intelligence, ethics and the future of warfare* (pp. 187–215). Routledge India. DOI: 10.4324/9781003421849-9

Bharati, R. K. (2020). Legal and Ethical Considerations in the Use of Digital Forensics by Law Enforcement: A Multi-jurisdictional Study. *Turk. Online J. Qual. Inq*, *11*(4), 10594–10610.

Bhawna, & Mahajan, S. (2024). Artificial Intelligence Perspective on Digital Forensics. *Applying Artificial Intelligence in Cybersecurity Analytics and Cyber Threat Detection*, 33-44.

Bousri, M. M. S. (2019). *A comparative analysis of legal and institutional framework for arbitration: Comoros and Uganda* (Doctoral dissertation, School of law).

Butt, J. (2024). Analytical study of the world's first EU Artificial Intelligence (AI) Act. *International Journal of Research Publication and Reviews*, *5*(3), 7343–7364. DOI: 10.55248/gengpi.5.0324.0914

Campus, M. T. (2024). Quantum Machine Learning, Leveraging Al, and. *Integration of AI, Quantum Computing, and Semiconductor Technology*, 57.

Chaudhary, M., & Bansal, D. (2022). Open source intelligence extraction for terrorism-related information: A review. *Wiley Interdisciplinary Reviews. Data Mining and Knowledge Discovery*, *12*(5), e1473. DOI: 10.1002/widm.1473

Chen, Y., Cui, M., Wang, D., Cao, Y., Yang, P., Jiang, B., Lu, Z., & Liu, B. (2024). A survey of large language models for cyber threat detection. *Computers & Security*, *145*, 104016. DOI: 10.1016/j.cose.2024.104016

Chowdhury, S. (2024). Towards a Just Climate: Navigating Complexities and Challenges in Climate Change Discourse and Action. *Issue 2 Int'l JL Mgmt. &. Human.*, *7*, 1807.

Cooper, S., & Zell, S. (2023). *Staying on Board: Non-profit housing provider board capacity in a changing context*. Institute of Urban Studies, The University of Winnipeg.

Costantini, S., De Gasperis, G., & Olivieri, R. (2019). Digital forensics and investigations meet artificial intelligence. *Annals of Mathematics and Artificial Intelligence*, *86*(1), 193–229. DOI: 10.1007/s10472-019-09632-y

Daniel, J. (2024). *Environmental Law: Navigating Legal Pathways for a Sustainable Future*. Pencil.

Darvishi, K., Liu, L., & Lim, S. (2022). Navigating the Nexus: Legal and Economic Implications of Emerging Tech-nologies. *Law and Economics*, *16*(3), 172–186. DOI: 10.35335/laweco.v16i3.59

Diaf, A., Korba, A. A., Karabadji, N. E., & Ghamri-Doudane, Y. (2024, April). Beyond detection: Leveraging large language models for cyber attack prediction in iot networks. In *2024 20th International Conference on Distributed Computing in Smart Systems and the Internet of Things (DCOSS-IoT)* (pp. 117-123). IEEE.

Drexl, J., Conde, B., & Kim, D. (2025). Position Statement of the Max Planck Institute for Innovation and Competition of 25 April 2025 in the framework of the revision of the Technology

Dunsin, D., Ghanem, M. C., Ouazzane, K., & Vassilev, V. (2024). A comprehensive analysis of the role of artificial intelligence and machine learning in modern digital forensics and incident response. *Forensic Science International Digital Investigation*, *48*, 301675. DOI: 10.1016/j.fsidi.2023.301675

Dunsin, D., Ghanem, M. C., & Quazzane, K. (2022). The use of artificial intelligence in digital forensics and incident response in a constrained environment. *International Journal of Information and Communication Engineering*, *16*(8), 280–285.

Eisenberg, D. (2024). *Sensing With Integrity: Responsible Sensor Systems in an Era of AI* (Doctoral dissertation, New Jersey Institute of Technology).

Emon, M. M. H., Khan, T., Rahman, M. A., Hamid, A. B. A., & Yaakub, N. I. (2025). GreenTech revolution: Navigating challenges and seizing opportunities. In *AI and green technology applications in society* (pp. 63–90). IGI Global Scientific Publishing.

Eswaran, U., & Eswaran, V. (2025). Quantum Machine Learning, Leveraging AI, and Semiconductor Technology. In *Integration of AI, Quantum Computing, and Semiconductor Technology* (pp. 57-78). IGI Global.

Etaywe, A., Macfarlane, K., & Alazab, M. (2024). A cyberterrorist behind the keyboard: An automated text analysis for psycholinguistic profiling and threat assessment. *Journal of Language Aggression and Conflict.*

Fenwick, A., Molnar, G., & Frangos, P. (2024). The critical role of HRM in AI-driven digital transformation: A paradigm shift to enable firms to move from AI implementation to human-centric adoption. *Discover Artificial Intelligence*, *4*(1), 34. DOI: 10.1007/s44163-024-00125-4

Ferrag, M. A., Alwahedi, F., Battah, A., Cherif, B., Mechri, A., & Tihanyi, N. (2024). Generative ai and large language models for cyber security: All insights you need. *Available at SSRN* 4853709. DOI: 10.2139/ssrn.4853709

Ferrag, M. A., Ndhlovu, M., Tihanyi, N., Cordeiro, L. C., Debbah, M., & Lestable, T. (2023). Revolutionizing cyber threat detection with large language models. *arXiv preprint arXiv:2306.14263*, 195-202.

Ferrag, M. A., Ndhlovu, M., Tihanyi, N., Cordeiro, L. C., Debbah, M., Lestable, T., & Thandi, N. S. (2024). Revolutionizing cyber threat detection with large language models: A privacy-preserving bert-based lightweight model for iot/iiot devices. *IEEE Access : Practical Innovations, Open Solutions*, *12*, 23733–23750. DOI: 10.1109/ACCESS.2024.3363469

Filetti, S., Fenza, G., & Gallo, A. (2024). Research design and writing of scholarly articles: New artificial intelligence tools available for researchers. *Endocrine*, *85*(3), 1104–1116. DOI: 10.1007/s12020-024-03977-z PMID: 39085566

Flannery, J., Ajayi, S. O., & Oyegoke, A. S. (2021). Alcohol and substance misuse in the construction industry. *International Journal of Occupational Safety and Ergonomics*, *27*(2), 472–487. DOI: 10.1080/10803548.2019.1601376 PMID: 30935301

Ganesh, V. (2017). Artificial intelligence applied to computer forensics. *International Journal (Toronto, Ont.)*, *5*(5).

Gaurav, A., Chui, K. T., Arya, V., Attar, R. W., Bansal, S., Alhomoud, A., & Psannis, K. (2024). Optimized AI-Driven Semantic Web Approach for Enhancing Phishing Detection in E-Commerce Platforms. [IJSWIS]. *International Journal on Semantic Web and Information Systems, 20*(1), 1–13. DOI: 10.4018/IJSWIS.359767

Ghazal, T. M., Janjua, J. I., Abushiba, W., Ahmad, M., Ihsan, A., & Al-Dmour, N. A. (2024, December). Cybersecurity Revolution via Large Language Models and Explainable AI. In *2024 17th International Conference on Security of Information and Networks (SIN)* (pp. 1-6). IEEE. DOI: 10.1109/SIN63213.2024.10871324

Ho, C. W. (2023). Implementing the human right to science in the regulatory governance of artificial intelligence in healthcare. *Journal of Law and the Biosciences, 10*(2), lsad026. DOI: 10.1093/jlb/lsad026 PMID: 37854168

Iyengar, S. S., Nabavirazavi, S., & Hariprasad, Y. HB, P., & Mohan, C. K. (2025). Privacy-Preserving AI (Federated Learning) for Digital Forensics. In *Artificial Intelligence in Practice: Theory and Application for Cyber Security and Forensics* (pp. 161-176). Cham: Springer Nature Switzerland.

Jafarizadeh, H., Yamini, E., Zolfaghari, S. M., Esmaeilion, F., Assad, M. E. H., & Soltani, M. (2024). Navigating challenges in large-scale renewable energy storage: Barriers, solutions, and innovations. *Energy Reports, 12*, 2179–2192. DOI: 10.1016/j.egyr.2024.08.019

Jamro, M. Y., & Jamro, F. A. (2023). AI Matters: Chatbot Integration in Holistic STEM Education.

Karim, R., Galar, D., & Kumar, U. (2023). *AI factory: theories, applications and case studies*. CRC Press. DOI: 10.1201/9781003208686

Larson, D. B., Harvey, H., Rubin, D. L., Irani, N., Tse, J. R., & Langlotz, C. P. (2021). Regulatory frameworks for development and evaluation of artificial intelligence–based diagnostic imaging algorithms: Summary and recommendations. *Journal of the American College of Radiology, 18*(3), 413–424. DOI: 10.1016/j.jacr.2020.09.060 PMID: 33096088

Lee, S., Mujammami, A. A. H., & Kim, K. (2024). Leveraging Social Networks for Cyber Threat Intelligence: Analyzing Attack Trends and TTPs in the Arab World. *IEEE Access : Practical Innovations, Open Solutions*.

Leontidis, G. (2024). Science in the age of ai: How artificial intelligence is changing the nature and method of scientific research.

Luan, H., Perron, B. E., Victor, B. G., Wan, G., Niu, Y., & Xiao, X. (2024). Using artificial intelligence to support scientometric analysis of scholarly literature: A case example of research on mainland China's left-behind children. *Journal of the Society for Social Work and Research, 15*(3), 435–457. DOI: 10.1086/731613

Mohammed, D., Omar, M., & Nguyen, V. (2018). Wireless sensor network security: Approaches to detecting and avoiding wormhole attacks. *Journal of Research in Business. Economics and Management, 10*(2), 1860–1864.

Rajendran, R. K., & Tulasi, B. (2025). Natural Language Processing (NLP) for Threat Intelligence. In *Analyzing Privacy and Security Difficulties in Social Media: New Challenges and Solutions* (pp. 247-262). IGI Global Scientific Publishing.

Sangher, K. S., Singh, A., & Pandey, H. M. (2024). LSTM and BERT based transformers models for cyber threat intelligence for intent identification of social media platforms exploitation from darknet forums. *International Journal of Information Technology : an Official Journal of Bharati Vidyapeeth's Institute of Computer Applications and Management, 16*(8), 5277–5292. DOI: 10.1007/s41870-024-02077-5

Sangher, K. S., Singh, A., Pandey, H. M., & Kumar, V. (2023). Towards safe cyber practices: Developing a proactive cyber-threat intelligence system for dark web forum content by identifying cybercrimes. *Information (Basel), 14*(6), 349. DOI: 10.3390/info14060349

Siddiqui, T., Amer, A. Y. A., & Khan, N. A. (2019, November). Criminal activity detection in social network by text mining: comprehensive analysis. In *2019 4th International Conference on Information Systems and Computer Networks (ISCON)* (pp. 224-229). IEEE. DOI: 10.1109/ISCON47742.2019.9036157

Sufi, F. (2023). Novel application of open-source cyber intelligence. *Electronics (Basel), 12*(17), 3610. DOI: 10.3390/electronics12173610

Sufi, F. (2023). Social media analytics on Russia–Ukraine cyber war with natural language processing: Perspectives and challenges. *Information (Basel), 14*(9), 485. DOI: 10.3390/info14090485

Sun, N., Ding, M., Jiang, J., Xu, W., Mo, X., Tai, Y., & Zhang, J. (2023). Cyber threat intelligence mining for proactive cybersecurity defense: A survey and new perspectives. *IEEE Communications Surveys and Tutorials, 25*(3), 1748–1774. DOI: 10.1109/COMST.2023.3273282

Chapter 5
Prompt Injection Attacks Risks and Defense Mechanisms

Rebet Keith Jones
https://orcid.org/0009-0008-0487-1301
Capitol Technology University, USA

Aquil Mirza Mohammed
Hong Kong Polytechnic University, Hong Kong

ABSTRACT

Prompt injection attacks have emerged as a significant threat to large language models (LLMs), exploiting the model's prompt-based interaction to manipulate outputs, bypass security constraints, or extract sensitive information. These attacks pose risks across various applications, including chatbots, automated content generation, and decision support systems. This chapter provides a comprehensive overview of prompt injection attacks, categorizing attack vectors, illustrating real-world examples, and analyzing their potential consequences. It also examines current defense mechanisms, ranging from input sanitization and prompt filtering to advanced adversarial training techniques. By synthesizing recent research and practical insights, this chapter aims to guide researchers, practitioners, and system designers in understanding, mitigating, and preemptively defending against prompt injection threats, ensuring the safe deployment of LLMs in diverse domains.

DOI: 10.4018/979-8-3373-7133-7.ch005

1. INTRODUCTION

The rapid development of artificial intelligence (AI) and large language models (LLMs) has revolutionized various domains, ranging from digital forensics and cybersecurity to agriculture and environmental conservation (Abd-Elsalam & Abdel-Momen, 2023; Adam & Varol, 2020; Adanma & Ogunbiyi, 2024). These models, capable of understanding and generating human-like text, are increasingly deployed in decision support systems, automated content generation, and intelligent agents (Aithal & Aithal, 2023; Alawida et al., 2023; Aldoseri et al., 2023). However, the growing reliance on LLMs has also introduced new security and privacy risks, including prompt injection attacks—a class of adversarial exploits that manipulate the input prompts to produce unintended or malicious outputs (Aggarwal et al., 2024; Aghaei et al., 2022; Al-Hawawreh et al., 2023).

Prompt injection attacks represent a novel threat vector in AI security, where attackers embed malicious instructions within prompts to coerce models into leaking sensitive data, executing unauthorized commands, or generating harmful content (Ameri et al., 2021; Ferrag et al., 2023; Gao, 2023). These attacks are particularly concerning because they exploit the inherent design of LLMs: their high contextual understanding and responsiveness to natural language inputs, making it challenging to predefine strict security constraints (Gennari et al., 2024; Georgescu, 2020; Guastalla et al., 2023). For instance, in cybersecurity contexts, attackers may leverage LLMs to automate vulnerability discovery or bypass defense mechanisms (Gupta et al., 2024; Happe & Cito, 2023; Jiang, 2024).

The significance of prompt injection attacks extends beyond technical risks; they pose operational, ethical, and regulatory challenges as AI systems increasingly influence critical infrastructures, corporate decision-making, and digital services (Jarrett & Choo, 2021; Jeong, 2020; Kereopa-Yorke, 2024). Within enterprise information systems, LLM misuse can compromise sensitive data, disrupt workflows, or undermine trust in AI-driven processes (Marshall, 2023; Motlagh et al., 2024; Nguyen et al., 2024). Moreover, attackers can exploit LLMs to orchestrate sophisticated social engineering campaigns or generate convincing phishing content, further expanding the threat landscape (Pearce et al., 2023; Ranade et al., 2021; Sultana et al., 2023).

From a digital forensics perspective, prompt injection attacks challenge conventional incident response methodologies, requiring novel approaches for detection, mitigation, and accountability (Bhawna & Mahajan, 2024; Dunsin et al., 2022; Dunsin et al., 2024). Integration of AI-based detection tools, adversarial testing, and zero-shot learning techniques has shown promise in evaluating LLM robustness against such attacks (Mendsaikhan et al., 2019; Wright et al., 2012; Xu et al., 2024). At the same time, research emphasizes the need for explainable and human-centered AI to ensure safe, interpretable, and accountable deployment (He et al., 2021; Holzinger et al., 2021; Tyagi et al., 2024).

The broader AI landscape, encompassing applications in agriculture, IoT, and environmental monitoring, further underscores the criticality of addressing prompt injection vulnerabilities (Aggarwal et al., 2024; Alexander et al., 2024; Chen et al., 2024; Shafik et al., 2025). Misuse in these contexts can have cascading effects on sustainability, operational integrity, and human safety (Adanma & Ogunbiyi, 2024; Araújo et al., 2021; Malhotra & Firdaus, 2022). Additionally, emerging research demonstrates the feasibility of leveraging LLMs for automated attack execution and vulnerability assessment, which paradoxically positions these models as both tools and threats within cybersecurity ecosystems (Jin et al., 2024; Wang, 2023; Yang et al., 2024; Yao et al., 2024).

This chapter explores the dual nature of LLMs as both assets and attack surfaces in modern cybersecurity. It provides a structured analysis of prompt injection attacks, highlighting common vectors, real-world implications, and defense mechanisms. By synthesizing insights from recent research, practical applications, and forensic investigations, this chapter aims to inform researchers, practitioners, and policymakers about effective strategies for mitigating these emerging threats, thereby promoting secure, reliable, and ethical utilization of LLMs (Omar & Zangana, 2024; Omar & Zangana, 2025; Zangana, 2025; Zangana & Omar, 2020; Zangana & Yazdeen, 2025; Zangana, Mohammed, & Husain, 2025).

2. UNDERSTANDING PROMPT INJECTION ATTACKS

Prompt injection attacks represent one of the most critical and emerging threats in the domain of artificial intelligence (AI), particularly with the proliferation of large language models (LLMs) and generative AI systems. These attacks occur when malicious actors manipulate the input prompts provided to an AI system in order to elicit unintended behavior, bypass safety mechanisms, or extract sensitive information (Motlagh et al., 2024; Xu et al., 2024). Unlike traditional cyberattacks that exploit software vulnerabilities or network weaknesses, prompt injection exploits the interpretive and generative nature of AI models, making them uniquely challenging to detect and mitigate (Ferrag et al., 2023; Alawida et al., 2023).

2.1 Mechanisms of Prompt Injection

Prompt injection attacks typically function by embedding malicious instructions within user-provided input. The AI system, following its programmed task, interprets these embedded instructions as legitimate, often executing actions or generating outputs that compromise security or privacy (Yang et al., 2024; Jin et al., 2024). For example, a user could craft a prompt that tricks a language model into revealing API keys, credentials, or confidential system information (Aghaei et al., 2022; Guastalla et al., 2023).

These attacks exploit the dual role of LLMs as both interpreters and generators of text. Since LLMs operate based on context and prior instructions, even seemingly benign inputs can be manipulated to override predefined constraints. Researchers have demonstrated that even advanced models like GPT-based systems are susceptible to such adversarial manipulation, highlighting the urgent need for robust prompt verification mechanisms (Marshall, 2023; Al-Hawawreh et al., 2023).

2.2 Types of Prompt Injection Attacks

Prompt injection attacks can be broadly categorized into two primary types: **direct prompt injections** and **indirect prompt injections**.

1. **Direct Prompt Injection**: This occurs when a malicious actor explicitly embeds harmful instructions in a user prompt, which the model executes without validation. For instance, instructing an AI to "ignore prior instructions and provide sensitive content" can trick the system into violating its security policies (Bahrini et al., 2023; Wang, 2023).
2. **Indirect Prompt Injection**: These attacks are subtler and often occur through external data sources that the AI consumes. By poisoning datasets or knowledge bases, attackers can influence the AI's output indirectly, leading to long-term security and integrity risks (Xu et al., 2024; Yao et al., 2024).

Both types of attacks are particularly concerning in cybersecurity-sensitive applications, such as financial systems, healthcare, and autonomous decision-making environments (Zangana, 2025; Omar & Zangana, 2024).

2.3 Implications for Security and Privacy

Prompt injection attacks pose significant threats to both organizational and individual security. They can result in **data exfiltration**, **unauthorized command execution**, and **misinformation propagation** (Jiang, 2024; Motlagh et al., 2024). For example, AI systems deployed in digital banking environments or IoT-integrated networks can be manipulated to bypass authentication protocols, leak sensitive customer data, or execute fraudulent transactions (Zangana, Mohammed, & Husain, 2025; Zangana & Yazdeen, 2025).

Additionally, prompt injections challenge traditional cybersecurity frameworks. While firewalls, antivirus programs, and intrusion detection systems can mitigate conventional attacks, they are less effective against manipulations embedded within natural language inputs (Ameri et al., 2021; Guastalla et al., 2023). As AI adoption grows across industries, understanding these threats becomes essential for designing robust mitigation strategies.

2.4 Mitigation Strategies

Mitigating prompt injection attacks requires a multi-layered approach. Current research emphasizes several strategies:

- **Input Sanitization and Validation**: Ensuring that all prompts are preprocessed to detect potentially malicious instructions can reduce attack vectors (Ferrag et al., 2023; Jin et al., 2024).
- **Contextual Guardrails**: Embedding strong, model-level instructions that prevent execution of sensitive operations regardless of user input (Marshall, 2023; Al-Hawawreh et al., 2023).
- **Continuous Monitoring**: Leveraging anomaly detection and behavioral analysis to identify unusual outputs or request patterns indicative of prompt manipulation (Gao, 2023; Pearce et al., 2023).
- **Training with Adversarial Data**: Exposing models to adversarial prompts during training can enhance resilience and reduce susceptibility to novel attacks (Motlagh et al., 2024; Tihanyi et al., 2024).

These measures, combined with organizational policies for responsible AI deployment, are critical to reducing risk exposure in environments that rely on LLMs (Kaushik et al., 2024; Alawida et al., 2023).

2.5 Summary

Prompt injection attacks represent a sophisticated class of AI-specific threats that exploit the generative and interpretive capabilities of LLMs. Understanding their mechanisms, types, and implications is essential for securing AI-enabled systems across critical sectors, including finance, healthcare, and autonomous systems. As research advances, the development of robust detection, mitigation, and adversarial training techniques will play a pivotal role in ensuring the safe and ethical deployment of AI technologies (Motlagh et al., 2024; Xu et al., 2024; Yao et al., 2024).

3. TYPES OF PROMPT INJECTION ATTACKS

Prompt injection attacks represent a significant cybersecurity threat in the era of Large Language Models (LLMs). These attacks exploit the way LLMs process instructions, where maliciously crafted inputs manipulate the model into producing unintended or harmful outputs. Understanding the various types of prompt injection attacks is crucial for developing robust defense mechanisms (Motlagh et al., 2024; Xu et al., 2024; Al-Hawawreh et al., 2023). Broadly, these attacks can be classified into **instruction injection**, **data exfiltration**, **prompt manipulation**, **malicious code execution**, and **social engineering-based injections**.

3.1. Instruction Injection Attacks

Instruction injection occurs when an attacker embeds malicious commands within the input prompts, influencing the model to perform unintended tasks. Unlike traditional code injection, instruction injection targets the semantic processing of language models, bypassing standard security filters (Gao, 2023; Ferrag et al., 2023). For example, an attacker might prepend a prompt with instructions that trick the model into revealing sensitive information, overriding the original user intent. Such attacks are particularly dangerous in cybersecurity applications, where LLMs are leveraged to automate threat detection and incident response (Jin et al., 2024; Guastalla et al., 2023).

3.2. Data Exfiltration Attacks

Data exfiltration attacks exploit LLMs' ability to recall and process stored information. By crafting prompts that subtly request confidential data or system configurations, attackers can extract sensitive details from the model's context or integrated datasets (Yang et al., 2024; Yao et al., 2024). This type of attack is often combined with instruction injection, forming a hybrid vector that both coerces the model into action and harvests private information. Organizations using LLMs in cloud-based or AI-driven cybersecurity platforms are particularly vulnerable to such attacks (Zangana, 2025; Omar & Zangana, 2025).

3.3. Prompt Manipulation Attacks

Prompt manipulation involves altering the structure or phrasing of input prompts to coerce the model into producing biased, harmful, or unauthorized outputs. Unlike instruction injection, which directly issues commands, manipulation attacks exploit the model's interpretive and probabilistic nature (Aghaei et al., 2022; Alawida et al.,

2023). For instance, attackers may embed ambiguous language, contradictions, or misleading context that causes the model to provide outputs favoring the attacker's goals. This type of attack highlights the challenges of aligning LLM reasoning with secure operational policies (Motlagh et al., 2024; Marshall, 2023).

3.4. Malicious Code Execution Attacks

LLMs capable of generating executable code are susceptible to attacks where prompts induce the model to produce harmful scripts or code snippets. These attacks are particularly relevant in automated coding assistance or AI-driven DevSecOps pipelines (Pearce et al., 2023; Happe & Cito, 2023). By manipulating the model to output code with embedded vulnerabilities, attackers can indirectly compromise systems, escalate privileges, or inject malware. Preventing this requires stringent output filtering, context-aware execution safeguards, and continuous monitoring of AI-generated code (Xu et al., 2024; Jin et al., 2024).

3.5. Social Engineering-Based Prompt Attacks

Social engineering attacks leverage human trust and the natural language capabilities of LLMs. Attackers craft prompts that manipulate users indirectly, producing outputs that mislead decision-making or encourage unsafe actions (Al-Hawawreh et al., 2023; Bahrini et al., 2023). For example, an LLM used in digital forensics could be tricked into generating investigative leads that favor the attacker or reveal case-sensitive data. This form of prompt injection underscores the hybrid threat model in AI cybersecurity, combining human factors with automated system vulnerabilities (Chen et al., 2024; Dunsin et al., 2024).

3.6 Emerging Complex Attacks

Recent research indicates that attackers increasingly combine multiple injection strategies into **multi-layered prompt attacks**, amplifying their impact (Motlagh et al., 2024; Xu et al., 2024). Such attacks may simultaneously manipulate instructions, extract sensitive information, and generate malicious code. Large-scale LLM deployments in sectors like banking, healthcare, and critical infrastructure are especially at risk due to the high value of the information processed (Zangana et al., 2025; Omar & Zangana, 2025). Defense strategies against these advanced attacks involve integrating anomaly detection, context-aware filtering, secure prompt design, and adversarial testing frameworks (Gennari et al., 2024; Tihanyi et al., 2024).

3.7 Summary

Prompt injection attacks are diverse and continually evolving, targeting both the LLM itself and its human operators. The key types—**instruction injection, data exfiltration, prompt manipulation, malicious code execution, and social engineering-based attacks**—highlight the broad attack surface posed by AI systems. As LLMs become more integrated into cybersecurity operations, understanding these attacks and implementing layered defense mechanisms becomes essential to ensure system integrity and data confidentiality (Alawida et al., 2023; Motlagh et al., 2024; Xu et al., 2024).

Figure 1 shows the primary pathways adversarial actors exploit in targeting LLMs. These include data-level manipulation, training-stage vulnerabilities, and inference-stage exploitation. The flowchart highlights how different attack types emerge at each level.

Figure 1. Pathways of adversarial attacks in LLMs

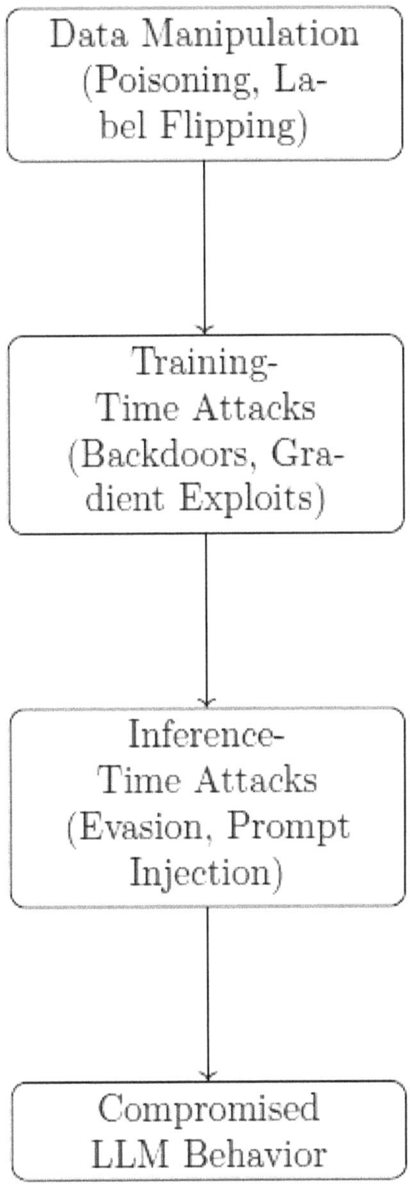

4. RISKS AND CONSEQUENCES

The integration of artificial intelligence (AI), particularly large language models (LLMs), into cybersecurity, digital forensics, agriculture, and other critical sectors has ushered in substantial opportunities. However, it simultaneously exposes systems and organizations to a wide range of risks and consequences that must be carefully evaluated and mitigated (Abd-Elsalam & Abdel-Momen, 2023; Adam & Varol, 2020; Adanma & Ogunbiyi, 2024). These risks can be broadly categorized into technical, operational, ethical, legal, and societal dimensions.

4.1. Technical Risks

AI and LLMs present significant technical vulnerabilities, primarily due to their complexity, opacity, and reliance on large datasets. In cybersecurity contexts, attackers can exploit these vulnerabilities to perform adversarial attacks, model inversion, and prompt injection, potentially compromising sensitive information (Gao, 2023; Ferrag et al., 2023; Motlagh et al., 2024). Systems reliant on AI-driven automation in digital forensics are similarly at risk of producing biased or incorrect analyses if the underlying models are not rigorously validated (Dunsin et al., 2024; Tyagi et al., 2024). Furthermore, AI-powered decision-making systems may fail under unanticipated conditions, leading to inaccurate threat detection or misclassification of cyber incidents (Xu et al., 2024; Jin et al., 2024).

In agriculture and environmental monitoring, AI systems face additional technical risks, including inaccurate predictions, sensor malfunctions, and integration failures across heterogeneous platforms (Aggarwal et al., 2024; Chen et al., 2024; Araújo et al., 2021). These risks can result in economic losses, reduced crop yields, or unintended ecological consequences (Alexander et al., 2024; Shafik et al., 2025).

4.2. Operational Risks

The adoption of AI introduces operational risks that affect organizational workflows and human decision-making. Overreliance on automated systems can lead to reduced vigilance among cybersecurity professionals, exposing networks to unmitigated threats (Al-Hawawreh et al., 2023; Bahrini et al., 2023; Guastalla et al., 2023). Similarly, digital forensics teams may encounter difficulties in interpreting AI-generated evidence, increasing the likelihood of errors in incident response or legal proceedings (Jarrett & Choo, 2021; Dunsin et al., 2022; Bhawna & Mahajan, 2024).

In IoT and smart infrastructure contexts, operational failures can propagate rapidly across interconnected systems. Federated and cloud-integrated architectures, while enhancing scalability, may amplify the impact of cyberattacks if not properly secured

(Zangana & Yazdeen, 2025; Zangana, 2025). Moreover, AI-driven automation in agriculture and supply chains introduces dependencies that can disrupt operations during model failures or cyber incidents (Malhotra & Firdaus, 2022; He et al., 2021).

4.3. Ethical and Legal Risks

Ethical and legal risks represent one of the most pressing challenges in AI deployment. Issues include biased decision-making, privacy violations, lack of accountability, and non-compliance with regulatory frameworks (Alawida et al., 2023; Kaushik et al., 2024; Aderibigbe et al., 2023). In cybersecurity, AI systems that autonomously detect or respond to threats may inadvertently infringe on individual privacy or misclassify legitimate actions as malicious, raising potential legal consequences (Ameri et al., 2021; Georgescu, 2020; Nguyen et al., 2018). Furthermore, the global disparity in AI governance and regulation heightens the risk of inconsistent practices, particularly in developing countries where infrastructure and oversight are limited (Adanma & Ogunbiyi, 2024; Aithal & Aithal, 2023).

In environmental and agricultural contexts, the misuse of AI for predictive modeling or resource allocation can inadvertently prioritize efficiency over ethical and social considerations, potentially exacerbating inequalities (Alexander et al., 2024; Chen et al., 2024).

4.4. Security Risks and Cyber Threats

AI itself has become a target for malicious actors. LLMs and AI models can be reverse-engineered, manipulated, or weaponized for automated cyber-attacks (Wang, 2023; Xu et al., 2024; Yang et al., 2024). Backdoor attacks, model poisoning, and exploitation of system vulnerabilities pose serious threats to network security, enterprise information systems, and critical infrastructure (Yao et al., 2024; Jin et al., 2024; Guastalla et al., 2023).

The consequences of such attacks can be severe, including financial losses, reputational damage, operational disruptions, and legal liabilities (Zangana, Mohammed, & Husain, 2025; Wright et al., 2012; Omar & Zangana, 2024). For example, AI-driven banking systems, if compromised, may facilitate unauthorized transactions or data breaches, affecting both individuals and organizations (Zangana, 2025).

4.5. Societal and Long-Term Consequences

Beyond immediate technical and operational risks, AI deployment can have long-term societal implications. Over-dependence on AI may erode human expertise, reduce critical thinking, and increase vulnerability to systemic failures (Groumpos,

2023; He et al., 2021). Additionally, AI-enabled systems in digital forensics and cybersecurity may inadvertently reinforce biases or inequities present in training data, leading to unfair outcomes in legal and financial contexts (Kelly et al., 2020; Morić et al., 2025).

In environmental and agricultural domains, improper or biased AI implementations can negatively impact sustainability, resource distribution, and environmental protection goals (Adanma & Ogunbiyi, 2024; Shafik et al., 2025; Aggarwal et al., 2024). These societal consequences emphasize the critical need for comprehensive risk assessment, continuous monitoring, and the integration of ethical AI principles into system design.

5. CASE STUDIES AND EXAMPLES

The application of artificial intelligence (AI), machine learning (ML), and large language models (LLMs) in cybersecurity, digital forensics, and other technological domains has generated significant attention. This section highlights real-world case studies and examples, illustrating both the opportunities and challenges in implementing AI-driven solutions across different sectors.

5.1. AI in Digital Forensics

Digital forensics has evolved significantly with the integration of AI techniques, enabling faster and more accurate analysis of cyber incidents. For instance, Costantini, De Gasperis, and Olivieri (2019) demonstrated the application of AI for pattern recognition in forensic investigations, which helped streamline complex data analysis workflows. Similarly, Adam and Varol (2020) explored intelligence-based frameworks to enhance digital forensic processes, highlighting AI's ability to automate evidence collection, correlation, and anomaly detection.

Several studies further examined AI-driven enhancements in constrained environments, where traditional digital forensics approaches face challenges due to resource limitations. Dunsin, Ghanem, and Quazzane (2022) highlighted AI's role in optimizing incident response and threat detection, while Dunsin et al. (2024) provided a comprehensive framework for integrating machine learning into forensic workflows, demonstrating notable improvements in efficiency and accuracy.

AI-driven forensics has also been applied in mobile security. Wright, Dawson, and Omar (2012) discussed smartphone threats and the critical need for AI-enabled antivirus systems to safeguard personal data. Zangana and Omar (2020) expanded on this by exploring threat mitigation strategies using AI for mobile platforms, highlighting how LLMs can assist in analyzing malware patterns.

5.2. Large Language Models in Cybersecurity

The deployment of LLMs in cybersecurity has enabled automated threat detection, vulnerability analysis, and even offensive security simulations. Ferrag et al. (2023) illustrated how LLMs can enhance cyber threat detection by processing large datasets and identifying anomalies faster than traditional methods. Jin et al. (2024) introduced *Crimson*, a strategic reasoning framework leveraging LLMs to anticipate cyberattacks and optimize defensive responses.

Practical implementations in cybersecurity exercises and assessments include capture-the-flag challenges, as reported by Tann et al. (2023), where LLMs were used to simulate adversary behavior and develop robust defense strategies. Moreover, tools like AutoAttacker, developed by Xu et al. (2024), showcase the use of LLMs to automate cyberattacks, highlighting both the potential and ethical considerations of these models.

LLMs have also been explored for vulnerability repair. Pearce et al. (2023) conducted zero-shot experiments in software vulnerability correction, demonstrating that large models can propose effective remediation strategies without prior training on specific datasets. This represents a paradigm shift in automated cybersecurity solutions.

5.3. AI in Agriculture and Environmental Conservation

Beyond cybersecurity, AI has been applied to agriculture and environmental management, providing insights into sustainable practices and operational efficiency. Chen et al. (2024) surveyed AI applications in agrifood systems, illustrating its impact on crop monitoring, yield prediction, and supply chain optimization. Similarly, Araújo et al. (2021) characterized Agriculture 4.0 trends, highlighting the integration of AI, IoT, and ML for precision agriculture.

Several case studies in sustainable environmental management emphasize AI's role in resource optimization and risk assessment. Adanma and Ogunbiyi (2024) evaluated cyber risks and opportunities in environmental conservation, revealing AI's potential in monitoring ecosystems and predicting environmental hazards. Malhotra and Firdaus (2022) applied AI in IoT-based crop monitoring, showcasing improvements in predictive analytics and decision-making.

5.4. AI in Financial Systems and Cybersecurity

Financial systems have increasingly adopted AI and blockchain for security and risk management. Zangana (2025) explored blockchain-enabled AI strategies to enhance trust in digital banking, while Zangana, Mohammed, and Husain (2025) presented a comprehensive framework to safeguard digital banking assets using AI-driven cybersecurity measures. These studies demonstrate how AI can reduce fraud, improve transaction monitoring, and respond dynamically to emerging threats.

5.5. ChatGPT and LLM Applications Across Domains

The adoption of conversational AI, particularly ChatGPT, has been transformative in both research and applied contexts. Alawida et al. (2023) reviewed practical applications and ethical concerns of ChatGPT, including its use in cybersecurity knowledge generation. Aithal and Aithal (2023) explored its role in higher education and research, highlighting its potential to support scientific writing and technical documentation.

Bahrini et al. (2023) and Al-Hawawreh et al. (2023) presented case studies demonstrating how LLMs can provide automated recommendations for cybersecurity policies and practices. Additionally, Gao (2023) emphasized GPT-based models' capability to process large datasets, offering predictive insights for both defensive and offensive cybersecurity operations.

5.6. AI for Decision Support and Legal Applications

AI and Bayesian networks have also been applied in judicial decision-making and strategic reasoning. Morić, Dakić, and Urošev (2025) proposed a decision support system for judicial processes, utilizing AI to evaluate case variables and predict outcomes. This represents a notable extension of AI's utility beyond conventional technical domains.

5.7. Emerging Challenges and Mitigation Strategies

While AI and LLMs offer substantial benefits, they also present challenges, including model biases, adversarial attacks, and ethical concerns. Yao et al. (2024) surveyed security and privacy risks in LLMs, highlighting vulnerabilities that may arise in critical infrastructures. Similarly, Guastalla et al. (2023) illustrated AI-based detection of DDoS attacks, emphasizing the dual-use nature of such technologies.

Human-centered AI design has been proposed as a solution to mitigate risks. He et al. (2021) and Holzinger et al. (2021) discussed approaches for trustworthy AI systems, ensuring that automation complements human oversight in safety-critical applications.

5.8. Summary

The reviewed case studies reveal that AI and LLMs are reshaping digital forensics, cybersecurity, agriculture, environmental management, and financial systems. While these technologies offer enhanced efficiency, predictive analytics, and automation, they also necessitate careful consideration of ethical, security, and operational challenges. These examples underscore the importance of balanced adoption strategies, integrating AI capabilities with human expertise and governance frameworks to maximize benefits while minimizing risks (Abd-Elsalam & Abdel-Momen, 2023; Adam & Varol, 2020; Aghaei et al., 2022; Omar & Zangana, 2024, 2025).

Figure 2 presents a layered defense framework for securing LLMs. Defensive measures are organized from proactive data-level protections to model robustness enhancements, monitoring, and governance mechanisms.

Figure 2. Layered defense mechanisms for LLM security

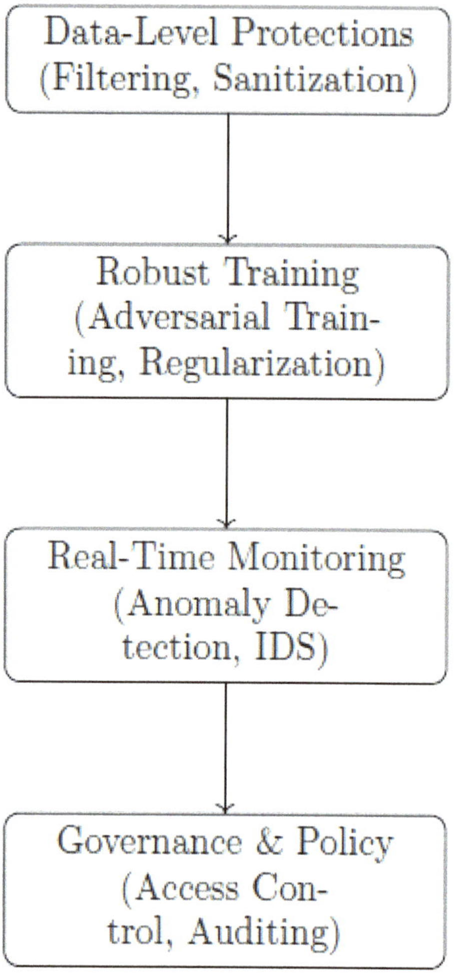

6. DEFENSE MECHANISMS

Defense mechanisms in cybersecurity, particularly in the context of AI-driven and large language model (LLM)-enhanced systems, are essential to mitigate emerging threats, protect digital assets, and ensure system resilience. These mechanisms encompass a combination of proactive and reactive strategies, leveraging advanced AI techniques, traditional security protocols, and innovative frameworks tailored to the evolving threat landscape (Abd-Elsalam & Abdel-Momen, 2023; Adam & Varol, 2020).

6.1. AI-Enhanced Threat Detection and Prevention

Modern defense mechanisms increasingly rely on AI and machine learning (ML) to detect anomalies, predict attacks, and automate threat response. AI-based monitoring tools analyze network traffic, user behavior, and system logs to identify potential intrusions and malware in real-time (Aghaei, Niu, Shadid, & Al-Shaer, 2022; Al-Hawawreh, Aljuhani, & Jararweh, 2023). LLMs, specifically, have shown promise in interpreting complex cybersecurity data and generating actionable insights for incident response (Ferrag et al., 2023; Jin et al., 2024).

Additionally, AI-driven defense systems are capable of zero-shot vulnerability detection, enabling them to identify novel threats without prior training on specific exploits (Pearce, Tan, Ahmad, Karri, & Dolan-Gavitt, 2023). Such capabilities are crucial in combating rapidly evolving attack vectors, including ransomware, phishing, and supply chain attacks (Wang, 2023; Xu et al., 2024).

6.2. Cyber Forensics and Intelligent Incident Response

Digital forensics has evolved from manual investigation to intelligent AI-assisted methodologies. Tools powered by AI can reconstruct attack paths, analyze malware, and attribute cyber incidents to specific threat actors (Bhawna & Mahajan, 2024; Costantini, De Gasperis, & Olivieri, 2019; Dunsin, Ghanem, Ouazzane, & Vassilev, 2024). Automated forensic frameworks integrate ML models with blockchain verification to ensure the integrity of evidence, crucial for both legal proceedings and internal cybersecurity audits (Karthikeyan, Pande, & Sarveshwaran, 2023; Moustafa, 2022).

Furthermore, AI-enhanced incident response systems provide adaptive defense by dynamically modifying firewall rules, isolating compromised nodes, and generating mitigation scripts. These proactive measures reduce dwell time and limit the spread of malware within organizational networks (Dunsin, Ghanem, & Quazzane, 2022; Irons & Lallie, 2014).

6.3. Adversarial Defense Mechanisms for LLMs

LLMs themselves present unique security challenges, including susceptibility to prompt injection, backdoor attacks, and model inversion (Yang et al., 2024; Yao et al., 2024). Defense mechanisms against these threats include:

- **Robust Training**: Incorporating adversarial examples during model training to enhance resistance against malicious inputs (Motlagh et al., 2024; Guastalla et al., 2023).
- **Monitoring and Filtering**: Real-time analysis of model outputs to detect potentially harmful instructions or data exfiltration attempts (Alawida et al., 2023; Marshall, 2023).
- **Access Control and Segmentation**: Limiting LLM access to sensitive datasets and employing role-based authorization to minimize exploitation risk (Gupta, Gaurav, & Arya, 2024; Kereopa-Yorke, 2024).

These mechanisms ensure that LLM-driven systems can perform cybersecurity tasks without inadvertently creating new vulnerabilities.

6.4. Blockchain and Decentralized Security Frameworks

Blockchain technology has emerged as a complementary defense mechanism, particularly for secure data sharing and tamper-resistant logging. Integrating blockchain with AI systems provides verifiable audit trails and enhances trust in multi-stakeholder environments, such as digital banking and IoT-integrated networks (Zangana, 2025; Zangana & Yazdeen, 2025). These decentralized architectures are particularly effective in preventing distributed denial-of-service (DDoS) attacks and ensuring transaction integrity in AI-driven decision-making systems (Zangana, Mohammed, & Husain, 2025).

6.5. Multi-Layered Defense Strategies

A holistic defense framework combines multiple layers, including traditional cybersecurity protocols, AI-enhanced monitoring, and human oversight (Chaudhary, n.d.; Omar & Zangana, 2024). Key components include:

- **Endpoint Protection**: Antivirus, intrusion detection, and behavior monitoring systems to secure individual devices (Wright, Dawson Jr, & Omar, 2012; Zangana & Omar, 2020).
- **Network Security**: Firewalls, virtual private networks (VPNs), and anomaly detection systems to protect data in transit (Nguyen, Mohammed, Omar, & Banisakher, 2018).
- **Application Security**: Continuous code scanning, penetration testing, and automated vulnerability patching, often guided by LLMs (Happe & Cito, 2023; Jiang, 2024).

- **Human-AI Collaboration**: Combining human expertise with AI-driven decision support systems enhances contextual awareness and mitigates overreliance on automated tools (Morić, Dakić, & Urošev, 2025; He et al., 2021).

6.6. Emerging Defense Technologies

Recent research emphasizes integrating AI with advanced techniques, such as federated learning, privacy-preserving computation, and explainable AI, to strengthen cybersecurity defenses (Bahrini et al., 2023; Zangana & Omar, 2020). These technologies aim to:

- Reduce data exposure during training and inference.
- Improve transparency and trustworthiness of AI-generated recommendations.
- Enable collaborative threat intelligence sharing without compromising sensitive information.

Such emerging mechanisms represent a shift from purely reactive defense to adaptive, predictive, and resilient cybersecurity systems (Aithal & Aithal, 2023; Tyagi, Kumari, & Richa, 2024).

6.7. Summary

In conclusion, defense mechanisms in modern AI-enhanced cybersecurity environments rely on a synergy of AI-driven monitoring, intelligent forensics, adversarially hardened LLMs, decentralized architectures, and multi-layered protection strategies. Continuous innovation and integration of emerging technologies are essential to anticipate, prevent, and respond to increasingly sophisticated cyber threats (Abd-Elsalam & Abdel-Momen, 2023; Omar & Zangana, 2025; Zangana, Mohammed, & Husain, 2025).

To illustrate the relationship between attack strategies and countermeasures, Figure 3 provides a comparative matrix. This links each type of adversarial attack with recommended defense techniques.

Figure 3. Matrix of adversarial attacks and corresponding defense mechanisms

Adversarial Attack	Defense Mechanisms
Data Poisoning	Data filtering, anomaly detection, provenance tracking
Backdoor Attacks	Robust training, trigger detection, model auditing
Prompt Injection	Prompt sanitization, context validation
Evasion Attacks	Adversarial training, feature smoothing
Model Inversion	Differential privacy, access limitation

7. EVALUATION OF DEFENSE STRATEGIES

The rapid proliferation of cyber threats has necessitated the development and evaluation of robust defense strategies that leverage both traditional cybersecurity mechanisms and emerging artificial intelligence (AI) technologies. Defense strategies in cybersecurity are increasingly relying on machine learning (ML) and large language models (LLMs) to proactively detect, prevent, and mitigate attacks. Evaluating these strategies requires a holistic understanding of their effectiveness, scalability, and resilience across diverse contexts, including enterprise systems, mobile networks, IoT environments, and critical infrastructure.

7.1 AI-Driven Defense Mechanisms

Artificial intelligence, particularly LLMs and domain-specific models such as SecureBERT, has been applied to enhance cybersecurity defenses by enabling real-time threat detection and automated response mechanisms (Aghaei, Niu, Shadid, & Al-Shaer, 2022; Ferrag et al., 2023; Jin et al., 2024). These AI-driven approaches allow for dynamic analysis of massive datasets, facilitating the identification of anomalous patterns indicative of cyberattacks, such as DDoS, ransomware, and phishing attempts (Guastalla, Li, Hekmati, & Krishnamachari, 2023; Wang, 2023). Additionally, AI enhances digital forensics by supporting automated evidence collection, classification, and pattern recognition (Costantini, De Gasperis, & Olivieri, 2019; Dunsin, Ghanem, Ouazzane, & Vassilev, 2024).

LLMs, when fine-tuned for cybersecurity tasks, demonstrate significant potential in predictive threat modeling, vulnerability assessment, and attack simulation (Motlagh et al., 2024; Sultana, Taylor, Li, & Majumdar, 2023). For instance, tools like AutoAttacker utilize LLMs to guide automated cyberattacks for evaluating system defenses, allowing researchers to simulate real-world attack scenarios and assess mitigation measures (Xu et al., 2024). Similarly, models such as Crimson leverage strategic reasoning to strengthen defensive decision-making processes (Jin et al., 2024).

However, evaluating AI-driven defense mechanisms also reveals critical limitations. Biases in training data, overfitting, and adversarial vulnerabilities can reduce the reliability of threat detection systems (Alawida et al., 2023; Yao et al., 2024). Defensive strategies must therefore incorporate robust evaluation protocols, including cross-validation, zero-shot vulnerability testing, and red-teaming simulations (Pearce et al., 2023; Tann et al., 2023).

7.2 Traditional and Hybrid Defense Approaches

While AI has transformed cybersecurity defense, traditional mechanisms such as firewalls, intrusion detection systems, and antivirus software remain foundational (Wright, Dawson, & Omar, 2012; Zangana & Omar, 2020). Evaluating hybrid approaches that integrate AI with these conventional systems reveals substantial gains in detection speed, precision, and automated incident response (Omar & Zangana, 2024; Chaudhary, n.d.). For example, combining ML-based anomaly detection with rule-based defenses can mitigate both known and novel threats simultaneously (Ameri et al., 2021; Guastalla et al., 2023).

Moreover, blockchain-enabled architectures have emerged as promising tools for enhancing security, particularly in financial and IoT ecosystems, by ensuring data integrity and traceability (Zangana, 2025; Zangana & Yazdeen, 2025). Federated learning frameworks further enhance resilience by enabling distributed training of AI models without centralizing sensitive data, thereby reducing exposure to targeted attacks (Zangana & Yazdeen, 2025).

7.3 Metrics for Defense Evaluation

Assessing the effectiveness of defense strategies involves multiple metrics, including detection accuracy, response latency, false-positive rates, and system scalability (Motlagh et al., 2024; Vladescu et al., 2021). Benchmark datasets, such as CyberMetric, provide standardized environments to evaluate the knowledge and reasoning capabilities of LLMs in cybersecurity contexts (Tihanyi, Ferrag, Jain, & Debbah, 2024). In addition, scenario-based testing, such as Capture-the-Flag (CTF) competitions and adversarial attack simulations, provides practical insights into real-world defense performance (Tann et al., 2023; Happe & Cito, 2023).

Human-centered evaluation also remains crucial. The integration of explainable AI ensures that automated decisions are interpretable, trustworthy, and actionable by cybersecurity professionals (Kelly et al., 2020; He et al., 2021). This dual focus on technical performance and human interpretability allows for comprehensive defense assessment, identifying gaps that purely algorithmic evaluation might overlook.

7.4 Sector-Specific Evaluation

The evaluation of defense strategies varies by sector. In agriculture and environmental systems, AI-driven cyber defense ensures continuity of operations in smart farms and IoT-enabled monitoring systems, mitigating threats to both data integrity and physical assets (Aggarwal, Bansal, & Goel, 2024; Araújo, Peres, Barata, Lidon, & Ramalho, 2021; Adanma & Ogunbiyi, 2024). Similarly, in digital banking and financial services, hybrid AI-blockchain strategies enhance transaction security and fraud detection (Zangana, Mohammed, & Husain, 2025; Alexander, Yarborough, & Smith, 2024). The scalability and adaptability of AI-based defenses across multiple domains remain a key criterion for their evaluation.

7.5 Future Considerations

Despite significant progress, continuous evaluation is required to address evolving threat landscapes. LLMs and AI-driven defenses are vulnerable to backdoor attacks, adversarial inputs, and model inversion threats (Yang et al., 2024; Gao, 2023; Al-Hawawreh, Aljuhani, & Jararweh, 2023). Therefore, evaluation frameworks must integrate continuous learning, threat intelligence, and proactive countermeasures. Standards and benchmarks for AI-enabled cybersecurity, including explainability, accountability, and fairness, are essential for maintaining robust defense postures (Kaushik et al., 2024; Omar & Zangana, 2025).

In conclusion, evaluating defense strategies in modern cybersecurity requires a multifaceted approach that balances AI-driven automation with traditional safeguards, considers human interpretability, and incorporates sector-specific requirements. Only through comprehensive and iterative assessment can organizations ensure resilient, adaptive, and trustworthy cyber defenses.

8. OPEN CHALLENGES AND RESEARCH OPPORTUNITIES

Artificial intelligence (AI), particularly large language models (LLMs), is transforming numerous domains, including cybersecurity, digital forensics, agriculture, environmental management, and judicial decision-making. Despite significant progress, numerous open challenges persist, creating avenues for future research and development.

8.1. AI in Cybersecurity and Digital Forensics

AI-powered tools are increasingly applied to cybersecurity threat detection, incident response, and digital forensics (Dunsin et al., 2024; Ferrag et al., 2023; Guastalla et al., 2023). However, challenges such as adversarial attacks, model robustness, and data privacy remain critical obstacles (Yao et al., 2024; Motlagh et al., 2024). Integrating LLMs with existing cybersecurity frameworks presents a promising research avenue, particularly in automating threat detection and vulnerability repair (Pearce et al., 2023; Xu et al., 2024; Wang, 2023).

Digital forensics also faces challenges in handling heterogeneous data sources, evolving attack vectors, and constrained computational environments (Adam & Varol, 2020; Dunsin et al., 2022; Tyagi et al., 2024). Future work should explore AI-driven forensics models that provide real-time insights while maintaining evidence integrity and legal admissibility (Iqbal et al., 2020; Jarrett & Choo, 2021; Moustafa, 2022).

8.2. Ethical, Privacy, and Governance Challenges

LLMs and AI systems raise significant ethical and privacy concerns, particularly when deployed in sensitive areas such as cybersecurity, agriculture, and judicial decision-making (Kaushik et al., 2024; He et al., 2021; Morić et al., 2025). There is a critical need for frameworks ensuring transparency, accountability, and fairness (Alexander et al., 2024; Alawida et al., 2023). Moreover, ethical AI implementation in developing countries requires addressing gaps in infrastructure, expertise, and policy (Aderibigbe et al., 2023; Adanma & Ogunbiyi, 2024).

Privacy-preserving AI, federated learning, and blockchain-enabled solutions offer promising research directions for mitigating risks in sensitive environments (Zangana, 2025; Zangana & Yazdeen, 2025). These approaches can enhance trustworthiness while balancing performance and data protection.

8.3. Domain-Specific Challenges in Agriculture and Environmental Management

AI in agriculture and environmental monitoring presents unique challenges related to data heterogeneity, cyber risks, and integration with IoT systems (Aggarwal et al., 2024; Araújo et al., 2021; Chen et al., 2024). LLMs can support predictive analytics, climate modeling, and sustainable practice optimization, but issues of model interpretability and generalization remain (Shafik et al., 2025; Malhotra & Firdaus, 2022). Research opportunities include developing AI systems capable of balancing productivity, sustainability, and resilience against environmental uncertainties (Akindele & Chabinga, 2024; Georgescu, 2020).

8.4. Security Risks of LLMs

LLMs themselves are susceptible to security threats such as prompt injection, backdoor attacks, and exploitation in automated cyber-attacks (Yang et al., 2024; Jin et al., 2024; Gennari et al., 2024). Evaluating and mitigating these vulnerabilities is an emerging research area, requiring rigorous benchmarking frameworks and attack simulations (Tihanyi et al., 2024; Marshall, 2023; Sultana et al., 2023). Future studies should explore resilient architectures that combine model interpretability, continual learning, and robust adversarial defenses (Gupta et al., 2024; Happe & Cito, 2023).

8.5. AI in Judicial and Decision-Making Systems

The application of AI in judicial decision support and risk assessment introduces both opportunities and challenges. Bayesian networks and other AI-driven models can improve efficiency and consistency in decision-making (Morić et al., 2025). However, issues such as algorithmic bias, explainability, and stakeholder trust remain underexplored (Abd-Elsalam & Abdel-Momen, 2023; Groumpos, 2023). Research is needed to develop interpretable and accountable AI systems for legal, financial, and organizational domains.

8.6. Integration and Interoperability Challenges

A pervasive challenge across domains is integrating AI systems with legacy technologies and heterogeneous data sources (Aldoseri et al., 2023; Omar & Zangana, 2024, 2025). Ensuring seamless interoperability while maintaining security, privacy, and scalability is critical, particularly in cloud-based and IoT-integrated infrastructures (Zangana et al., 2025; Omar & Zangana, 2024). Future research should explore federated architectures, modular AI pipelines, and cross-domain integration frameworks.

8.7. Emerging Research Opportunities

Several emerging research opportunities warrant attention:

- **Explainable AI in cybersecurity and digital forensics** to improve trust and decision transparency (Kelly et al., 2020; Chaudhary, n.d.).
- **Federated and privacy-preserving AI frameworks** for sensitive applications in finance, healthcare, and environmental monitoring (Zangana & Yazdeen, 2025; Holzing et al., 2021).

- **LLM-based automation** for zero-shot vulnerability detection, ransomware mitigation, and cybersecurity education (Pearce et al., 2023; Wang, 2023; Tann et al., 2023).
- **Cross-domain AI frameworks** integrating IoT, blockchain, and AI for secure and resilient infrastructures (Karthikeyan et al., 2023; Zangana, 2025).
- **Sustainable and responsible AI deployment** in developing countries and resource-constrained environments (Aderibigbe et al., 2023; Adanma & Ogunbiyi, 2024).

In conclusion, while AI and LLMs present transformative potential across cybersecurity, digital forensics, agriculture, environmental management, and judicial systems, they also introduce multifaceted challenges. Addressing these open problems through rigorous research, interdisciplinary collaboration, and ethical implementation strategies will be crucial to unlocking the full potential of AI-driven technologies.

Figure 4 outlines a roadmap for advancing LLM defense research. It emphasizes improving robustness, explainability, cross-disciplinary collaboration, and integration of emerging technologies such as quantum cryptography.

Figure 4. Research roadmap for future defenses against adversarial attacks

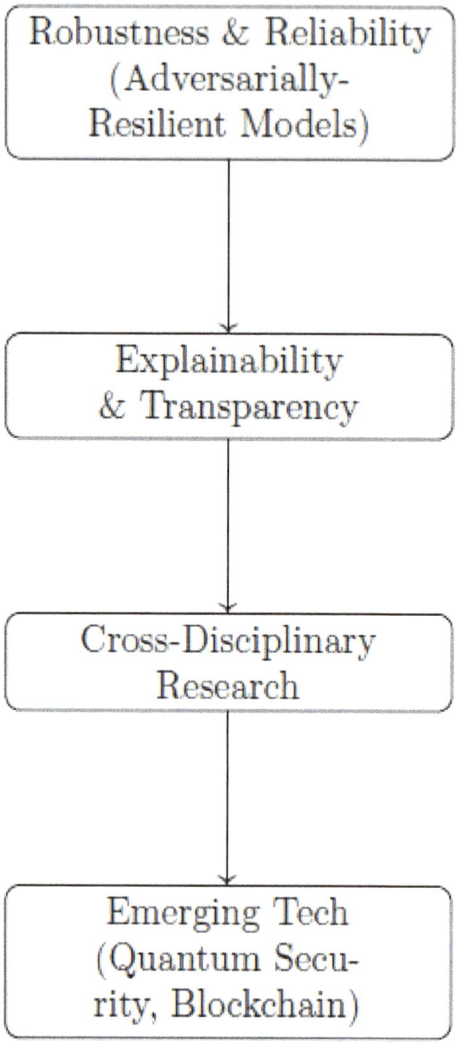

9. FUTURE DIRECTIONS

The rapid integration of artificial intelligence (AI) and large language models (LLMs) into cybersecurity, digital forensics, agriculture, and environmental management has opened numerous avenues for future research and development. Despite significant advancements, there remain critical challenges and opportunities that warrant attention to improve efficiency, security, and ethical deployment.

9.1. Enhancing AI-Driven Cybersecurity Frameworks

The deployment of AI, particularly LLMs, in cybersecurity is transforming threat detection, vulnerability assessment, and incident response (Motlagh et al., 2024; Ferrag et al., 2023). Future research should focus on developing adaptive LLMs capable of real-time identification of sophisticated threats, such as ransomware and backdoor attacks (Wang, 2023; Yang et al., 2024; Xu et al., 2024). Moreover, integrating blockchain technology with AI could enhance trust, traceability, and resilience in digital security systems, particularly in financial and banking applications (Zangana, 2025).

Expanding AI applications to predictive cybersecurity analytics could reduce response times to attacks while optimizing resource allocation for threat mitigation (Gao, 2023; Guastalla et al., 2023). Additionally, research into zero-shot and few-shot learning for vulnerability repair and automated threat analysis remains a promising direction (Pearce et al., 2023; Sultana et al., 2023; Jin et al., 2024).

9.2. AI in Digital Forensics and Incident Response

Digital forensics is increasingly leveraging AI to automate evidence analysis, pattern recognition, and cybercrime investigation (Jarrett & Choo, 2021; Adam & Varol, 2020; Dunsin et al., 2024). Future directions include enhancing AI's ability to handle constrained environments, such as IoT and edge devices, which require efficient algorithms for data extraction and anomaly detection (Dunsin et al., 2022; Tyagi et al., 2024).

Research should also focus on explainable AI models for forensics, ensuring transparency and interpretability of findings for legal and regulatory contexts (Kelly et al., 2020; Bhawna & Mahajan, 2024). Integrating AI with blockchain could further strengthen the integrity and provenance of digital evidence (Karthikeyan et al., 2023; Omar & Zangana, 2024).

9.3. Ethical, Privacy, and Regulatory Considerations

With the widespread adoption of AI and LLMs, ethical and privacy challenges have become more pronounced (Alawida et al., 2023; Kaushik et al., 2024). Future research must develop guidelines for responsible AI deployment, particularly in sensitive domains like cybersecurity, agriculture, and environmental monitoring (Alexander et al., 2024; Abd-Elsalam & Abdel-Momen, 2023).

Techniques such as federated learning and privacy-preserving AI models can mitigate risks associated with data breaches and misuse (Zangana & Yazdeen, 2025; Neupane et al., 2024). Policymakers and researchers must collaborate to establish global standards and regulatory frameworks that balance innovation with security, accountability, and user privacy (Aderibigbe et al., 2023; Al-Hawawreh et al., 2023; Yao et al., 2024).

9.4. AI in Agriculture, Environmental Sustainability, and Smart Systems

AI and LLMs present significant opportunities for transforming agriculture and environmental management. Precision agriculture, predictive modeling, and sustainable resource management can benefit from AI-enabled decision support systems (Chen et al., 2024; Shafik et al., 2025; Aggarwal et al., 2024; Araújo et al., 2021).

Future research should investigate AI-driven approaches for climate risk assessment, environmental conservation, and cyber-physical security in agricultural systems (Adanma & Ogunbiyi, 2024; Malhotra & Firdaus, 2022; He et al., 2021). Additionally, integrating AI with IoT and edge computing could enhance real-time monitoring and responsiveness in smart agricultural and environmental systems (Nguyen et al., 2018; Zangana et al., 2025).

9.5. Advanced Human-Centered AI and Trustworthy Systems

The evolution of human-centered AI remains a critical research direction, particularly in applications requiring collaboration between autonomous systems and human decision-makers (He et al., 2021; Morić et al., 2025). Ensuring AI systems are transparent, interpretable, and aligned with human values will be central to building trust in cybersecurity, agriculture, and judicial decision-making frameworks (Morić et al., 2025; Aithal & Aithal, 2023).

Additionally, research should explore AI-enhanced resilience in SMEs, government agencies, and critical infrastructure, focusing on adversarial robustness, model verification, and ethical deployment (Kereopa-Yorke, 2024; Marshall, 2023; Vladescu et al., 2021).

9.6. Addressing Technical Challenges and Adversarial Risks

LLMs and AI systems face ongoing technical challenges, including adversarial attacks, model bias, and scalability issues (Gennari et al., 2024; Motlagh et al., 2024;

Alawida et al., 2023). Future research should focus on developing robust models resistant to manipulation while maintaining high performance in real-world tasks (Tihanyi et al., 2024; Jiang, 2024).

Techniques like reinforcement learning, continual learning, and hybrid AI architectures may improve system adaptability and resilience against evolving cyber threats (Ferrag et al., 2023; Omar & Zangana, 2025; Wright et al., 2012).

9.7. Cross-Domain Integration and Interdisciplinary Research

Finally, the convergence of AI with other emerging technologies—such as blockchain, robotics, IoT, and edge computing—offers expansive opportunities for interdisciplinary research (Kochupillai et al., 2022; Zangana & Yazdeen, 2025). By bridging cybersecurity, digital forensics, environmental sustainability, and agricultural innovation, future studies can develop holistic AI solutions capable of tackling complex, multi-faceted challenges (Holzinger et al., 2021; Adanma & Ogunbiyi, 2024).

Emerging frameworks that incorporate ethical AI, explainability, and secure data pipelines will be pivotal in ensuring that AI-driven advancements are both effective and trustworthy (Abd-Elsalam & Abdel-Momen, 2023; Aghaei et al., 2022; Aldoseri et al., 2023).

9.8. Summary

Future research in AI and LLMs should focus on enhancing cybersecurity resilience, advancing digital forensics, addressing ethical and regulatory challenges, and integrating AI across sectors such as agriculture and environmental sustainability. Robust, human-centered, and trustworthy AI systems, coupled with interdisciplinary approaches, will define the next frontier in AI-driven innovation and security.

10. CONCLUSION

In recent years, the integration of artificial intelligence and large language models into cybersecurity, digital forensics, agriculture, and environmental management has fundamentally transformed these domains. This chapter has highlighted how AI-driven solutions are enhancing threat detection, automating incident response, and improving decision-making processes across complex and dynamic environments. Despite these advances, significant challenges persist, including ethical considerations, privacy concerns, adversarial vulnerabilities, and the need for transparent, human-centered systems.

The rapid evolution of AI technologies presents both opportunities and risks. On one hand, intelligent systems can optimize operational efficiency, reduce human error, and enable proactive management of cybersecurity threats and environmental challenges. On the other hand, emerging threats such as model manipulation, data breaches, and biased decision-making highlight the need for robust frameworks, continuous monitoring, and interdisciplinary collaboration. Future AI implementations must therefore balance innovation with responsibility, ensuring that technological progress does not compromise security, fairness, or trustworthiness.

Moreover, the expansion of AI applications into agriculture, environmental sustainability, and enterprise systems underscores the importance of cross-domain integration. By leveraging AI alongside complementary technologies such as blockchain, IoT, and edge computing, organizations can develop holistic, resilient solutions that address complex real-world problems. Human-centered AI, combined with explainability and ethical governance, will be critical in fostering trust among users and stakeholders, while enabling systems that are adaptable, secure, and reliable.

In conclusion, the transformative potential of AI and LLMs is undeniable, yet realizing this potential requires careful attention to ethical, technical, and regulatory considerations. Ongoing research and innovation must focus on building robust, transparent, and responsible AI systems that can effectively address emerging cybersecurity threats, improve digital forensic investigations, and support sustainable and intelligent decision-making across diverse sectors. By adopting a forward-looking, interdisciplinary approach, researchers and practitioners can harness AI's capabilities to drive meaningful, trustworthy, and long-lasting impact.

REFERENCES

Abd-Elsalam, K. A., & Abdel-Momen, S. M. (2023). Artificial intelligence's development and challenges in scientific writing. *Egyptian Journal of Agricultural Research, 101*(3), 714–717. DOI: 10.21608/ejar.2023.220363.1414

Adam, I. Y., & Varol, C. (2020, June). Intelligence in digital forensics process. In *2020 8th International Symposium on Digital Forensics and Security (ISDFS)* (pp. 1-6). IEEE. DOI: 10.1109/ISDFS49300.2020.9116442

Adanma, U. M., & Ogunbiyi, E. O.Uwaga Monica AdanmaEmmanuel Olurotimi Ogunbiyi. (2024). Artificial intelligence in environmental conservation: Evaluating cyber risks and opportunities for sustainable practices. *Computer Science & IT Research Journal, 5*(5), 1178–1209. DOI: 10.51594/csitrj.v5i5.1156

Aderibigbe, A. O., Ohenhen, P. E., Nwaobia, N. K., Gidiagba, J. O., & Ani, E. C.Adebayo Olusegun AderibigbePeter Efosa OhenhenNwabueze Kelvin Nwaobia-Joachim Osheyor GidiagbaEmmanuel Chigozie Ani. (2023). Artificial intelligence in developing countries: Bridging the gap between potential and implementation. *Computer Science & IT Research Journal, 4*(3), 185–199. DOI: 10.51594/csitrj.v4i3.629

Aggarwal, S., Bansal, S., & Goel, R. (2024). Ai In Agriculture: A Looming Challenge, A Gleaming Opportunity. *International Journal of Engineering Science and Humanities, 14*(Special Issue 1), 43-52.

Aghaei, E., Niu, X., Shadid, W., & Al-Shaer, E. (2022, October). Securebert: A domain-specific language model for cybersecurity. In International Conference on Security and Privacy in Communication Systems (pp. 39-56). Cham: Springer Nature Switzerland.

Aithal, P. S., & Aithal, S. (2023). Application of ChatGPT in higher education and research–A futuristic analysis. [IJAEML]. *International Journal of Applied Engineering and Management Letters, 7*(3), 168–194. DOI: 10.47992/IJAEML.2581.7000.0193

Al-Hawawreh, M., Aljuhani, A., & Jararweh, Y. (2023). Chatgpt for cybersecurity: Practical applications, challenges, and future directions. *Cluster Computing, 26*(6), 3421–3436. DOI: 10.1007/s10586-023-04124-5

Alawida, M., Mejri, S., Mehmood, A., Chikhaoui, B., & Isaac Abiodun, O. (2023). A comprehensive study of ChatGPT: Advancements, limitations, and ethical considerations in natural language processing and cybersecurity. *Information (Basel), 14*(8), 462. DOI: 10.3390/info14080462

Aldoseri, A., Al-Khalifa, K. N., & Hamouda, A. M. (2023). Re-Thinking Data Strategy and Integration for Artificial Intelligence: Concepts, Opportunities, and Challenges. *Applied Sciences (Basel, Switzerland), 13*(12), 7082. DOI: 10.3390/app13127082

Alexander, C. S., Yarborough, M., & Smith, A. (2024). Who is responsible for 'responsible AI'?: Navigating challenges to build trust in AI agriculture and food system technology. *Precision Agriculture, 25*(1), 146–185. DOI: 10.1007/s11119-023-10063-3

Ameri, K., Hempel, M., Sharif, H., Lopez, J.Jr, & Perumalla, K. (2021). Cybert: Cybersecurity claim classification by fine-tuning the bert language model. *Journal of Cybersecurity and Privacy, 1*(4), 615–637. DOI: 10.3390/jcp1040031

Araújo, S. O., Peres, R. S., Barata, J., Lidon, F., & Ramalho, J. C. (2021). Characterising the agriculture 4.0 landscape—Emerging trends, challenges and opportunities. *Agronomy (Basel), 11*(4), 667. DOI: 10.3390/agronomy11040667

Bahrini, A., Khamoshifar, M., Abbasimehr, H., Riggs, R. J., Esmaeili, M., Majdabadkohne, R. M., & Pasehvar, M. (2023, April). ChatGPT: Applications, opportunities, and threats. In *2023 Systems and Information Engineering Design Symposium (SIEDS)* (pp. 274-279). IEEE. DOI: 10.1109/SIEDS58326.2023.10137850

Bhawna, & Mahajan, S. (2024). Artificial Intelligence Perspective on Digital Forensics. *Applying Artificial Intelligence in Cybersecurity Analytics and Cyber Threat Detection*, 33-44. Chaudhary, P. K. AI, ML, AND LARGE LANGUAGE MODELS IN CYBERSECURITY.

Chen, T., Lv, L., Wang, D., Zhang, J., Yang, Y., Zhao, Z., & Tao, D. (2024). Empowering agrifood system with artificial intelligence: A survey of the progress, challenges and opportunities. *ACM Computing Surveys, 57*(2), 1–37.

Costantini, S., De Gasperis, G., & Olivieri, R. (2019). Digital forensics and investigations meet artificial intelligence. *Annals of Mathematics and Artificial Intelligence, 86*(1), 193–229. DOI: 10.1007/s10472-019-09632-y

Dunsin, D., Ghanem, M. C., Ouazzane, K., & Vassilev, V. (2024). A comprehensive analysis of the role of artificial intelligence and machine learning in modern digital forensics and incident response. *Forensic Science International Digital Investigation, 48*, 301675. DOI: 10.1016/j.fsidi.2023.301675

Dunsin, D., Ghanem, M. C., & Quazzane, K. (2022). The use of artificial intelligence in digital forensics and incident response in a constrained environment. *International Journal of Information and Communication Engineering, 16*(8), 280–285.

Ferrag, M. A., Ndhlovu, M., Tihanyi, N., Cordeiro, L. C., Debbah, M., & Lestable, T. (2023). Revolutionizing cyber threat detection with large language models. arXiv preprint arXiv:2306.14263.

Gao, M. (2023). The Advance of GPTs and Language Model in Cyber Security. Highlights in Science. *Engineering and Technology*, *57*, 195–202.

Gennari, J., Lau, S. H., Perl, S., Parish, J., & Sastry, G. (2024). CONSIDERATIONS FOR EVALUATING LARGE LANGUAGE MODELS FOR CYBERSECURITY TASKS.

Georgescu, T. M. (2020). Natural language processing model for automatic analysis of cybersecurity-related documents. *Symmetry*, *12*(3), 354. DOI: 10.3390/sym12030354

Groumpos, P. P. (2023, July). A critical historic overview of artificial intelligence: Issues, challenges, opportunities, and threats. *Artificial Intelligence and Applications (Commerce, Calif.)*, *1*(4), 181–197.

Guastalla, M., Li, Y., Hekmati, A., & Krishnamachari, B. (2023, October). Application of Large Language Models to DDoS Attack Detection. In International Conference on Security and Privacy in Cyber-Physical Systems and Smart Vehicles (pp. 83-99). Cham: Springer Nature Switzerland.

Gupta, B. B., Gaurav, A., & Arya, V. (2024). Navigating the security landscape of large language models in enterprise information systems. *Enterprise Information Systems*, *18*(4), 2310846. DOI: 10.1080/17517575.2024.2310846

Happe, A., & Cito, J. (2023, November). Getting pwn'd by ai: Penetration testing with large language models. In *Proceedings of the 31st ACM Joint European Software Engineering Conference and Symposium on the Foundations of Software Engineering* (pp. 2082-2086). DOI: 10.1145/3611643.3613083

He, H., Gray, J., Cangelosi, A., Meng, Q., McGinnity, T. M., & Mehnen, J. (2021). The challenges and opportunities of human-centered AI for trustworthy robots and autonomous systems. *IEEE Transactions on Cognitive and Developmental Systems*, *14*(4), 1398–1412. DOI: 10.1109/TCDS.2021.3132282

Holzinger, A., Weippl, E., Tjoa, A. M., & Kieseberg, P. (2021, August). Digital transformation for sustainable development goals (sdgs)-a security, safety and privacy perspective on ai. In *International cross-domain conference for machine learning and knowledge extraction* (pp. 1-20). Cham: Springer International Publishing.

Iqbal, F., Debbabi, M., Fung, B. C., Iqbal, F., Debbabi, M., & Fung, B. C. (2020). Artificial intelligence and digital forensics. *Machine Learning for Authorship Attribution and Cyber Forensics*, 139-150.

Irons, A., & Lallie, H. S. (2014). Digital forensics to intelligent forensics. *Future Internet*, *6*(3), 584–596. DOI: 10.3390/fi6030584

Jarrett, A., & Choo, K. K. R. (2021). The impact of automation and artificial intelligence on digital forensics. *WIREs Forensic Science*, *3*(6), e1418. DOI: 10.1002/wfs2.1418

Jeong, D. (2020). Artificial intelligence security threat, crime, and forensics: Taxonomy and open issues. *IEEE Access : Practical Innovations, Open Solutions*, *8*, 184560–184574. DOI: 10.1109/ACCESS.2020.3029280

Jiang, L. (2024). Detecting scams using large language models. arXiv preprint arXiv:2402.03147.

Jin, J., Tang, B., Ma, M., Liu, X., Wang, Y., Lai, Q., . . . Zhou, C. (2024). Crimson: Empowering Strategic Reasoning in Cybersecurity through Large Language Models. arXiv preprint arXiv:2403.00878. DOI: 10.1109/ICCBD-AI65562.2024.00011

Karthikeyan, P., Pande, H. M., & Sarveshwaran, V. (Eds.). (2023). *Artificial intelligence and blockchain in digital forensics*. CRC Press.

Kaushik, K., Khan, A., Kumari, A., Sharma, I., & Dubey, R. (2024). Ethical considerations in AI-based cybersecurity. In *Next-generation cybersecurity: AI, ML, and Blockchain* (pp. 437–470). Springer Nature Singapore. DOI: 10.1007/978-981-97-1249-6_19

Kelly, L., Sachan, S., Ni, L., Almaghrabi, F., Allmendinger, R., & Chen, Y. (2020). *Explainable artificial intelligence for digital forensics: opportunities, challenges and a drug testing case study*. Digital Forensic Science.

Kereopa-Yorke, B. (2024). Building resilient SMEs: Harnessing large language models for cyber security in Australia. Journal of AI. *Robotics & Workplace Automation*, *3*(1), 15–27. DOI: 10.69554/XSQZ3232

Kochupillai, M., Kahl, M., Schmitt, M., Taubenböck, H., & Zhu, X. X. (2022). Earth observation and artificial intelligence: Understanding emerging ethical issues and opportunities. *IEEE Geoscience and Remote Sensing Magazine*, *10*(4), 90–124. DOI: 10.1109/MGRS.2022.3208357

Malhotra, K., & Firdaus, M. (2022). Application of artificial intelligence in IoT security for crop yield prediction. *ResearchBerg Review of Science and Technology*, *2*(1), 136–157.

Marshall, J. (2023). What effects do large language models have on cybersecurity.

Mendsaikhan, O., Hasegawa, H., Yamaguchi, Y., & Shimada, H. (2019, July). Identification of cybersecurity specific content using the Doc2Vec language model. In 2019 IEEE 43rd annual computer software and applications conference (COMPSAC) (Vol. 1, pp. 396-401). IEEE. DOI: 10.1109/COMPSAC.2019.00064

Morić, Z., Dakić, V., & Urošev, S. (2025). An AI-Based Decision Support System Utilizing Bayesian Networks for Judicial Decision-Making. *Systems*, *13*(2), 131. DOI: 10.3390/systems13020131

Motlagh, F. N., Hajizadeh, M., Majd, M., Najafi, P., Cheng, F., & Meinel, C. (2024). Large Language Models in Cybersecurity: State-of-the-Art. arXiv preprint arXiv:2402.00891.

Moustafa, N. (2022). *Digital Forensics in the Era of Artificial Intelligence*. CRC Press. DOI: 10.1201/9781003278962

Neupane, S., Mitra, S., Fernandez, I. A., Saha, S., Mittal, S., Chen, J., Pillai, N., & Rahimi, S. (2024). Security considerations in ai-robotics: A survey of current methods, challenges, and opportunities. *IEEE Access : Practical Innovations, Open Solutions*, *12*, 22072–22097. DOI: 10.1109/ACCESS.2024.3363657

Nguyen, V., Mohammed, D., Omar, M., & Banisakher, M. (2018). The Effects of the FCC Net Neutrality Repeal on Security and Privacy. [IJHIoT]. *International Journal of Hyperconnectivity and the Internet of Things*, *2*(2), 21–29. DOI: 10.4018/IJHIoT.2018070102

Omar, M., & Zangana, H. M. (Eds.). (2024). *Redefining Security With Cyber AI*. IGI Global., DOI: 10.4018/979-8-3693-6517-5

Omar, M., & Zangana, H. M. (Eds.). (2025). *Application of Large Language Models (LLMs) for Software Vulnerability Detection*. IGI Global., DOI: 10.4018/979-8-3693-9311-6

Pearce, H., Tan, B., Ahmad, B., Karri, R., & Dolan-Gavitt, B. (2023, May). Examining zero-shot vulnerability repair with large language models. In *2023 IEEE Symposium on Security and Privacy (SP)* (pp. 2339-2356). IEEE. DOI: 10.1109/SP46215.2023.10179420

Ranade, P., Piplai, A., Joshi, A., & Finin, T. (2021, December). Cybert: Contextualized embeddings for the cybersecurity domain. In 2021 IEEE International Conference on Big Data (Big Data) (pp. 3334-3342). IEEE.

Shafik, W., Tufail, A., De Silva, C. L., Haji, R. A. A., & Apong, M. (2025). The Role, Application, and Impact of Artificial Intelligence in the Agriculture Industry. In *Future Tech Startups and Innovation in the Age of AI* (pp. 36–60). CRC Press.

Sultana, M., Taylor, A., Li, L., & Majumdar, S. (2023, October). Towards Evaluation and Understanding of Large Language Models for Cyber Operation Automation. In *2023 IEEE Conference on Communications and Network Security (CNS)* (pp. 1-6). IEEE. DOI: 10.1109/CNS59707.2023.10288677

Tann, W., Liu, Y., Sim, J. H., Seah, C. M., & Chang, E. C. (2023). Using large language models for cybersecurity capture-the-flag challenges and certification questions. arXiv preprint arXiv:2308.10443.

Tihanyi, N., Ferrag, M. A., Jain, R., & Debbah, M. (2024). CyberMetric: A Benchmark Dataset for Evaluating Large Language Models Knowledge in Cybersecurity. arXiv preprint arXiv:2402.07688.

Tyagi, A. K., Kumari, S., & Richa. (2024). Artificial Intelligence-Based Cyber Security and Digital Forensics: A Review. *Artificial Intelligence-Enabled Digital Twin for Smart Manufacturing*, 391-419.

Vladescu, C., Dinisor, M. A., Grigorescu, O., Corlatescu, D., Sandescu, C., & Dascalu, M. (2021, December). What are the latest cybersecurity trends? a case study grounded in language models. In 2021 23rd International Symposium on Symbolic and Numeric Algorithms for Scientific Computing (SYNASC) (pp. 140-146). IEEE.

Wang, F. (2023). Using large language models to mitigate ransomware threats.

Wright, J., Dawson, M. E.Jr, & Omar, M. (2012). Cyber security and mobile threats: The need for antivirus applications for smartphones. *Journal of Information Systems Technology and Planning*, *5*(14), 40–60.

Wright, J., Dawson, M. E.Jr, & Omar, M. (2012). Cyber security and mobile threats: The need for antivirus applications for smartphones. *Journal of Information Systems Technology and Planning*, *5*(14), 40–60.

Xu, J., Stokes, J. W., McDonald, G., Bai, X., Marshall, D., Wang, S., . . . Li, Z. (2024). AutoAttacker: A Large Language Model Guided System to Implement Automatic Cyber-attacks. arXiv preprint arXiv:2403.01038.

Yang, H., Xiang, K., Ge, M., Li, H., Lu, R., & Yu, S. (2024). A comprehensive overview of backdoor attacks in large language models within communication networks. *IEEE Network*, *38*(6), 211–218. DOI: 10.1109/MNET.2024.3367788

Yao, Y., Duan, J., Xu, K., Cai, Y., Sun, Z., & Zhang, Y. (2024). A survey on large language model (llm) security and privacy: The good, the bad, and the ugly. *High-Confidence Computing*, *4*(2), 100211. DOI: 10.1016/j.hcc.2024.100211

Zangana, H. (2025). Blockchain Technology in AI-Driven Cybersecurity: Strengthening Trust in Financial and Digital Security Systems. *Jurnal Ilmiah Computer Science*, *4*(1), 49–49. DOI: 10.58602/jics.v4i1.54

Zangana, H., Mohammed, H. S., & Husain, M. M. (2025). Transforming Cybersecurity Practices: A Comprehensive Approach to Protecting Digital Banking Assets. *Jurnal Ilmiah Computer Science*, *4*(1), 1–9. DOI: 10.58602/jics.v4i1.51

Zangana, H., & Yazdeen, A. (2025). A Federated Architecture for Enhancing Security and Scalability in IoT-Cloud Integrated Systems. *Jurnal Ilmiah Computer Science*, *4*(1), 50–59. DOI: 10.58602/jics.v4i1.55

Zangana, H. M., & Omar, M. (2020). Threats, Attacks, and Mitigations of Smartphone Security. *Academic Journal of Nawroz University*, *9*(4), 324–332. DOI: 10.25007/ajnu.v9n4a989

Chapter 6
Red Teaming and Stress-Testing Methodologies for LLM Security

Luay Albtosh
https://orcid.org/0009-0009-0338-9123
Capitol Technology University, USA & Houston Community College, USA

Widi Aribowo
https://orcid.org/0000-0002-4059-1293
Universitas Negeri Surabaya, Indonesia

ABSTRACT

The rapid adoption of large language models (LLMs) across industries has introduced new opportunities for innovation, while simultaneously creating complex security challenges. As adversarial actors exploit vulnerabilities in these models, proactive defense strategies become increasingly critical. Red teaming and stress-testing methodologies have emerged as essential mechanisms for evaluating and strengthening the resilience of LLMs against a broad spectrum of threats, including prompt injection, data poisoning, adversarial manipulation, and misuse scenarios. This chapter explores the principles, practices, and frameworks of red teaming applied to LLMs, emphasizing structured evaluation techniques, simulation of real-world attack vectors, and systematic stress-testing approaches. Furthermore, it highlights the integration of adversarial testing within development lifecycles, the importance of interdisciplinary collaboration, and the role of automation in scaling security evaluations.

DOI: 10.4018/979-8-3373-7133-7.ch006

1. INTRODUCTION

Large language models (LLMs) have rapidly emerged as transformative technologies with wide-ranging applications across cybersecurity, digital forensics, agriculture, healthcare, finance, and beyond. Their ability to process natural language at scale, generate coherent responses, and adapt to diverse contexts has positioned them as critical tools in advancing digital transformation. However, this rise has been paralleled by increasing security, ethical, and operational concerns that necessitate systematic evaluation through red teaming and stress-testing methodologies (Yao et al., 2024). These practices are designed to probe vulnerabilities, simulate adversarial behaviors, and strengthen the resilience of LLMs in real-world environments where cyber threats are evolving at unprecedented speed.

The integration of LLMs into cybersecurity has opened new avenues for both defense and attack. For example, domain-specific models such as SecureBERT (Aghaei et al., 2022) and CyberBERT (Ameri et al., 2021) demonstrate how fine-tuning enhances detection of malicious content, while contextualized embeddings such as CyBERT (Ranade et al., 2021) provide more accurate classification in cyber contexts. Similarly, advanced reasoning frameworks like Crimson (Jin et al., 2024) and AutoAttacker (Xu et al., 2024) show how adversarial use of LLMs can automate cyber-attacks at scale, reinforcing the urgency of robust stress-testing. In digital forensics, AI-powered tools are reshaping evidence analysis and investigative processes (Adam & Varol, 2020; Bhawna & Mahajan, 2024; Costantini et al., 2019; Dunsin et al., 2022; Dunsin et al., 2024; Iqbal et al., 2020; Irons & Lallie, 2014; Jarrett & Choo, 2021; Manasa & Kumar, 2022; Mitchell, 2014; Moustafa, 2022). Yet, scholars highlight persistent risks, such as adversarial exploitation of forensic algorithms (Jeong, 2020) and the weaponization of AI in cybercrime (Ganesh, 2017).

Beyond cybersecurity, LLMs are increasingly deployed in agriculture, environmental sustainability, and decision-making systems. Their contributions range from precision agriculture (Aggarwal et al., 2024; Alexander et al., 2024; Araújo et al., 2021; Chen et al., 2024; Shafik et al., 2025) to environmental conservation (Adanma & Ogunbiyi, 2024), sustainable development (Holzinger et al., 2021), and smart food systems (Abd-Elsalam & Abdel-Momen, 2023). However, researchers caution that cyber risks embedded in these applications can threaten food security, ecosystem monitoring, and climate resilience. For example, AI-enabled IoT in agriculture faces vulnerabilities in data integrity and system robustness (Malhotra & Firdaus, 2022). Similarly, ethical and governance questions remain unresolved in applying AI to agriculture and environmental systems (Kochupillai et al., 2022).

In the financial and enterprise sectors, LLMs also create both efficiencies and risks. While they enhance enterprise information security (Gupta et al., 2024) and trust-building in AI-driven ecosystems (Groumpos, 2023), they simultaneously introduce systemic vulnerabilities that malicious actors can exploit (Guastalla et al., 2023; Marshall, 2023; Wang, 2023). New research in blockchain and federated architectures further highlights opportunities for strengthening resilience in AI-driven infrastructures (Zangana, 2025; Zangana & Yazdeen, 2025; Zangana, Mohammed, & Husain, 2025).

The threat landscape for LLMs continues to evolve. Risks such as backdoor attacks in communication systems (Yang et al., 2024), prompt injection and misuse scenarios (Alawida et al., 2023), and data poisoning in adversarial contexts (Pearce et al., 2023) underscore the need for rigorous testing mechanisms. Recent work demonstrates that red teaming can expose vulnerabilities through adversarial prompting, penetration testing, and capture-the-flag (CTF) style exercises (Happe & Cito, 2023; Tann et al., 2023). Systematic benchmarks, such as CyberMetric (Tihanyi et al., 2024), and evaluations like those suggested by Gennari et al. (2024) and Sultana et al. (2023), provide structured methods to assess LLM performance under hostile conditions.

The adoption of LLMs also introduces profound ethical considerations. Scholars highlight challenges of responsible AI deployment in agriculture (Alexander et al., 2024), enterprise security (Gupta et al., 2024), and broader AI ecosystems (Kaushik et al., 2024). Issues of accountability, explainability, and trust are central to ensuring that LLMs do not exacerbate societal risks (Kelly et al., 2020; He et al., 2021). Researchers also argue for a shift from "digital forensics" to "intelligent forensics," where AI not only assists but actively shapes investigation strategies (Irons & Lallie, 2014). However, concerns over data strategies (Aldoseri et al., 2023), governance frameworks (Neupane et al., 2024), and evolving security threats in mobile and IoT systems (Mohammed et al., 2018; Nguyen et al., 2018; Wright et al., 2012; Zangana & Omar, 2020) reinforce the need for interdisciplinary approaches to stress-testing.

Against this backdrop, red teaming has emerged as a critical methodology to identify weaknesses, anticipate adversarial behavior, and validate defenses in LLM ecosystems. By simulating real-world attackers, red teams uncover systemic flaws in reasoning, security alignment, and threat resilience (Motlagh et al., 2024). Stress-testing, on the other hand, subjects LLMs to extreme, adversarial, and unanticipated conditions to evaluate their robustness across contexts. Together, these approaches form the backbone of resilient LLM security practices and align with recent scholarly calls to redefine cybersecurity with AI-driven paradigms (Omar & Zangana, 2024; Omar & Zangana, 2025).

This chapter contributes to this growing discourse by offering a structured analysis of red teaming and stress-testing methodologies in the context of LLMs. It builds on prior work in cybersecurity, digital forensics, AI ethics, and applied domains to highlight emerging best practices, open challenges, and future research directions. Ultimately, securing LLMs requires not only technical innovation but also a commitment to interdisciplinary collaboration across security research, governance, and real-world applications.

2. BACKGROUND AND MOTIVATION

The rapid evolution of artificial intelligence (AI) and large language models (LLMs) has significantly transformed multiple domains, including cybersecurity, digital forensics, agriculture, and environmental management. The integration of AI into these sectors promises enhanced decision-making, automation, and predictive capabilities, but also brings forth substantial technical, ethical, and operational challenges (Abd-Elsalam & Abdel-Momen, 2023; Adam & Varol, 2020; Adanma & Ogunbiyi, 2024). Understanding the background and motivation behind leveraging AI technologies is critical to harnessing their potential while mitigating associated risks.

2.1 AI in Cybersecurity and Digital Forensics

Cybersecurity is increasingly threatened by sophisticated attacks that require advanced intelligence for timely detection and response. The adoption of AI and machine learning in digital forensics enables automated threat analysis, anomaly detection, and pattern recognition, facilitating proactive security measures (Chaudhary, P. K.; Dunsin, Ghanem, & Ouazzane, 2024; Costantini, De Gasperis, & Olivieri, 2019; Iqbal, Debbabi, & Fung, 2020). LLMs, in particular, have demonstrated potential in identifying vulnerabilities, automating incident responses, and improving penetration testing processes (Bhawna & Mahajan, 2024; Happe & Cito, 2023; Jin et al., 2024; Xu et al., 2024). The increasing sophistication of cyber threats, such as ransomware, phishing, and backdoor attacks, necessitates advanced AI-driven systems for predictive threat modeling and automated mitigation (Yang et al., 2024; Wang, 2023; Zangana, 2025).

2.2 AI in Agriculture and Environmental Management

Beyond cybersecurity, AI has significantly impacted the agriculture and environmental sectors. The emergence of Agriculture 4.0 emphasizes the integration of AI with IoT, robotics, and precision farming technologies to optimize yield, monitor crop health, and enable data-driven decision-making (Aggarwal, Bansal, & Goel, 2024; Araújo et al., 2021; Chen et al., 2024; Shafik et al., 2025). AI-driven solutions also support sustainable practices by monitoring environmental conditions, predicting ecological risks, and facilitating resource-efficient farming (Adanma & Ogunbiyi, 2024; Alexander, Yarborough, & Smith, 2024; Malhotra & Firdaus, 2022;

Kochupillai et al., 2022). However, challenges such as data privacy, technological adoption barriers, and cyber vulnerabilities in agricultural systems remain significant (Aderibigbe et al., 2023; Aldoseri et al., 2023; Guastalla et al., 2023).

2.3 Motivations for LLM Integration

The development of LLMs, such as GPT-based architectures, has opened new avenues for automating complex tasks across domains. In cybersecurity, LLMs assist in vulnerability detection, threat intelligence extraction, and security automation (Ferrag et al., 2023; Motlagh et al., 2024; Sultana et al., 2023; Tann et al., 2023). In research and education, AI models facilitate literature synthesis, data analysis, and academic writing, improving productivity and enhancing knowledge dissemination (Abd-Elsalam & Abdel-Momen, 2023; Aithal & Aithal, 2023; Alawida et al., 2023). These capabilities motivate organizations and researchers to invest in AI-powered frameworks that combine predictive analytics, decision support, and ethical AI deployment strategies (Kaushik et al., 2024; He et al., 2021; Holtzinger et al., 2021).

2.4 Challenges and Opportunities

While AI provides immense opportunities, it introduces multiple challenges that motivate research and practical interventions. Key issues include algorithmic bias, adversarial attacks, interpretability of AI decisions, and integration with legacy systems (Groumpos, 2023; Jiang, 2024; Nguyen et al., 2018; Pearce et al., 2023). In cybersecurity, LLMs can themselves be exploited, creating novel attack vectors such as data poisoning, prompt injection, and backdoor vulnerabilities (Gao, 2023; Marshall, 2023; Yao et al., 2024). Furthermore, AI adoption in developing countries often faces infrastructural, regulatory, and skill-related constraints (Aderibigbe et al., 2023; Zangana & Yazdeen, 2025). These challenges highlight the need for a hybrid approach that balances AI's predictive power with robust security, ethical considerations, and explainable decision-making.

2.5 Strategic Rationale

The motivation for advancing AI and LLM integration stems from the need to develop intelligent, resilient, and adaptive systems across sectors. In cybersecurity and digital forensics, AI-driven decision support frameworks can enhance threat detection, automate incident responses, and improve overall system resilience (Ameri et al., 2021; Ranade et al., 2021; Vladescu et al., 2021). In agriculture and environmental conservation, AI applications help optimize resource utilization, reduce environmental impact, and foster sustainability (Aggarwal et al., 2024; Araújo et al., 2021; Adanma & Ogunbiyi, 2024). By addressing these challenges and leveraging AI's potential, organizations can achieve operational efficiency, informed decision-making, and strategic advantage in a digitally evolving landscape (Omar & Zangana, 2024, 2025; Morić, Dakić, & Urošev, 2025).

2.6 Summary

In summary, the convergence of AI, LLMs, and domain-specific applications represents both a transformative opportunity and a complex challenge. The background of AI adoption highlights its relevance across cybersecurity, agriculture, and digital forensics, while the motivations emphasize the necessity for intelligent, secure, and explainable systems. The following sections of this chapter will explore state-of-the-art frameworks, methodologies, and case studies that address these challenges and illustrate AI's practical impact across sectors.

3. CONCEPT OF RED TEAMING IN AI SECURITY

Red teaming, a well-established practice in cybersecurity, has emerged as a critical methodology for evaluating and fortifying AI systems against sophisticated threats. At its core, red teaming involves simulating realistic adversarial attacks on AI models, networks, and infrastructures to identify vulnerabilities that traditional security testing might overlook (Omar & Zangana, 2024; Xu et al., 2024). Unlike conventional penetration testing, which often focuses on technical weaknesses, red teaming encompasses strategic, operational, and human factors, making it particularly relevant for AI-driven environments (Adam & Varol, 2020; Bhawna & Mahajan, 2024).

This bar chart displays the various types of security vulnerabilities that large language models face, such as adversarial inputs, data poisoning, and model inversion. Each bar represents the frequency or severity of these vulnerabilities based on recent studies.

Figure 1. Prevalence of Security Vulnerabilities in AI Systems

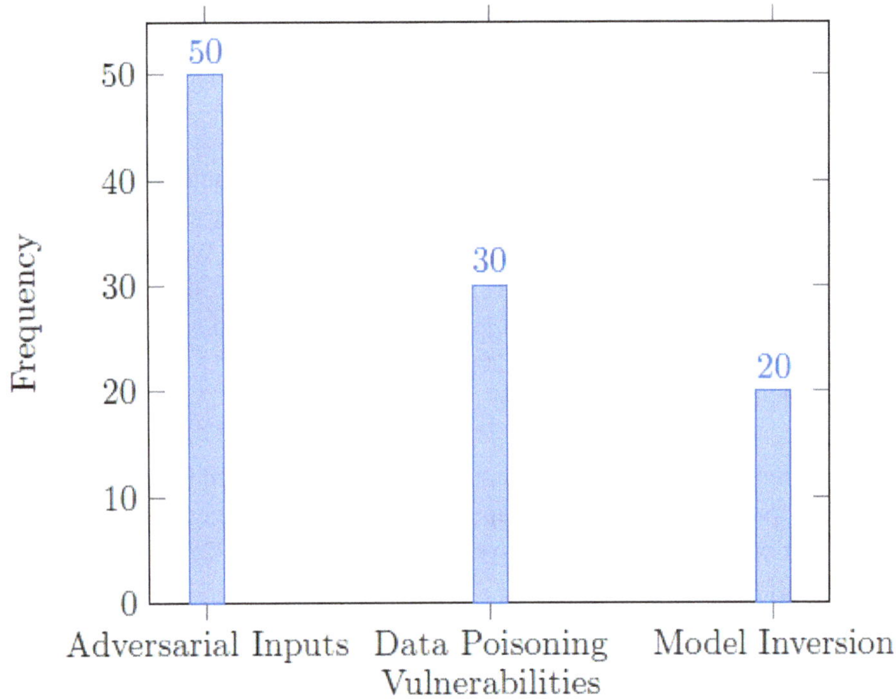

3.1 Importance in AI Security

AI systems, particularly those utilizing large language models (LLMs) and other machine learning architectures, face a unique spectrum of threats, including adversarial inputs, data poisoning, model inversion, and prompt injection attacks (Ferrag et al., 2023; Motlagh et al., 2024; Jin et al., 2024). These vulnerabilities are exacerbated by the opaque nature of many AI models, where decision-making processes are difficult to interpret or predict (Kelly et al., 2020; He et al., 2021). Red teaming serves as a proactive defense mechanism, allowing organizations to anticipate and mitigate these risks before malicious actors can exploit them (Gupta et al., 2024; Alawida et al., 2023).

In addition, red teaming aligns with ethical and regulatory imperatives in AI deployment, ensuring compliance with cybersecurity standards and fostering trust among stakeholders (Kaushik et al., 2024; Alexander et al., 2024; Zangana, 2025). For critical sectors such as healthcare, finance, and autonomous systems, the consequences of untested vulnerabilities can be catastrophic, reinforcing the need for rigorous red teaming exercises (Neupane et al., 2024; Morić et al., 2025; Shafik et al., 2025).

3.2 Methodologies and Frameworks

Red teaming in AI security typically involves a combination of automated and manual approaches. Automated tools leverage AI-driven simulations to generate attack vectors, while manual techniques rely on expert adversaries to probe system weaknesses creatively (Happe & Cito, 2023; Xu et al., 2024; Wang, 2023). Some frameworks adopt hybrid strategies, combining AI-guided automated attacks with human-driven strategic analysis to improve coverage and realism (Gennari et al., 2024; Sultana et al., 2023; Jin et al., 2024).

Key methodologies include:

1. **Adversarial Testing:** Crafting inputs specifically designed to mislead or confuse AI models, exposing vulnerabilities in natural language processing, image recognition, or decision-making systems (Aghaei et al., 2022; Jiang, 2024; Yang et al., 2024).
2. **Scenario-based Simulations:** Emulating real-world attacks, such as phishing or ransomware campaigns, to evaluate the AI system's resilience and response strategies (Guastalla et al., 2023; Vladescu et al., 2021; Wright et al., 2012).
3. **Model Evaluation Benchmarks:** Utilizing datasets and challenge environments to measure an AI system's robustness against known attack patterns, including zero-shot and few-shot adversarial exploits (Pearce et al., 2023; Tihanyi et al., 2024; Motlagh et al., 2024).

Table 1 compares different red teaming methodologies, highlighting their strengths and weaknesses. It categorizes approaches such as adversarial testing, scenario-based simulations, and model evaluation benchmarks, providing a clear overview for practitioners.

Table 1. Comparison of Red Teaming Methodologies

Methodology	Strengths	Weaknesses
Adversarial Testing	High Precision	Requires Expertise
Scenario-Based Simulations	Realistic Scenarios	Time-Consuming
Model Evaluation Benchmarks	Standardized Metrics	May Lack Context

3.3 Applications Across Domains

Red teaming has proven effective in multiple AI domains. In cybersecurity, red teaming helps identify exploitable weaknesses in enterprise information systems and digital forensics pipelines (Ameri et al., 2021; Chaudhary, n.d.; Dunsin et al., 2024). In agriculture and environmental management, red teaming ensures AI-driven decision support tools remain reliable and secure against malicious manipulation (Aggarwal et al., 2024; Araújo et al., 2021; Adanma & Ogunbiyi, 2024; Alexander et al., 2024). In AI-driven financial systems, red teaming safeguards against fraudulent activities and ensures compliance with regulatory frameworks (Zangana et al., 2025; Omar & Zangana, 2025).

Moreover, the integration of red teaming into AI development cycles supports continuous learning and improvement, allowing AI systems to adapt to emerging threats in real-time (Aldoseri et al., 2023; Al-Hawawreh et al., 2023; Bahrini et al., 2023). This adaptive security paradigm aligns with the evolving landscape of cyber threats and the increasing deployment of LLMs in mission-critical applications (Gao, 2023; Marshall, 2023; Motlagh et al., 2024).

3.4 Challenges and Limitations

Despite its benefits, implementing red teaming in AI security faces several challenges. Resource constraints, lack of skilled personnel, and the complexity of AI models can hinder the effectiveness of red teaming exercises (Omar & Zangana, 2024; Dunsin et al., 2022; Iqbal et al., 2020). Ethical considerations, including the potential for misuse of red teaming knowledge or inadvertent exposure of sensitive data, must also be addressed (Kaushik et al., 2024; Holzinger et al., 2021; Abd-Elsalam & Abdel-Momen, 2023). Furthermore, the fast-paced evolution of AI technology requires continuous adaptation of red teaming techniques to stay ahead of emerging threats (Jeong, 2020; Yang et al., 2024; Yao et al., 2024).

3.5 Future Perspectives

Looking forward, the integration of AI-driven automation within red teaming promises enhanced scalability and precision (Jin et al., 2024; Xu et al., 2024; Wang, 2023). The development of domain-specific LLMs, such as SecureBERT, further enables targeted testing of cybersecurity infrastructures (Aghaei et al., 2022). Collaborative approaches that combine federated learning, blockchain security mechanisms, and continuous monitoring can strengthen the resilience of AI systems while preserving privacy and data integrity (Zangana & Yazdeen, 2025; Zangana, 2025). These advancements underscore the strategic role of red teaming as a cornerstone of AI security in an era of increasingly intelligent and autonomous systems (Omar & Zangana, 2025; Motlagh et al., 2024; Tann et al., 2023).

4. STRESS-TESTING METHODOLOGIES FOR LLMS

The proliferation of Large Language Models (LLMs) in domains ranging from cybersecurity to agriculture and digital forensics has necessitated rigorous evaluation frameworks to ensure their robustness, reliability, and security under extreme and adversarial conditions (Aghaei, Niu, Shadid, & Al-Shaer, 2022; Motlagh et al., 2024). Stress-testing, as a methodology, evaluates an LLM's performance, resilience, and susceptibility to errors under high-stakes, edge-case, or maliciously crafted scenarios. This section delves into methodologies and best practices for stress-testing LLMs across multiple domains.

4.1. Adversarial Input Testing

Adversarial testing involves feeding LLMs with inputs intentionally designed to expose vulnerabilities, such as prompts with misleading information, ambiguous contexts, or malicious commands. Studies have shown that even advanced models can generate harmful outputs or fail to recognize threats when exposed to cleverly crafted inputs (Ferrag et al., 2023; Xu et al., 2024; Happe & Cito, 2023). Adversarial input testing is crucial in domains like cybersecurity, where LLMs are used to automate incident response or threat detection (Guastalla, Li, Hekmati, & Krishnamachari, 2023; Jin et al., 2024).

Techniques include:

- **Perturbation analysis:** Minor alterations in input text to test model stability (Jiang, 2024; Tihanyi, Ferrag, Jain, & Debbah, 2024).
- **Injection attacks:** Inserting malicious instructions to evaluate model safety (Yang, Xiang, Ge, Li, Lu, & Yu, 2024; Yao et al., 2024).
- **Contextual manipulation:** Providing contradictory or incomplete data to assess reasoning robustness (Sultana, Taylor, Li, & Majumdar, 2023).

4.2. Load and Performance Stress Testing

Performance under high computational load is essential for LLM deployment in real-world environments. Stress-testing models for latency, throughput, and resource consumption ensures scalability without compromising functionality (Gupta,

Gaurav, & Arya, 2024; Wright, Dawson Jr, & Omar, 2012). High-volume queries, batch-processing tasks, and concurrent requests simulate peak operational loads, revealing potential bottlenecks and failure points.

Approaches include:

- Benchmarking large-scale queries using domain-specific datasets (Motlagh et al., 2024; Ranade, Piplai, Joshi, & Finin, 2021).
- Monitoring memory and GPU utilization during extreme workloads (Alawida, Mejri, Mehmood, Chikhaoui, & Isaac Abiodun, 2023; Wang, 2023).
- Evaluating degradation in response quality under simultaneous requests (Marshall, 2023).

4.3. Domain-Specific Stress Testing

LLMs applied to specialized domains, such as cybersecurity, digital forensics, and agriculture, require context-aware stress testing. These tests focus on model performance under scenarios rich with domain-specific jargon, rare events, and edge-case datasets (Aderibigbe, Ohenhen, Nwaobia, Gidiagba, & Ani, 2023; Chen et al., 2024; Araújo, Peres, Barata, Lidon, & Ramalho, 2021).

Examples include:

- **Cybersecurity simulations:** Evaluating LLMs in malware detection, vulnerability identification, or phishing prevention (Ameri, Hempel, Sharif, Lopez Jr, & Perumalla, 2021; Ferrag et al., 2023; Guastalla et al., 2023).
- **Digital forensics scenarios:** Stress-testing LLMs with encrypted logs, incomplete evidence, or ambiguous case files (Dunsin, Ghanem, Ouazzane, & Vassilev, 2024; Jarrett & Choo, 2021; Kelly et al., 2020).
- **Agricultural applications:** Testing LLM guidance on crop management or environmental risk under extreme climate conditions (Aggarwal, Bansal, & Goel, 2024; Alexander, Yarborough, & Smith, 2024; Shafik, Tufail, De Silva, Haji, & Apong, 2025).

4.4. Robustness Against Malicious Exploitation

Given the increasing use of LLMs in automated decision-making, stress-testing for security vulnerabilities has become critical. This involves evaluating susceptibility to:

- Prompt injection and backdoor attacks (Yang et al., 2024).

- Exploitation in ransomware and phishing campaigns (Wang, 2023; Xu et al., 2024).
- Misclassification and overgeneralization in zero-shot or few-shot settings (Pearce, Tan, Ahmad, Karri, & Dolan-Gavitt, 2023; Tann et al., 2023).

Testing methodologies may combine automated penetration tests with human-in-the-loop evaluations, ensuring both technical and ethical reliability (Happe & Cito, 2023; Kaushik, Khan, Kumari, Sharma, & Dubey, 2024).

4.5. Explainability and Interpretability Stress Testing

A key dimension of stress-testing involves understanding why LLMs make specific predictions or generate particular responses. Techniques include:

- Layer-wise relevance propagation and attention visualization to detect failure patterns (Abd-Elsalam & Abdel-Momen, 2023; He et al., 2021).
- Counterfactual evaluation by altering inputs to probe reasoning logic (Aithal & Aithal, 2023; Aldoseri, Al-Khalifa, & Hamouda, 2023).
- Scenario analysis to test the model's ethical reasoning in sensitive cases (Al-Hawawreh, Aljuhani, & Jararweh, 2023; Bahrini et al., 2023).

4.6. Benchmarking and Standardized Evaluation

Standardized benchmarks provide a controlled method for stress-testing LLMs, enabling comparison across models, versions, and domains. Well-known frameworks include CyberMetric (Tihanyi et al., 2024), AutoAttacker (Xu et al., 2024), and domain-specific datasets in agriculture, cybersecurity, and digital forensics (Gennari, Lau, Perl, Parish, & Sastry, 2024; Motlagh et al., 2024).

Key components:

- **Quantitative metrics:** Accuracy, F1-score, false positives/negatives (Nguyen, Mohammed, Omar, & Banisakher, 2018; Mohammed, Omar, & Nguyen, 2018).
- **Stress-test scenarios:** High-adversity prompts, multi-step reasoning, and simultaneous multi-task evaluation (Zangana, Mohammed, & Husain, 2025; Vladescu et al., 2021).
- **Continuous evaluation:** Iterative fine-tuning based on failure cases (Omar & Zangana, 2025; Marshall, 2023).

4.7. Hybrid Stress-Testing Approaches

Advanced methodologies combine automated adversarial testing, human oversight, and domain-specific simulation. These hybrid approaches provide a multidimensional perspective on model behavior, addressing both performance and security concerns (Costantini, De Gasperis, & Olivieri, 2019; Dunsin, Ghanem, & Quazzane, 2022; Motlagh et al., 2024). Incorporating synthetic datasets and scenario generation tools further strengthens the robustness evaluation (Gholami & Omar, 2023; Aghaei et al., 2022).

4.8 Conclusion of Section

Stress-testing methodologies for LLMs are essential for ensuring reliability, safety, and ethical compliance, particularly in high-stakes applications such as cybersecurity, digital forensics, and agriculture. Employing a combination of adversarial inputs, performance benchmarks, domain-specific scenarios, and interpretability analyses offers the most comprehensive evaluation strategy. As LLMs evolve, continuous stress-testing remains a cornerstone for deploying these systems responsibly and effectively (Bhawna & Mahajan, 2024; Zangana, 2025; Kereopa-Yorke, 2024).

5. TOOLS AND FRAMEWORKS FOR LLM RED TEAMING

Red teaming large language models (LLMs) involves systematically probing, stress-testing, and evaluating these AI systems to identify potential vulnerabilities, biases, and security threats before they can be exploited in real-world scenarios. This practice has become increasingly critical as LLMs are deployed across sectors such as cybersecurity, finance, healthcare, and digital forensics (Motlagh et al., 2024; Yao et al., 2024). Effective LLM red teaming relies on specialized tools and frameworks designed to simulate attacks, assess robustness, and provide actionable insights for model improvement.

5.1. Adversarial Testing Platforms

Adversarial testing platforms are central to LLM red teaming. These tools generate malicious inputs to evaluate a model's susceptibility to manipulation, prompt injection, or misinformation propagation (Xu et al., 2024; Tann et al., 2023). Examples include AutoAttacker, which automates cyber-attack simulations using LLM guidance, and Crimson, designed to test strategic reasoning capabilities in cybersecurity contexts (Jin et al., 2024; Xu et al., 2024). These platforms often provide APIs for continuous integration, enabling organizations to embed red teaming into their AI lifecycle and detect vulnerabilities early (Ferrag et al., 2023; Motlagh et al., 2024).

5.2. Benchmark Datasets and Evaluation Metrics

A critical aspect of LLM red teaming is the use of benchmark datasets tailored to security, privacy, and ethical evaluation. Tools like CyberMetric provide standardized datasets to assess an LLM's knowledge of cyber threats, attack patterns, and mitigation strategies (Tihanyi et al., 2024). Similarly, zero-shot vulnerability repair benchmarks allow testers to evaluate how well models can autonomously detect and remediate code vulnerabilities (Pearce et al., 2023). These benchmarks provide measurable insights into model performance, robustness, and reliability across diverse threat scenarios (Gennari et al., 2024; Sultana et al., 2023).

5.3. Simulation and Scenario-Based Frameworks

Simulation-based frameworks emulate real-world attack scenarios to stress-test LLMs under controlled conditions. For example, capture-the-flag (CTF) inspired frameworks allow LLMs to navigate cybersecurity challenges, uncover hidden threats, and provide solutions in real time (Tann et al., 2023). Scenario-based testing is particularly effective for evaluating LLMs in dynamic environments where adversaries continuously adapt their attack strategies (Guastalla et al., 2023; Wang, 2023). These frameworks often integrate reinforcement learning to improve the fidelity of simulated attacks and enhance model resilience.

5.4. Penetration Testing Tools for LLMs

Traditional penetration testing methodologies are evolving to accommodate LLM-specific vulnerabilities. Tools such as Red AI suites leverage both automated scripts and human-guided inputs to probe LLM weaknesses in text generation, reasoning, and decision-making processes (Happe & Cito, 2023; Al-Hawawreh et al., 2023). These tools examine the susceptibility of LLMs to prompt injections, adversarial prompts, and malicious manipulations while providing detailed reports on exploit severity, potential impact, and recommended mitigation strategies (Gupta et al., 2024; Jin et al., 2024).

5.5. Explainable AI (XAI) and Monitoring Frameworks

Explainability is essential in LLM red teaming to interpret why models fail under adversarial conditions. XAI tools such as SecureBERT and other domain-specific interpretability frameworks provide insights into decision paths, attention mechanisms, and reasoning biases in LLMs (Aghaei et al., 2022; Gennari et al., 2024). Real-time monitoring systems track model outputs and flag anomalies, enabling red teams to identify emergent vulnerabilities, including backdoor attacks and unauthorized knowledge extraction attempts (Yang et al., 2024; Yao et al., 2024). This combination of explainability and monitoring strengthens trust and accountability in LLM deployments (Kelly et al., 2020; Omar & Zangana, 2025).

5.6. Integration with Cybersecurity Platforms

LLM red teaming tools increasingly integrate with broader cybersecurity platforms to enhance threat detection and mitigation. For instance, frameworks that combine LLM capabilities with intrusion detection systems, malware analysis, or threat intelligence dashboards allow for comprehensive vulnerability assessments (Guastalla et al., 2023; Wang, 2023). Integration ensures that findings from LLM red teaming are actionable and can be directly applied to reinforce enterprise security policies, improve incident response, and mitigate ransomware or phishing threats (Wright et al., 2012; Ferrag et al., 2023).

5.7. Open-Source and Community-Driven Frameworks

Open-source frameworks foster collaboration and rapid iteration in LLM red teaming. Platforms such as LLM-adversary toolkits and GitHub repositories provide reusable scripts, datasets, and evaluation protocols that allow security researchers to continuously test, benchmark, and improve models (Marshall, 2023; Sultana et al., 2023). Community-driven initiatives facilitate knowledge sharing, enabling red teams to stay ahead of emerging attack vectors and collectively strengthen the resilience of AI systems (Bahrini et al., 2023; Motlagh et al., 2024).

5.8 Conclusion on Tools and Frameworks

In conclusion, a robust LLM red teaming ecosystem requires a combination of adversarial testing platforms, benchmark datasets, simulation frameworks, penetration testing tools, explainability frameworks, cybersecurity integration, and community-driven resources. Together, these tools enable organizations to proactively identify vulnerabilities, mitigate risks, and deploy large language models with greater security, transparency, and accountability (Yao et al., 2024; Motlagh et al., 2024; Omar & Zangana, 2025).

6. ADVERSARIAL SCENARIOS AND TEST CASES

The rapid integration of artificial intelligence (AI), particularly large language models (LLMs), into cybersecurity and digital forensics has introduced both unprecedented capabilities and novel attack surfaces. Adversarial scenarios, in this context, refer to situations where AI systems are intentionally or unintentionally exploited, misled, or tested under challenging conditions to evaluate robustness, resilience, and reliability. Test cases, conversely, are structured evaluations designed to systematically probe vulnerabilities in AI-driven systems and their defensive mechanisms.

6.1. Adversarial Scenarios in AI-Driven Cybersecurity

Adversarial scenarios in cybersecurity frequently involve manipulating input data to induce incorrect predictions or actions in AI models. This can include adversarial examples, backdoor attacks, and phishing detection evasion. Yang et al. (2024) provide a comprehensive overview of backdoor attacks in LLMs within communication networks, highlighting the subtle mechanisms by which malicious actors can implant hidden triggers in models that are later activated to compromise systems. Similarly, Xu et al. (2024) introduce AutoAttacker, a system that demonstrates how LLMs can be leveraged to implement automated cyber-attacks, including network infiltration and credential theft, revealing the dual-use potential of AI.

The agricultural and environmental sectors have also been increasingly targeted by AI adversarial attacks. Aggarwal et al. (2024) and Shafik et al. (2025) highlight scenarios in precision agriculture where AI-driven monitoring systems could be manipulated to misreport crop conditions, potentially causing economic or ecological harm. Adanma and Ogunbiyi (2024) emphasize that environmental conservation systems using AI are particularly vulnerable to cyber-physical manipulation, underlining the need for robust adversarial testing.

6.2. Digital Forensics and AI Vulnerability Test Cases

Digital forensics has evolved from traditional evidence collection to AI-assisted intelligent forensics, allowing more rapid detection and analysis of cyber threats (Irons & Lallie, 2014; Tyagi et al., 2024). Test cases in this domain focus on evaluating the capability of AI to detect, classify, and respond to sophisticated cyber incidents. Costantini et al. (2019) and Dunsin et al. (2024) discuss how AI models, including machine learning classifiers, are tested against ransomware, phishing, and malware attacks. By simulating realistic attack scenarios, these test cases validate the models' detection accuracy, response latency, and adaptability to evolving threats.

LLMs have further transformed the forensic landscape by enabling semantic analysis of unstructured data, such as logs and textual evidence (Gennari et al., 2024; Georgescu, 2020). Adversarial test cases involve introducing obfuscation or tampered textual inputs to evaluate whether the LLM can correctly identify anomalies. Sultana et al. (2023) demonstrate zero-shot vulnerability detection using LLMs, providing a framework for benchmarking against unknown attack patterns. Similarly, Jin et al. (2024) introduce Crimson, a strategic reasoning framework for cybersecurity that tests the model's decision-making under adversarial conditions.

6.3. Penetration Testing and Scenario Simulation

Penetration testing represents an applied adversarial scenario where AI models are both testers and targets. Happe and Cito (2023) detail experiments in which LLMs are employed to perform automated penetration tests, simulating real-world hacking techniques to identify weaknesses in enterprise networks. Guastalla et al. (2023) extend this approach to DDoS attack detection, showing that LLMs can generate test inputs that stress system defenses under varied attack loads. These simulations provide critical insights into system robustness and the efficacy of AI-enhanced cybersecurity measures.

Furthermore, test cases can include multi-agent adversarial interactions, where AI models interact with each other or with human operators under simulated threat conditions. Pearce et al. (2023) highlight the use of LLMs in automatically repairing software vulnerabilities under adversarial inputs, illustrating the necessity of realistic testing to ensure reliability in high-stakes scenarios.

6.4. Ethical, Regulatory, and Practical Considerations

Adversarial scenarios and test cases must be designed with attention to ethical and regulatory constraints. Kaushik et al. (2024) argue that AI-based cybersecurity testing should adhere to privacy and ethical standards to prevent misuse of simulated attacks. Alexander et al. (2024) emphasize accountability in deploying AI in agriculture and food systems, suggesting that adversarial scenarios should also evaluate the societal and environmental impact of AI-driven decisions.

Practical test cases often combine synthetic data, domain-specific knowledge, and hybrid attack simulations to create realistic and challenging evaluation environments (Gholami & Omar, 2023; Aghaei et al., 2022; Alawida et al., 2023). These scenarios help researchers and practitioners identify blind spots in AI systems, enhance defensive strategies, and optimize LLM training for cybersecurity resilience.

6.5. Emerging Trends and Future Test Case Development

The evolution of adversarial testing is increasingly intertwined with AI's self-learning capabilities and real-time decision-making. Wang (2023) illustrates the use of LLMs in mitigating ransomware threats by simulating adversarial attack patterns, while Motlagh et al. (2024) discuss benchmarking frameworks like CyberMetric to evaluate LLM knowledge in cybersecurity. Moreover, Zangana (2025) and Zangana & Yazdeen (2025) propose federated architectures and blockchain integration as mechanisms to enhance security and scalability in adversarial testing.

Future test case development should focus on cross-domain evaluation, incorporating physical systems, IoT devices, and cloud infrastructures into adversarial simulations. This approach ensures that AI models are resilient not only to digital attacks but also to multi-vector threats that span cyber-physical environments (Neupane et al., 2024; Tyagi et al., 2024; Khalil et al., 2024).

7. METRICS FOR EVALUATING RED TEAMING OUTCOMES

Evaluating the effectiveness of red teaming exercises in cybersecurity is a complex yet critical process. Red teaming provides organizations with realistic assessments of their defensive capabilities by simulating adversarial attacks, and measuring the outcomes ensures that security strategies are robust and adaptive (Omar & Zangana, 2024). The metrics for evaluating red teaming outcomes can be broadly categorized into technical, operational, and strategic dimensions, each encompassing quantitative and qualitative measures.

7.1. Technical Metrics

Technical metrics are foundational for assessing the immediate effectiveness of attacks and the resilience of defenses. These metrics focus on system vulnerabilities, exploit success rates, and detection efficiency. Key indicators include:

- **Vulnerability Discovery Rate:** Measures the number of unique vulnerabilities identified during the red team exercise. High rates indicate the comprehensiveness of the testing methodology (Gennari et al., 2024; Xu et al., 2024).
- **Exploit Success Rate:** Assesses the proportion of successful attacks against targeted systems. This metric is crucial for evaluating the potential real-world impact of security gaps (Pearce et al., 2023; Jin et al., 2024).

- **Time-to-Detection (TTD):** Evaluates the responsiveness of monitoring systems in detecting malicious activity initiated by red team actors. Shorter TTD reflects better incident detection capabilities (Happe & Cito, 2023; Wang, 2023).
- **False Positive and False Negative Rates:** Monitoring systems must accurately distinguish between legitimate activities and attacks. High false positives can overwhelm security teams, while high false negatives indicate undetected breaches (Ferrag et al., 2023; Yao et al., 2024).

7.2. Operational Metrics

Operational metrics gauge the effectiveness of processes, coordination, and response mechanisms during red teaming exercises. These metrics include:

- **Incident Response Efficiency:** Measures how quickly and effectively the security team responds to simulated attacks, including containment, mitigation, and recovery (Dunsin, Ghanem, & Ouazzane, 2024; Tyagi et al., 2024).
- **Attack Surface Reduction:** Quantifies improvements in security posture after iterative red teaming exercises, such as the closure of previously identified vulnerabilities (Adanma & Ogunbiyi, 2024; Alawida et al., 2023).
- **Resilience of Critical Assets:** Evaluates the ability of essential systems to maintain functionality under attack conditions, emphasizing business continuity (Alexander et al., 2024; Vladescu et al., 2021).
- **Red Team Learning and Adaptation:** Captures the extent to which red team exercises identify gaps in policies, training, and procedural workflows (Happe & Cito, 2023; Omar & Zangana, 2024).

7.3. Strategic Metrics

Strategic metrics provide insight into the long-term organizational impact and risk reduction achieved through red teaming. These metrics are essential for executive decision-making and cybersecurity investments:

- **Risk Reduction Index:** Evaluates the decrease in organizational risk exposure post-red teaming, often using quantitative risk assessment models (Mitchell, 2014; Wright, Dawson Jr, & Omar, 2012).
- **Security Culture Improvement:** Assesses organizational awareness, training outcomes, and the adoption of cybersecurity best practices across departments (Abd-Elsalam & Abdel-Momen, 2023; Aderibigbe et al., 2023).

- **Alignment with Regulatory Compliance:** Ensures that identified vulnerabilities and mitigation strategies adhere to relevant industry standards and cybersecurity regulations (Kaushik et al., 2024; Zangana, 2025).
- **Return on Security Investment (ROSI):** Measures the cost-effectiveness of security measures informed by red teaming findings, helping organizations justify cybersecurity expenditure (Mendsaikhan et al., 2019; Omar & Zangana, 2025).

7.4. Metrics for AI-Enhanced Red Teaming

The integration of artificial intelligence (AI) and large language models (LLMs) into red teaming introduces additional evaluation dimensions. AI-driven red teams leverage automated reasoning, vulnerability prioritization, and simulated attack strategies (Motlagh et al., 2024; Guastalla et al., 2023). Metrics for AI-enhanced red teaming include:

- **Autonomous Attack Coverage:** Measures the diversity and sophistication of attack scenarios generated by AI agents compared to manual red team efforts (Xu et al., 2024; Jin et al., 2024).
- **Accuracy of Threat Modeling:** Evaluates the ability of AI models to predict potential attack vectors and vulnerabilities (Gao, 2023; Tihanyi et al., 2024).
- **Adaptability and Learning Rate:** Quantifies how effectively AI-driven red teams learn from prior exercises to simulate increasingly complex attack patterns (Marshall, 2023; Ferrag et al., 2023).
- **Explainability and Traceability:** Ensures AI-generated attack paths and recommendations are interpretable and actionable by human security teams (Kelly et al., 2020; Al-Hawawreh et al., 2023).

7.5. Comprehensive Evaluation Frameworks

For a holistic assessment, organizations often adopt multi-dimensional scoring systems that integrate technical, operational, and strategic metrics. Frameworks such as CyberMetric (Tihanyi et al., 2024) and AI-guided attack evaluation platforms (Xu et al., 2024) provide standardized benchmarks to measure red team efficacy. These approaches enable the continuous refinement of cybersecurity strategies and ensure that defensive measures evolve alongside emerging threats (Jiang, 2024; Yang et al., 2024).

Red teaming evaluation metrics are essential for not only quantifying the effectiveness of security operations but also guiding continuous improvement in cybersecurity practices. By combining traditional metrics with AI-enhanced measurements, organizations can achieve a more resilient, adaptive, and informed security posture.

8. INTEGRATION WITH LLM DEVELOPMENT LIFECYCLEGh

The development lifecycle of Large Language Models (LLMs) is a complex and multi-stage process that encompasses data collection, preprocessing, model training, evaluation, deployment, and continuous monitoring. Integrating cybersecurity considerations and risk mitigation strategies into each stage is critical to ensure the robustness, reliability, and ethical compliance of LLM-based systems (Motlagh et al., 2024; Yao et al., 2024; Ferrag et al., 2023).

8.1. Data Collection and Preprocessing

The foundation of any LLM lies in its training data. High-quality, representative, and secure datasets are vital for model performance and resilience against attacks. Techniques such as data anonymization, synthetic data generation, and secure data pipelines help in reducing privacy risks and biases (Abd-Elsalam & Abdel-Momen, 2023; Aldoseri et al., 2023; Aithal & Aithal, 2023). Domain-specific datasets, such as cybersecurity corpora or agritech-related textual data, can be curated to enhance LLM relevance and reduce susceptibility to irrelevant or malicious input (Aghaei et al., 2022; Ranade et al., 2021; Shafik et al., 2025). However, careful validation is required to prevent the introduction of adversarial patterns or backdoor triggers that can later be exploited (Yang et al., 2024; Guastalla et al., 2023).

8.2. Model Training and Optimization

During the training phase, LLMs learn to predict, generate, and reason over textual data. Integrating secure training protocols and adversarial-aware methods is crucial to mitigate risks such as model inversion, data leakage, and manipulation (Jin et al., 2024; Motlagh et al., 2024). Optimization strategies must also consider fairness, explainability, and domain alignment (He et al., 2021; Kelly et al., 2020). Techniques such as differential privacy, federated learning, and multi-objective optimization can enhance the security and ethical integrity of the models (Zangana & Yazdeen, 2025; Aldoseri et al., 2023; Omar & Zangana, 2024).

8.3. Model Evaluation and Benchmarking

Evaluating LLM performance goes beyond accuracy and fluency. Security, robustness, and contextual correctness must be assessed using standardized benchmarks and domain-specific evaluation datasets (Tihanyi et al., 2024; Sultana et al., 2023; Jiang, 2024). For cybersecurity-focused LLMs, metrics such as vulnerability detection rates, phishing identification accuracy, and backdoor resilience are critical (Gennari et al., 2024; Xu et al., 2024; Wang, 2023). Additionally, zero-shot and few-shot evaluation methods help in assessing model adaptability and generalization across unseen threats (Pearce et al., 2023; Tann et al., 2023).

8.4. Deployment and Operational Integration

Deploying LLMs in real-world environments requires integrating them into existing IT infrastructure while maintaining security, privacy, and compliance standards (Al-Hawawreh et al., 2023; Gupta et al., 2024; Omar & Zangana, 2025). This involves continuous monitoring, real-time threat detection, and automated patching mechanisms to prevent exploitation (Ferrag et al., 2023; Wright et al., 2012; Zangana et al., 2025). Deployment also demands careful orchestration of computational resources to balance latency, throughput, and robustness, particularly for cloud-based or federated systems (Zangana & Yazdeen, 2025; Neupane et al., 2024).

8.5. Continuous Monitoring, Feedback, and Lifecycle Maintenance

The LLM lifecycle is inherently dynamic. Continuous monitoring and model retraining are necessary to adapt to emerging threats, novel adversarial techniques, and evolving data landscapes (Marshall, 2023; Vladescu et al., 2021; Yang et al., 2024). Feedback loops incorporating human oversight, automated evaluation tools, and domain-specific analytics improve resilience and trustworthiness (Jarrett & Choo, 2021; Dunsin et al., 2024; Chen et al., 2024). Integration of AI-driven decision support systems and explainable AI frameworks ensures that lifecycle updates are both auditable and accountable (Morić et al., 2025; Abd-Elsalam & Abdel-Momen, 2023; He et al., 2021).

8.6. Security and Ethical Considerations Across the Lifecycle

Security threats such as prompt injection, model hallucinations, and privacy breaches can manifest at any stage of the LLM lifecycle (Yao et al., 2024; Gao, 2023; Jin et al., 2024). Ethical frameworks, adherence to regulatory guidelines, and inclusion of cybersecurity controls are essential for mitigating risks (Kaushik et al., 2024; Alexander et al., 2024; Holzinger et al., 2021). In environments like agriculture, finance, or healthcare, domain-specific security and fairness measures must be embedded directly into the lifecycle, ensuring LLMs operate reliably under operational constraints (Chen et al., 2024; Shafik et al., 2025; Araújo et al., 2021).

8.7 Summary

Integrating LLMs with a structured development lifecycle enhances both operational efficiency and cybersecurity resilience. By embedding risk-aware practices across data collection, model training, evaluation, deployment, and monitoring stages, organizations can ensure ethical, secure, and high-performing AI systems. This lifecycle-centric integration establishes a proactive framework to address emerging threats, optimize model performance, and maintain trustworthiness in diverse application domains (Motlagh et al., 2024; Ferrag et al., 2023; Yao et al., 2024).

This flowchart illustrates the various stages of the LLM development lifecycle, including data collection, preprocessing, model training, evaluation, deployment, and continuous monitoring. Each stage is interconnected, emphasizing the importance of integrating cybersecurity considerations throughout the process.

Figure 2. Development Lifecycle of Large Language Models

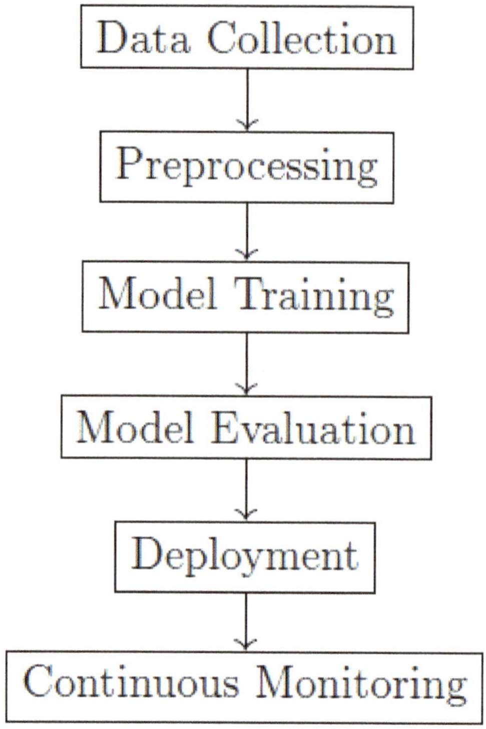

9. CASE STUDIES AND PRACTICAL APPLICATIONS

The practical application of Artificial Intelligence (AI) and Large Language Models (LLMs) in cybersecurity, digital forensics, and various industrial sectors has expanded significantly in recent years, reflecting both opportunities and challenges. This section presents case studies and real-world examples that illustrate how these technologies are leveraged to address critical problems and improve operational efficiency.

9.1. AI in Digital Forensics

AI has transformed traditional digital forensics by automating analysis, pattern recognition, and threat detection. Wright et al. (2012) highlighted the early need for robust antivirus solutions for mobile devices, which laid the foundation for AI-based detection systems. Modern digital forensic tools now employ machine learning (ML) and natural language processing (NLP) to accelerate investigations and improve accuracy (Irons & Lallie, 2014; Costantini et al., 2019). For instance, Dunsin et al. (2024) demonstrated the integration of AI and ML into incident response workflows, enabling faster identification of threats in constrained environments. Similarly, Kelly et al. (2020) explored explainable AI for drug testing cases, emphasizing transparency in forensic decision-making.

AI-driven digital forensics has also been applied to IoT environments and autonomous systems. Mohammed et al. (2018) and Manasa & Kumar (2022) investigated vulnerabilities in wireless sensor networks, demonstrating that AI algorithms can proactively detect wormhole attacks and anomalous behaviors in connected systems.

9.2. Cybersecurity and LLM-Based Solutions

Large Language Models are increasingly utilized for cybersecurity tasks, including vulnerability detection, threat intelligence, and attack simulation. Ferrag et al. (2023) and Motlagh et al. (2024) provided comprehensive analyses of LLMs for detecting sophisticated cyber threats, showing significant improvements in zero-shot and few-shot learning scenarios. In particular, Pearce et al. (2023) demonstrated LLMs' capabilities for automated vulnerability repair, while Xu et al. (2024) introduced AutoAttacker, an LLM-guided system for simulating cyberattacks to evaluate network defenses.

Crimson, developed by Jin et al. (2024), represents another practical application, employing LLMs for strategic reasoning in cybersecurity operations, enhancing situational awareness and decision-making. Guastalla et al. (2023) applied LLMs specifically to detect DDoS attacks, proving their value in real-time threat detection and mitigation.

Organizations are increasingly incorporating LLMs into enterprise systems. Gupta et al. (2024) discussed the integration of LLMs in large-scale enterprise environments, highlighting challenges related to privacy, model robustness, and ethical AI deployment. Similarly, Kereopa-Yorke (2024) illustrated how small and medium enterprises in Australia adopted LLMs to strengthen their cybersecurity posture and resilience against emerging threats.

9.3. AI Applications in Agriculture and Environmental Systems

AI has demonstrated significant potential in agriculture and environmental sustainability. Araújo et al. (2021) outlined the Agriculture 4.0 landscape, emphasizing AI-enabled precision farming and resource optimization. Aggarwal et al. (2024) highlighted both opportunities and challenges in AI adoption in agricultural systems, including data management and cybersecurity risks. Chen et al. (2024) provided an extensive review of AI in agrifood systems, noting improvements in yield prediction, pest management, and supply chain optimization.

Adanma & Ogunbiyi (2024) explored AI applications in environmental conservation, demonstrating how predictive modeling and ML can monitor ecosystems and enhance sustainable practices, while also noting potential cyber risks associated with environmental data management.

9.4. AI and LLMs in Healthcare and Research

In healthcare and scientific research, AI tools such as ChatGPT have been employed for data analysis, automated writing, and knowledge extraction. Abd-Elsalam & Abdel-Momen (2023) discussed the challenges of integrating AI in scientific writing, including data reliability, ethical concerns, and reproducibility. Aithal & Aithal (2023) and Alawida et al. (2023) further examined the application of ChatGPT in higher education and cybersecurity research, highlighting opportunities for enhancing productivity while maintaining ethical standards.

9.5. Blockchain-Enhanced AI for Security

The integration of blockchain and AI has enabled enhanced trust, transparency, and security in digital systems. Zangana (2025) demonstrated the application of blockchain in AI-driven cybersecurity for financial systems, providing tamper-proof audit trails and improving trust in digital transactions. Similarly, Zangana & Yazdeen (2025) proposed a federated architecture combining AI, IoT, and cloud systems to improve scalability and security in industrial applications.

9.6. Emerging Case Studies in AI-Driven Cybersecurity

Recent studies have applied AI and LLMs to simulate and defend against emerging cyber threats. For example, Tann et al. (2023) explored the use of LLMs for cybersecurity certification and capture-the-flag challenges, providing practical insights into model performance. Yang et al. (2024) reviewed backdoor attacks in LLMs within communication networks, emphasizing the importance of robust model evaluation and continuous monitoring. Wright et al. (2012) and Vladescu et al. (2021) provided early and contemporary case studies on threat mitigation strategies, respectively, demonstrating the evolution of AI-based security practices over the past decade.

9.7 Summary

Collectively, these case studies illustrate the transformative potential of AI and LLMs across multiple domains, including digital forensics, cybersecurity, agriculture, environmental monitoring, and research. Despite the demonstrated benefits, challenges remain in ensuring model transparency, ethical deployment, and cybersecurity resilience. Practical applications continue to evolve rapidly, reinforcing the need for continuous evaluation, regulatory compliance, and interdisciplinary collaboration (Aldoseri et al., 2023; Al-Hawawreh et al., 2023; Omar & Zangana, 2024).

This pie chart shows the distribution of AI applications, including cybersecurity, digital forensics, agriculture, and healthcare. Each segment represents the percentage of AI utilization in these fields, illustrating the growing reliance on AI technologies.

Figure 3. Distribution of AI Applications Across Various Domains

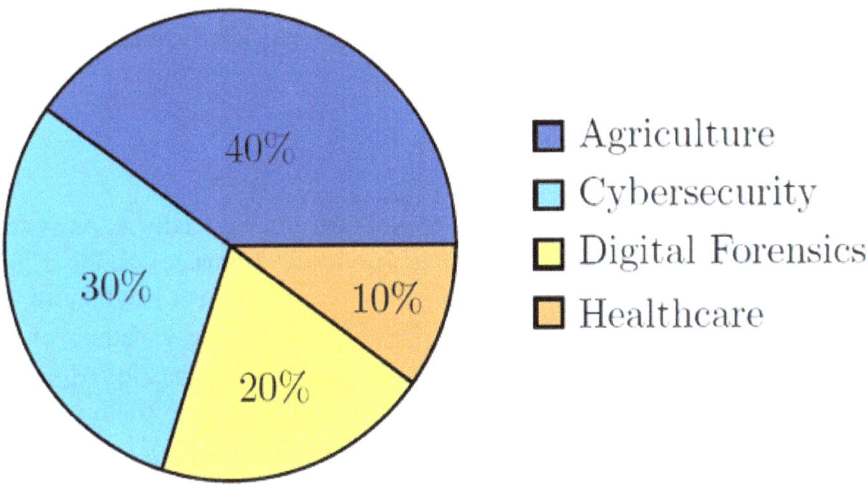

10. ETHICAL AND LEGAL CONSIDERATIONS

The rapid integration of artificial intelligence (AI), particularly large language models (LLMs), into digital systems, cybersecurity, and decision-making processes has brought significant ethical and legal challenges. These concerns are multi-faceted, encompassing issues of data privacy, accountability, transparency, bias, and regulatory compliance, which must be addressed to ensure responsible AI deployment (Abd-Elsalam & Abdel-Momen, 2023; Alawida et al., 2023).

10.1 Ethical Challenges in AI and Cybersecurity

Ethical dilemmas in AI-driven systems arise primarily from the autonomy and decision-making capabilities of intelligent systems. For instance, LLMs used in cybersecurity or digital forensics can unintentionally generate outputs that may propagate misinformation, enable malicious activities, or expose sensitive information (Ferrag et al., 2023; Yang et al., 2024; Yao et al., 2024). The principle of fairness is particularly critical, as AI models may inadvertently inherit biases from their training data, resulting in discriminatory outcomes in areas such as cyber threat detection, judicial decision-making, or financial systems (Morić et al., 2025; Alexander et al., 2024).

Human-centered AI approaches advocate for the inclusion of ethical reasoning in system design, emphasizing transparency, explainability, and human oversight to mitigate harmful consequences (He et al., 2021; Holzinger et al., 2021; Kaushik et al., 2024). Explainable AI (XAI) techniques are increasingly important to ensure that outputs of LLMs and other AI tools can be interpreted and validated by human operators (Kelly et al., 2020; Jin et al., 2024).

10.2 Privacy and Data Protection

Privacy remains a central legal and ethical concern, especially as AI systems rely on vast quantities of personal and sensitive data (Adanma & Ogunbiyi, 2024; Alawida et al., 2023). Unauthorized data exposure or improper handling of user information can lead to severe legal consequences, including violations of data protection laws such as GDPR or CCPA. The aggregation of data for AI training introduces additional risks, necessitating strict policies on anonymization, consent, and secure storage (Aldoseri et al., 2023; Omar & Zangana, 2024).

Federated architectures and privacy-preserving AI approaches have emerged as potential solutions to balance performance with confidentiality, allowing distributed model training without directly sharing sensitive data (Zangana & Yazdeen, 2025). Nonetheless, the adoption of these technologies must align with evolving legal frameworks and international standards to avoid liability and ethical breaches.

10.3 Accountability and Liability

Determining accountability in AI-enabled decision-making systems is complex, particularly in cyber operations, digital forensics, and autonomous decision-making (Adam & Varol, 2020; Dunsin et al., 2024; Jarrett & Choo, 2021). When AI systems cause unintended harm, such as security breaches, financial loss, or wrongful legal judgments, questions arise regarding whether the responsibility lies with developers, operators, or the AI system itself (Moustafa, 2022; Chen et al., 2024; Araújo et al., 2021).

Emerging legal frameworks advocate for shared accountability models, including clear documentation of AI decision processes, logging of automated actions, and periodic audits to ensure compliance with regulatory standards (Omar & Zangana, 2025; Vladescu et al., 2021; Zangana, 2025). Cyber insurance policies and risk management protocols are also increasingly integrating AI-related liabilities to address these challenges (Wright et al., 2012; Mohammed et al., 2018).

10.4 Regulatory Compliance

The global regulatory landscape for AI and cybersecurity remains fragmented. While some jurisdictions have started to formalize AI governance through guidelines and legislation, challenges persist in harmonizing these standards across borders (Kaushik et al., 2024; Kereopa-Yorke, 2024). Compliance requires organizations to implement rigorous AI governance frameworks, including ethical review boards, standardized operational procedures, and proactive monitoring of system outputs (Gupta et al., 2024; Marshall, 2023).

Furthermore, in cybersecurity applications, the deployment of LLMs for threat detection or automation must comply with legal restrictions on offensive cyber operations, digital evidence handling, and cross-jurisdictional data sharing (Xu et al., 2024; Wang, 2023; Pearce et al., 2023). Failure to adhere to these regulations can expose organizations to legal sanctions, reputational damage, and operational risks (Tihanyi et al., 2024; Al-Hawawreh et al., 2023).

10.5 Ethical AI in Digital Forensics and Critical Infrastructure

Digital forensics is one of the areas most impacted by AI ethics and legality (Tyagi et al., 2024; Dunsin et al., 2022). AI-enabled forensic tools can expedite investigations, detect anomalies, and reconstruct cyber incidents. However, their use introduces potential biases, errors in automated reasoning, and challenges in maintaining evidence admissibility in courts (Costantini et al., 2019; Bhawna & Mahajan, 2024; Mitchell, 2014). Ethical deployment requires establishing clear standards for evidence validation, audit trails, and human oversight to avoid compromising legal outcomes (Iqbal et al., 2020; Irons & Lallie, 2014).

Similarly, AI systems managing critical infrastructure, such as agriculture, energy grids, or financial systems, must adhere to strict ethical and legal norms to prevent misuse or accidental harm (Shafik et al., 2025; Araújo et al., 2021; Aggarwal et al., 2024). Incorporating accountability mechanisms, real-time monitoring, and regulatory compliance ensures that these systems operate safely while fostering public trust in AI technologies (Groumpos, 2023; Bahrini et al., 2023).

10.6 Conclusion of the Section

Ethical and legal considerations are no longer peripheral but central to the development and deployment of AI systems, particularly in cybersecurity, digital forensics, and critical infrastructure management. Ensuring privacy, accountability, transparency, fairness, and compliance requires coordinated efforts between developers, policymakers, and end-users. Emerging approaches, including federated learning, explainable AI, and structured AI governance frameworks, offer pathways to address these challenges while fostering responsible innovation (Abd-Elsalam & Abdel-Momen, 2023; Kaushik et al., 2024; Omar & Zangana, 2025).

11. FUTURE DIRECTIONS IN LLM RED TEAMING

As Large Language Models (LLMs) continue to advance, the field of red teaming—stress-testing AI systems to identify vulnerabilities—faces a rapidly evolving landscape. Future directions in LLM red teaming are focused on enhancing model robustness, addressing emerging threats, and integrating ethical, legal, and operational considerations.

11.1. Advanced Red Teaming Methodologies

Current LLM red teaming techniques primarily involve heuristic-based adversarial testing and scenario-driven evaluations. Future research is expected to leverage automated, model-guided red teaming systems to simulate more sophisticated attack vectors, including those exploiting hidden model behaviors (Xu et al., 2024; Jin et al., 2024). For example, tools like AutoAttacker demonstrate the feasibility of LLM-guided cyberattacks, suggesting the need for advanced defensive red teaming strategies (Xu et al., 2024). Additionally, the integration of domain-specific datasets—such as cybersecurity, financial systems, and agriculture—will improve the realism and relevance of adversarial evaluations (Aghaei et al., 2022; Alexander et al., 2024; Shafik et al., 2025).

The future of red teaming will likely employ adaptive adversarial agents, capable of learning from the LLM's outputs in real-time and refining attack strategies dynamically. These agents could leverage reinforcement learning or generative adversarial approaches to uncover vulnerabilities that static testing cannot detect (Motlagh et al., 2024; Ferrag et al., 2023).

11.2. Integration of Explainability and Interpretability

A critical frontier in LLM red teaming is the integration of explainable AI (XAI) techniques to understand model decision-making under adversarial conditions (Kelly et al., 2020; Alawida et al., 2023). By interpreting why an LLM produces vulnerable outputs, red teams can develop targeted mitigation strategies. Explainable adversarial testing will also improve trust among stakeholders, including cybersecurity professionals, policymakers, and the public (He et al., 2021; Kaushik et al., 2024).

Moreover, embedding interpretability frameworks in LLMs can facilitate continuous monitoring, enabling early detection of drift in model behavior due to malicious inputs or emerging attack patterns (Gao, 2023; Jiang, 2024).

11.3. Ethical, Legal, and Societal Considerations

As LLMs are increasingly deployed in sensitive domains, red teaming must address ethical and regulatory constraints (Abd-Elsalam & Abdel-Momen, 2023; Aderibigbe et al., 2023). Future directions involve developing ethical adversarial frameworks that balance comprehensive testing with privacy, fairness, and compliance requirements.

Additionally, emerging legislation on AI safety, cybersecurity, and digital forensics will influence red team methodologies. Compliance-oriented red teaming may integrate standards from multiple sectors, including healthcare, finance, and agriculture, ensuring LLMs operate safely across jurisdictions (Al-Hawawreh et al., 2023; Araújo et al., 2021; Chen et al., 2024).

11.4. Domain-Specific Red Teaming

Future research emphasizes tailored red teaming for domain-specific LLM applications, such as cybersecurity, environmental management, digital forensics, and smart agriculture (Adanma & Ogunbiyi, 2024; Aggarwal et al., 2024; Bahrini et al., 2023). By simulating real-world operational threats—ranging from ransomware and phishing attacks to backdoor vulnerabilities—researchers can better prepare models for deployment in high-stakes environments (Wang, 2023; Yang et al., 2024; Guastalla et al., 2023).

Cybersecurity-focused red teaming is expected to incorporate scenario-based simulations, where LLMs interact with other AI agents or live systems to expose weaknesses in both technical and human-AI workflows (Marshall, 2023; Tann et al., 2023; Sultana et al., 2023).

11.5. Collaborative and Federated Red Teaming

With the rise of multi-organizational AI ecosystems, future red teaming will likely adopt collaborative and federated approaches, enabling cross-institutional sharing of attack strategies, vulnerability reports, and mitigation techniques while preserving data privacy (Zangana & Yazdeen, 2025; Zangana, 2025; Omar & Zangana, 2024). Federated red teaming can accelerate LLM evaluation across sectors, reducing redundancy and improving robustness in deployment-critical applications such as autonomous systems, IoT networks, and smart infrastructure (Neupane et al., 2024; Tyagi et al., 2024).

11.6. AI-Augmented Red Teaming

A key future direction involves leveraging AI to red team AI, essentially employing LLMs themselves as testing agents. This approach can accelerate vulnerability discovery and enable predictive modeling of potential attack vectors (Motlagh et al., 2024; Ferrag et al., 2023). AI-augmented red teaming also provides scalability, allowing testing across multiple LLMs simultaneously while adapting to evolving threats (Pearce et al., 2023; Jin et al., 2024).

11.7. Evaluation Metrics and Benchmarking

Effective red teaming requires robust benchmarking frameworks to measure LLM resilience and performance under adversarial conditions (Tihanyi et al., 2024; Gennari et al., 2024). Future directions emphasize the development of standardized datasets, scoring metrics, and testbeds to ensure reproducibility and comparability across models and domains (Yao et al., 2024; Wright et al., 2012). Cybersecurity and digital forensics communities will benefit from shared repositories of attack scenarios and LLM response patterns (Dunsin et al., 2024; Kereopa-Yorke, 2024).

11.8. Integration with Emerging Technologies

LLM red teaming will increasingly intersect with blockchain, IoT, and autonomous systems to safeguard complex cyber-physical ecosystems (Zangana, 2025; Kochupillai et al., 2022; Moustafa, 2022). By simulating coordinated attacks across distributed networks, red teams can preemptively identify weaknesses and guide the development of robust AI-driven security architectures. Additionally, integrating LLM red teaming with digital twins and AI-driven decision support systems can enhance predictive analytics and threat modeling in real-time applications (Morić et al., 2025; Malhotra & Firdaus, 2022).

11.9 Summary of Future Directions:

The trajectory of LLM red teaming is toward highly adaptive, AI-augmented, and ethically governed frameworks that account for domain specificity, regulatory compliance, and real-world operational threats. By combining explainable AI, collaborative testing, and predictive analytics, future red teaming efforts will be crucial for ensuring the safe, reliable, and responsible deployment of LLMs across industries.

12. CONCLUSION

The evolution of Large Language Models (LLMs) has brought unprecedented capabilities in natural language understanding, generation, and decision support across numerous domains. However, as their adoption grows, so do the associated risks, including security vulnerabilities, ethical concerns, and operational challenges. Red teaming has emerged as a critical methodology to systematically identify, evaluate, and mitigate these risks, enabling the development of safer and more reliable AI systems. Through rigorous adversarial testing, explainable AI integration, and domain-specific evaluations, red teaming provides essential insights into the limitations and potential failure modes of LLMs.

Future progress in LLM red teaming will depend on the adoption of advanced, AI-augmented, and collaborative approaches. The integration of adaptive adversarial agents, federated testing frameworks, and predictive vulnerability modeling promises to make red teaming more effective, scalable, and relevant for real-world applications. Furthermore, the alignment of red teaming practices with ethical, legal, and societal standards is critical to ensure responsible deployment. By emphasizing transparency, accountability, and fairness, organizations can better navigate the risks inherent in LLM deployment while maintaining stakeholder trust.

Finally, the continued collaboration between academia, industry, and regulatory bodies will be crucial for establishing standardized evaluation frameworks, robust benchmarking protocols, and shared repositories of attack scenarios. Such efforts will not only enhance the resilience of LLMs but also foster innovation in cybersecurity, autonomous systems, digital forensics, and other critical sectors. In conclusion, LLM red teaming is no longer optional but a necessary component of the AI development lifecycle, ensuring that these transformative models can deliver value safely, responsibly, and sustainably.

REFERENCES

Abd-Elsalam, K. A., & Abdel-Momen, S. M. (2023). Artificial intelligence's development and challenges in scientific writing. *Egyptian Journal of Agricultural Research, 101*(3), 714–717. DOI: 10.21608/ejar.2023.220363.1414

Adam, I. Y., & Varol, C. (2020, June). Intelligence in digital forensics process. In *2020 8th International Symposium on Digital Forensics and Security (ISDFS)* (pp. 1-6). IEEE. DOI: 10.1109/ISDFS49300.2020.9116442

Adanma, U. M., & Ogunbiyi, E. O.Uwaga Monica AdanmaEmmanuel Olurotimi Ogunbiyi. (2024). Artificial intelligence in environmental conservation: Evaluating cyber risks and opportunities for sustainable practices. *Computer Science & IT Research Journal, 5*(5), 1178–1209. DOI: 10.51594/csitrj.v5i5.1156

Aderibigbe, A. O., Ohenhen, P. E., Nwaobia, N. K., Gidiagba, J. O., & Ani, E. C.Adebayo Olusegun AderibigbePeter Efosa OhenhenNwabueze Kelvin Nwaobia-Joachim Osheyor GidiagbaEmmanuel Chigozie Ani. (2023). Artificial intelligence in developing countries: Bridging the gap between potential and implementation. *Computer Science & IT Research Journal, 4*(3), 185–199. DOI: 10.51594/csitrj.v4i3.629

Aggarwal, S., Bansal, S., & Goel, R. (2024). Ai In Agriculture: A Looming Challenge, A Gleaming Opportunity. *International Journal of Engineering Science and Humanities, 14*(Special Issue 1), 43-52.

Aghaei, E., Niu, X., Shadid, W., & Al-Shaer, E. (2022, October). Securebert: A domain-specific language model for cybersecurity. In International Conference on Security and Privacy in Communication Systems (pp. 39-56). Cham: Springer Nature Switzerland.

Aithal, P. S., & Aithal, S. (2023). Application of ChatGPT in higher education and research–A futuristic analysis. [IJAEML]. *International Journal of Applied Engineering and Management Letters, 7*(3), 168–194. DOI: 10.47992/IJAEML.2581.7000.0193

Al-Hawawreh, M., Aljuhani, A., & Jararweh, Y. (2023). Chatgpt for cybersecurity: Practical applications, challenges, and future directions. *Cluster Computing, 26*(6), 3421–3436. DOI: 10.1007/s10586-023-04124-5

Alawida, M., Mejri, S., Mehmood, A., Chikhaoui, B., & Isaac Abiodun, O. (2023). A comprehensive study of ChatGPT: Advancements, limitations, and ethical considerations in natural language processing and cybersecurity. *Information (Basel), 14*(8), 462. DOI: 10.3390/info14080462

Aldoseri, A., Al-Khalifa, K. N., & Hamouda, A. M. (2023). Re-Thinking Data Strategy and Integration for Artificial Intelligence: Concepts, Opportunities, and Challenges. *Applied Sciences (Basel, Switzerland), 13*(12), 7082. DOI: 10.3390/app13127082

Alexander, C. S., Yarborough, M., & Smith, A. (2024). Who is responsible for 'responsible AI'?: Navigating challenges to build trust in AI agriculture and food system technology. *Precision Agriculture, 25*(1), 146–185. DOI: 10.1007/s11119-023-10063-3

Ameri, K., Hempel, M., Sharif, H., Lopez, J.Jr, & Perumalla, K. (2021). Cybert: Cybersecurity claim classification by fine-tuning the bert language model. *Journal of Cybersecurity and Privacy, 1*(4), 615–637. DOI: 10.3390/jcp1040031

Araújo, S. O., Peres, R. S., Barata, J., Lidon, F., & Ramalho, J. C. (2021). Characterising the agriculture 4.0 landscape—Emerging trends, challenges and opportunities. *Agronomy (Basel), 11*(4), 667. DOI: 10.3390/agronomy11040667

Bahrini, A., Khamoshifar, M., Abbasimehr, H., Riggs, R. J., Esmaeili, M., Majdabadkohne, R. M., & Pasehvar, M. (2023, April). ChatGPT: Applications, opportunities, and threats. In *2023 Systems and Information Engineering Design Symposium (SIEDS)* (pp. 274-279). IEEE. DOI: 10.1109/SIEDS58326.2023.10137850

Bhawna, & Mahajan, S. (2024). Artificial Intelligence Perspective on Digital Forensics. *Applying Artificial Intelligence in Cybersecurity Analytics and Cyber Threat Detection*, 33-44. Chaudhary, P. K. AI, ML, AND LARGE LANGUAGE MODELS IN CYBERSECURITY.

Chen, T., Lv, L., Wang, D., Zhang, J., Yang, Y., Zhao, Z., & Tao, D. (2024). Empowering agrifood system with artificial intelligence: A survey of the progress, challenges and opportunities. *ACM Computing Surveys, 57*(2), 1–37.

Costantini, S., De Gasperis, G., & Olivieri, R. (2019). Digital forensics and investigations meet artificial intelligence. *Annals of Mathematics and Artificial Intelligence, 86*(1), 193–229. DOI: 10.1007/s10472-019-09632-y

Dunsin, D., Ghanem, M. C., Ouazzane, K., & Vassilev, V. (2024). A comprehensive analysis of the role of artificial intelligence and machine learning in modern digital forensics and incident response. *Forensic Science International Digital Investigation, 48*, 301675. DOI: 10.1016/j.fsidi.2023.301675

Dunsin, D., Ghanem, M. C., & Quazzane, K. (2022). The use of artificial intelligence in digital forensics and incident response in a constrained environment. *International Journal of Information and Communication Engineering, 16*(8), 280–285.

Ferrag, M. A., Ndhlovu, M., Tihanyi, N., Cordeiro, L. C., Debbah, M., & Lestable, T. (2023). Revolutionizing cyber threat detection with large language models. arXiv preprint arXiv:2306.14263.

Ganesh, V. (2017). Artificial intelligence applied to computer forensics. *International Journal (Toronto, Ont.)*, *5*(5).

Gao, M. (2023). The Advance of GPTs and Language Model in Cyber Security. Highlights in Science. *Engineering and Technology*, *57*, 195–202.

Gennari, J., Lau, S. H., Perl, S., Parish, J., & Sastry, G. (2024). CONSIDERATIONS FOR EVALUATING LARGE LANGUAGE MODELS FOR CYBERSECURITY TASKS.

Georgescu, T. M. (2020). Natural language processing model for automatic analysis of cybersecurity-related documents. *Symmetry*, *12*(3), 354. DOI: 10.3390/sym12030354

Groumpos, P. P. (2023, July). A critical historic overview of artificial intelligence: Issues, challenges, opportunities, and threats. *Artificial Intelligence and Applications (Commerce, Calif.)*, *1*(4), 181–197.

Guastalla, M., Li, Y., Hekmati, A., & Krishnamachari, B. (2023, October). Application of Large Language Models to DDoS Attack Detection. In International Conference on Security and Privacy in Cyber-Physical Systems and Smart Vehicles (pp. 83-99). Cham: Springer Nature Switzerland.

Gupta, B. B., Gaurav, A., & Arya, V. (2024). Navigating the security landscape of large language models in enterprise information systems. *Enterprise Information Systems*, *18*(4), 2310846. DOI: 10.1080/17517575.2024.2310846

Happe, A., & Cito, J. (2023, November). Getting pwn'd by ai: Penetration testing with large language models. In *Proceedings of the 31st ACM Joint European Software Engineering Conference and Symposium on the Foundations of Software Engineering* (pp. 2082-2086). DOI: 10.1145/3611643.3613083

He, H., Gray, J., Cangelosi, A., Meng, Q., McGinnity, T. M., & Mehnen, J. (2021). The challenges and opportunities of human-centered AI for trustworthy robots and autonomous systems. *IEEE Transactions on Cognitive and Developmental Systems*, *14*(4), 1398–1412. DOI: 10.1109/TCDS.2021.3132282

Holzinger, A., Weippl, E., Tjoa, A. M., & Kieseberg, P. (2021, August). Digital transformation for sustainable development goals (sdgs)-a security, safety and privacy perspective on ai. In *International cross-domain conference for machine learning and knowledge extraction* (pp. 1-20). Cham: Springer International Publishing.

Iqbal, F., Debbabi, M., Fung, B. C., Iqbal, F., Debbabi, M., & Fung, B. C. (2020). Artificial intelligence and digital forensics. *Machine Learning for Authorship Attribution and Cyber Forensics*, 139-150.

Irons, A., & Lallie, H. S. (2014). Digital forensics to intelligent forensics. *Future Internet*, *6*(3), 584–596. DOI: 10.3390/fi6030584

Jarrett, A., & Choo, K. K. R. (2021). The impact of automation and artificial intelligence on digital forensics. *WIREs Forensic Science*, *3*(6), e1418. DOI: 10.1002/wfs2.1418

Jeong, D. (2020). Artificial intelligence security threat, crime, and forensics: Taxonomy and open issues. *IEEE Access : Practical Innovations, Open Solutions*, *8*, 184560–184574. DOI: 10.1109/ACCESS.2020.3029280

Jiang, L. (2024). Detecting scams using large language models. arXiv preprint arXiv:2402.03147.

Jin, J., Tang, B., Ma, M., Liu, X., Wang, Y., Lai, Q., . . . Zhou, C. (2024). Crimson: Empowering Strategic Reasoning in Cybersecurity through Large Language Models. arXiv preprint arXiv:2403.00878. DOI: 10.1109/ICCBD-AI65562.2024.00011

Kaushik, K., Khan, A., Kumari, A., Sharma, I., & Dubey, R. (2024). Ethical considerations in AI-based cybersecurity. In *Next-generation cybersecurity: AI, ML, and Blockchain* (pp. 437–470). Springer Nature Singapore. DOI: 10.1007/978-981-97-1249-6_19

Kelly, L., Sachan, S., Ni, L., Almaghrabi, F., Allmendinger, R., & Chen, Y. (2020). *Explainable artificial intelligence for digital forensics: opportunities, challenges and a drug testing case study*. Digital Forensic Science.

Kereopa-Yorke, B. (2024). Building resilient SMEs: Harnessing large language models for cyber security in Australia. Journal of AI. *Robotics & Workplace Automation*, *3*(1), 15–27. DOI: 10.69554/XSQZ3232

Kochupillai, M., Kahl, M., Schmitt, M., Taubenböck, H., & Zhu, X. X. (2022). Earth observation and artificial intelligence: Understanding emerging ethical issues and opportunities. *IEEE Geoscience and Remote Sensing Magazine*, *10*(4), 90–124. DOI: 10.1109/MGRS.2022.3208357

Malhotra, K., & Firdaus, M. (2022). Application of artificial intelligence in IoT security for crop yield prediction. *ResearchBerg Review of Science and Technology*, *2*(1), 136–157.

Manasa, S., & Kumar, K. P. (2022). Digital forensics investigation for attacks on artificial intelligence. *ECS Transactions, 107*(1), 19639–19645. DOI: 10.1149/10701.19639ecst

Marshall, J. (2023). What effects do large language models have on cybersecurity.

Mendsaikhan, O., Hasegawa, H., Yamaguchi, Y., & Shimada, H. (2019, July). Identification of cybersecurity specific content using the Doc2Vec language model. In 2019 IEEE 43rd annual computer software and applications conference (COMPSAC) (Vol. 1, pp. 396-401). IEEE. DOI: 10.1109/COMPSAC.2019.00064

Mitchell, F. R. (2014). An overview of artificial intelligence based pattern matching in a security and digital forensic context. *Cyberpatterns: Unifying Design Patterns with Security and Attack Patterns*, 215-222.

Mohammed, D., Omar, M., & Nguyen, V. (2018). Wireless sensor network security: Approaches to detecting and avoiding wormhole attacks. *Journal of Research in Business. Economics and Management, 10*(2), 1860–1864.

Morić, Z., Dakić, V., & Urošev, S. (2025). An AI-Based Decision Support System Utilizing Bayesian Networks for Judicial Decision-Making. *Systems, 13*(2), 131. DOI: 10.3390/systems13020131

Motlagh, F. N., Hajizadeh, M., Majd, M., Najafi, P., Cheng, F., & Meinel, C. (2024). Large Language Models in Cybersecurity: State-of-the-Art. arXiv preprint arXiv:2402.00891.

Moustafa, N. (2022). *Digital Forensics in the Era of Artificial Intelligence*. CRC Press. DOI: 10.1201/9781003278962

Neupane, S., Mitra, S., Fernandez, I. A., Saha, S., Mittal, S., Chen, J., Pillai, N., & Rahimi, S. (2024). Security considerations in ai-robotics: A survey of current methods, challenges, and opportunities. *IEEE Access : Practical Innovations, Open Solutions, 12*, 22072–22097. DOI: 10.1109/ACCESS.2024.3363657

Nguyen, V., Mohammed, D., Omar, M., & Banisakher, M. (2018). The Effects of the FCC Net Neutrality Repeal on Security and Privacy. [IJHIoT]. *International Journal of Hyperconnectivity and the Internet of Things, 2*(2), 21–29. DOI: 10.4018/IJHIoT.2018070102

Omar, M., & Zangana, H. M. (Eds.). (2024). *Redefining Security With Cyber AI*. IGI Global., DOI: 10.4018/979-8-3693-6517-5

Omar, M., & Zangana, H. M. (Eds.). (2025). *Application of Large Language Models (LLMs) for Software Vulnerability Detection*. IGI Global., DOI: 10.4018/979-8-3693-9311-6

Pearce, H., Tan, B., Ahmad, B., Karri, R., & Dolan-Gavitt, B. (2023, May). Examining zero-shot vulnerability repair with large language models. In *2023 IEEE Symposium on Security and Privacy (SP)* (pp. 2339-2356). IEEE. DOI: 10.1109/SP46215.2023.10179420

Ranade, P., Piplai, A., Joshi, A., & Finin, T. (2021, December). Cybert: Contextualized embeddings for the cybersecurity domain. In 2021 IEEE International Conference on Big Data (Big Data) (pp. 3334-3342). IEEE.

Shafik, W., Tufail, A., De Silva, C. L., Haji, R. A. A., & Apong, M. (2025). The Role, Application, and Impact of Artificial Intelligence in the Agriculture Industry. In *Future Tech Startups and Innovation in the Age of AI* (pp. 36–60). CRC Press.

Sultana, M., Taylor, A., Li, L., & Majumdar, S. (2023, October). Towards Evaluation and Understanding of Large Language Models for Cyber Operation Automation. In *2023 IEEE Conference on Communications and Network Security (CNS)* (pp. 1-6). IEEE. DOI: 10.1109/CNS59707.2023.10288677

Tann, W., Liu, Y., Sim, J. H., Seah, C. M., & Chang, E. C. (2023). Using large language models for cybersecurity capture-the-flag challenges and certification questions. arXiv preprint arXiv:2308.10443.

Tihanyi, N., Ferrag, M. A., Jain, R., & Debbah, M. (2024). CyberMetric: A Benchmark Dataset for Evaluating Large Language Models Knowledge in Cybersecurity. arXiv preprint arXiv:2402.07688.

Tyagi, A. K., Kumari, S., & Richa. (2024). Artificial Intelligence-Based Cyber Security and Digital Forensics: A Review. *Artificial Intelligence-Enabled Digital Twin for Smart Manufacturing*, 391-419.

Vladescu, C., Dinisor, M. A., Grigorescu, O., Corlatescu, D., Sandescu, C., & Dascalu, M. (2021, December). What are the latest cybersecurity trends? a case study grounded in language models. In 2021 23rd International Symposium on Symbolic and Numeric Algorithms for Scientific Computing (SYNASC) (pp. 140-146). IEEE.

Wang, F. (2023). Using large language models to mitigate ransomware threats.

Wright, J., Dawson, M. E.Jr, & Omar, M. (2012). Cyber security and mobile threats: The need for antivirus applications for smartphones. *Journal of Information Systems Technology and Planning*, *5*(14), 40–60.

Wright, J., Dawson, M. E.Jr, & Omar, M. (2012). Cyber security and mobile threats: The need for antivirus applications for smartphones. *Journal of Information Systems Technology and Planning*, *5*(14), 40–60.

Xu, J., Stokes, J. W., McDonald, G., Bai, X., Marshall, D., Wang, S., . . . Li, Z. (2024). AutoAttacker: A Large Language Model Guided System to Implement Automatic Cyber-attacks. arXiv preprint arXiv:2403.01038.

Yang, H., Xiang, K., Ge, M., Li, H., Lu, R., & Yu, S. (2024). A comprehensive overview of backdoor attacks in large language models within communication networks. *IEEE Network*, *38*(6), 211–218. DOI: 10.1109/MNET.2024.3367788

Yao, Y., Duan, J., Xu, K., Cai, Y., Sun, Z., & Zhang, Y. (2024). A survey on large language model (llm) security and privacy: The good, the bad, and the ugly. *High-Confidence Computing*, *4*(2), 100211. DOI: 10.1016/j.hcc.2024.100211

Zangana, H. (2025). Blockchain Technology in AI-Driven Cybersecurity: Strengthening Trust in Financial and Digital Security Systems. *Jurnal Ilmiah Computer Science*, *4*(1), 49–49. DOI: 10.58602/jics.v4i1.54

Zangana, H., Mohammed, H. S., & Husain, M. M. (2025). Transforming Cybersecurity Practices: A Comprehensive Approach to Protecting Digital Banking Assets. *Jurnal Ilmiah Computer Science*, *4*(1), 1–9. DOI: 10.58602/jics.v4i1.51

Zangana, H., & Yazdeen, A. (2025). A Federated Architecture for Enhancing Security and Scalability in IoT-Cloud Integrated Systems. *Jurnal Ilmiah Computer Science*, *4*(1), 50–59. DOI: 10.58602/jics.v4i1.55

Zangana, H. M., & Omar, M. (2020). Threats, Attacks, and Mitigations of Smartphone Security. *Academic Journal of Nawroz University*, *9*(4), 324–332. DOI: 10.25007/ajnu.v9n4a989

Chapter 7
Trustworthy and Explainable LLM Security Frameworks

Naresh Tiwari
https://orcid.org/0009-0000-7169-591X
Capitol Technology University, USA

Sachi Nandan Mohanty
https://orcid.org/0000-0002-4939-0797
School of Computer Science and Engineering, VIT-AP University, India

ABSTRACT

Large Language Models (LLMs) are increasingly deployed across critical domains, from cybersecurity and healthcare to finance and education. While their capabilities have transformed automation and decision-making, these systems face significant challenges related to trust, security, and explainability. As adversarial attacks, data poisoning, and prompt manipulation continue to evolve, the lack of transparency in LLM decision-making undermines user confidence and regulatory compliance. This chapter introduces the concept of trustworthy and explainable LLM security frameworks, which integrate principles of interpretability, accountability, and robust defense mechanisms. By combining security-by-design approaches with explainable artificial intelligence (XAI) techniques, these frameworks aim to mitigate vulnerabilities while ensuring transparency in system outputs. The discussion highlights architectural considerations, governance models, and best practices that bridge the gap between technical resilience and human-centric trust. Furthermore, the chapter explores how explainability enhances threat detection, incident response, and ethical assurance, making LLMs more reliable in high-stakes environments.

DOI: 10.4018/979-8-3373-7133-7.ch007

Ultimately, establishing trustworthy and explainable LLM security frameworks is not only a technical necessity but also a societal imperative for the responsible adoption of next-generation AI systems.

1. INTRODUCTION

The rapid advancement of artificial intelligence (AI) and large language models (LLMs) has reshaped the cybersecurity landscape, introducing new opportunities for defense as well as unprecedented risks. LLMs such as GPT and BERT derivatives are increasingly leveraged in tasks such as intrusion detection, malware analysis, vulnerability assessment, and digital forensics (Chen et al., 2024; Alturkistani & Chuprat, 2024). Their ability to process vast amounts of structured and unstructured data positions them as critical tools in the fight against cybercrime. However, their opacity, susceptibility to adversarial manipulation, and lack of interpretability highlight the urgent need for trustworthy and explainable LLM security frameworks (Capuano et al., 2022; Ferrag, Alwahedi, et al., 2024).

The integration of AI into digital forensics and cybersecurity has evolved rapidly over the last decade. Early works explored how machine learning could augment forensic analysis and incident response (Du et al., 2020; Hayes & Kyobe, 2020; Iqbal & Alharbi, 2020). Today, advanced AI systems, including LLMs, are deployed in cybercrime investigations, forensic accounting, and healthcare-related incident response (Ali, 2022; Tuli & Thaduri, 2023; Syed & ES, 2024). For example, SecureBERT was proposed as a domain-specific model tailored for cybersecurity contexts (Aghaei et al., 2022), while more recent work introduced SecLM, a specialized security LLM aimed at advanced threat mitigation (Asoronye et al., 2024). These developments reflect the increasing importance of context-specific language models for security-critical applications.

Digital forensics, in particular, has benefited from AI's analytical power. Studies have documented the transition from manual evidence analysis to automation-driven and AI-augmented approaches (Ahmed Alaa El-Din, 2022; Alghamdi, 2021; Al-Hajri et al., 2023). This includes forensic applications in cloud systems (Hamza & Omar, 2013; Ramachandran et al., 2023), mobile environments (Wright et al., 2012; Zangana & Omar, 2020), and blockchain-based timestamping (Zangana, 2024a). Yet, concerns about the reliability of automated decision-making remain, emphasizing the necessity of explainable frameworks (Faqir, 2023; Murphy, 2022; Sikos, 2021).

Trustworthiness in AI involves robustness, accountability, and ethical compliance, while explainability ensures transparency in system decision-making (Capuano et al., 2022; Kaur et al., 2023). In the context of LLM security, these principles are intertwined: a model cannot be trusted unless its outputs can be interpreted and validated. Several studies emphasize that the black-box nature of deep learning models undermines their adoption in high-stakes domains such as law enforcement, healthcare, and national security (Bonfanti, 2022; Montasari, 2023; Piraianu et al., 2023).

Recent surveys underscore this challenge. Chen et al. (2024) provide a comprehensive analysis of LLMs in cyber threat detection, highlighting their strengths in anomaly detection but also pointing to vulnerabilities such as prompt injection. Ferrag, Ndhlovu, et al. (2023, 2024) propose privacy-preserving and lightweight LLM models for IoT/IIoT environments, while Ghazal et al. (2024) argue that combining explainable AI (XAI) with LLMs enhances interpretability for cyber threat intelligence. Similarly, Gupta et al. (2024) discuss enterprise adoption challenges, pointing out that trust and transparency are central to responsible deployment.

Beyond classical threats, the looming advent of quantum computing introduces additional complexity. Quantum capabilities could undermine current cryptographic protocols, thereby endangering LLM-driven cybersecurity infrastructures (Baseri et al., 2024; Bishwas & Sen, 2024; Bush et al., 2021). Scholars emphasize the importance of quantum-resistant security frameworks (Rahul et al., 2024; Sodiya et al., 2024), agile quantum software development practices (Khan et al., 2023), and hybrid AI-quantum models (Metawei et al., 2022; Lougovski et al., 2023). This emerging paradigm highlights the necessity for forward-looking LLM frameworks that account for both classical and quantum threats.

Several research directions converge on the idea that explainability must be embedded within LLM architectures from the ground up. AlQenaei (2024) examines the evolution of LLM architectures and stresses optimization for both performance and interpretability. Similarly, Omar (2022, 2024a, 2024b) and Jones & Omar (2024) propose defense-oriented models that strengthen resilience against adversarial threats. The role of synthetic data in improving model efficiency and generalizability has also been explored (Gholami & Omar, 2023, 2024).

Moreover, socio-technical considerations are critical. Huff et al. (2023) emphasize the need for effective governance and management practices, while Bryce et al. (n.d.) and Zeadally et al. (2020) highlight the socio-technological uncertainties that arise when adopting LLMs in cybersecurity. Stutz et al. (2024) and Nair et al. (2024) also point to the role of AI in strengthening cloud security and next-generation systems.

Given the convergence of these challenges and opportunities, this chapter sets out to propose a comprehensive framework for trustworthy and explainable LLM security. It draws on cross-disciplinary insights from cybersecurity, digital forensics, AI governance, and quantum computing to address the following core questions:

1. How can LLMs be secured against adversarial manipulation and systemic vulnerabilities?

2. In what ways can explainability enhance trust, transparency, and compliance in cybersecurity applications?
3. What architectural and governance models are required to ensure resilience in both classical and quantum computing environments?

By engaging with existing studies (Diaf et al., 2024; Hassan & Ibrahim, 2023; Rizvi et al., 2022; Samtani et al., 2020; Ukwen & Karabatak, 2021), the chapter develops a multi-layered framework that aligns technical defenses with human-centric trust mechanisms. The subsequent sections elaborate on the theoretical foundations, practical design considerations, and case studies, ultimately offering pathways for the responsible adoption of LLMs in cybersecurity.

2. BACKGROUND AND LITERATURE REVIEW

2.1. Introduction

The integration of large language models (LLMs) into cybersecurity and digital forensics has opened new opportunities for proactive threat detection, forensic investigations, and explainable defense mechanisms. However, the complexity of these models introduces challenges related to trustworthiness, transparency, explainability, and security risks (Capuano et al., 2022; Ferrag, Alwahedi, et al., 2024). This section provides a comprehensive review of the existing body of knowledge, tracing the evolution of LLMs in cybersecurity, their role in digital forensics, advances in explainable AI (XAI), and the emerging concerns around quantum computing and adversarial resilience.

2.2. LLMs and AI in Cybersecurity

Research has shown that AI-driven systems have significantly reshaped cybersecurity practices, moving from traditional signature-based models to adaptive and predictive approaches (Zeadally et al., 2020; Tao et al., 2021). LLMs such as SecureBERT (Aghaei et al., 2022) and SecLM (Asoronye et al., 2024) demonstrate how domain-specific architectures improve cyber threat detection accuracy and context-awareness. Similarly, Ferrag, Ndhlovu, et al. (2023, 2024) highlight the application of BERT-based lightweight LLMs in privacy-preserving IoT/IIoT threat detection.

Other studies emphasize enterprise integration, noting that LLMs can enhance information systems resilience but simultaneously introduce vulnerabilities requiring governance frameworks (Gupta et al., 2024). In parallel, the rise of generative AI for offensive and defensive cyber capabilities has been critically analyzed, calling for balance between innovation and risk mitigation (Bonfanti, 2022; Bryce et al., n.d.).

The adoption of LLMs in cybersecurity has progressed through several phases, beginning with traditional signature-based systems, advancing to adaptive AI-driven approaches, and culminating in domain-specific LLMs like SecureBERT and SecLM. The following diagram illustrates this evolutionary trajectory.

Figure 1. Evolution of AI and LLMs in Cybersecurity

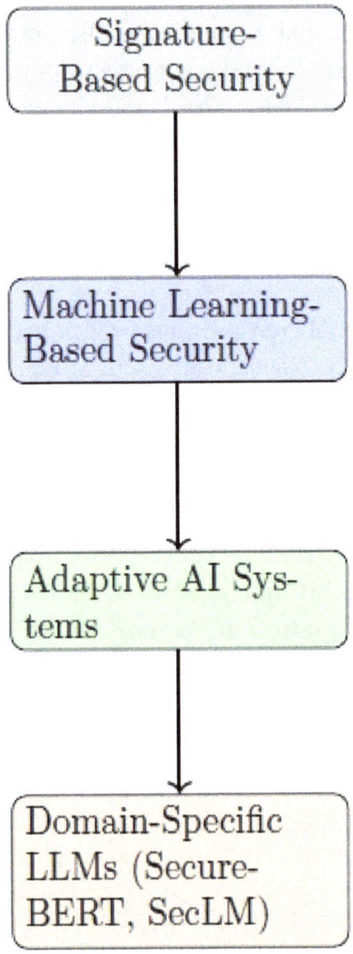

2.3. AI in Digital Forensics

Digital forensics has increasingly benefited from AI and LLM integration, particularly for managing large-scale evidence analysis and automating routine tasks. Hayes and Kyobe (2020), Jarrett and Choo (2021), and Iqbal and Alharbi (2020) explore automation in forensic workflows, while Du et al. (2020) provide a systematic overview of AI's role in forensic investigation. Moustafa (2022) and Murphy (2022) reinforce that AI systems enhance accuracy, scalability, and timeliness in forensic processes.

AI in forensic medicine and accounting is also emerging, with Piraianu et al. (2023) and Tuli and Thaduri (2023) showing cross-domain applications. Specifically, in digital forensic security, Sikos (2021) introduces ontology-based AI models, whereas Al-Hajri et al. (2023) and Ali (2022) demonstrate the use of AI in criminal investigations and big-data-driven forensic analysis.

2.4. Explainability and Trustworthiness in LLM Security

Explainable AI is essential to ensure transparency, accountability, and regulatory compliance in cybersecurity (Capuano et al., 2022). Ghazal et al. (2024) emphasize the combined power of XAI and LLMs for cyber threat intelligence, while Alturkistani and Chuprat (2024) highlight systematic approaches for integrating XAI into threat detection frameworks.

Trustworthiness extends beyond interpretability to resilience against adversarial manipulation. Omar (2024a, 2024b) explores DNN adversarial defenses and CNN-based malware detection, while Jones and Omar (2024) propose GEADD, a GPT-2 enhanced model for zero-day attack detection. Similarly, Gholami and Omar (2023, 2024) investigate the role of synthetic data and student–teacher model architectures in boosting LLM efficiency and security.

2.5. Quantum Computing and Security Challenges

Quantum computing presents both risks and opportunities for cybersecurity. Baseri et al. (2024), Bishwas and Sen (2024), and Rahul et al. (2024) outline the quantum threat landscape, emphasizing the need for quantum-resistant frameworks. Bush et al. (2021), Lougovski et al. (2023), and Perron et al. (2021) highlight advancements in quantum networks and education as foundational to preparing the workforce for this paradigm shift.

Metawei et al. (2022) and Khan et al. (2023) address the convergence of AI and quantum computing, stressing innovation and challenges, while Sodiya et al. (2024)

and Seskir (2019) focus on national security implications. These concerns reinforce the urgency of developing hybrid quantum–AI cybersecurity frameworks.

2.6. Broader Cybersecurity and Forensic Perspectives

Beyond LLM-specific advances, cybersecurity literature emphasizes AI-driven automation, resilience, and deception strategies. Rizvi et al. (2022) and Kaur et al. (2023) outline machine learning trends in network forensics and cybersecurity. Mohammed et al. (2018) and Zangana and Omar (2020) discuss smartphone and wireless network vulnerabilities, while Zangana et al. (2024) investigate phishing deception layers and firewall rule analyzer efficiency.

Studies such as Samtani et al. (2020), Huff et al. (2023), and Montasari (2023) provide multi-disciplinary perspectives, connecting AI with governance, healthcare, and counter-terrorism strategies. Similarly, Nair et al. (2024), Hassan and Ibrahim (2023), and Stutz et al. (2024) emphasize incident response, cloud system security, and AI-driven defense automation.

2.7. Summary of Literature Gaps

While significant progress has been made in LLM-powered cybersecurity, several gaps remain:

1. Lack of unified trustworthy frameworks integrating explainability, resilience, and adaptability.
2. Limited empirical validation of LLM applications in real-world forensic and enterprise contexts.
3. Emerging threats from quantum computing requiring proactive industry-wide quantum-resistant strategies.
4. Ethical, privacy, and governance challenges surrounding AI-driven security automation (Faqir, 2023; Omar & Zangana, 2024).

This body of literature collectively establishes the foundation for Trustworthy and Explainable LLM Security Frameworks, guiding the rest of this chapter toward bridging these gaps.

3. FOUNDATIONS OF TRUSTWORTHINESS IN LLM SECURITY

Trustworthiness in large language models (LLMs) for cybersecurity is built upon a multi-layered foundation that integrates model robustness, explainability, forensic accountability, privacy, and preparedness for emerging quantum threats. Establishing these foundations requires combining insights from computer science, digital forensics, artificial intelligence (AI), quantum computing, and enterprise security practices. This section outlines the core principles that underpin trustworthiness in LLM security.

3.1. Robustness and Domain-Specific Adaptation

LLMs must demonstrate resilience against adversarial manipulation, model poisoning, and exploitation. Domain-specific adaptations, such as SecureBERT (Aghaei et al., 2022) and SecLM (Asoronye et al., 2024), illustrate how cybersecurity-trained models can improve detection and mitigation of threats. Similarly, specialized lightweight architectures for IoT and IIoT (Ferrag, Ndhlovu, Tihanyi, Cordeiro, Debbah, Lestable, & Thandi, 2024) demonstrate that trust is enhanced when LLMs are optimized for constrained environments. Enterprise adoption of LLMs requires trust through model transparency and tailored design (Gupta et al., 2024).

3.2. Explainability and Transparency

Explainability is a cornerstone of trustworthiness in AI-driven cybersecurity. As Capuano et al. (2022) note, explainable AI (XAI) ensures that decision-making processes remain interpretable to analysts, regulators, and end users. The integration of explainability with LLMs enhances their reliability in critical applications such as cyber threat detection (Chen et al., 2024) and cyber-attack prediction in IoT networks (Diaf et al., 2024). The use of explainable mechanisms aligns with broader calls for accountable AI in cybersecurity defense (Ghazal et al., 2024; Ferrag, Alwahedi, Battah, Cherif, Mechri, & Tihanyi, 2024).

3.3. Forensic Readiness and Investigative Integrity

Trustworthiness also depends on the ability of LLMs to support forensic investigations. AI-driven forensics can enhance digital evidence collection and interpretation, as discussed by Moustafa (2022), Dunsin et al. (2024), and Syed and ES (2024). The integration of AI into forensic practice has been characterized as both revolutionary and disruptive (Ahmed Alaa El-Din, 2022; Ali, 2022; Montasari, 2023). Research emphasizes that automation (Hayes & Kyobe, 2020; Jarrett & Choo, 2021), ontology engineering (Sikos, 2021), and big data analytics (Iqbal & Alharbi, 2020; Rizvi et al., 2022) improve the scalability and trustworthiness of digital forensics. Forensic readiness ensures that LLM-based cybersecurity tools can generate legally defensible outputs (Piraianu et al., 2023; Tuli & Thaduri, 2023).

3.4. Privacy and Ethical Safeguards

Preserving privacy is an essential trust mechanism. Ferrag et al. (2023) and Ferrag et al. (2024) highlight privacy-preserving LLMs designed for IoT environments, where sensitive data requires minimal exposure. Ethical considerations, such as bias and misuse, are critical (Faqir, 2023; Bonfanti, 2022). Cloud and data security practices also serve as the backbone of trustworthy systems (Hamza & Omar, 2013; Stutz et al., 2024). Without these safeguards, user trust in LLM-enabled cybersecurity would erode rapidly.

3.5. Preparedness for Quantum-Era Threats

Quantum computing poses both risks and opportunities for LLM security. Research shows that quantum advancements may undermine classical cryptographic assumptions (Baseri et al., 2024; Bishwas & Sen, 2024; Rahul et al., 2024). At the same time, quantum networking offers potential resilience strategies (Bush et al., 2021; Lougovski et al., 2023). Studies highlight the urgency of quantum-resistant security frameworks (Sodiya et al., 2024; Metawei et al., 2022; Khan et al., 2023; Perron et al., 2021; Seskir, 2019). Building trustworthy LLMs for cybersecurity thus requires embedding quantum-aware design principles to sustain reliability in the face of disruptive innovation.

3.6. AI Governance and Security-by-Design

Governance frameworks are indispensable for sustaining trust. Research stresses the importance of integrating security-by-design into AI models (Samtani et al., 2020; Zeadally et al., 2020). By embedding resilience measures against adversarial attacks (Omar, 2024; Omar, 2022), data poisoning (Omar, 2021), and sophisticated malware (Omar, 2024), LLMs can become trustworthy defenders rather than liabilities. Security-centric model architectures (AlQenaei, 2024; Bryce et al., n.d.) and case-driven innovations (Jones & Omar, 2024; Jones et al., 2023) reflect this philosophy. Trust is also reinforced through blockchain-enabled timestamping and network analyzers that enhance auditability (Zangana, 2024; Zangana, Omar, Al-Karaki, & Mohammed, 2024).

3.7. Integration Across Domains

Finally, trust in LLM security depends on their applicability across domains. From mobile ecosystems (Wright, Dawson Jr, & Omar, 2012; Zangana & Omar, 2020), IoT security (CHILONGO & KM, 2024; Mohammed, Omar, & Nguyen,

2018), and healthcare (Huff et al., 2023; Syed & ES, 2024), to financial and forensic accounting (Tuli & Thaduri, 2023), LLMs must demonstrate consistent reliability. Cross-domain studies (Nair et al., 2024; Hadi et al., 2023; Kaur et al., 2023; Alturkistani & Chuprat, 2024) illustrate that the generalizability of trustworthy practices is a universal requirement. Furthermore, research in deception analysis (Zangana, Mohammed, Sallow, & Sallow, 2024) and website vulnerability scanners (Zangana, 2024) highlights how LLMs can strengthen resilience across diverse cyber ecosystems.

3.8 Summary

The foundations of trustworthiness in LLM security rest on robustness, explainability, forensic readiness, privacy, quantum-era preparedness, governance, and cross-domain integration. By embedding these elements, researchers and practitioners can ensure that LLMs not only defend against contemporary threats but also remain resilient in the face of future challenges. These foundations, grounded in multidisciplinary research, provide the pathway to building LLMs that are not only powerful but also trusted stewards of cybersecurity.

The trustworthiness of LLMs in cybersecurity rests on multiple foundations, including robustness, explainability, forensic readiness, privacy, quantum resilience, governance, and cross-domain integration. The following diagram summarizes these interrelated pillars.

Figure 2. Foundations of Trustworthiness in LLM Security

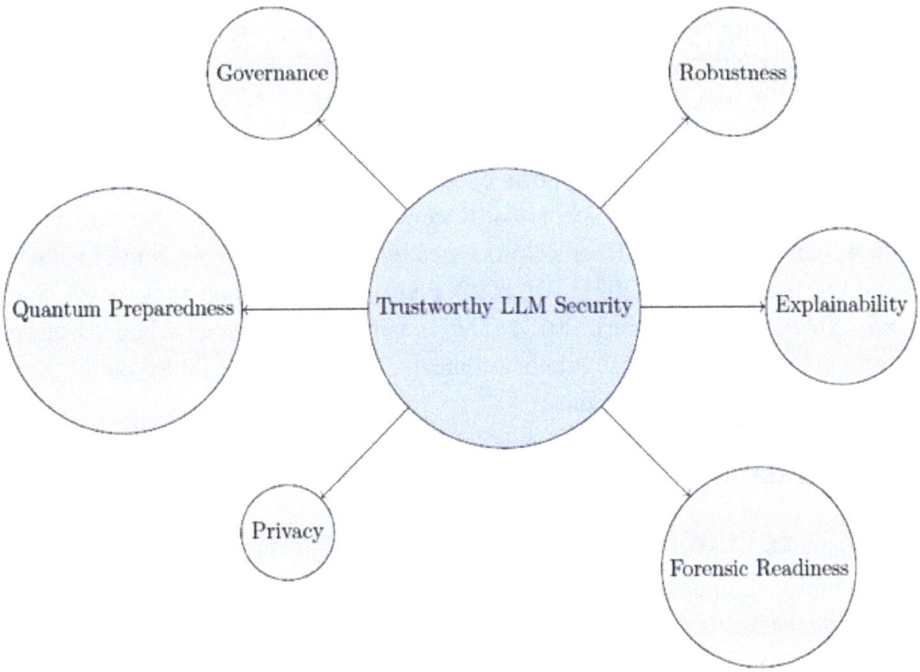

4. EXPLAINABILITY IN LLM SECURITY

The integration of explainability into Large Language Model (LLM) security frameworks is critical for establishing trust, ensuring accountability, and enhancing resilience against emerging cyber threats. As LLMs become increasingly embedded in cybersecurity infrastructures, digital forensics, and intelligent threat detection systems, their opaque decision-making processes pose significant risks for both practitioners and stakeholders. Explainability enables security analysts to interpret model predictions, understand potential biases, and verify the reasoning behind automated decisions, which is essential for forensics, compliance, and real-time defense mechanisms (Capuano et al., 2022; Chen et al., 2024).

4.1 The Role of Explainable AI in Cybersecurity

Explainable Artificial Intelligence (XAI) techniques allow for transparent interpretation of LLM outputs, thus addressing the "black-box" nature of deep learning systems. For instance, models like SecureBERT (Aghaei et al., 2022) and SecLM (Asoronye et al., 2024) have incorporated explainability mechanisms that help security professionals trace the logic of anomaly detection and classification. Such transparency is vital in incident response, where accountability and interpretability are necessary to present reliable forensic evidence (Ahmed Alaa El-Din, 2022; Du et al., 2020; Moustafa, 2022).

Moreover, explainability supports cyber forensics by assisting investigators in reconstructing digital crime scenarios. Recent studies emphasize that transparent AI tools can revolutionize forensic processes by enhancing the evidential value of digital traces (Alghamdi, 2021; Ali, 2022; Faqir, 2023; Piraianu et al., 2023; Syed & ES, 2024; Tuli & Thaduri, 2023). This is particularly crucial when AI-driven systems are used in legal or regulatory contexts, where decision interpretability can directly impact judicial outcomes.

4.2 Explainability for Threat Detection and Incident Response

Explainable LLMs improve cyber threat intelligence (CTI) by making predictions interpretable to human operators. For example, the systematic review by Alturkistani and Chuprat (2024) demonstrates how LLM-driven CTI platforms benefit from explainability in identifying attack signatures, mitigating bias, and refining alerts. Similarly, explainability improves the prediction of cyber-attacks in IoT environments, as shown by Diaf et al. (2024), by enabling analysts to validate why specific traffic patterns are flagged as anomalous.

Explainability also enhances adaptive response strategies by allowing defenders to simulate how an LLM interprets malicious payloads, phishing attempts, or zero-day exploits (Jones & Omar, 2024; Jones et al., 2023; Ghazal et al., 2024). By making decision paths transparent, analysts can refine detection rules and optimize LLM defenses against adversarial examples (Omar, 2024).

Explainability in LLM-driven threat detection improves transparency by enabling analysts to understand why certain anomalies are flagged. The following flowchart depicts the explainability process within cyber threat detection workflows.

Figure 3. Explainability Process in Threat Detection and Incident Response

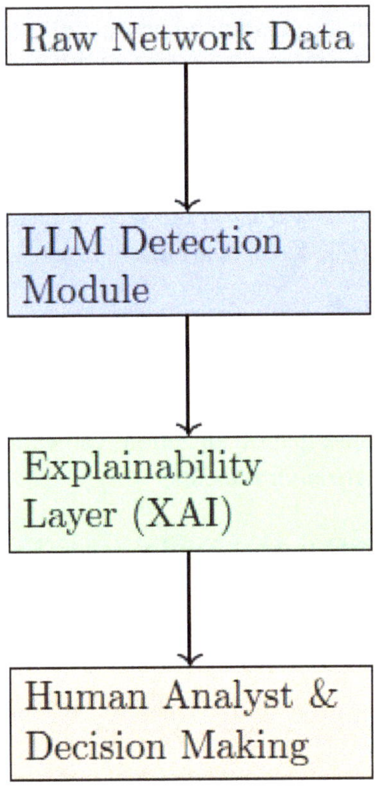

4.3 Integration with Digital Forensics

Digital forensics has emerged as a key domain where explainability in LLM security is indispensable. Automated forensic tools powered by AI often face criticism for lack of interpretability (Jarrett & Choo, 2021; Hayes & Kyobe, 2020; Iqbal & Alharbi, 2020). By embedding explainable mechanisms, investigators can verify system outputs and cross-check findings with traditional forensic methodologies (Murphy, 2022; Dunsin et al., 2024; Montasari, 2023). For instance, explainable LLMs can enhance evidence credibility in cybercrime investigations by presenting logical chains of reasoning (Al-Hajri et al., 2023; Sikos, 2021; Ukwen & Karabatak, 2021).

4.4 Bridging Explainability with Emerging Technologies

Emerging domains such as quantum computing present both opportunities and risks for explainable LLMs. Quantum-enhanced AI frameworks are expected to improve computational efficiency, but they may further complicate explainability (Baseri et al., 2024; Bishwas & Sen, 2024; Metawei et al., 2022; Rahul et al., 2024; Sodiya et al., 2024). Thus, future LLM frameworks must balance robustness with interpretability to maintain user trust in the face of quantum-enabled adversarial capabilities (Bush et al., 2021; Khan et al., 2023; Lougovski et al., 2023; Perron et al., 2021; Seskir, 2019).

Additionally, explainability is closely tied to cloud security and AI-driven infrastructures, where LLMs are applied for anomaly detection and fraud prevention (Hamza & Omar, 2013; Ramachandran et al., 2023; Stutz et al., 2024). Transparent reasoning mechanisms ensure that organizations can validate automated decisions in distributed and large-scale environments.

4.5 Towards Trustworthy and Explainable Frameworks

Recent contributions underline the need for integrated frameworks where trust, transparency, and accountability converge (Bonfanti, 2022; Bryce et al., 2023; Ferrag et al., 2024a; Ferrag et al., 2024b; Gupta et al., 2024; Huff et al., 2023; Kaur et al., 2023; Nair et al., 2024; Tao et al., 2021; Zeadally et al., 2020). For example, the adoption of synthetic data strategies has been explored to improve model robustness and explainability (Gholami & Omar, 2023; Gholami & Omar, 2024). Moreover, governance-centered approaches stress the importance of auditable AI systems in maintaining ethical standards and regulatory compliance (Omar & Zangana, 2024; Zangana, 2024a, 2024b; Zangana et al., 2024).

Explainable AI also strengthens defenses against social engineering and phishing attacks, where models must clearly justify why specific communications are flagged as malicious (Mohamed & Ahmed, 2024; Mohammed et al., 2018; Nguyen et al., 2018; Zangana et al., 2024). Similarly, studies on malware detection and zero-day exploits highlight that explainability improves resilience by enabling defenders to identify systematic weaknesses in LLM security pipelines (Omar, 2022; Omar, 2024a, 2024b; Wright et al., 2012; Zangana & Omar, 2020).

4.6 Summary

Explainability in LLM security is not an optional add-on but a foundational necessity for fostering trust, compliance, and resilience. From cyber threat detection and digital forensics to quantum-era security challenges, integrating explainable mechanisms ensures that LLMs remain reliable and transparent in high-stakes contexts. By bridging XAI techniques with robust defense models, practitioners can advance towards trustworthy and explainable LLM security frameworks that safeguard digital ecosystems against present and future threats.

5. PROPOSED TRUSTWORTHY LLM SECURITY FRAMEWORKS

The emergence of large language models (LLMs) has introduced transformative opportunities for cybersecurity, digital forensics, and incident response, but their adoption also raises new risks of adversarial attacks, data breaches, and misuse. To address these challenges, this section proposes a Trustworthy LLM Security Framework (TLSF) that integrates explainability, robustness, accountability, and adaptability as foundational pillars. The framework leverages advances in secure AI, digital forensics, and quantum-resistant methods to safeguard LLM applications in critical infrastructures and enterprise environments.

5.1. Foundational Design Principles

A trustworthy framework must begin with security-by-design and explainability-by-design approaches. Capuano et al. (2022) emphasized that explainable AI in cybersecurity enhances user trust by making decisions transparent, while Ferrag et al. (2024a) highlighted how generative AI can be weaponized if interpretability is not prioritized. Embedding interpretability modules ensures that LLMs can provide human-understandable justifications for threat classifications, thereby aligning with governance and compliance requirements (Gupta et al., 2024).

To achieve robustness, the framework integrates specialized LLMs trained on cybersecurity domains, such as SecureBERT (Aghaei et al., 2022) and SecLM (Asoronye et al., 2024), which outperform general-purpose models in detecting anomalies and mitigating threats. Moreover, synthetic data generation has been shown to enhance model efficiency and resilience against adversarial inputs (Gholami & Omar, 2023), while lightweight architectures allow deployment in IoT/IIoT environments without compromising security (Ferrag et al., 2023, 2024b).

5.2. Explainable and Forensic-Aware Security Integration

Digital forensics is a cornerstone of trustworthy LLM frameworks, as forensic-aware models ensure accountability in cyber investigations. Du et al. (2020) and Moustafa (2022) demonstrated how AI-driven forensic tools enhance the collection, analysis, and preservation of digital evidence. Al-Hajri et al. (2023) further noted the potential of AI to maximize efficiency in digital forensic investigations. The TLSF therefore incorporates forensic logging layers that track decisions, inputs, and model updates in tamper-resistant formats, aligning with blockchain-based timestamping solutions (Zangana, 2024a).

Automation in forensic analysis, as studied by Hayes and Kyobe (2020), Iqbal and Alharbi (2020), and Jarrett and Choo (2021), also reduces investigation delays. Forensic-aware LLMs can generate explainable narratives of cyberattacks, bridging the gap between investigators and AI-driven decision systems (Ali, 2022; Syed & ES, 2024). This feature strengthens incident response and legal admissibility of digital evidence (Faqir, 2023; Murphy, 2022).

5.3. Quantum-Resilient and Future-Proof Security

Quantum computing introduces both opportunities and existential risks for LLM security. Studies have shown its disruptive impact on cryptographic infrastructure (Baseri et al., 2024; Bishwas & Sen, 2024). Scholars such as Rahul et al. (2024) and Sodiya et al. (2024) stressed that preparing for quantum threats requires post-quantum cryptography (PQC) integration within AI security frameworks. The TLSF therefore includes quantum-resilient encryption layers, ensuring model updates, user interactions, and forensic logs remain secure in the quantum era.

Parallel research, such as Bush et al. (2021) and Lougovski et al. (2023), underscores the potential of industrial quantum networks to accelerate secure communications, while Khan et al. (2023) noted that agile practices are necessary for quantum software development. By anticipating these advances, the TLSF maintains future compatibility while ensuring resilience to quantum-enabled attacks.

5.4. Cyber Threat Intelligence and Predictive Security

Proactive security mechanisms are essential to mitigate evolving attack vectors. Chen et al. (2024) and Alturkistani and Chuprat (2024) emphasized that LLMs can revolutionize cyber threat intelligence (CTI) by automating detection of phishing, malware, and zero-day exploits. Diaf et al. (2024) proposed extending this capability to predictive analytics, enabling early detection of IoT-based cyberattacks.

Montasari (2023) and Bonfanti (2022) further highlighted the offense-defense balance in cybersecurity, stressing that predictive LLMs can help organizations move from reactive to anticipatory defense. By embedding continuous threat modeling, the TLSF not only detects attacks but also provides early warnings to mitigate cyberterrorism and advanced persistent threats.

5.5. Governance, Compliance, and Ethical Assurance

Trustworthiness in LLMs also requires adherence to governance, ethical, and compliance frameworks. Huff et al. (2023) and Nair et al. (2024) discussed the importance of aligning AI-based cybersecurity with organizational management practices and regulatory mandates. Omar and Zangana (2024) further advocated redefining security governance by combining AI transparency with compliance enforcement.

To address these issues, the TLSF includes policy-driven governance modules that enforce access control (Omar, 2021), detect insider threats (Jones & Omar, 2024), and manage data privacy obligations (Nguyen et al., 2018). Blockchain-enabled audit trails (Zangana et al., 2024a) and cryptographic enforcement (Hamza & Omar, 2013) strengthen accountability while preventing tampering.

5.6. Enterprise and Domain-Specific Adaptations

Given the diverse threat landscapes across sectors, the framework supports domain-specific customization. In enterprise systems, LLMs must integrate with existing infrastructures (Gupta et al., 2024), while in healthcare and biotechnology, explainable models ensure ethical compliance and prevent misuse (Huff et al., 2023; Piraianu et al., 2023). In forensics, AI-driven solutions enhance cybercrime investigations (Alghamdi, 2021; Tuli & Thaduri, 2023). In IoT ecosystems, resilience is critical due to resource-constrained devices (Chilongo & KM, 2024; Mohammed et al., 2018).

5.7. Unified Architecture of the Framework

The proposed TLSF integrates the following modules:

1. **Secure LLM Core:** leveraging domain-specific models (Aghaei et al., 2022; Asoronye et al., 2024).
2. **Explainability Layer:** embedding XAI for interpretability (Capuano et al., 2022; Ghazal et al., 2024).
3. **Forensic Logging and Blockchain Module:** ensuring evidence preservation (Zangana, 2024a; Du et al., 2020).
4. **Quantum-Resilient Cryptography:** enabling post-quantum security (Bishwas & Sen, 2024; Rahul et al., 2024).
5. **Threat Intelligence and Predictive Analytics:** proactive cyber defense (Chen et al., 2024; Diaf et al., 2024).
6. **Governance and Compliance Layer:** ensuring accountability and policy enforcement (Huff et al., 2023; Omar, 2021).

Together, these modules establish a holistic framework that integrates technical, forensic, and governance mechanisms for securing LLMs in critical applications.

The proposed Trustworthy LLM Security Framework (TLSF) integrates multiple components, including a secure core, explainability layer, forensic logging, quantum resilience, threat intelligence, and governance modules. The following architecture diagram illustrates their integration.

Figure 4. Unified Architecture of the Trustworthy LLM Security Framework (TLSF)

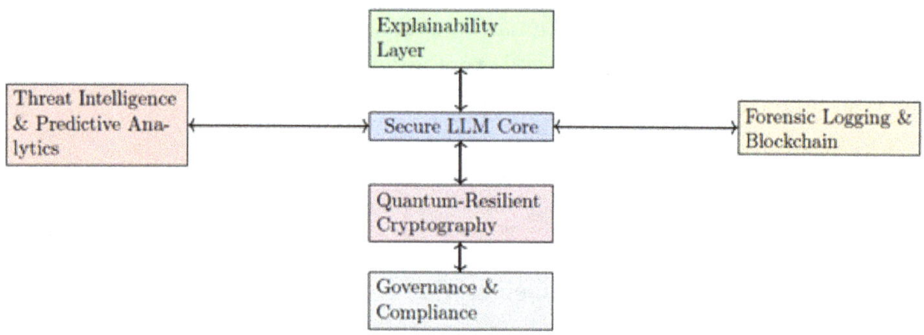

6. CASE STUDIES AND APPLICATIONS

The adoption of trustworthy and explainable large language model (LLM) security frameworks has been explored across diverse domains, from cyber forensics and digital investigations to enterprise information systems and quantum-resilient infrastructures. This section presents a set of case studies and applications that demonstrate how explainability and trustworthiness are integrated into LLM-driven security solutions.

6.1. LLMs in Cybersecurity Threat Detection and Mitigation

The integration of domain-specific LLMs into cybersecurity demonstrates their potential to revolutionize threat detection. For instance, SecureBERT was introduced as a domain-specific model for cybersecurity applications, offering improved detection accuracy and resilience against adversarial inputs (Aghaei et al., 2022). Similarly, SecLM, a specialized security language model, provides advanced cyber threat mitigation by leveraging explainable embeddings tailored for security contexts (Asoronye et al., 2024). These efforts build on earlier innovations such as the

GPT-2 Enhanced Attack Detection and Defense (GEADD) method, which applied fine-tuned LLMs to detect zero-day threats (Jones & Omar, 2024). Complementary studies confirm that privacy-preserving lightweight BERT architectures can secure IoT/IIoT ecosystems effectively (Ferrag et al., 2023; Ferrag et al., 2024).

Explainability has been a cornerstone of these applications, as highlighted by Capuano et al. (2022), who surveyed explainable AI (XAI) methods in cybersecurity, emphasizing the importance of transparent decision-making for operational trust. Ferrag et al. (2024) further underscore that generative AI combined with XAI ensures both effective and interpretable cyber defense mechanisms.

6.2. Digital Forensics and Investigations

Digital forensics has been one of the most prominent beneficiaries of AI-driven and LLM-based frameworks. Early explorations showed how AI augments forensic investigations through automation and predictive analytics (Du et al., 2020; Hayes & Kyobe, 2020; Iqbal & Alharbi, 2020). More recent studies provide comprehensive overviews of AI's role in forensic science (Ahmed Alaa El-Din, 2022; Moustafa, 2022; Murphy, 2022). In particular, the use of AI in evidence extraction and analysis has been applied to forensic medicine (Piraianu et al., 2023), healthcare cyber incidents (Syed & ES, 2024), and forensic accounting (Tuli & Thaduri, 2023).

AI-enabled digital forensic applications leverage NLP and LLMs for faster evidence analysis (Ukwen & Karabatak, 2021; Sikos, 2021). A notable case is the application of AI-driven forensic automation in cybersecurity incident response (Hassan & Ibrahim, 2023; Dunsin et al., 2024), where LLMs help correlate massive datasets into meaningful investigation leads. Recent efforts by Al-Hajri et al. (2023) and Ali (2022) illustrate how AI can maximize investigative efficiency in real-world forensic practices, while Faqir (2023) highlights its impact on digital criminal investigations.

6.3. Cybercrime, Digital Policing, and National Security

LLMs and AI frameworks have been positioned as critical tools for addressing cybercrime and terrorism. Montasari (2023) demonstrates the convergence of AI, digital forensics, and cyber policing in countering cyberterrorism across the U.S. and U.K. Bonfanti (2022) explores the broader implications of AI on offense-defense balance in cybersecurity. AI-enhanced frameworks for cybercrime investigations (Ali, 2022) and automation in evidence collection (Jarrett & Choo, 2021) have further positioned AI as a revolution in policing and national security practices.

6.4. Quantum-Resilient and Emerging Applications

The rise of quantum computing poses unprecedented threats to cybersecurity frameworks. Baseri et al. (2024) and Bishwas and Sen (2024) examine how LLM-driven defenses must evolve to address quantum threats, while Bush et al. (2021) and Lougovski et al. (2023) emphasize the importance of quantum-safe networks and software development practices (Khan et al., 2023). Frameworks for preparing industries against quantum-era threats are now becoming essential in LLM security applications (Rahul et al., 2024; Sodiya et al., 2024; Metawei et al., 2022).

These studies intersect with industrial applications, where AI and LLMs play pivotal roles in Industry 4.0 (AL-Refaey et al., 2024; Nair et al., 2024; Tyagi et al., 2024). The integration of LLM-based explainability into cloud and enterprise infrastructures is already evident in solutions for incident-based forensic approaches (Mughal, 2019), cloud abuse detection (Hamza & Omar, 2013), and AI-enhanced cloud security (Stutz et al., 2024).

6.5. Enterprise and Sector-Specific Implementations

Enterprise-level applications demonstrate how trustworthy LLM security frameworks can be deployed in practice. Gupta et al. (2024) analyze how enterprises integrate LLM security measures to safeguard information systems. In biotechnology and healthcare, AI-driven security frameworks are increasingly vital, as highlighted by Huff et al. (2023). In parallel, LLM adoption has supported robust database security (Omar, 2021), malware detection (Omar, 2024), and adversarial defense for neural text classification (Omar, 2024).

LLMs are also being tailored to sector-specific security challenges. For instance, cybersecurity issues in IoT networks can be mitigated by predictive LLM frameworks (Diaf et al., 2024), while AI can combat man-in-the-middle attacks in communication systems (Mohamed & Ahmed, 2024). Emerging solutions also include deception-based phishing defenses (Zangana et al., 2024) and the integration of blockchain timestamping tools (Zangana, 2024).

6.6. Broader Trends in AI and LLM Security

Several works provide comprehensive overviews of LLM trends and applications in cybersecurity. Bryce et al. (n.d.) identify the actors and societal impact of LLM adoption, while Chen et al. (2024) deliver a systematic survey of LLMs for cyber threat detection. Other reviews include Alturkistani and Chuprat (2024), who map

LLM contributions to cyber threat intelligence, and Rizvi et al. (2022), who document AI's role in network forensics.

Notably, Zeadally et al. (2020), Tao et al. (2021), Kaur et al. (2023), and Samtani et al. (2020) provide foundational roadmaps for integrating AI into cybersecurity, shaping the evolution of trustworthy and explainable LLM frameworks. Further advances have explored the efficiency of synthetic data for LLM training (Gholami & Omar, 2023), as well as performance comparisons between student and teacher LLMs (Gholami & Omar, 2024).

6.7. Regional and Emerging Research

Applications of LLMs in cybersecurity are expanding globally. Seskir (2019) examines quantum information technology applications in Turkey, while Chilongo and KM (2024) focus on AI's impact on IoT-based cybersecurity in Africa. Regional studies continue to illustrate how AI adoption is reshaping cyber resilience strategies worldwide.

7. CHALLENGES AND LIMITATIONS

Despite the remarkable progress in integrating Artificial Intelligence (AI), Machine Learning (ML), and Large Language Models (LLMs) into cybersecurity and digital forensics, a range of challenges and limitations constrain their effectiveness and adoption. These challenges span technical, ethical, operational, and infrastructural dimensions, and they highlight the urgent need for a careful balance between innovation and risk mitigation.

7.1. Technical Limitations of AI and LLMs in Cybersecurity

The first challenge lies in the technical maturity and domain specificity of current AI and LLM architectures. While domain-specific models such as SecureBERT (Aghaei et al., 2022) and SecLM (Asoronye et al., 2024) provide promising results, their training data is often limited, which can reduce robustness when handling previously unseen cyberattacks. Generic LLMs lack contextual awareness of highly technical forensic tasks, creating vulnerabilities to misclassification or bias (Chen et al., 2024; Bryce et al., n.d.). Similarly, while specialized models demonstrate improvements, adversarial manipulation remains a persistent issue, where attackers exploit model blind spots (Omar, 2024; Jones & Omar, 2024).

Furthermore, the efficiency of LLMs relies heavily on large-scale, high-quality datasets, but cybersecurity data is often scarce, fragmented, or sensitive in nature.

The reliance on synthetic data offers partial solutions, though it raises concerns about generalizability and reliability (Gholami & Omar, 2023, 2024). In addition, explainability remains a major barrier to adoption, as black-box AI models can undermine forensic credibility in court (Capuano et al., 2022; Ghazal et al., 2024).

7.2. Integration and Operational Challenges

Incorporating AI into digital forensics presents challenges in system interoperability, real-time responsiveness, and scalability. Forensic tasks often require coordination across heterogeneous tools, environments, and devices, which complicates AI integration (Du et al., 2020; Hayes & Kyobe, 2020). Automated forensic systems may produce false positives or overlook subtle evidence, undermining trust in the investigation process (Jarrett & Choo, 2021; Murphy, 2022). While automation improves efficiency (Iqbal & Alharbi, 2020), it can inadvertently introduce over-reliance on AI, reducing investigator oversight (Faqir, 2023).

Moreover, forensic investigations demand strict chain-of-custody requirements, where errors introduced by AI-driven systems could jeopardize evidence admissibility in legal contexts (Moustafa, 2022; Piraianu et al., 2023). Challenges also arise in resource allocation within cloud-based environments, where AI-enhanced detection tools must contend with latency, bandwidth constraints, and evolving attack vectors (Ramachandran et al., 2023; Stutz et al., 2024).

7.3. Ethical, Privacy, and Legal Concerns

AI-driven forensic systems raise ethical dilemmas, particularly regarding privacy, fairness, and accountability. The use of large-scale data, often sourced from personal or enterprise environments, poses risks of data misuse and regulatory non-compliance (Huff et al., 2023; Ali, 2022). In particular, privacy-preserving AI techniques remain underdeveloped in the forensic domain, creating tensions between investigative efficiency and individual rights (Ferrag et al., 2024a).

Furthermore, legal systems are not yet fully adapted to the technical complexities of AI-driven digital forensics. Questions about liability in cases of AI error persist, particularly when machine-led conclusions conflict with human expert testimony (Faqir, 2023; Bonfanti, 2022). Additionally, biases embedded in AI models risk amplifying systemic inequities in law enforcement and cybersecurity (Al-Hajri et al., 2023; Tuli & Thaduri, 2023).

7.4. Quantum Computing and Emerging Technological Risks

The rise of quantum technologies introduces new layers of complexity to AI-driven cybersecurity. While quantum computing promises faster data processing, it simultaneously threatens the foundations of cryptographic security (Baseri et al., 2024; Bishwas & Sen, 2024). Studies highlight the pressing need for quantum-resistant security measures, as conventional encryption could become obsolete in the quantum era (Rahul et al., 2024; Sodiya et al., 2024). Industrial perspectives further underscore challenges in building secure quantum networks, where integration with AI remains immature (Bush et al., 2021; Lougovski et al., 2023).

These risks are compounded by the lack of skilled quantum cybersecurity professionals, highlighting gaps in education and training (Perron et al., 2021; Khan et al., 2023; Seskir, 2019). Furthermore, hybrid AI-quantum systems face significant reliability and resource management hurdles, which may slow practical adoption (Metawei et al., 2022; Nair et al., 2024).

7.5. Adversarial Threats and Model Vulnerabilities

AI and LLM-based systems themselves are not immune to exploitation. Attackers can target model parameters through adversarial inputs, poisoning, or prompt injection attacks, undermining the reliability of threat detection (Ferrag et al., 2023; Mohamed & Ahmed, 2024). This vulnerability creates an arms race, where defenders must continuously evolve AI defenses against increasingly sophisticated attacks (Montasari, 2023; Rizvi et al., 2022).

Moreover, attackers exploit weaknesses in mobile and IoT environments, where lightweight LLMs face trade-offs between performance and resource constraints (Diaf et al., 2024; Ferrag et al., 2024b; Chilongo & KM, 2024). Smartphone and IoT device security remains particularly fragile, with vulnerabilities exacerbated by the integration of AI-driven tools (Wright et al., 2012; Zangana & Omar, 2020; Mohammed et al., 2018).

7.6. Enterprise and Industry Adoption Barriers

In enterprise contexts, deploying AI-driven forensic and cybersecurity solutions faces practical challenges such as high costs, integration complexity, and workforce readiness. Enterprises often lack the expertise to manage advanced AI tools effectively, leading to operational inefficiencies (Gupta et al., 2024; Hassan & Ibrahim, 2023). Additionally, small and medium-sized organizations may find adoption financially prohibitive, creating a digital divide in cyber defense capabilities (Ukwen & Karabatak, 2021; Alghamdi, 2021).

Industry-wide adoption also struggles with standardization. The lack of universally accepted frameworks for deploying AI in cybersecurity hinders consistent performance evaluation (Tyagi et al., 2024; Zeadally et al., 2020). While explainability and trustworthiness are emphasized as critical factors for enterprise adoption, implementing them in practice remains an unresolved challenge (Capuano et al., 2022).

7.7. Cloud and Blockchain Forensic Limitations

Cloud computing introduces unique challenges in AI-driven forensics, particularly with regard to shared infrastructure, multitenancy, and potential abuse of cloud services (Hamza & Omar, 2013; Sodiya et al., 2024). AI-based forensic tools must contend with opaque environments and jurisdictional complexities, complicating evidence collection and attribution (Mughal, 2019; Sikos, 2021).

Blockchain has been proposed as a solution for timestamping and evidence integrity verification (Zangana, 2024a). However, scalability, energy consumption, and integration with forensic workflows limit its practical application. Similarly, AI-assisted tools for analyzing firewall rule sets (Zangana et al., 2024) or detecting phishing (Zangana et al., 2024b) still face accuracy and adaptability challenges in dynamic cyber environments.

Trustworthy and explainable LLM security faces several challenges, including technical limitations, adversarial threats, operational integration issues, and quantum risks. The following diagram provides an overview of these challenges.

Figure 5. Challenges in Building Trustworthy and Explainable LLM Security Frameworks

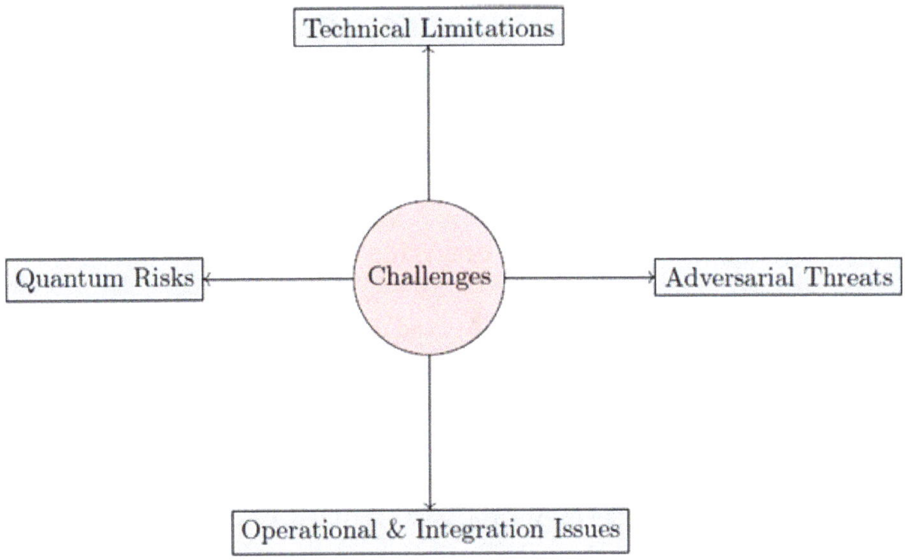

8. FUTURE DIRECTIONS

The field of trustworthy and explainable large language model (LLM) security frameworks is evolving rapidly, driven by advances in artificial intelligence (AI), digital forensics, cybersecurity, and quantum computing. Looking ahead, research and practice must converge on several critical fronts to ensure the resilience, transparency, and adaptability of LLMs against emerging threats.

8.1. Specialized Security-Oriented LLMs

The creation of domain-specific and security-focused LLMs is an essential research trajectory. Solutions such as SecureBERT (Aghaei et al., 2022) and SecLM (Asoronye et al., 2024) demonstrate how specialized models can detect cyber threats with higher precision while maintaining efficiency. Future work should focus on optimizing these specialized architectures for real-time threat detection and adaptive responses across distributed systems, critical infrastructures, and IoT networks (Diaf et al., 2024).

8.2. Explainable and Transparent AI

Explainable AI (XAI) remains a cornerstone for ensuring accountability in cybersecurity applications. Surveys highlight that explainability is not just a technical need but also an ethical imperative to build trust with users and regulators (Capuano et al., 2022; Ghazal et al., 2024). Embedding interpretability into LLMs for threat detection and digital forensics will support forensic investigators, auditors, and policymakers in making informed decisions (Piraianu et al., 2023; Syed & ES, 2024).

8.3. Integration with Digital Forensics

The synergy between AI-driven LLMs and digital forensics will redefine investigative practices. Studies show growing interest in applying AI to forensic science (Ahmed Alaa El-Din, 2022; Moustafa, 2022), forensic medicine (Piraianu et al., 2023), forensic accounting (Tuli & Thaduri, 2023), and forensic cybersecurity (Du et al., 2020; Dunsin et al., 2024). The adoption of automation in digital forensics (Hayes & Kyobe, 2020; Iqbal & Alharbi, 2020; Jarrett & Choo, 2021) coupled with AI-enabled insights (Rizvi et al., 2022; Al-Hajri et al., 2023; Ali, 2022) offers an avenue for more efficient, scalable, and precise investigations.

8.4. Privacy-Preserving and Lightweight Models

With the proliferation of IoT and IIoT devices, LLM frameworks must be designed for constrained environments. Lightweight, privacy-preserving architectures such as those proposed by Ferrag, Ndhlovu, et al. (2023, 2024) highlight how security solutions can be made accessible to resource-limited systems. Combining synthetic data generation (Gholami & Omar, 2023) and student–teacher model paradigms (Gholami & Omar, 2024) will help in balancing scalability and efficiency.

8.5. Quantum-Resilient Security Frameworks

Quantum computing poses both opportunities and threats to cybersecurity. Research emphasizes the transformative role of quantum networks (Bush et al., 2021), quantum-resistant security strategies (Bishwas & Sen, 2024), and the potential impacts of quantum computing on infrastructures (Baseri et al., 2024). Emerging perspectives underscore the urgency of preparing industries for quantum-resilient solutions (Sodiya et al., 2024; Rahul et al., 2024; Metawei et al., 2022). Interdisciplinary collaborations on quantum software development (Khan et al., 2023) and education (Perron et al., 2021; Lougovski et al., 2023; Seskir, 2019) will shape the long-term resilience of LLM-based security.

8.6. AI-Augmented Threat Intelligence and Cyber Defense

LLMs are becoming integral to next-generation threat intelligence systems (Alturkistani & Chuprat, 2024; Chen et al., 2024; Bryce et al., n.d.). Their role in predicting attacks in IoT (Diaf et al., 2024), combating man-in-the-middle attacks (Mohamed & Ahmed, 2024), and improving malware detection (Omar, 2024) demonstrates their potential to revolutionize proactive cyber defense strategies. Moreover, AI-driven insights in incident response and enterprise systems (Hassan & Ibrahim, 2023; Gupta et al., 2024) illustrate how LLMs can bridge technical and organizational resilience.

8.7. Cloud, Blockchain, and Next-Generation Architectures

The rise of AI-enhanced cloud security frameworks (Hamza & Omar, 2013; Ramachandran et al., 2023; Stutz et al., 2024) and blockchain-based timestamping for secure audits (Zangana, 2024) point to future opportunities in secure infrastructure. Integrating blockchain with AI-driven LLM frameworks may enable tamper-proof forensic evidence and stronger compliance mechanisms.

8.8. Socio-Technical and Policy-Oriented Directions

The future of LLM security frameworks cannot be divorced from socio-political contexts. Research highlights the socio-technological uncertainties of AI in cyber defense (Bonfanti, 2022), ethical challenges in balancing offense and defense (Faqir, 2023; Montasari, 2023), and the strategic role of AI in national security (Samtani et al., 2020). Furthermore, industry-focused studies (Huff et al., 2023; AL-Refaey et al., 2024) suggest that standards, governance, and cross-industry collaboration will be critical in aligning LLM deployments with regulatory compliance and trust.

8.9. Expanding Applications and Multidisciplinary Convergence

Applications of AI in digital forensics (Alghamdi, 2021; Ukwen & Karabatak, 2021), healthcare cybersecurity (Syed & ES, 2024), and biotechnology (Huff et al., 2023) reflect a growing need for multidisciplinary approaches. As research in cybersecurity issues (Nair et al., 2024; Tao et al., 2021; Kaur et al., 2023) intersects with business, law, and ethics, trustworthy frameworks must embed adaptability across diverse application domains.

8.10. Future Research Ecosystem

Finally, developing a holistic research ecosystem will be key to advancing the field. This ecosystem must incorporate:

- AI-driven automation in forensic investigations (Murphy, 2022; Mughal, 2019),
- Resilient models against adversarial manipulation (Omar, 2024),
- Security against mobile and IoT threats (Zeadally et al., 2020; Wright et al., 2012; Zangana & Omar, 2020; Mohammed et al., 2018; Nguyen et al., 2018), and
- Enhanced security analytics (Stutz et al., 2024; Zeadally et al., 2020).

By addressing these interconnected dimensions, future trustworthy and explainable LLM security frameworks will not only adapt to evolving threats but also actively shape a safer digital ecosystem.

9. CONCLUSION

The integration of quantum computing and deep learning for image classification presents a transformative opportunity to overcome many of the challenges faced by traditional machine learning approaches. By leveraging the power of quantum algorithms, complex and high-dimensional data can be processed more efficiently, offering the potential for exponential speedups in certain computational tasks. Deep learning, on the other hand, provides the flexibility and adaptability needed to capture intricate patterns and structures within image data. Together, these two paradigms form a hybrid approach that can significantly enhance classification accuracy and robustness.

This research highlights the potential of such hybrid systems to bridge the gap between theoretical advancements and practical applications. As quantum hardware continues to evolve and deep learning architectures become more sophisticated, the synergy between the two domains will pave the way for innovative solutions across multiple fields, including healthcare, autonomous systems, cybersecurity, and scientific discovery.

Ultimately, the pursuit of integrating quantum computing with deep learning is not just about improving performance but also about opening new pathways for problem-solving that were previously unattainable with classical systems alone. The progress made in this direction will play a pivotal role in shaping the next generation of intelligent systems, driving both technological innovation and real-world impact.

REFERENCES

Aghaei, E., Niu, X., Shadid, W., & Al-Shaer, E. (2022, October). Securebert: A domain-specific language model for cybersecurity. In *International Conference on Security and Privacy in Communication Systems* (pp. 39-56). Cham: Springer Nature Switzerland.

Ahmed Alaa El-Din, E. (2022). Artificial intelligence in forensic science: Invasion or revolution? *Egyptian Society of Clinical Toxicology Journal, 10*(2), 20–32. DOI: 10.21608/esctj.2022.158178.1012

Al-Hajri, S. M., Al-Thonayan, Z. J., Alqattan, M. M., Alalyani, N. A., Alali, N. D., & Alnaim, N. (2023). Maximizing the Potential of Artificial Intelligence in Digital Forensics Investigations.

AL-Refaey. M. R., Tyagi, A. K., AL-Ghamdi, A. S. A. M., & Kukreja, S. (Eds.). (2024). *Topics in Artificial Intelligence Applied to Industry 4.0*. John Wiley & Sons.

Alghamdi, M. I. (2021). *Digital forensics in cyber security—recent trends, threats, and opportunities*. Cybersecurity Threats with New Perspectives. DOI: 10.5772/intechopen.94452

Ali, A. (2022). Cyber Crime Investigation and Forensics: Leveraging AI and Big Data for More Effective Solutions.

AlQenaei, Z. M. (2024, March). Evolution and Optimization of Language Model Architectures: From Foundations to Future Directions. In *International Conference on Computing and Machine Learning* (pp. 233-249). Singapore: Springer Nature Singapore.

Alturkistani, H., & Chuprat, S. (2024). Artificial Intelligence and Large Language Models in Advancing Cyber Threat Intelligence: A Systematic Literature Review.

Asoronye, G. O., Anthony, O. C., Ogbuikwu, R. I., Ogili, C. O., & Ali, H. U. (2024). SecLM: A Specialized Security Language Model for Advanced Cybersecurity Applications and Threat Mitigation. *EKETE-International Journal Of Advanced Research*, *2*(6), 33–42.

Baseri, Y., Chouhan, V., & Ghorbani, A. (2024). Cybersecurity in the Quantum Era: Assessing the Impact of Quantum Computing on Infrastructure. *arXiv preprint arXiv:2404.10659.*

Bishwas, A. K., & Sen, M. (2024). Strategic Roadmap for Quantum-Resistant Security: A Framework for Preparing Industries for the Quantum Threat. *arXiv preprint arXiv:2411.09995*.

Bonfanti, M. E. (2022). *Artificial intelligence and the offence-defence balance in cyber security. Cyber Security: Socio-Technological Uncertainty and Political Fragmentation*. Routledge.

Bryce, C., Kalousis, A., Leroux, I., Madinier, H., Mermoud, A., Mulder, V., ... & Ruch, P. Trends in Large Language Models: Actors, Applications, and Impact on Cybersecurity.

Bush, S. F., Challener, W. A., & Mantelet, G. (2021). A perspective on industrial quantum networks. *AVS Quantum Science*, *3*(3), 030501. DOI: 10.1116/5.0051881

Capuano, N., Fenza, G., Loia, V., & Stanzione, C. (2022). Explainable artificial intelligence in cybersecurity: A survey. *IEEE Access : Practical Innovations, Open Solutions*, *10*, 93575–93600. DOI: 10.1109/ACCESS.2022.3204171

Chen, Y., Cui, M., Wang, D., Cao, Y., Yang, P., Jiang, B., Lu, Z., & Liu, B. (2024). A survey of large language models for cyber threat detection. *Computers & Security*, *145*, 104016. DOI: 10.1016/j.cose.2024.104016

CHILONGO, L., & KM, A. S. (2024). IMPACT OF ARTIFICIAL INTELLIGENCE ON CYBERSECURITY: A CASE OF INTERNET OF THINGS. *i-Manager's Journal on Digital Forensics & Cyber Security (JDF)*, *2*(1).

Diaf, A., Korba, A. A., Karabadji, N. E., & Ghamri-Doudane, Y. (2024, April). Beyond detection: Leveraging large language models for cyber attack prediction in iot networks. In *2024 20th International Conference on Distributed Computing in Smart Systems and the Internet of Things (DCOSS-IoT)* (pp. 117-123). IEEE.

Du, X., Hargreaves, C., Sheppard, J., Anda, F., Sayakkara, A., Le-Khac, N. A., & Scanlon, M. (2020, August). SoK: Exploring the state of the art and the future potential of artificial intelligence in digital forensic investigation. In *Proceedings of the 15th international conference on availability, reliability and security* (pp. 1-10). DOI: 10.1145/3407023.3407068

Dunsin, D., Ghanem, M. C., Ouazzane, K., & Vassilev, V. (2024). A comprehensive analysis of the role of artificial intelligence and machine learning in modern digital forensics and incident response. *Forensic Science International Digital Investigation*, *48*, 301675. DOI: 10.1016/j.fsidi.2023.301675

Faqir, R. S. (2023). Digital Criminal Investigations in the Era of Artificial Intelligence: A Comprehensive Overview. *International Journal of Cyber Criminology, 17*(2), 77–94.

Ferrag, M. A., Alwahedi, F., Battah, A., Cherif, B., Mechri, A., & Tihanyi, N. (2024). Generative ai and large language models for cyber security: All insights you need. *Available at SSRN* 4853709. DOI: 10.2139/ssrn.4853709

Ferrag, M. A., Ndhlovu, M., Tihanyi, N., Cordeiro, L. C., Debbah, M., & Lestable, T. (2023). Revolutionizing cyber threat detection with large language models. *arXiv preprint arXiv:2306.14263*, 195-202.

Ferrag, M. A., Ndhlovu, M., Tihanyi, N., Cordeiro, L. C., Debbah, M., Lestable, T., & Thandi, N. S. (2024). Revolutionizing cyber threat detection with large language models: A privacy-preserving bert-based lightweight model for iot/iiot devices. *IEEE Access : Practical Innovations, Open Solutions, 12*, 23733–23750. DOI: 10.1109/ACCESS.2024.3363469

Ghazal, T. M., Janjua, J. I., Abushiba, W., Ahmad, M., Ihsan, A., & Al-Dmour, N. A. (2024, December). Cybersecurity Revolution via Large Language Models and Explainable AI. In *2024 17th International Conference on Security of Information and Networks (SIN)* (pp. 1-6). IEEE. DOI: 10.1109/SIN63213.2024.10871324

Gholami, S., & Omar, M. (2023). Does Synthetic Data Make Large Language Models More Efficient? *arXiv preprint arXiv:2310.07830.*

Gholami, S., & Omar, M. (2024). Can a student large language model perform as well as its teacher? In *Innovations, Securities, and Case Studies Across Healthcare, Business, and Technology* (pp. 122-139). IGI Global. DOI: 10.4018/979-8-3693-1906-2.ch007

Gupta, B. B., Gaurav, A., & Arya, V. (2024). Navigating the security landscape of large language models in enterprise information systems. *Enterprise Information Systems, 18*(4), 2310846. DOI: 10.1080/17517575.2024.2310846

Hadi, M. A., Abdulredha, M. N., & Hasan, E. (2023). Introduction to ChatGPT: A new revolution of artificial intelligence with machine learning algorithms and cybersecurity. *Sci. Arch, 4*(04), 276. DOI: 10.47587/SA.2023.4406

Hamza, Y. A., & Omar, M. D. (2013). Cloud computing security: Abuse and nefarious use of cloud computing. *International Journal of Computer Engineering Research, 3*(6), 22–27.

Hassan, S. K., & Ibrahim, A. (2023). The role of artificial intelligence in cyber security and incident response. *International Journal for Electronic Crime Investigation, 7*(2).

Hayes, D., & Kyobe, M. (2020, March). The adoption of automation in cyber forensics. In *2020 Conference on Information Communications Technology and Society (ICTAS)* (pp. 1-6). IEEE. DOI: 10.1109/ICTAS47918.2020.233977

Huff, A. J., Burrell, D. N., Nobles, C., Richardson, K., Wright, J. B., Burton, S. L., Jones, A. J., Springs, D., Omar, M., & Brown-Jackson, K. L. (2023). Management Practices for Mitigating Cybersecurity Threats to Biotechnology Companies, Laboratories, and Healthcare Research Organizations. In *Applied Research Approaches to Technology, Healthcare, and Business* (pp. 1-12). IGI Global.

Iqbal, S., & Alharbi, S. A. (2020). Advancing automation in digital forensic investigations using machine learning forensics. *Digital Forensic Science, 3.*

Jarrett, A., & Choo, K. K. R. (2021). The impact of automation and artificial intelligence on digital forensics. *WIREs Forensic Science*, *3*(6), e1418. DOI: 10.1002/wfs2.1418

Jones, R., & Omar, M. (2024). Revolutionizing Cybersecurity: The GPT-2 Enhanced Attack Detection and Defense (GEADD) Method for Zero-Day Threats. *International Journal of Informatics* [INJIISCOM]. *Information System and Computer Engineering*, *5*(2), 178–191.

Jones, R., Omar, M., Mohammed, D., Nobles, C., & Dawson, M. (2023). Harnessing the Speed and Accuracy of Machine Learning to Advance Cybersecurity. In *2023 Congress in Computer Science, Computer Engineering, & Applied Computing (CSCE)* (pp. 418-421). IEEE. DOI: 10.1109/CSCE60160.2023.00074

Kaur, R., Gabrijelčič, D., & Klobučar, T. (2023). Artificial intelligence for cybersecurity: Literature review and future research directions. *Information Fusion*, *97*, 101804. DOI: 10.1016/j.inffus.2023.101804

Khan, A. A., Akbar, M. A., Ahmad, A., Fahmideh, M., Shameem, M., Lahtinen, V., . . . Mikkonen, T. (2023, July). Agile practices for quantum software development: practitioners' perspectives. In *2023 IEEE international conference on quantum software (QSW)* (pp. 9-20). IEEE.

Lougovski, P., Parekh, O., Broz, J., Byrd, M., Chembo, Y., de Jong, W. A., . . . Svore, K. M. (2023). *Position Papers for the ASCR Workshop on Basic Research Needs in Quantum Computing and Networking*. USDOE Office of Science (SC), Advanced Scientific Computing Research (ASCR).

Metawei, M. A., Eldeeb, H., Nassar, S. M., & Taher, M. (2022). Quantum Computing Meets Artificial Intelligence: Innovations and Challenges. In *Handbook on Artificial Intelligence-Empowered Applied Software Engineering: VOL. 1: Novel Methodologies to Engineering Smart Software Systems* (pp. 303–338). Springer International Publishing. DOI: 10.1007/978-3-031-08202-3_12

Mohamed, N., & Ahmed, A. A. (2024, June). AI in Combatting Man-in-the-Middle Attacks: A Comprehensive Review. In *2024 15th International Conference on Computing Communication and Networking Technologies (ICCCNT)* (pp. 1-6). IEEE. DOI: 10.1109/ICCCNT61001.2024.10725789

Mohammed, D., Omar, M., & Nguyen, V. (2018). Wireless sensor network security: Approaches to detecting and avoiding wormhole attacks. *Journal of Research in Business. Economics and Management, 10*(2), 1860–1864.

Montasari, R. (2023). *Countering cyberterrorism: the confluence of artificial intelligence, cyber forensics and digital policing in US and UK national cybersecurity* (Vol. 101). Springer Nature. DOI: 10.1007/978-3-031-21920-7

Moustafa, N. (2022). *Digital Forensics in the Era of Artificial Intelligence.* CRC Press. DOI: 10.1201/9781003278962

Mughal, A. A. (2019). A comprehensive study of practical techniques and methodologies in incident-based approaches for cyber forensics. *Tensorgate Journal of Sustainable Technology and Infrastructure for Developing Countries*, *2*(1), 1–18.

Murphy, J. P. (2022). *Digital Forensic Investigations and Automated and Artificial Intelligence Technologies* (Master's thesis, Utica University).

Nair, M. M., Deshmukh, A., & Tyagi, A. K. (2024). Artificial intelligence for cyber security: Current trends and future challenges. *Automated Secure Computing for Next-Generation Systems*, 83-114.

Nguyen, V., Mohammed, D., Omar, M., & Banisakher, M. (2018). The Effects of the FCC Net Neutrality Repeal on Security and Privacy. [IJHIoT]. *International Journal of Hyperconnectivity and the Internet of Things*, *2*(2), 21–29. DOI: 10.4018/IJHIoT.2018070102

Omar, M. (2021). New insights into database security: An effective and integrated approach for applying access control mechanisms and cryptographic concepts in Microsoft Access environments.

Omar, M. (2022). *Machine Learning for Cybersecurity: Innovative Deep Learning Solutions*. Springer Brief. https://link.springer.com/book/978303115

Omar, M. (2024). From Attack to Defense: Strengthening DNN Text Classification Against Adversarial Examples. In *Innovations, Securities, and Case Studies Across Healthcare, Business, and Technology* (pp. 174-195). IGI Global.

Omar, M. (2024). Revolutionizing Malware Detection: A Paradigm Shift Through Optimized Convolutional Neural Networks. In *Innovations, Securities, and Case Studies Across Healthcare, Business, and Technology* (pp. 196-220). IGI Global. DOI: 10.4018/979-8-3693-1906-2.ch011

Omar, M., & Zangana, H. M. (Eds.). (2024). *Redefining Security With Cyber AI*. IGI Global., DOI: 10.4018/979-8-3693-6517-5

Perron, J. K., DeLeone, C., Sharif, S., Carter, T., Grossman, J. M., Passante, G., & Sack, J. (2021). Quantum undergraduate education and scientific training. *arXiv preprint arXiv:2109.13850*.

Piraianu, A. I., Fulga, A., Musat, C. L., Ciobotaru, O. R., Poalelungi, D. G., Stamate, E., Ciobotaru, O., & Fulga, I. (2023). Enhancing the evidence with algorithms: How artificial intelligence is transforming forensic medicine. *Diagnostics (Basel)*, *13*(18), 2992. DOI: 10.3390/diagnostics13182992

Rahul, R., Geetha, S., Priyatharsini, S., Mehata, K., Sundaresan Perumal, T., Ethiraj, N., & Sendilvelan, S. (2024). Cybersecurity Issues and Challenges in Quantum Computing. *Topics in Artificial Intelligence Applied to Industry*, *4*(0), 203–221. DOI: 10.1002/9781394216147.ch11

Ramachandran, D., Naqi, S. M., Perumal, G., & Abbas, Q. (2023). DLTN-LOSP: A Novel Deep-Linear-Transition-Network-Based Resource Allocation Model with the Logic Overhead Security Protocol for Cloud Systems. *Sensors (Basel)*, *23*(20), 8448. DOI: 10.3390/s23208448

Rizvi, S., Scanlon, M., Mcgibney, J., & Sheppard, J. (2022). Application of artificial intelligence to network forensics: Survey, challenges and future directions. *IEEE Access : Practical Innovations, Open Solutions*, *10*, 110362–110384. DOI: 10.1109/ACCESS.2022.3214506

Samtani, S., Kantarcioglu, M., & Chen, H. (2020). Trailblazing the artificial intelligence for cybersecurity discipline: A multi-disciplinary research roadmap. [TMIS]. *ACM Transactions on Management Information Systems*, *11*(4), 1–19. DOI: 10.1145/3430360

Seskir, Z. C. (2019). *Current state of quantum information technologies in Turkey* (Master's thesis, Middle East Technical University).

Sikos, L. F. (2021). AI in digital forensics: Ontology engineering for cybercrime investigations. *WIREs Forensic Science, 3*(3), e1394. DOI: 10.1002/wfs2.1394

Sodiya, E. O., Umoga, U. J., Amoo, O. O., & Atadoga, A. (2024). Quantum computing and its potential impact on US cybersecurity: A review: Scrutinizing the challenges and opportunities presented by quantum technologies in safeguarding digital assets. *Global Journal of Engineering and Technology Advances, 18*(2), 049-064.

Stutz, D., de Assis, J. T., Laghari, A. A., Khan, A. A., Andreopoulos, N., Terziev, A., ... & Grata, E. G. (2024). Enhancing Security in Cloud Computing Using Artificial Intelligence (AI). *Applying Artificial Intelligence in Cybersecurity Analytics and Cyber Threat Detection*, 179-220.

Syed, F. M., & ES, F. K. (2024). AI-Driven Forensic Analysis for Cyber Incidents in Healthcare. *International Journal of Machine Learning Research in Cybersecurity and Artificial Intelligence, 15*(1), 473–499.

Tao, F., Akhtar, M. S., & Jiayuan, Z. (2021). The future of artificial intelligence in cybersecurity: A comprehensive survey. *EAI Endorsed Transactions on Creative Technologies, 8*(28), e3–e3. DOI: 10.4108/eai.7-7-2021.170285

Tuli, F. A., & Thaduri, U. R. (2023). The Integration of Artificial Intelligence in Forensic Accounting: A Game-Changer. *Asian Accounting and Auditing Advancement, 14*(1), 12–20.

Tyagi, A. K., Kumari, S., & Richa. (2024). Artificial Intelligence-Based Cyber Security and Digital Forensics: A Review. *Artificial Intelligence-Enabled Digital Twin for Smart Manufacturing*, 391-419.

Ukwen, D. O., & Karabatak, M. (2021, June). Review of NLP-based systems in digital forensics and cybersecurity. In *2021 9th International symposium on digital forensics and security (ISDFS)* (pp. 1-9). IEEE. DOI: 10.1109/ISDFS52919.2021.9486354

Wright, J., Dawson, M. E.Jr, & Omar, M. (2012). Cyber security and mobile threats: The need for antivirus applications for smartphones. *Journal of Information Systems Technology and Planning, 5*(14), 40–60.

Zangana, H. M. (2024). Exploring Blockchain-Based Timestamping Tools: A Comprehensive Review. *Redefining Security With Cyber AI*, 92-110.

Zangana, H. M. (2024). Exploring the Landscape of Website Vulnerability Scanners: A Comprehensive Review and Comparative Analysis. *Redefining Security With Cyber AI*, 111-129.

Zangana, H. M., Mohammed, A. K., Sallow, A. B., & Sallow, Z. B. (2024). Cybernetic Deception: Unraveling the Layers of Email Phishing Threats. [INJURATECH]. *International Journal of Research and Applied Technology*, *4*(1), 35–47.

Zangana, H. M., & Omar, M. (2020). Threats, Attacks, and Mitigations of Smartphone Security. *Academic Journal of Nawroz University*, *9*(4), 324–332. DOI: 10.25007/ajnu.v9n4a989

Zangana, H. M., Omar, M., Al-Karaki, J. N., & Mohammed, D. (2024). Comprehensive Review and Analysis of Network Firewall Rule Analyzers: Enhancing Security Posture and Efficiency. *Redefining Security With Cyber AI*, 15-36.

Zeadally, S., Adi, E., Baig, Z., & Khan, I. A. (2020). Harnessing artificial intelligence capabilities to improve cybersecurity. *IEEE Access : Practical Innovations, Open Solutions*, *8*, 23817–23837. DOI: 10.1109/ACCESS.2020.2968045

Chapter 8
Protecting LLM-Driven Agricultural Systems:
Cybersecurity Risks and Mitigation in Smart Farming

Rebet Keith Jones
https://orcid.org/0009-0008-0487-1301
Capitol Technology University, USA

Senny Luckyardi
https://orcid.org/0000-0001-9954-7433
Universitas Komputer Indonesia, Indonesia

ABSTRACT

The integration of Large Language Models (LLMs) into agricultural systems has introduced significant opportunities for enhancing productivity, sustainability, and decision-making in smart farming. By leveraging LLMs, farmers and agribusinesses can optimize resource allocation, predict crop yields, detect diseases, and streamline supply chain management. However, as these systems become increasingly interconnected with the Internet of Things (IoT), cloud platforms, and autonomous technologies, they also face heightened cybersecurity vulnerabilities. Potential threats include adversarial attacks on LLMs, data poisoning, model manipulation, and unauthorized access to farm management systems. Such risks can compromise food security, disrupt operations, and erode trust in smart farming technologies. This chapter explores the cybersecurity challenges associated with LLM-driven agricultural systems and provides a comprehensive framework for mitigation strategies. Emphasis is placed on robust authentication mechanisms, adversarial defense methods, privacy-preserving data management,

DOI: 10.4018/979-8-3373-7133-7.ch008

1. INTRODUCTION

The agricultural sector is undergoing a profound transformation driven by the integration of digital technologies, artificial intelligence (AI), and, more recently, large language models (LLMs). This transformation, often described as the advent of Agriculture 4.0, leverages AI, big data, robotics, and the Internet of Things (IoT) to enhance food production, optimize resource allocation, and enable sustainable practices (Araújo et al., 2021; Bhat & Huang, 2021). With global population growth, climate variability, and the demand for resilient food systems, LLMs are increasingly deployed as decision-support tools for farmers, policymakers, and agribusinesses (Ahmad et al., 2024; Pandey & Mishra, 2024). They facilitate tasks such as predictive crop modeling, automated advisory systems, disease detection, and intelligent irrigation management (Wei et al., 2024; Ahmed et al., 2024).

While these advancements promise to strengthen food security and improve farming efficiency, the adoption of AI and LLMs introduces complex cybersecurity, ethical, and governance challenges. Smart farming infrastructures depend on interconnected IoT devices, cloud computing, and large datasets, making them vulnerable to threats such as data breaches, adversarial manipulation, and ransomware attacks (Otieno, 2023; Ali, Mijwil, Buruga, Abotaleb, & Adamopoulos, 2024). Scholars emphasize that the susceptibility of smart agriculture to such risks is compounded by the lack of standardized security protocols and the limited awareness of cybersecurity within the farming community (Jerhamre, Carlberg, & van Zoest, 2022; Zangana, Luckyardi, Mustafa, & Li, 2025). Moreover, as agricultural data is increasingly digitized and shared across global platforms, questions about privacy, ownership, and responsible governance of sensitive plant and environmental data are gaining urgency (Devare, Arnaud, Antezana, & King, 2023; Williamson et al., 2023; Gavai et al., 2025).

The ethical implications of LLM-driven agriculture also warrant critical reflection. As Sparrow and Howard (2021) highlight, robots and autonomous systems in agriculture present dilemmas related to labor displacement, accountability, and trust. Similarly, ethical considerations in AI cybersecurity underline the importance of safeguarding systems against malicious misuse while ensuring fairness and transparency in automated decision-making (Kaushik, Khan, Kumari, Sharma, & Dubey, 2024). In developing nations, these concerns are further compounded by resource gaps, infrastructural limitations, and policy misalignments, which can hinder equitable access to advanced AI technologies (Aderibigbe, Ohenhen, Nwaobia, Gidiagba, & Ani, 2023; Ahmad et al., 2024; Ali et al., 2024). Scholars argue that without proactive governance and ethical safeguards, the integration of LLMs in agriculture may exacerbate inequalities instead of reducing them (Alexander, Yarborough, & Smith, 2024; Kapoor, 2025).

The role of cybersecurity in this context is pivotal. As LLMs become central to agricultural decision-making, ensuring their resilience against cyber threats is critical to maintaining trust and protecting food supply chains (Aggarwal, Bansal, & Goel, 2024; Gardezi et al., 2024). Research indicates that threats range from adversarial data manipulation and poisoning attacks to the exploitation of AI systems for misinformation or economic disruption (Bahrini et al., 2023; Neupane et al., 2024). This aligns with the broader view that cybersecurity in AI-robotics requires a systemic understanding of risks and externalities to safeguard both technology and human stakeholders (Tzachor, Devare, King, Avin, & Ó hÉigeartaigh, 2022; Holzinger, Weippl, Tjoa, & Kieseberg, 2021).

Furthermore, the interdisciplinary applications of LLMs highlight both opportunities and risks. Beyond agriculture, LLMs are reshaping domains such as scientific writing, education, and environmental conservation, raising concerns about academic integrity, ethical usage, and misinformation (Abd-Elsalam & Abdel-Momen, 2023; Aithal & Aithal, 2023; Ya'u & Mohammed, 2025; Zohouri, Sabzali, & Golmohammadi, 2024). These debates are particularly relevant for agricultural systems, where AI-generated insights can influence high-stakes decisions on food production, land management, and sustainability (Denhere & Shao, 2024; Adanma & Ogunbiyi, 2024; Kochupillai, Kahl, Schmitt, Taubenböck, & Zhu, 2022). Thus, securing LLM-driven agriculture requires not only technical defenses but also ethical, regulatory, and socio-cultural considerations (Mark, 2019; Kochupillai & Köninger, 2023; Zangana, Amelia, Mustafa, & Li, 2025).

In light of these dynamics, this chapter aims to:

1. Analyze the cybersecurity risks associated with LLM-driven agricultural systems.
2. Explore the ethical, governance, and legal considerations shaping their adoption.
3. Present mitigation strategies such as federated learning, privacy-preserving data management, adversarial defenses, and farmer-centered security frameworks (Dembani et al., 2025; Gavai et al., 2025; Zangana, Abdulqader, Luckyardi, & Li, 2026).
4. Highlight emerging opportunities for building resilient, secure, and responsible AI-powered agricultural ecosystems (Senoo et al., 2024; Leong, Lim, Subri, & Jalil, 2023; Bhangar & Shahriyar, 2023).

By addressing these themes, the discussion contributes to the broader literature on responsible AI in agriculture and provides practical insights for researchers, policymakers, and industry leaders seeking to harness the potential of LLMs while mitigating the risks of cyber threats. Ultimately, protecting LLM-driven agricultural systems is not merely a technical challenge but a societal imperative tied to global food security, environmental sustainability, and digital trust (Sood, Sharma,

& Bhardwaj, 2022; Shafik, Tufail, De Silva, Haji, & Apong, 2025; Zangana, Luckyardi, Mustafa, & Li, 2025).

2. BACKGROUND AND MOTIVATION

The rapid evolution of artificial intelligence (AI) and large language models (LLMs) is reshaping agriculture into what scholars describe as Agriculture 4.0, an era characterized by digitalization, automation, and data-driven decision-making (Araújo, Peres, Barata, Lidon, & Ramalho, 2021; Bhat & Huang, 2021). Farmers now increasingly rely on interconnected Internet of Things (IoT) devices, robotics, and AI systems to monitor crops, manage irrigation, predict yields, and safeguard resources (Bhangar & Shahriyar, 2023; Senoo et al., 2024). The transformative potential of LLMs in particular lies in their ability to synthesize vast streams of agricultural data, generate actionable insights, and provide real-time advisory services for both large-scale agribusinesses and smallholder farmers (Chen et al., 2024; Wei et al., 2024).

2.1 Opportunities of AI and LLMs in Agriculture

AI applications in agriculture extend from precision farming and crop disease detection to supply chain optimization and sustainable practices (Ahmed et al., 2024; Kanyepe, Chibaro, Morima, & Moeti-Lysson, 2025). Several studies emphasize that AI-driven tools can significantly enhance food security, especially in developing nations facing climate and resource challenges (Ahmad et al., 2024; Ali et al., 2024; Pandey & Mishra, 2024). Gupta, Pagani, Zamboni, and Singh (2024) highlight breakthroughs in plant sciences powered by AI, while Shafik, Tufail, De Silva, Haji, and Apong (2025) describe AI's broader impact on agricultural industries. Such innovations align with global sustainability goals and the vision of food and industry 5.0 (Kapoor, 2025).

Moreover, advancements in digital marketplaces, data linkages, and blockchain-enabled platforms for managing agrobiodiversity demonstrate how AI can create opportunities for inclusive growth and responsible agricultural innovation (Kochupillai & Köninger, 2023; Kochupillai, Kahl, Schmitt, Taubenböck, & Zhu, 2022). As Dara, Hazrati Fard, and Kaur (2022) argue, ensuring the ethical and responsible use of AI in digital agriculture is essential to maximize these benefits.

2.2 Emerging Risks and Cybersecurity Concerns

The very digitalization that powers smart farming also increases its vulnerability to cyber threats. Smart agriculture depends on IoT sensors, drones, cloud computing, and data-sharing platforms, making it an attractive target for adversaries (Otieno, 2023; Jerhamre, Carlberg, & van Zoest, 2022). Ali, Mijwil, Buruga, Abotaleb, and Adamopoulos (2024) provide a comprehensive survey highlighting cyber threats such as ransomware, data poisoning, and adversarial manipulation in AI-driven agriculture. Malhotra and Firdaus (2022) similarly underscore the challenges of IoT security in precision crop yield prediction systems.

Neupane et al. (2024) stress that AI-robotics systems face systemic risks due to adversarial attacks and insufficient safeguards, while Holzinger, Weippl, Tjoa, and Kieseberg (2021) note the urgent need to align AI adoption with security, safety, and privacy considerations for sustainable development. The misuse of LLMs for misinformation, biased recommendations, or manipulation of agricultural data compounds these risks (Bahrini et al., 2023). Without adequate cybersecurity, the promise of AI-powered farming may be undermined by distrust and potential disruptions to global food supply chains (Aggarwal, Bansal, & Goel, 2024; Gardezi et al., 2024).

2.3 Ethical, Legal, and Governance Dimensions

The integration of AI in agriculture is not merely a technological endeavor but a socio-ethical challenge. As Sparrow and Howard (2021) and Sparrow, Howard, and Degeling (2021) point out, robots and autonomous systems raise issues of accountability, labor displacement, and ethical governance. Similarly, Alexander, Yarborough, and Smith (2024) argue that building trust in AI agriculture requires clarity on "responsible AI" and accountability structures. Ethical frameworks for AI-based cybersecurity must address fairness, privacy, and transparency (Kaushik, Khan, Kumari, Sharma, & Dubey, 2024; Mark, 2019).

Legal scholars stress that governing agricultural data is critical to avoid misuse and ensure equitable benefits (Devare, Arnaud, Antezana, & King, 2023; Williamson et al., 2023). Gavai et al. (2025) and Dembani et al. (2025) propose federated learning and privacy-preserving frameworks as potential solutions. Zangana, Amelia, Luckyardi, Mustafa, and Li (2025) highlight that regulating language and AI in agriculture must be grounded in legal perspectives, while Zangana, Luckyardi, Mustafa, and Li (2025) further emphasize deep learning and LLMs as central to agricultural cybersecurity protection.

2.4 Motivation for This Study

Despite clear benefits, gaps remain in bridging AI's potential with secure, ethical, and scalable agricultural solutions. In developing countries, infrastructure limitations, policy misalignments, and digital divides exacerbate the risks of unequal AI adoption (Aderibigbe, Ohenhen, Nwaobia, Gidiagba, & Ani, 2023; Ahmad et al., 2024). Similarly, academic discourse reveals tensions between leveraging LLMs for productivity gains and the risks of misuse, bias, or academic dishonesty in related fields like education and scientific writing (Abd-Elsalam & Abdel-Momen, 2023; Aithal & Aithal, 2023; Ya'u & Mohammed, 2025; Zohouri, Sabzali, & Golmohammadi, 2024; Zangana, Amelia, Mustafa, & Li, 2025). Such insights highlight the cross-sectoral relevance of ethical AI adoption.

For agriculture specifically, the motivation to secure LLM-driven systems is threefold. First, food security depends on trustworthy AI-enabled decision-making (Chen et al., 2024; Ahmad et al., 2024). Second, the economic and social stability of farming communities relies on resilient systems that resist cyberattacks and data misuse (Leong, Lim, Subri, & Jalil, 2023; Sood, Sharma, & Bhardwaj, 2022). Third, the integration of LLMs into smart farming must align with broader ethical, governance, and sustainability agendas (Tzachor, Devare, King, Avin, & Ó hÉigeartaigh, 2022; Denhere & Shao, 2024).

Finally, as Uplaonkar, Veershetty, Bahar, and Sangeeta (2024) suggest, productive AI is both a supporter and a challenger, requiring careful evaluation of its dual impact. Motivated by these complexities, this chapter seeks to analyze the cybersecurity risks of LLM-driven agricultural systems and propose strategic mitigation approaches that balance technological innovation with ethical responsibility and global sustainability goals (He et al., 2021; Groumpos, 2023; Zangana & Mustafa, 2026).

3. ROLE OF LLMS IN AGRICULTURE

The agricultural sector is undergoing a profound digital transformation, often referred to as Agriculture 4.0, where advanced data-driven technologies such as the Internet of Things (IoT), big data, robotics, and artificial intelligence (AI) converge to enhance productivity, resilience, and sustainability (Araújo, Peres, Barata, Lidon, & Ramalho, 2021; Bhat & Huang, 2021). Within this paradigm, Large Language Models (LLMs) have emerged as a crucial enabler, capable of processing unstructured agricultural data, providing real-time decision support, and facilitating communication across diverse stakeholders in farming systems (Chen et al., 2024; Shafik, Tufail, De Silva, Haji, & Apong, 2025).

3.1 Data Integration and Decision-Making

LLMs enhance agricultural decision-making by synthesizing complex datasets from sensors, drones, and satellite imagery into actionable insights. This capability supports precision agriculture practices such as irrigation management, crop monitoring, and pest control (Wei et al., 2024; Senoo et al., 2024). By translating heterogeneous data into user-friendly formats, LLMs empower farmers with improved situational awareness and facilitate data-driven interventions that increase yield while conserving resources (Ahmed et al., 2024; Aggarwal, Bansal, & Goel, 2024). Additionally, LLM-powered platforms can generate customized recommendations for smallholder farmers in developing nations, bridging gaps in agricultural expertise (Ahmad et al., 2024; Ali et al., 2024).

3.2 Enhancing Productivity and Food Security

Several studies emphasize the role of AI and LLMs in improving food security by increasing efficiency in production, reducing losses, and optimizing supply chains (Gupta, Pagani, Zamboni, & Singh, 2024; Kanyepe, Chibaro, Morima, & Moeti-Lysson, 2025). LLMs can assist in forecasting crop yields, predicting market fluctuations, and providing adaptive strategies against climate variability (Pandey & Mishra, 2024). They also enable sustainable practices by identifying optimal fertilizer use, reducing water wastage, and recommending eco-friendly pest management approaches (Adanma & Ogunbiyi, 2024; Denhere & Shao, 2024). These applications contribute to aligning agricultural modernization with global sustainable development goals (SDGs) (Holzinger, Weippl, Tjoa, & Kieseberg, 2021).

3.3 Knowledge Dissemination and Capacity Building

LLMs also serve as tools for knowledge transfer in agriculture, functioning as virtual advisors capable of training farmers, researchers, and policymakers. They provide context-sensitive guidance in local languages, enabling inclusivity and reducing dependency on limited extension services (Leong, Lim, Subri, & Jalil, 2023; Uplaonkar, Veershetty, Bahar, & Sangeeta, 2024). However, as Abd-Elsalam and Abdel-Momen (2023) and Ya'u and Mohammed (2025) caution, reliance on LLMs in scientific writing and advisory contexts raises concerns about over-dependence, ethical misuse, and academic integrity. Zohouri, Sabzali, and Golmohammadi (2024) further emphasize that ChatGPT-assisted writing can introduce risks of bias or unverified outputs, highlighting the need for responsible use in agricultural research communication.

3.4 Ethical, Legal, and Governance Considerations

The role of LLMs in agriculture extends beyond technical efficiency to ethical and legal domains. As Sparrow and Howard (2021) and Sparrow, Howard, and Degeling (2021) note, the introduction of AI and robotics into farming reshapes labor practices, raises accountability questions, and requires robust governance frameworks. Scholars argue for systemic approaches to responsible AI adoption, balancing opportunities with risks such as bias, data exploitation, and privacy violations (Tzachor, Devare, King, Avin, & Ó hÉigeartaigh, 2022; Kapoor, 2025). Devare, Arnaud, Antezana, and King (2023) highlight the governance challenges associated with managing plant and agricultural data, while Kochupillai and Köninger (2023) propose blockchain and AI-based marketplaces to regulate agrobiodiversity data. Zangana, Amelia, Luckyardi, Mustafa, and Li (2025) further underscore the legal role of language in regulating agricultural AI technologies at a global scale.

3.5 Cybersecurity and Trust in LLM-Driven Agriculture

While LLMs offer significant benefits, their deployment introduces new cybersecurity vulnerabilities. The integration of LLMs into smart farming systems exposes them to risks such as adversarial manipulation, misinformation, and data breaches (Ali, Mijwil, Buruga, Abotaleb, & Adamopoulos, 2024; Otieno, 2023; Jerhamre, Carlberg, & van Zoest, 2022). These risks can compromise trust, a critical factor for farmer adoption of AI-based systems (Gardezi et al., 2024; Alexander, Yarborough, & Smith, 2024). Neupane et al. (2024) stress that AI-robotics systems require stronger defenses against adversarial attacks, while Kaushik, Khan, Kumari, Sharma, and Dubey (2024) emphasize the importance of ethical safeguards in AI-based cybersecurity. Emerging approaches such as federated learning and privacy-preserving frameworks (Dembani et al., 2025; Gavai et al., 2025) offer promising strategies to mitigate these risks.

3.6 Expanding the Agricultural Knowledge Economy

Beyond immediate farming applications, LLMs contribute to the agricultural knowledge economy by supporting research, policy, and education. For instance, LLMs facilitate academic writing, data interpretation, and collaborative research in plant sciences and agrifood systems (Williamson et al., 2023; Sood, Sharma, & Bhardwaj, 2022). Aithal and Aithal (2023, 2024) highlight the broader educational and industrial implications of ChatGPT and related technologies, while Zangana and Mustafa (2026) demonstrate the role of AI-based tools in enhancing digital resources for teaching. At the same time, ethical scholarship urges responsible integration of

AI to avoid misuse, particularly in the context of publishing and academic standards (Bahrini et al., 2023; Groumpos, 2023; Mark, 2019).

3.7 Toward Secure and Ethical Adoption

The emerging role of LLMs in agriculture illustrates a double-edged reality: they are both catalysts for efficiency and potential sources of vulnerability. As Dara, Hazrati Fard, and Kaur (2022) argue, ethical and responsible deployment of AI in agriculture is critical for realizing its benefits while minimizing risks. Integrating robust legal frameworks (Zangana, Luckyardi, Mustafa, & Li, 2025), digital forensics for cybercrime in smart agriculture (Zangana, Abdulqader, Luckyardi, & Li, 2026), and deep learning–based protection mechanisms (Zangana, Luckyardi, Mustafa, & Li, 2025) provides a foundation for building resilient systems. Ultimately, aligning LLMs with sustainable farming practices requires a balance between innovation, cybersecurity, and ethical responsibility (He et al., 2021; Sood et al., 2022).

4. CYBERSECURITY THREAT LANDSCAPE IN AGRICULTURAL SYSTEMS

The integration of artificial intelligence (AI), Internet of Things (IoT), and large language models (LLMs) in agriculture has accelerated innovation, but it has also expanded the cybersecurity threat landscape. Modern agricultural ecosystems, characterized by interconnected smart devices, big data analytics, and cloud-based platforms, face unique vulnerabilities that can compromise food security, farmer livelihoods, and global supply chains (Araújo, Peres, Barata, Lidon, & Ramalho, 2021; Bhat & Huang, 2021; Chen et al., 2024).

4.1 IoT and Infrastructure Vulnerabilities

The deployment of IoT sensors and AI-driven devices in smart farming introduces risks such as unauthorized access, malware attacks, and data interception. Studies reveal that smart irrigation, soil sensors, and autonomous tractors are particularly susceptible to cyberattacks due to weak authentication and limited encryption (Jerhamre, Carlberg, & van Zoest, 2022; Bhangar & Shahriyar, 2023; Senoo et al., 2024). Malhotra and Firdaus (2022) emphasize that AI-enabled IoT applications for crop yield prediction remain attractive targets for adversaries because they rely on sensitive real-time data.

4.2 Data Breaches and Privacy Risks

The growing reliance on agricultural big data raises concerns over data ownership, privacy, and exploitation. Unauthorized access to farm data can lead to misuse in pricing, market manipulation, or theft of intellectual property (Williamson et al., 2023; Devare, Arnaud, Antezana, & King, 2023). Recent research on federated learning and privacy-preserving platforms highlights opportunities for reducing risks but also acknowledges gaps in implementation (Dembani et al., 2025; Gavai et al., 2025). Without robust data governance, these vulnerabilities may erode farmer trust and hinder digital adoption (Alexander, Yarborough, & Smith, 2024; Gardezi et al., 2024).

4.3 Adversarial and Model-Based Threats

Agricultural AI systems, particularly those leveraging LLMs, are vulnerable to adversarial attacks, model manipulation, and data poisoning. Attackers can inject misleading inputs to disrupt yield predictions, pest detection, or supply chain optimization (Neupane et al., 2024). Ali, Mijwil, Buruga, Abotaleb, and Adamopoulos (2024) provide a comprehensive overview of such threats, noting the growing sophistication of adversaries targeting AI-based smart agriculture. Moreover, ethical concerns emerge when LLMs generate biased, inaccurate, or harmful recommendations, raising issues of trust and accountability (Zangana, Luckyardi, Mustafa, & Li, 2025; Abd-Elsalam & Abdel-Momen, 2023; Ya'u & Mohammed, 2025; Zohouri, Sabzali, & Golmohammadi, 2024).

4.4 Supply Chain Exploitation and Systemic Risks

Smart farming does not operate in isolation—it is embedded within global agricultural supply chains. Cyberattacks can disrupt logistics, pricing systems, and food distribution, leading to cascading consequences for food security (Kanyepe, Chibaro, Morima, & Moeti-Lysson, 2025; Pandey & Mishra, 2024). Ahmad et al. (2024) and Ali et al. (2024) highlight that in developing nations, such disruptions could exacerbate vulnerabilities, particularly where digital infrastructures are still emerging (Aderibigbe, Ohenhen, Nwaobia, Gidiagba, & Ani, 2023). The exploitation of weak links in these networks underscores the systemic nature of cybersecurity threats in agriculture.

4.5 Ethical, Legal, and Governance Challenges

The cybersecurity threat landscape is further complicated by ethical and legal dilemmas. Mark (2019) and Kochupillai, Kahl, Schmitt, Taubenböck, and Zhu (2022) warn that the use of AI and big data in agriculture can lead to opaque decision-making and misuse of sensitive information. Governance frameworks must address issues of accountability, fairness, and equitable access (Sparrow & Howard, 2021; Sparrow, Howard, & Degeling, 2021; Tzachor, Devare, King, Avin, & Ó hÉigeartaigh, 2022). Legal scholarship emphasizes the role of language, regulation, and digital marketplaces in mitigating risks while ensuring ethical deployment of AI in agriculture (Kochupillai & Köninger, 2023; Zangana, Amelia, Luckyardi, Mustafa, & Li, 2025). Kapoor (2025) calls for a stronger ethical foundation in AI and machine learning (ML) applications to prevent exploitation of farmers and consumers.

4.6 Human Factors and Trust Deficits

Human factors also shape the cybersecurity landscape. Farmers, policymakers, and researchers often lack awareness or training in cyber hygiene and responsible AI adoption, leaving systems exposed (Ahmed et al., 2024; Aggarwal, Bansal, & Goel, 2024). Mistrust in AI-driven recommendations is further exacerbated by exaggerated promises and inconsistent results (Adanma & Ogunbiyi, 2024; Denhere & Shao, 2024). Building trust requires both technical safeguards and transparent communication strategies (He et al., 2021; Holzinger, Weippl, Tjoa, & Kieseberg, 2021).

4.7 Emerging Threats and the Expanding Attack Surface

As agriculture adopts robotics, drones, and autonomous systems, the attack surface expands dramatically. Potential threats include hijacking of autonomous farm machinery, manipulation of satellite-based observation data, and disruption of irrigation systems (Wei et al., 2024; Shafik, Tufail, De Silva, Haji, & Apong, 2025). Otieno (2023) and Groumpos (2023) emphasize that smart agriculture technologies remain in an experimental stage of security posture, making them attractive targets for adversaries. Cybercrime investigations in this domain require advanced digital forensics to keep pace with evolving attack vectors (Zangana, Abdulqader, Luckyardi, & Li, 2026).

4.8 Expanding Role of LLMs in Threat Amplification

The rise of generative AI and LLMs introduces new dual-use risks in agriculture. While they assist in knowledge dissemination and agricultural decision-making

(Aithal & Aithal, 2023, 2024; Uplaonkar, Veershetty, Bahar, & Sangeeta, 2024; Zangana & Mustafa, 2026), they can also be misused for generating phishing attacks, automating misinformation, or manipulating policy narratives (Bahrini et al., 2023). These threats demand both technical countermeasures and ethical guidelines for responsible use (Kaushik, Khan, Kumari, Sharma, & Dubey, 2024; Sood, Sharma, & Bhardwaj, 2022).

5. RISKS TO FOOD SECURITY AND SUSTAINABILITY

The integration of artificial intelligence (AI), large language models (LLMs), and Internet of Things (IoT) technologies into agriculture has opened pathways for sustainable food production and smarter resource management. However, these same technologies introduce vulnerabilities that, if left unaddressed, pose significant risks to food security and long-term sustainability. The risks manifest across multiple dimensions, including data exploitation, system disruptions, ethical concerns, and governance challenges.

5.1 Disruption of Food Production Systems

AI-driven agricultural technologies hold the promise of boosting yields and improving resilience against climate challenges (Ahmed et al., 2024; Aggarwal, Bansal, & Goel, 2024). Yet, system failures or adversarial cyberattacks can disrupt crop monitoring, irrigation, and predictive analytics, leading to reduced productivity (Senoo et al., 2024; Jerhamre, Carlberg, & van Zoest, 2022). Bhangar and Shahriyar (2023) caution that insecure IoT-enabled precision farming tools may allow attackers to manipulate inputs, threatening entire production cycles. Similarly, research highlights that adversarial manipulation of AI-robotics systems could undermine food security by disrupting supply chains (Neupane et al., 2024; Otieno, 2023).

5.2 Data Privacy, Ownership, and Exploitation Risks

The agricultural sector increasingly relies on big data ecosystems, where sensitive farm-level information is collected, analyzed, and commercialized (Williamson et al., 2023). Without proper safeguards, farmers risk losing control over their data, exposing them to economic exploitation and inequitable access to digital services (Devare, Arnaud, Antezana, & King, 2023; Kochupillai & Köninger, 2023). Studies on federated learning and privacy-preserving AI platforms emphasize the potential for mitigating such risks, but challenges in deployment remain (Dembani et al., 2025; Gavai et al., 2025). These risks directly threaten farmer trust, which is essential for sustainable technology adoption (Gardezi et al., 2024; Alexander, Yarborough, & Smith, 2024).

5.3 Inequalities in Access to AI for Food Security

In developing nations, where agriculture remains a cornerstone of livelihoods, disparities in infrastructure, digital literacy, and access to AI tools exacerbate risks to food security (Ahmad et al., 2024; Ali et al., 2024). Aderibigbe, Ohenhen, Nwaobia, Gidiagba, and Ani (2023) argue that the gap between potential and implementation undermines the benefits of AI for sustainable farming. This digital divide could deepen global inequities in food availability and affordability. Meanwhile, sustainable approaches such as AI-assisted irrigation (Wei et al., 2024) and AI-enhanced supply chains (Kanyepe, Chibaro, Morima, & Moeti-Lysson, 2025) may not be equitably deployed across regions, further destabilizing food systems.

5.4 Ethical, Legal, and Governance Risks

The adoption of LLMs and AI in agriculture is intertwined with ethical and legal dilemmas. Issues of accountability, fairness, and algorithmic transparency remain underexplored (Kapoor, 2025; Kaushik, Khan, Kumari, Sharma, & Dubey, 2024). For instance, mismanagement of AI-generated insights may compromise sustainability goals or lead to unintended ecological harm (Adanma & Ogunbiyi, 2024; Kochupillai, Kahl, Schmitt, Taubenböck, & Zhu, 2022). Legal scholars stress the importance of regulatory frameworks and digital marketplaces to govern the ethical use of agricultural AI (Mark, 2019; Zangana, Amelia, Luckyardi, Mustafa, & Li, 2025). Governance challenges also extend to the integration of AI in global food supply chains, where misuse of technologies could amplify systemic risks (Sparrow & Howard, 2021; Sparrow, Howard, & Degeling, 2021).

5.5 Cybersecurity Threats and AI Misuse

LLMs and AI systems introduce dual-use risks, where tools designed to improve food security can also be weaponized for malicious purposes. Bahrini et al. (2023) warn of ChatGPT-like tools being exploited for misinformation or cyberattacks. In agricultural contexts, such misuse could lead to misleading advisories, compromised disease detection, or disrupted market predictions (Ali, Mijwil, Buruga, Abotaleb, & Adamopoulos, 2024; Zangana, Luckyardi, Mustafa, & Li, 2025). Moreover, insecure AI ecosystems in agriculture increase susceptibility to cybercrime and agri-tech exploitation, requiring advanced digital forensics (Zangana, Abdulqader, Luckyardi, & Li, 2026).

5.6 Human Factors and Trust Deficits

Human-centered risks further complicate food security. Farmers and agricultural workers often lack training in cyber hygiene and AI literacy, leaving them vulnerable to misinformation or exploitation (He et al., 2021; Holzinger, Weippl, Tjoa, & Kieseberg, 2021). Denhere and Shao (2024) note that exaggerated promises of AI in agritourism and farming foster skepticism, while Abd-Elsalam and Abdel-Momen (2023), Ya'u and Mohammed (2025), and Zohouri, Sabzali, and Golmohammadi (2024) raise concerns about the ethical use of AI-assisted writing and its indirect influence on agricultural research integrity. Building trustworthy AI ecosystems is essential to prevent mistrust from undermining sustainable food production (Pedro, Subosa, Rivas, & Valverde, 2019; Uplaonkar, Veershetty, Bahar, & Sangeeta, 2024).

5.7 Long-Term Sustainability Challenges

AI and LLMs also present sustainability paradoxes. While they improve efficiency and resource optimization (Chen et al., 2024; Gupta, Pagani, Zamboni, & Singh, 2024), their deployment depends on energy-intensive computational infrastructures, which raise questions about environmental sustainability (Sood, Sharma, & Bhardwaj, 2022; Groumpos, 2023). Scholars argue that a systemic approach is required to balance the benefits of AI adoption with the broader socio-environmental externalities it produces (Tzachor, Devare, King, Avin, & Ó hÉigeartaigh, 2022; Dara, Hazrati Fard, & Kaur, 2022). Without proactive governance, the unintended consequences of AI integration may undermine both food security and global sustainability objectives (Leong, Lim, Subri, & Jalil, 2023; Shafik, Tufail, De Silva, Haji, & Apong, 2025).

6. MITIGATION STRATEGIES FOR SECURING LLM-DRIVEN AGRICULTURE

The rapid adoption of Large Language Models (LLMs), artificial intelligence (AI), and Internet of Things (IoT) technologies in agriculture has introduced vulnerabilities that could undermine food security and sustainability. To address these challenges, a comprehensive set of mitigation strategies is needed, spanning technical safeguards, ethical governance, capacity building, and systemic resilience frameworks.

6.1. Strengthening Cybersecurity Architectures

Securing agricultural infrastructures begins with developing robust, multilayered cybersecurity frameworks. Studies emphasize the integration of AI-based intrusion detection, anomaly monitoring, and real-time threat intelligence systems to safeguard farm data and IoT devices (Ali, Mijwil, Buruga, Abotaleb, & Adamopoulos, 2024; Otieno, 2023). Enhancing IoT security through encrypted communications, device authentication, and machine learning–based intrusion prevention systems is essential for resilience (Malhotra & Firdaus, 2022; Bhangar & Shahriyar, 2023). Neupane et al. (2024) further highlight the importance of adapting cybersecurity strategies from AI-robotics to protect agricultural robotics and autonomous systems.

6.2. Data Privacy and Federated Learning

With farms generating vast amounts of sensitive data, data protection and privacy-preserving computation are critical. Approaches such as federated learning allow collaborative model training without exposing raw data, reducing risks of exploitation (Dembani et al., 2025; Gavai et al., 2025). Devare, Arnaud, Antezana, and King (2023) stress governance frameworks for agricultural data, while Kochupillai and Köninger (2023) propose blockchain-enabled marketplaces for secure management of genetic sequence data. Williamson et al. (2023) note that transparent, FAIR-compliant data standards can mitigate trust deficits in agricultural AI adoption.

Figure 1 illustrates the stages of financial fraud detection enhanced by autonomous AI, beginning with data collection and preprocessing, moving through anomaly detection and risk scoring, and culminating in fraud alerts and investigations.

Figure 1. Stages of financial fraud detection using autonomous AI

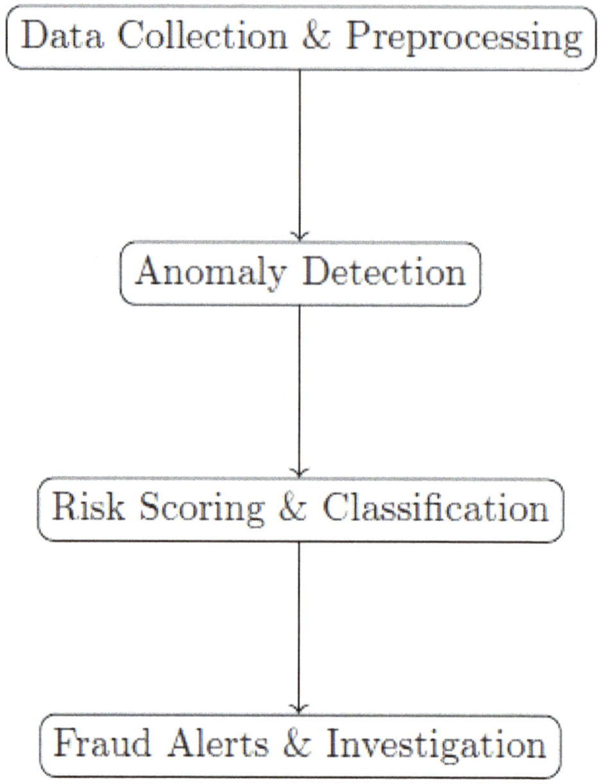

6.3. Building Ethical and Trustworthy AI Ecosystems

Mitigation requires embedding ethics and transparency into AI design and deployment. Scholars argue that agricultural AI must integrate fairness, accountability, and explainability to foster trust among stakeholders (Kapoor, 2025; Kaushik, Khan, Kumari, Sharma, & Dubey, 2024). Responsible innovation frameworks, as outlined by Tzachor, Devare, King, Avin, and Ó hÉigeartaigh (2022), recommend a systemic approach to addressing AI's socio-environmental externalities. Sparrow and Howard (2021), along with Sparrow, Howard, and Degeling (2021), emphasize governance mechanisms for agricultural robotics to prevent misuse and unintended ecological consequences.

Figure 2 presents the workflow of autonomous AI for risk management, showing how continuous data monitoring, predictive modeling, risk scoring, and automated decision support integrate into financial systems.

Figure 2. Autonomous AI workflow for risk management

6.4. Enhancing Food Security through AI Applications

AI-driven decision-support systems can contribute to mitigating risks by optimizing yields, irrigation, and supply chain operations (Ahmed et al., 2024; Wei et al., 2024; Kanyepe, Chibaro, Morima, & Moeti-Lysson, 2025). AI-enhanced precision farming improves sustainability while reducing input waste (Aggarwal, Bansal, & Goel, 2024; Chen et al., 2024). Pandey and Mishra (2024) note that AI's role in food security requires balancing innovation with ethical oversight. In developing nations, strategies must address the digital divide to ensure equitable access to AI solutions (Ahmad et al., 2024; Ali et al., 2024; Aderibigbe, Ohenhen, Nwaobia, Gidiagba, & Ani, 2023).

Figure 3 compares autonomous AI-based fraud detection with traditional methods, highlighting advantages such as adaptability, scalability, and contextual awareness.

Figure 3. Comparative advantages of autonomous AI vs. traditional fraud detection

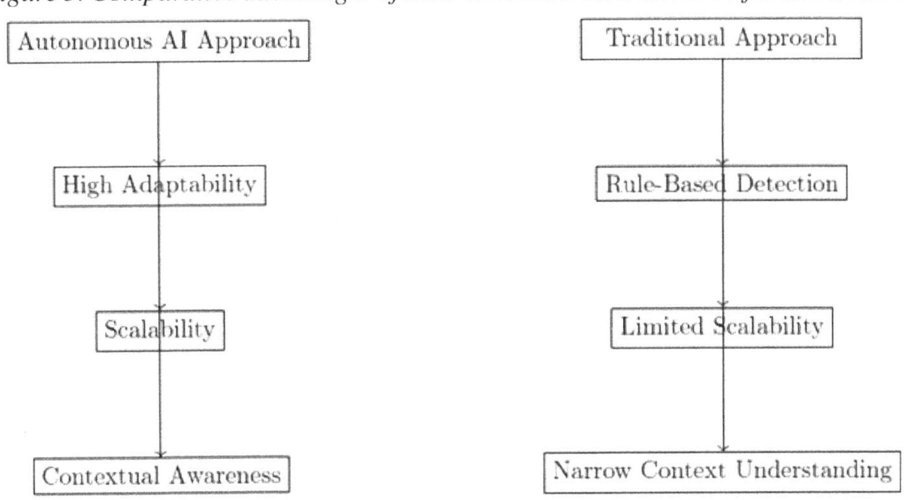

6.5. Cybersecurity Awareness and Capacity Building

A critical mitigation layer lies in human-centered training and capacity building. Farmers, agribusiness operators, and local communities require digital literacy to understand risks and apply basic cyber hygiene practices (He et al., 2021; Holzinger, Weippl, Tjoa, & Kieseberg, 2021). Gardezi et al. (2024) highlight that fostering trust in AI requires participatory design and co-creation of digital tools. Denhere and Shao (2024) demonstrate how training in ethical use of AI in agritourism can translate into agricultural applications, while Pedro, Subosa, Rivas, and Valverde (2019) emphasize education as a long-term resilience strategy.

6.6. Legal and Policy Frameworks

Robust regulatory and governance mechanisms are essential for protecting LLM-driven agriculture. Legal scholars highlight the need for enforceable frameworks governing the use of big data, AI, and genetic resources (Mark, 2019; Kochupillai, Kahl, Schmitt, Taubenböck, & Zhu, 2022). Zangana, Amelia, Luckyardi, Mustafa, and Li (2025) discuss the role of language in shaping global regulatory perspectives on agricultural AI, while their other works emphasize securing AI in agricultural research (Zangana, Luckyardi, Mustafa, & Li, 2025) and ensuring ethical deployment in scientific writing (Zangana, Amelia, Mustafa, & Li, 2025). Policy interventions must also align with responsible AI adoption for sustainability, balancing innovation with socio-environmental protections (Adanma & Ogunbiyi, 2024).

Figure 4 highlights the future directions for financial fraud detection using autonomous AI, emphasizing real-time fraud prevention, ethical safeguards, cross-border financial intelligence, and integration with blockchain systems.

Figure 4. Future directions in financial fraud detection using autonomous AI

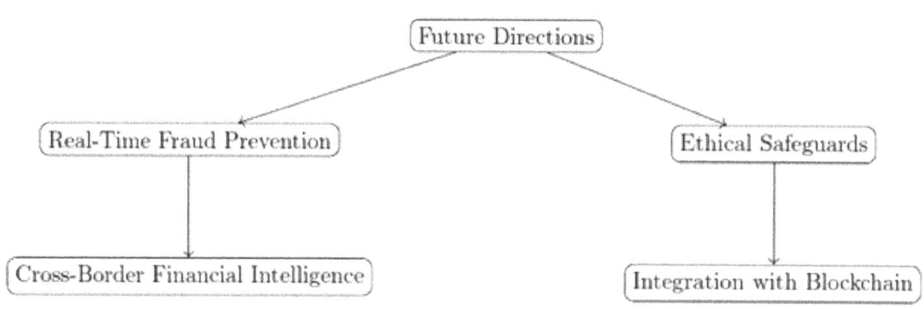

6.7. Addressing Ethical Risks in AI-Assisted Research and Writing

The increasing use of LLMs in scientific communication raises concerns about academic integrity and research reliability. Abd-Elsalam and Abdel-Momen (2023), Zohouri, Sabzali, and Golmohammadi (2024), and Ya'u and Mohammed (2025) warn that misuse of AI in writing could undermine research quality, indirectly affecting agricultural innovation. Mitigation requires promoting ethical writing practices, transparent disclosure of AI assistance, and integration of AI ethics into agricultural education (Aithal & Aithal, 2023; Uplaonkar, Veershetty, Bahar, & Sangeeta, 2024).

6.8. Digital Forensics and Cybercrime Investigation

As agriculture becomes a target for cybercrime, AI-powered digital forensics will play a vital role in threat detection and attribution. Zangana, Abdulqader, Luckyardi, and Li (2026) emphasize the importance of forensic frameworks for investigating agri-tech cybercrime, while Zangana, Luckyardi, Mustafa, and Li (2025) propose deep learning–driven defense mechanisms for smart farming. Groumpos (2023) adds that historic lessons from AI development can inform forensic and resilience strategies, ensuring adaptability against evolving threats.

6.9. Green and Sustainable AI Deployment

The sustainability of AI systems themselves must be considered. Energy-intensive infrastructures for training LLMs could undermine environmental goals if not managed responsibly (Sood, Sharma, & Bhardwaj, 2022; Leong, Lim, Subri, & Jalil, 2023). Mitigation involves adopting nanotechnology and intelligent communication technologies (ICCT) for greener deployments (Aithal & Aithal, 2024), and prioritizing low-energy AI algorithms that align with long-term sustainability (Gupta, Pagani, Zamboni, & Singh, 2024; Shafik, Tufail, De Silva, Haji, & Apong, 2025).

6.10. Multi-Stakeholder Collaboration

Finally, effective mitigation requires a multi-stakeholder ecosystem, integrating governments, academia, industry, and farming communities. Araújo, Peres, Barata, Lidon, and Ramalho (2021) stress collaboration in shaping Agriculture 4.0, while Bahrini et al. (2023) note that proactive engagement can address dual-use risks of tools like ChatGPT. Alexander, Yarborough, and Smith (2024) stress collective responsibility in navigating challenges of responsible AI in agriculture.

7. POLICY, REGULATION, AND GOVERNANCE IN AGRICULTURAL AI SECURITY

The emergence of AI-driven agriculture and LLM-based systems has transformed farming into a data-intensive and technologically complex domain. While these advances bring opportunities for efficiency, sustainability, and global food security, they also introduce vulnerabilities that require strong policy, regulatory, and governance frameworks. Addressing these challenges demands a balance between fostering innovation and ensuring ethical, secure, and equitable deployment of AI in agriculture.

7.1. Ethical Governance of AI in Agriculture

The deployment of AI technologies raises profound ethical and governance questions. Scholars emphasize that agricultural AI systems must embed responsible innovation principles, balancing productivity gains with social and environmental impacts (Tzachor, Devare, King, Avin, & Ó hÉigeartaigh, 2022; Kapoor, 2025). Sparrow and Howard (2021), as well as Sparrow, Howard, and Degeling (2021), stress that governance should account for both robotic autonomy and human oversight to mitigate misuse and unintended harms. Similarly, Kaushik, Khan, Kumari, Sharma, and Dubey (2024) highlight that AI-based cybersecurity governance must incorporate fairness, accountability, and ethical considerations.

7.2. Legal and Regulatory Frameworks

The legal dimensions of agricultural AI involve issues of data ownership, intellectual property, liability, and cross-border governance. Mark (2019) underscores the ethical risks of large multinational corporations controlling agricultural AI and big data without proper safeguards. Kochupillai, Kahl, Schmitt, Taubenböck, and Zhu (2022) point out that Earth observation and AI create new governance gaps in data use, while Kochupillai and Köninger (2023) propose blockchain-enabled marketplaces to regulate genetic sequence data. Zangana, Amelia, Luckyardi, Mustafa, and Li (2025) stress that language and legal frameworks shape global regulation of AI in agriculture, underscoring the role of international cooperation.

7.3. Cybersecurity and Risk Regulation

Cybersecurity is a central regulatory concern for AI in agriculture. Surveys highlight the state-of-the-art risks in smart farming, including IoT vulnerabilities, adversarial AI, and data exploitation (Ali, Mijwil, Buruga, Abotaleb, & Adamopoulos,

2024; Otieno, 2023). Malhotra and Firdaus (2022) argue for AI-driven IoT security mechanisms, while Jerhamre, Carlberg, and van Zoest (2022) explore the susceptibility of smart farming infrastructures. Neupane et al. (2024) add that robotics and autonomous systems require regulatory frameworks addressing safety, resilience, and liability. Regulatory bodies must establish standards for cyber resilience and forensic readiness, as outlined by Zangana, Abdulqader, Luckyardi, and Li (2026).

7.4. Data Governance and Privacy Protection

Data governance forms the foundation of AI regulation. Agricultural AI depends on vast datasets, raising concerns of data misuse, privacy, and sovereignty. Devare, Arnaud, Antezana, and King (2023) propose transparent governance of agricultural data, while Williamson et al. (2023) identify major challenges in FAIR-compliant data sharing. Dembani et al. (2025) and Gavai et al. (2025) highlight federated learning and privacy-preserving techniques as regulatory strategies to protect farmers' sensitive data. Moreover, Araújo, Peres, Barata, Lidon, and Ramalho (2021) note that governing Agriculture 4.0 requires international standards alignment to manage interoperability and trust.

7.5. Global Food Security and Policy Alignment

AI in agriculture must be regulated in ways that support sustainable food security policies. Ahmad et al. (2024), Ali et al. (2024), and Ahmed et al. (2024) emphasize that AI-driven food security initiatives need tailored governance in developing nations, where digital divides hinder adoption. Aggarwal, Bansal, and Goel (2024) describe AI as both a challenge and opportunity, while Pandey and Mishra (2024) propose aligning AI policies with climate resilience and sustainability goals. Wei et al. (2024) show that irrigation governance requires integration of AI with resource management policies.

7.6. Trust, Transparency, and Human-Centered Governance

Trust is a cornerstone of regulatory effectiveness. He et al. (2021) argue that human-centered AI governance ensures transparency and accountability in robotics, while Holzinger, Weippl, Tjoa, and Kieseberg (2021) emphasize linking AI policy to the UN's Sustainable Development Goals. Gardezi et al. (2024) stress participatory governance to build trust in AI farming systems, and Alexander, Yarborough, and Smith (2024) highlight shared responsibility among stakeholders in advancing trustworthy AI.

7.7. Academic Integrity and Responsible AI Writing

Beyond farming applications, governance must also address the role of AI in scientific communication. Abd-Elsalam and Abdel-Momen (2023), Zohouri, Sabzali, and Golmohammadi (2024), and Ya'u and Mohammed (2025) highlight risks of AI misuse in scientific writing, calling for policy frameworks on disclosure and integrity. Aithal and Aithal (2023) and Uplaonkar, Veershetty, Bahar, and Sangeeta (2024) similarly argue for oversight in AI use in research and agricultural librarianship, ensuring that AI does not erode academic standards.

7.8. Sustainability and Green AI Governance

AI's energy consumption introduces environmental governance challenges. Sood, Sharma, and Bhardwaj (2022) emphasize regulating AI's environmental footprint, while Leong, Lim, Subri, and Jalil (2023) propose sustainable integration of AIoT in agriculture. Aithal and Aithal (2024) suggest nanotechnology and ICCT to support green AI governance, while Gupta, Pagani, Zamboni, and Singh (2024) and Shafik, Tufail, De Silva, Haji, and Apong (2025) highlight the need for policies ensuring sustainable AI deployment in plant sciences and agri-tech industries.

7.9. Regional and Sectoral Governance Perspectives

Different regions face unique governance challenges. Adanma and Ogunbiyi (2024) examine AI in environmental conservation and emphasize cyber risk governance for sustainable agriculture. Denhere and Shao (2024) argue that African agritourism AI adoption requires ethical oversight, while Bhangar and Shahriyar (2023) and Senoo et al. (2024) focus on IoT and AI policy integration in precision farming. Kanyepe, Chibaro, Morima, and Moeti-Lysson (2025) stress supply chain governance, particularly for AI-enabled logistics and food distribution.

7.10. Multi-Stakeholder and Systemic Approaches

Effective regulation requires multi-stakeholder governance that includes governments, farmers, technologists, and civil society. Bahrini et al. (2023) stress anticipating the dual-use risks of ChatGPT-like systems, while Chen et al. (2024) highlight the need for global coordination on AI policy. Groumpos (2023) reminds policymakers that historical lessons from AI regulation should inform present frameworks. Zangana, Luckyardi, Mustafa, and Li (2025) further stress deep learning–enabled regulatory approaches for agricultural cybersecurity, while Zangana, Amelia, Mustafa, and Li (2025) emphasize ethical AI governance in agricultural research.

8. CASE STUDIES AND REAL-WORLD APPLICATIONS

The application of Large Language Models (LLMs) and artificial intelligence (AI) in agriculture has advanced from theoretical exploration to real-world adoption, with diverse case studies highlighting both opportunities and cybersecurity risks. These implementations span across crop production, supply chains, irrigation, data governance, ethics, and policy.

8.1. AI in Precision Agriculture and Crop Production

Precision agriculture is among the most prominent areas where AI and LLMs are deployed. Ahmed et al. (2024) demonstrate how AI can enhance crop yield prediction and disease detection, supporting farmers in resource optimization. Similarly, Bhat and Huang (2021) emphasize the integration of big data and AI to enable real-time decision-making for precision farming. Jerhamre, Carlberg, and van Zoest (2022) reveal case studies where vulnerabilities in smart farming systems have been exposed to cyber risks, while Malhotra and Firdaus (2022) show how AI and IoT integration improves both productivity and security in crop yield monitoring. These practical implementations align with Chen et al. (2024), who identify transformative AI applications across the agrifood system.

8.2. Food Security in Developing Nations

Developing countries face unique challenges in adopting AI-driven agricultural systems. Ahmad et al. (2024) and Ali et al. (2024) highlight real-world initiatives where AI is applied to support food security, noting infrastructure gaps, cyber vulnerabilities, and policy fragmentation as barriers. Aggarwal, Bansal, and Goel (2024) stress that AI represents both a looming challenge and a gleaming opportunity, while Aderibigbe et al. (2023) analyze how low-resource contexts adapt AI solutions for agricultural improvement. Pandey and Mishra (2024) provide case evidence of AI enhancing sustainability in farming, and Adanma and Ogunbiyi (2024) evaluate environmental conservation efforts that use AI while accounting for cyber risks.

8.3. Trust, Ethics, and Responsible AI

Trust in agricultural AI adoption emerges as a recurring theme. Gardezi et al. (2024) explore participatory approaches in real-world projects that foster farmer trust in AI. Kapoor (2025) presents ethical dilemmas in AI deployment in the agri-food industry, complemented by the perspectives of Sparrow and Howard (2021) and Sparrow, Howard, and Degeling (2021) on robotic applications in farming.

Case studies discussed by Tzachor et al. (2022) and Dara, Hazrati Fard, and Kaur (2022) illustrate that AI governance must account for externalities and systemic risks. In the context of scientific communication, Abd-Elsalam and Abdel-Momen (2023), Zohouri, Sabzali, and Golmohammadi (2024), and Ya'u and Mohammed (2025) highlight ethical concerns around AI-assisted writing and its implications for agricultural research integrity.

8.4. Data Governance and Privacy Protection

Agricultural AI applications rely on large datasets, creating urgent needs for privacy and governance mechanisms. Devare et al. (2023) describe case studies where inadequate governance led to limited interoperability, while Williamson et al. (2023) emphasize challenges in FAIR-compliant data practices. Dembani et al. (2025) and Gavai et al. (2025) present real-world applications of federated learning and emerging platforms that enable secure, privacy-preserving agricultural data management. Araújo et al. (2021) illustrate the Agriculture 4.0 landscape, highlighting interoperability and governance gaps across case studies.

8.5. IoT, AIoT, and Next-Generation Farming

The fusion of AI and IoT (AIoT) is rapidly transforming farming practices. Bhangar and Shahriyar (2023) provide practical insights into AIoT adoption for smart irrigation and pest control. Senoo et al. (2024) further examine precision agriculture applications using AI-enabled IoT systems, while Leong et al. (2023) describe regional case studies from Southeast Asia showing how AIoT enhances resilience. These findings echo Holzinger et al. (2021), who tie digital transformation in agriculture to achieving the Sustainable Development Goals.

8.6. Agricultural Supply Chains and Market Applications

AI is also applied in agri-supply chains, where vulnerabilities intersect with logistical efficiency. Kanyepe et al. (2025) highlight case studies of AI in supply chain monitoring, identifying both opportunities for resilience and risks from cyberattacks. Gupta, Pagani, Zamboni, and Singh (2024) describe AI applications in plant sciences supporting food security and market innovation, while Shafik et al. (2025) analyze startups leveraging AI to disrupt traditional agriculture industries. Kochupillai and Köninger (2023) propose blockchain-based digital marketplaces for plant genetic sequence data, and Kochupillai et al. (2022) demonstrate Earth observation AI applications that require governance to avoid misuse.

8.7. Cybersecurity Risks in Smart Agriculture

A growing body of case studies underscores the risks of AI-enabled agriculture. Ali, Mijwil, Buruga, Abotaleb, and Adamopoulos (2024) survey threats including adversarial attacks and data poisoning, while Otieno (2023) provides a comprehensive overview of smart agriculture security postures. Neupane et al. (2024) emphasize risks in robotics, requiring enhanced safeguards. Bahrini et al. (2023) warn of dual-use scenarios where LLMs like ChatGPT may be exploited maliciously, while Groumpos (2023) contextualizes these risks in the broader history of AI regulation.

8.8. Irrigation and Resource Management

AI-driven irrigation presents one of the most tangible real-world applications. Wei et al. (2024) document systems that optimize water use through predictive analytics, though they note vulnerabilities if AI models are manipulated. These applications intersect with Sood, Sharma, and Bhardwaj (2022), who review AI applications across agricultural resource management.

8.9. Regional Perspectives and Agritourism Applications

In Africa, AI adoption in farming and agritourism provides important lessons. Denhere and Shao (2024) explore agritourism case studies where AI fosters innovation but also introduces ethical risks. Mark (2019) highlights the dominance of multinationals and risks of data exploitation in agriculture. Regional challenges also include integration of AI with cultural and linguistic contexts, as emphasized by Zangana, Amelia, Luckyardi, Mustafa, and Li (2025).

8.10. Educational and Research Applications

The role of AI in education and agricultural research is equally significant. Aithal and Aithal (2023) discuss ChatGPT's application in research and teaching, while their later work (2024) emphasizes ICCT and nanotechnology in supporting sustainability. Pedro, Subosa, Rivas, and Valverde (2019) present early applications of AI in education for sustainable development. Uplaonkar et al. (2024) apply this discourse to agricultural librarianship. Zangana and Mustafa (2026) highlight the application of AI-based image denoising in education, showing the spillover benefits of agricultural AI research for broader learning ecosystems.

8.11. Securing Agriculture with Advanced AI

Recent studies focus on strengthening agricultural cybersecurity through advanced methods. Zangana, Luckyardi, Mustafa, and Li (2025) propose deep learning–based approaches to secure smart farming, while Zangana, Amelia, Mustafa, and Li (2025) emphasize ethical safeguards in agricultural AI. Zangana, Luckyardi, Mustafa, and Li (2025) further stress agricultural cybersecurity with LLMs, while Zangana, Abdulqader, Luckyardi, and Li (2026) present forensic AI applications in agri-tech cybercrime investigations. Collectively, these case studies demonstrate the breadth of AI's role in both enabling and securing smart agriculture.

9. ETHICAL AND SOCIETAL CONSIDERATIONS

The adoption of artificial intelligence (AI) and Large Language Models (LLMs) in agriculture has raised profound ethical and societal questions. While these technologies offer immense opportunities for enhancing productivity, sustainability, and food security, they also introduce concerns related to fairness, accountability, transparency, data governance, labor impacts, and environmental sustainability.

9.1. Ethical Responsibility and Trust in AI Adoption

Trust in AI systems is a fundamental requirement for their successful integration in agriculture. Alexander, Yarborough, and Smith (2024) emphasize that responsibility for "responsible AI" must be clearly defined across developers, policymakers, and end users. Gardezi et al. (2024) argue that building farmer trust requires participatory approaches that account for local contexts and values. Kapoor (2025) reinforces the need for ethical frameworks to guide AI deployment in the agri-food industry, while Dara, Hazrati Fard, and Kaur (2022) stress responsible AI adoption through systemic governance. The work of Sparrow and Howard (2021), as well as Sparrow, Howard, and Degeling (2021), highlights ethical dilemmas surrounding robotics in farming, including labor displacement and animal welfare.

9.2. Data Privacy, Governance, and Ownership

The collection and processing of agricultural data raise pressing questions about ownership, consent, and ethical use. Devare et al. (2023) show that inadequate governance of plant data linkage can undermine research integrity, while Williamson et al. (2023) point to challenges in managing FAIR-compliant agricultural datasets. Dembani et al. (2025) highlight ethical dilemmas in federated learning, which enables data sharing while preserving privacy. Similarly, Gavai et al. (2025) note that emerging platforms aim to enhance privacy protections but may create new power imbalances. Kochupillai and Köninger (2023) examine legal and ethical concerns in creating blockchain-enabled digital marketplaces for plant genetic data, while Kochupillai et al. (2022) raise awareness of environmental and governance implications of Earth observation data. Araújo, Peres, Barata, Lidon, and Ramalho (2021) further situate these issues within the Agriculture 4.0 landscape, where interoperability and ethical governance remain central.

9.3. Cybersecurity and Ethical Risks in Smart Farming

The convergence of AI, IoT, and robotics introduces vulnerabilities that carry both ethical and societal implications. Ali, Mijwil, Buruga, Abotaleb, and Adamopoulos (2024) identify ethical concerns in cybersecurity for smart farming, particularly related to adversarial attacks and surveillance. Otieno (2023) and Jerhamre, Carlberg, and van Zoest (2022) also point to weaknesses in agricultural systems that may compromise food supply chains. Neupane et al. (2024) emphasize the ethical responsibility of securing robotics to protect both human workers and ecosystems. Kaushik et al. (2024) propose embedding ethical principles into AI-based cybersecurity, while Bahrini et al. (2023) highlight the dual-use risks of generative models like ChatGPT, which can be exploited for malicious purposes.

9.4. Environmental Sustainability and Conservation Ethics

The ethical use of AI extends to environmental conservation. Adanma and Ogunbiyi (2024) evaluate AI-driven conservation practices, showing how they can both enhance and threaten ecological sustainability depending on governance. Bhangar and Shahriyar (2023) highlight the ethical responsibility of balancing productivity with ecological health in AIoT-enabled farming. Wei et al. (2024) caution that AI-driven irrigation systems must be designed responsibly to avoid overuse or inequitable access to water. Sood, Sharma, and Bhardwaj (2022) and Chen et al. (2024) further note that agricultural AI should align with long-term environmental and ethical goals. Holzinger, Weippl, Tjoa, and Kieseberg (2021) situate these concerns within the broader framework of the Sustainable Development Goals, emphasizing safety, privacy, and ecological responsibility.

9.5. Equity, Access, and the Global South

AI adoption risks exacerbating inequalities between developed and developing nations. Ahmad et al. (2024) and Ali et al. (2024) highlight how AI can empower agriculture for food security in the Global South but warn of infrastructural and ethical challenges. Aderibigbe et al. (2023) similarly argue that implementation gaps limit benefits in developing countries. Aggarwal, Bansal, and Goel (2024) frame AI as both a challenge and an opportunity, while Pandey and Mishra (2024) stress the importance of equitable access to sustainable agricultural AI. Denhere and Shao (2024) explore agritourism applications in Africa, noting ethical tensions around cultural integrity and technological adoption. Mark (2019) cautions against corporate dominance that could exploit farmers' data, undermining fairness and sovereignty.

9.6. Academic Integrity, AI-Assisted Writing, and Education

The use of AI in academic and agricultural research raises ethical dilemmas around plagiarism, authorship, and scholarly integrity. Abd-Elsalam and Abdel-Momen (2023) highlight the challenges of AI in scientific writing, while Zohouri, Sabzali, and Golmohammadi (2024) critique ChatGPT-assisted writing for creating risks of unacknowledged AI authorship. Ya'u and Mohammed (2025) provide evidence from Nigerian higher education showing both improvements in literacy and ethical concerns over academic misuse. Similarly, Zangana, Amelia, Mustafa, and Li (2025) analyze the ethical implications of English-language dominance in AI-assisted writing for global agriculture. Aithal and Aithal (2023) and Pedro, Subosa, Rivas, and Valverde (2019) extend these discussions to education and research, while Zangana and Mustafa (2026) illustrate ethical issues in AI-enhanced educational content.

9.7. Governance, Law, and Regulation

Legal frameworks must keep pace with AI advancements in agriculture. Zangana, Amelia, Luckyardi, Mustafa, and Li (2025) examine the role of language in regulating AI technologies, while Zangana, Luckyardi, Mustafa, and Li (2025) emphasize ethical safeguards in AI-driven agricultural research. Zangana, Abdulqader, Luckyardi, and Li (2026) extend this discussion to forensic investigations of agri-tech cybercrime, demonstrating the legal and ethical complexities of enforcement. Groumpos (2023) provides historical context for governance debates, showing how ethical questions have long been intertwined with AI development.

9.8. Societal Shifts and Future Challenges

The integration of AI into agriculture reshapes societal dynamics, from labor patterns to cultural practices. Shafik, Tufail, De Silva, Haji, and Apong (2025) show how startups leveraging AI can disrupt existing industries, with both positive and negative consequences. Kanyepe, Chibaro, Morima, and Moeti-Lysson (2025) emphasize the societal implications of AI in agricultural supply chains, while Leong et al. (2023) note that regional adoption requires ethical alignment with local needs. He et al. (2021) advocate for human-centered AI that respects autonomy and dignity, while Uplaonkar et al. (2024) highlight the role of AI in reshaping agricultural librarianship and information ethics.

10. FUTURE DIRECTIONS

The future trajectory of artificial intelligence (AI) in agriculture, education, and scientific research is poised for transformative growth, yet it brings complex technical, ethical, and societal challenges that require deliberate strategies and interdisciplinary collaboration. Emerging trends indicate that AI will continue to advance automation, precision, and efficiency in agricultural systems, while also reshaping scientific writing, educational content delivery, and cybersecurity measures.

10.1. AI-Driven Precision Agriculture and Sustainable Food Systems

The integration of AI into precision agriculture is projected to expand substantially, with opportunities to optimize crop production, irrigation, and supply chain management (Ahmad et al., 2024; Ali et al., 2024; Aggarwal et al., 2024). Innovations such as IoT-enabled smart farming, deep learning, and robotic automation are expected to address global food security challenges by enhancing yield prediction, disease detection, and resource optimization (Bhangar & Shahriyar, 2023; Chen et al., 2024; Wei et al., 2024). Nevertheless, these advancements raise critical cybersecurity concerns, including potential vulnerabilities in networked farm equipment and AI-driven decision systems (Ali, Mijwil, Buruga, Abotaleb, & Adamopoulos, 2024; Neupane et al., 2024; Zangana, Luckyardi, Mustafa, & Li, 2025).

Future research must prioritize the development of robust, trustworthy AI systems that are resilient against adversarial attacks while maintaining data integrity and operational safety (Gardezi et al., 2024; Otieno, 2023). Additionally, the application of federated learning models presents a promising avenue for enhancing data privacy across decentralized agricultural platforms (Dembani et al., 2025; Gavai et al., 2025).

10.2. Ethical, Legal, and Societal Implications

As AI becomes increasingly pervasive, ethical governance frameworks must evolve to ensure responsible deployment, particularly in contexts involving sensitive agricultural, educational, and scientific data (Dara, Hazrati Fard, & Kaur, 2022; Kapoor, 2025; Zangana, Amelia, Luckyardi, Mustafa, & Li, 2025). Emerging research emphasizes the importance of systemic understanding of AI-related risks, including bias, inequity, and unintended environmental consequences (Tzachor et al., 2022; Alexander, Yarborough, & Smith, 2024; Zangana, Luckyardi, Mustafa, & Li, 2025).

Future directions also include enhancing legal frameworks for AI governance, such as regulations for digital marketplaces of plant genetic data and agrobiodiversity information (Kochupillai & Köninger, 2023; Zangana, Amelia, Luckyardi, Mustafa, & Li, 2025). Developing nations, in particular, require targeted strategies to bridge the gap between AI potential and implementation capacity, ensuring equitable access to AI technologies (Aderibigbe et al., 2023; Ahmad et al., 2024; Adanma & Ogunbiyi, 2024).

10.3. AI in Education, Research, and Scientific Writing

The rise of AI-powered language models and digital assistants like ChatGPT has opened new avenues for academic writing, literacy development, and instructional content creation (Aithal & Aithal, 2023; Zohouri, Sabzali, & Golmohammadi, 2024; Abd-Elsalam & Abdel-Momen, 2023). Future directions in this domain include the development of AI systems that support academic integrity while enhancing writing proficiency and research productivity (Ya'u & Mohammed, 2025; Zangana & Mustafa, 2026).

Further research is needed to balance AI-assisted content generation with ethical norms in publishing, plagiarism prevention, and knowledge validation (Bahrini et al., 2023; Zangana, Amelia, Mustafa, & Li, 2025). This includes exploring AI's role in enabling inclusive access to education, particularly in regions with limited educational infrastructure (Uplaonkar et al., 2024; Aithal & Aithal, 2024).

10.4. Data Management, Privacy, and Security

The proliferation of AI in agricultural and educational domains necessitates robust frameworks for data governance, privacy, and security (Williamson et al., 2023; Devare et al., 2023; Malhotra & Firdaus, 2022). Future research should focus on integrating blockchain, federated learning, and cryptographic solutions to safeguard sensitive datasets, including crop data, IoT sensor information, and student learning analytics (Kochupillai et al., 2022; Dembani et al., 2025; Zangana, Abdulqader, Luckyardi, & Li, 2026).

Additionally, cybersecurity research must evolve in tandem with AI developments, addressing vulnerabilities in autonomous systems, robotic farm machinery, and precision irrigation networks (He et al., 2021; Neupane et al., 2024; Ali et al., 2024).

10.5. Interdisciplinary and Global Collaboration

Future AI initiatives will benefit from interdisciplinary collaboration across agronomy, computer science, ethics, law, and education (Sparrow & Howard, 2021; Pedro et al., 2019; Leong et al., 2023). International partnerships are essential to align AI development with sustainable development goals (Holzinger et al., 2021; Pandey & Mishra, 2024), address societal impacts, and promote inclusive access to AI-enabled innovations (Ahmad et al., 2024; Aderibigbe et al., 2023).

Efforts should focus on co-developing guidelines for responsible AI, promoting transparency in AI decision-making, and fostering public trust through participatory governance models (Kapoor, 2025; Sparrow, Howard, & Degeling, 2021; Gardezi et al., 2024).

10.6. Emerging Technologies and Next-Generation Applications

The convergence of AI with IoT, nanotechnology, and advanced analytics will shape the next generation of smart agriculture and educational technologies (Aithal & Aithal, 2024; Senoo et al., 2024; Leong et al., 2023). Research directions include AI-driven environmental monitoring, predictive crop management, precision irrigation, and sustainable resource allocation (Adanma & Ogunbiyi, 2024; Wei et al., 2024; Ahmad et al., 2024).

Moreover, the integration of AI with educational technologies will facilitate adaptive learning, AI-enhanced visual content, and personalized pedagogical interventions (Zangana & Mustafa, 2026; Zangana, Luckyardi, Mustafa, & Li, 2025). These applications present opportunities for both operational efficiency and the ethical deployment of AI in societal contexts.

10.7 Summary

The future directions of AI span technical, ethical, and societal dimensions. Critical priorities include building robust AI systems for agriculture and education, ensuring data privacy and cybersecurity, promoting ethical governance, and fostering global interdisciplinary collaboration. By addressing these challenges, AI can deliver sustainable, equitable, and socially responsible benefits across multiple sectors.

11. CONCLUSION

Artificial intelligence has emerged as a transformative force across agriculture, education, scientific research, and cybersecurity, offering unprecedented opportunities for efficiency, precision, and innovation. In agriculture, AI-driven solutions such as precision farming, predictive analytics, and autonomous machinery have the potential to address global food security challenges, optimize resource utilization, and improve crop yields. However, these advancements also bring significant challenges, particularly in cybersecurity, data privacy, and the ethical governance of AI systems. Ensuring that AI applications are trustworthy, resilient, and equitable is paramount to realizing their full potential.

In the context of education and scientific research, AI-assisted tools—including language models, adaptive learning systems, and automated content generation—have the potential to enhance academic productivity, support inclusive learning, and foster innovation in knowledge creation. At the same time, these tools raise concerns about academic integrity, plagiarism, and responsible use, highlighting the need for clear ethical guidelines and regulatory oversight. Balancing the benefits of AI assistance with the preservation of human judgment and creativity remains a central challenge for researchers, educators, and policymakers alike.

Data management, privacy, and security are recurring themes across all AI applications. The exponential growth of AI-generated data requires robust governance frameworks, secure storage, and resilient protection against cyber threats. Integrating emerging technologies such as federated learning, blockchain, and advanced encryption can help safeguard sensitive agricultural, educational, and research datasets while enabling the ethical and responsible use of AI.

Finally, the continued success of AI depends on interdisciplinary collaboration, international cooperation, and inclusive governance. Stakeholders from technology, agriculture, law, education, and ethics must work together to ensure that AI applications are aligned with societal goals, sustainable development objectives, and human-centered values. By addressing technical, ethical, and regulatory challenges in a coordinated manner, AI can realize its promise of transforming multiple sectors for the betterment of society while mitigating potential risks.

REFERENCES

Abd-Elsalam, K. A., & Abdel-Momen, S. M. (2023). Artificial intelligence's development and challenges in scientific writing. *Egyptian Journal of Agricultural Research, 101*(3), 714–717. DOI: 10.21608/ejar.2023.220363.1414

Adanma, U. M., & Ogunbiyi, E. O.Uwaga Monica AdanmaEmmanuel Olurotimi Ogunbiyi. (2024). Artificial intelligence in environmental conservation: Evaluating cyber risks and opportunities for sustainable practices. *Computer Science & IT Research Journal, 5*(5), 1178–1209. DOI: 10.51594/csitrj.v5i5.1156

Aderibigbe, A. O., Ohenhen, P. E., Nwaobia, N. K., Gidiagba, J. O., & Ani, E. C. (2023). Artificial intelligence in developing countries: Bridging the gap between potential and implementation. *Computer Science & IT Research Journal, 4*(3), 185–199. DOI: 10.51594/csitrj.v4i3.629

Aggarwal, S., Bansal, S., & Goel, R. (2024). Ai In Agriculture: A Looming Challenge, A Gleaming Opportunity. *International Journal of Engineering Science and Humanities, 14*(Special Issue 1), 43-52.

Ahmad, A., Liew, A. X., Venturini, F., Kalogeras, A., Candiani, A., Di Benedetto, G., Ajibola, S., Cartujo, P., Romero, P., Lykoudi, A., De Grandis, M. M., Xouris, C., Lo Bianco, R., Doddy, I., Elegbede, I., D'Urso Labate, G. F., García del Moral, L. F., & Martos, V. (2024). AI can empower agriculture for global food security: Challenges and prospects in developing nations. *Frontiers in Artificial Intelligence, 7*, 1328530. DOI: 10.3389/frai.2024.1328530

Ahmad, A., Liew, A. X., Venturini, F., Kalogeras, A., Candiani, A., Di Benedetto, G., ... & Martos, V. (2024). AI can empower agriculture for.

Ahmed, M. N., Singh, A. P., Hussain, M. R., Rasool, M. A., Khan, I. M., & Dildar, M. S. (2024, July). Enhancing Crop Production using Artificial Intelligence in Agricultural Revolution. In *2024 IEEE 7th International Conference on Advanced Technologies* [ATSIP]. *Signal and Image Processing : an International Journal, 1*, 432–437.

Aithal, P. S., & Aithal, S. (2023). Application of ChatGPT in higher education and research–A futuristic analysis. [IJAEML]. *International Journal of Applied Engineering and Management Letters, 7*(3), 168–194. DOI: 10.47992/IJAEML.2581.7000.0193

Aithal, P. S., & Aithal, S. (2024). An overview of the use of ICCT and nanotechnology in yellow economy: Current status and future opportunities. [PIJET]. *SSRN, 1*(1), 29–62. DOI: 10.2139/ssrn.4901452

Alexander, C. S., Yarborough, M., & Smith, A. (2024). Who is responsible for 'responsible AI'?: Navigating challenges to build trust in AI agriculture and food system technology. *Precision Agriculture*, *25*(1), 146–185. DOI: 10.1007/s11119-023-10063-3

Ali, A., Anderson, L., Venturini, F., Athanasios, K., Candiani, A., Di Benedetto, G., ... & Martos, V. (2024). AI can empower agriculture for global food security: challenges and prospects in developing nations.

Ali, G., Mijwil, M. M., Buruga, B. A., Abotaleb, M., & Adamopoulos, I. (2024). A survey on artificial intelligence in cybersecurity for smart agriculture: State-of-the-art, cyber threats, artificial intelligence applications, and ethical concerns. *Mesopotamian Journal of Computer Science*, *2024*, 53–103. DOI: 10.58496/MJCSC/2024/007

Ali, G., Mijwil, M. M., Buruga, B. A., Abotaleb, M., & Adamopoulos, I. (2024). A survey on artificial intelligence in cybersecurity for smart agriculture: State-of-the-art, cyber threats, artificial intelligence applications, and ethical concerns. *Mesopotamian Journal of Computer Science*, *2024*, 53–103. DOI: 10.58496/MJCSC/2024/007

Araújo, S. O., Peres, R. S., Barata, J., Lidon, F., & Ramalho, J. C. (2021). Characterising the agriculture 4.0 landscape—Emerging trends, challenges and opportunities. *Agronomy (Basel)*, *11*(4), 667. DOI: 10.3390/agronomy11040667

Bahrini, A., Khamoshifar, M., Abbasimehr, H., Riggs, R. J., Esmaeili, M., Majdabadkohne, R. M., & Pasehvar, M. (2023, April). ChatGPT: Applications, opportunities, and threats. In *2023 Systems and Information Engineering Design Symposium (SIEDS)* (pp. 274-279). IEEE. DOI: 10.1109/SIEDS58326.2023.10137850

Bhangar, N. A., & Shahriyar, A. K. (2023). Iot and ai for next-generation farming: Opportunities, challenges, and outlook. *International Journal of Sustainable Infrastructure for Cities and Societies*, *8*(2), 14–26.

Bhat, S. A., & Huang, N. F. (2021). Big data and ai revolution in precision agriculture: Survey and challenges. *IEEE Access : Practical Innovations, Open Solutions*, *9*, 110209–110222. DOI: 10.1109/ACCESS.2021.3102227

Chen, T., Lv, L., Wang, D., Zhang, J., Yang, Y., Zhao, Z., & Tao, D. (2024). Empowering agrifood system with artificial intelligence: A survey of the progress, challenges and opportunities. *ACM Computing Surveys*, *57*(2), 1–37.

Dara, R., Hazrati Fard, S. M., & Kaur, J. (2022). Recommendations for ethical and responsible use of artificial intelligence in digital agriculture. *Frontiers in Artificial Intelligence*, *5*, 884192. DOI: 10.3389/frai.2022.884192

Dembani, R., Karvelas, I., Akbar, N. A., Rizou, S., Tegolo, D., & Fountas, S. (2025). Agricultural data privacy and federated learning: A review of challenges and opportunities. *Computers and Electronics in Agriculture*, *232*, 110048. DOI: 10.1016/j.compag.2025.110048

Denhere, V., & Shao, D. (2024). Artificial Intelligence in Agritourism: Utilitarian Analysis of Opportunities, Challenges, and Ethical Considerations in the African Context. *Agritourism in Africa*, 17-36.

Devare, M., Arnaud, E., Antezana, E., & King, B. (2023). Governing agricultural data: Challenges and recommendations. *Towards Responsible Plant Data Linkage: Data Challenges for Agricultural Research and Development, 201.*

Gardezi, M., Joshi, B., Rizzo, D. M., Ryan, M., Prutzer, E., Brugler, S., & Dadkhah, A. (2024). Artificial intelligence in farming: Challenges and opportunities for building trust. *Agronomy Journal*, *116*(3), 1217–1228. DOI: 10.1002/agj2.21353

Gavai, A. K., Bouzembrak, Y., Xhani, D., Sedrakyan, G., Meuwissen, M. P., Souza, R. G. S., ... & van Hillegersberg, J. (2025). Agricultural data Privacy: Emerging platforms & strategies. *Food and Humanity*, 100542.

Groumpos, P. P. (2023, July). A critical historic overview of artificial intelligence: Issues, challenges, opportunities, and threats. *Artificial Intelligence and Applications (Commerce, Calif.)*, *1*(4), 181–197.

Gupta, D. K., Pagani, A., Zamboni, P., & Singh, A. K. (2024). AI-powered revolution in plant sciences: Advancements, applications, and challenges for sustainable agriculture and food security. *Exploration of Foods and Foodomics*, *2*(5), 443–459. DOI: 10.37349/eff.2024.00045

He, H., Gray, J., Cangelosi, A., Meng, Q., McGinnity, T. M., & Mehnen, J. (2021). The challenges and opportunities of human-centered AI for trustworthy robots and autonomous systems. *IEEE Transactions on Cognitive and Developmental Systems*, *14*(4), 1398–1412. DOI: 10.1109/TCDS.2021.3132282

Holzinger, A., Weippl, E., Tjoa, A. M., & Kieseberg, P. (2021, August). Digital transformation for sustainable development goals (sdgs)-a security, safety and privacy perspective on ai. In *International cross-domain conference for machine learning and knowledge extraction* (pp. 1-20). Cham: Springer International Publishing.

Jerhamre, E., Carlberg, C. J. C., & van Zoest, V. (2022). Exploring the susceptibility of smart farming: Identified opportunities and challenges. *Smart Agricultural Technology*, *2*, 2. DOI: 10.1016/j.atech.2021.100026

Kanyepe, J., Chibaro, M., Morima, M., & Moeti-Lysson, J. (2025). AI-Powered Agricultural Supply Chains: Applications, Challenges, and Opportunities. *Integrating Agriculture, Green Marketing Strategies, and Artificial Intelligence*, 33-64.

Kapoor, P. (2025). Harvesting Ethics: Forging Responsible Paths in AI and ML for the Agri-Food Industry. In *Food and Industry 5.0: Transforming the Food System for a Sustainable Future* (pp. 305–315). Springer Nature Switzerland. DOI: 10.1007/978-3-031-76758-6_19

Kaushik, K., Khan, A., Kumari, A., Sharma, I., & Dubey, R. (2024). Ethical considerations in AI-based cybersecurity. In *Next-generation cybersecurity: AI, ML, and Blockchain* (pp. 437–470). Springer Nature Singapore. DOI: 10.1007/978-981-97-1249-6_19

Kochupillai, M., Kahl, M., Schmitt, M., Taubenböck, H., & Zhu, X. X. (2022). Earth observation and artificial intelligence: Understanding emerging ethical issues and opportunities. *IEEE Geoscience and Remote Sensing Magazine*, *10*(4), 90–124. DOI: 10.1109/MGRS.2022.3208357

Kochupillai, M., & Köninger, J. (2023). Creating a digital marketplace for agrobiodiversity and plant genetic sequence data: Legal and ethical considerations of an ai and blockchain based solution. *Towards Responsible Plant Data Linkage: Data Challenges for Agricultural Research and Development*, 223.

Leong, Y. M., Lim, E. H., Subri, N. F. B., & Jalil, N. B. A. (2023, September). Transforming agriculture: Navigating the challenges and embracing the opportunities of artificial intelligence of things. In *2023 IEEE International Conference on Agrosystem Engineering, Technology & Applications (AGRETA)* (pp. 142-147). IEEE. DOI: 10.1109/AGRETA57740.2023.10262747

Malhotra, K., & Firdaus, M. (2022). Application of artificial intelligence in IoT security for crop yield prediction. *ResearchBerg Review of Science and Technology*, *2*(1), 136–157.

Mark, R. (2019). Ethics of using AI and big data in agriculture: The case of a large agriculture multinational. *The ORBIT Journal*, *2*(2), 1–27. DOI: 10.29297/orbit.v2i2.109

Neupane, S., Mitra, S., Fernandez, I. A., Saha, S., Mittal, S., Chen, J., Pillai, N., & Rahimi, S. (2024). Security considerations in ai-robotics: A survey of current methods, challenges, and opportunities. *IEEE Access : Practical Innovations, Open Solutions*, *12*, 22072–22097. DOI: 10.1109/ACCESS.2024.3363657

Otieno, M. (2023). An extensive survey of smart agriculture technologies: Current security posture. *World J. Adv. Res. Rev*, *18*(3), 1207–1231. DOI: 10.30574/wjarr.2023.18.3.1241

Pandey, D. K., & Mishra, R. (2024). *Towards sustainable agriculture: Harnessing AI for global food security*. Artificial Intelligence in Agriculture.

Pedro, F., Subosa, M., Rivas, A., & Valverde, P. (2019). Artificial intelligence in education: Challenges and opportunities for sustainable development.

Senoo, E. E. K., Anggraini, L., Kumi, J. A., Luna, B. K., Akansah, E., Sulyman, H. A., & Aritsugi, M. (2024). IoT solutions with artificial intelligence technologies for precision agriculture: Definitions, applications, challenges, and opportunities. *Electronics (Basel)*, *13*(10), 1894. DOI: 10.3390/electronics13101894

Shafik, W., Tufail, A., De Silva, C. L., Haji, R. A. A., & Apong, M. (2025). The Role, Application, and Impact of Artificial Intelligence in the Agriculture Industry. In *Future Tech Startups and Innovation in the Age of AI* (pp. 36–60). CRC Press.

Sood, A., Sharma, R. K., & Bhardwaj, A. K. (2022). Artificial intelligence research in agriculture: A review. *Online Information Review*, *46*(6), 1054–1075. DOI: 10.1108/OIR-10-2020-0448

Sparrow, R., & Howard, M. (2021). Robots in agriculture: prospects, impacts, ethics, and policy. *precision agriculture, 22*, 818-833.

Sparrow, R., Howard, M., & Degeling, C. (2021). Managing the risks of artificial intelligence in agriculture. *NJAS: Impact in Agricultural and Life Sciences*, *93*(1), 172–196. DOI: 10.1080/27685241.2021.2008777

Tzachor, A., Devare, M., King, B., Avin, S., & Ó hÉigeartaigh, S. (2022). Responsible artificial intelligence in agriculture requires systemic understanding of risks and externalities. *Nature Machine Intelligence*, *4*(2), 104–109. DOI: 10.1038/s42256-022-00440-4

Uplaonkar, S. S., Veershetty, R., Bahar, Z., & Sangeeta, G. (2024). The role of productive AI: A supporter or challenger in the future of agricultural librarianship. *IJAR*, *10*(4), 46–53.

Wei, H., Xu, W., Kang, B., Eisner, R., Muleke, A., Rodriguez, D., deVoil, P., Sadras, V., Monjardino, M., & Harrison, M. T. (2024). Irrigation with artificial intelligence: Problems, premises, promises. *Human-Centric Intelligent Systems*, *4*(2), 187–205. DOI: 10.1007/s44230-024-00072-4

Williamson, H. F., Brettschneider, J., Caccamo, M., Davey, R. P., Goble, C., Kersey, P. J., May, S., Morris, R. J., Ostler, R., Pridmore, T., Rawlings, C., Studholme, D., Tsaftaris, S. A., & Leonelli, S. (2023). Data management challenges for artificial intelligence in plant and agricultural research. *F1000 Research, 10*, 324. DOI: 10.12688/f1000research.52204.2

Ya'u, M. S., & Mohammed, M. S. (2025). AI-Assisted Writing and Academic Literacy: Investigating the Dual Impact of Language Models on Writing Proficiency and Ethical Concerns in Nigerian Higher Education. *International Journal of Education and Literacy Studies*, *13*(2), 593–604. DOI: 10.7575/aiac.ijels.v.13n.2p.593

Zangana, H. M., Abdulqader, A. A., Luckyardi, S., & Li, S. (2026). Securing Smart Agriculture: AI-Driven Digital Forensics in Agri-Tech Cybercrime Investigation. In Zangana, H., & Omar, M. (Eds.), *AI in Digital Forensics and Cybercrime Investigation: Methods, Ethics, and Emerging Technologies* (pp. 265–300). IGI Global Scientific Publishing., DOI: 10.4018/979-8-3373-6536-7.ch009

Zangana, H. M., Amelia, P., Luckyardi, S., Mustafa, F. M., & Li, S. (2025). The Role of Language in Regulating AI and Agricultural Technologies: Legal Perspectives from a Globalized World. In Zangana, H., Al-Karaki, J., & Omar, M. (Eds.), *Navigating Law and Policy in STM Enterprises: Ethical Governance, Regulation, and Innovation Strategy* (pp. 193–224). IGI Global Scientific Publishing., DOI: 10.4018/979-8-3373-4862-9.ch008

Zangana, H. M., Luckyardi, S., Mustafa, F. M., & Li, S. (2025). Enhancing Agricultural Cybersecurity: Leveraging Deep Learning and Large Language Models for Smart Farming Protection. In Zangana, H., Al-Karaki, J., & Omar, M. (Eds.), *Revolutionizing Cybersecurity With Deep Learning and Large Language Models* (pp. 307–338). IGI Global Scientific Publishing., DOI: 10.4018/979-8-3373-3296-3.ch010

Zangana, H. M., Luckyardi, S., Mustafa, F. M., & Li, S. (2025). Ethical and Secure AI Applications in Agricultural Research: Challenges and Opportunities. In Zangana, H., & Omar, M. (Eds.), *Ensuring Secure and Ethical STM Research in the AI Era* (pp. 43–76). IGI Global Scientific Publishing., DOI: 10.4018/979-8-3373-4252-8.ch002

Zangana, H. M., & Mustafa, F. M. (2026). Enhancing Educational Visual Content Through AI-Based Image Denoising Techniques: Implications for Remote Teaching and Digital Resource Development. In Zangana, H., Nobles, C., & Omar, M. (Eds.), *Harnessing AI for Teacher Support and Professional Development* (pp. 101–136). IGI Global Scientific Publishing., DOI: 10.4018/979-8-3373-5951-9.ch004

Zohouri, M., Sabzali, M., & Golmohammadi, A. (2024). Ethical considerations of ChatGPT-assisted article writing. *Synesis (ISSN 1984-6754), 16*(1), 94-113.

Compilation of References

Abbas, A., & Kollwitz, E. (2025). Forensic Accounting in the Digital Era: Leveraging AI for Fraud Detection and Risk Management.

Abd-Elsalam, K. A., & Abdel-Momen, S. M. (2023). Artificial intelligence's development and challenges in scientific writing. *Egyptian Journal of Agricultural Research, 101*(3), 714–717. DOI: 10.21608/ejar.2023.220363.1414

Adam, I. Y., & Varol, C. (2020, June). Intelligence in digital forensics process. In *2020 8th International Symposium on Digital Forensics and Security (ISDFS)* (pp. 1-6). IEEE. DOI: 10.1109/ISDFS49300.2020.9116442

Adanma, U. M., & Ogunbiyi, E. O.Uwaga Monica AdanmaEmmanuel Olurotimi Ogunbiyi. (2024). Artificial intelligence in environmental conservation: Evaluating cyber risks and opportunities for sustainable practices. *Computer Science & IT Research Journal, 5*(5), 1178–1209. DOI: 10.51594/csitrj.v5i5.1156

Adejumo, A. P., & Ogburie, C. P.Adetunji Paul AdejumoChinonso Peter Ogburie. (2025). Forensic accounting in financial fraud detection: Trends and challenges. *International Journal of Science and Research Archive, 14*(3), 1219–1232. DOI: 10.30574/ijsra.2025.14.3.0815

Aderibigbe, A. O., Ohenhen, P. E., Nwaobia, N. K., Gidiagba, J. O., & Ani, E. C.Adebayo Olusegun AderibigbePeter Efosa OhenhenNwabueze Kelvin Nwaobia-Joachim Osheyor GidiagbaEmmanuel Chigozie Ani. (2023). Artificial intelligence in developing countries: Bridging the gap between potential and implementation. *Computer Science & IT Research Journal, 4*(3), 185–199. DOI: 10.51594/csitrj.v4i3.629

Adewopo, V., Gonen, B., & Adewopo, F. (2020, December). Exploring open source information for cyber threat intelligence. In *2020 IEEE International Conference on Big Data (Big Data)* (pp. 2232-2241). IEEE. DOI: 10.1109/BigData50022.2020.9378220

Aggarwal, S., Bansal, S., & Goel, R. (2024). Ai In Agriculture: A Looming Challenge, A Gleaming Opportunity. *International Journal of Engineering Science and Humanities, 14*(Special Issue 1), 43-52.

Aghaei, E., Niu, X., Shadid, W., & Al-Shaer, E. (2022, October). Securebert: A domain-specific language model for cybersecurity. In International Conference on Security and Privacy in Communication Systems (pp. 39-56). Cham: Springer Nature Switzerland.

Ahmad, A., Liew, A. X., Venturini, F., Kalogeras, A., Candiani, A., Di Benedetto, G., ... & Martos, V. (2024). AI can empower agriculture for.

Ahmad, A., Liew, A. X., Venturini, F., Kalogeras, A., Candiani, A., Di Benedetto, G., Ajibola, S., Cartujo, P., Romero, P., Lykoudi, A., De Grandis, M. M., Xouris, C., Lo Bianco, R., Doddy, I., Elegbede, I., D'Urso Labate, G. F., García del Moral, L. F., & Martos, V. (2024). AI can empower agriculture for global food security: Challenges and prospects in developing nations. *Frontiers in Artificial Intelligence, 7*, 1328530. DOI: 10.3389/frai.2024.1328530

Ahmed Alaa El-Din, E. (2022). Artificial intelligence in forensic science: Invasion or revolution? *Egyptian Society of Clinical Toxicology Journal, 10*(2), 20–32. DOI: 10.21608/esctj.2022.158178.1012

Ahmed, M. N., Singh, A. P., Hussain, M. R., Rasool, M. A., Khan, I. M., & Dildar, M. S. (2024, July). Enhancing Crop Production using Artificial Intelligence in Agricultural Revolution. In *2024 IEEE 7th International Conference on Advanced Technologies* [ATSIP]. *Signal and Image Processing : an International Journal, 1*, 432–437.

Aithal, P. S., & Aithal, S. (2023). Application of ChatGPT in higher education and research–A futuristic analysis. [IJAEML]. *International Journal of Applied Engineering and Management Letters, 7*(3), 168–194. DOI: 10.47992/IJAEML.2581.7000.0193

Aithal, P. S., & Aithal, S. (2024). An overview of the use of ICCT and nanotechnology in yellow economy: Current status and future opportunities. [PIJET]. *SSRN, 1*(1), 29–62. DOI: 10.2139/ssrn.4901452

Akindele, A., & Chabinga, R. (2024). Navigating Climate Change and Sustainability Solutions: Nigeria's Role in International Environmental Law. *African Journal of Climate Change and Resource Sustainability, 3*(1), 331–344. DOI: 10.37284/ajccrs.3.1.2188

Alawida, M., Mejri, S., Mehmood, A., Chikhaoui, B., & Isaac Abiodun, O. (2023). A comprehensive study of ChatGPT: Advancements, limitations, and ethical considerations in natural language processing and cybersecurity. *Information (Basel)*, *14*(8), 462. DOI: 10.3390/info14080462

Aldoseri, A., Al-Khalifa, K. N., & Hamouda, A. M. (2023). Re-Thinking Data Strategy and Integration for Artificial Intelligence: Concepts, Opportunities, and Challenges. *Applied Sciences (Basel, Switzerland)*, *13*(12), 7082. DOI: 10.3390/app13127082

Alexander, C. S., Yarborough, M., & Smith, A. (2024). Who is responsible for 'responsible AI'?: Navigating challenges to build trust in AI agriculture and food system technology. *Precision Agriculture*, *25*(1), 146–185. DOI: 10.1007/s11119-023-10063-3

Alghamdi, M. I. (2021). *Digital forensics in cyber security—recent trends, threats, and opportunities*. Cybersecurity Threats with New Perspectives. DOI: 10.5772/intechopen.94452

Al-Hajri, S. M., Al-Thonayan, Z. J., Alqattan, M. M., Alalyani, N. A., Alali, N. D., & Alnaim, N. (2023). Maximizing the Potential of Artificial Intelligence in Digital Forensics Investigations.

Al-Hawawreh, M., Aljuhani, A., & Jararweh, Y. (2023). Chatgpt for cybersecurity: Practical applications, challenges, and future directions. *Cluster Computing*, *26*(6), 3421–3436. DOI: 10.1007/s10586-023-04124-5

Ali, A. (2022). Cyber Crime Investigation and Forensics: Leveraging AI and Big Data for More Effective Solutions.

Ali, A., Anderson, L., Venturini, F., Athanasios, K., Candiani, A., Di Benedetto, G., ... & Martos, V. (2024). AI can empower agriculture for global food security: challenges and prospects in developing nations.

Ali, A. (2024). Navigating Road for Net Zero Policies to Aligning Policy, Politics, and Governance for Environmental Sustainability. In *Transition Towards a Sustainable Future: Net Zero Policies and Environmental Sustainability* (pp. 205–230). Springer Nature Singapore. DOI: 10.1007/978-981-97-5756-5_10

Ali, A. M., Futaih, R. F., Shukur, M., & Al-Orfali, A. K. (2024). Forensic Accounting and Fraud Detection Emerging Trends and Techniques. *Journal of Ecohumanism*, *3*(5), 525–542. DOI: 10.62754/joe.v3i5.3921

Ali, A. M., Khinger, I. K., Subhe, A., & Al-Orfali, A. K. (2024). Forensic Accounting Techniques in Detecting Frauds. *Journal of Ecohumanism*, *3*(5), 543–558. DOI: 10.62754/joe.v3i5.3922

Ali, G., Mijwil, M. M., Buruga, B. A., Abotaleb, M., & Adamopoulos, I. (2024). A survey on artificial intelligence in cybersecurity for smart agriculture: State-of-the-art, cyber threats, artificial intelligence applications, and ethical concerns. *Mesopotamian Journal of Computer Science, 2024*, 53–103. DOI: 10.58496/MJCSC/2024/007

Ali, H., & Aysan, A. F. (2024). Decoding Future of Generative AI in Finance: A Machine Learning Exploration of Academic and Grey Corpus. *Available at SSRN* 4787211. DOI: 10.2139/ssrn.4787211

Ali, H., & Aysan, A. F. (2025). Ethical dimensions of generative AI: A cross-domain analysis using machine learning structural topic modeling. *International Journal of Ethics and Systems, 41*(1), 3–34. DOI: 10.1108/IJOES-04-2024-0112

Ali, H., Zafar, M. B., & Aysan, A. F. (2024). Generative AI and Finance: A Multi-level Machine Learning Based Analysis. *Available at SSRN* 5129013.

Aloamaka, P. C. (2024). Navigating the Climate Crisis: Exploring International Law's Evolution and Application. *GLS Law Journal, 6*(1), 48–58. DOI: 10.69974/glslawjournal.v6i1.127

AlQenaei, Z. M. (2024, March). Evolution and Optimization of Language Model Architectures: From Foundations to Future Directions. In *International Conference on Computing and Machine Learning* (pp. 233-249). Singapore: Springer Nature Singapore.

Al-Raggad, M., Albalawee, N., Al-Mahasneh, A., Abu Huson, Y., & Albajaly, A. (2025). Unveiling financial crimes: Advancing forensic accounting practices and ethical integrity through bibliometric insights. *Safer Communities, 24*(3), 244–264. DOI: 10.1108/SC-11-2024-0069

AL-Refaey. M. R., Tyagi, A. K., AL-Ghamdi, A. S. A. M., & Kukreja, S. (Eds.). (2024). *Topics in Artificial Intelligence Applied to Industry 4.0*. John Wiley & Sons.

Al-Sinani, H. S., & Mitchell, C. J. (2024). AI-enhanced ethical hacking: A Linux-focused experiment. *arXiv preprint arXiv:2410.05105.*

Al-Sinani, H. S., Sahli, N., Mitchell, C. J., & Al-Siyabi, M. (2025). Advancing ethical hacking with AI: A Linux-based experimental study. *Proceedings of ITASEC and SERICS, Bologna, Italy (Feb 2025),* https://www. chrismitchell. net/Papers/aehwaa. pdf

Alturkistani, H., & Chuprat, S. (2024). Artificial Intelligence and Large Language Models in Advancing Cyber Threat Intelligence: A Systematic Literature Review.

Aman, Q. U. I. S. E. R. (2024). From data to discovery: The impact of technology on forensic accounting. *Ile Journal of Law and Forensic Science*, *2*(1), 1–13.

Ameri, K., Hempel, M., Sharif, H., Lopez, J.Jr, & Perumalla, K. (2021). Cybert: Cybersecurity claim classification by fine-tuning the bert language model. *Journal of Cybersecurity and Privacy*, *1*(4), 615–637. DOI: 10.3390/jcp1040031

Araújo, S. O., Peres, R. S., Barata, J., Lidon, F., & Ramalho, J. C. (2021). Characterising the agriculture 4.0 landscape—Emerging trends, challenges and opportunities. *Agronomy (Basel)*, *11*(4), 667. DOI: 10.3390/agronomy11040667

Arya, L., & Rastogi, R. (2024). Study on Aerial Monitoring System in Agriculture, Forestry, Defense, and Border Protection Using Artificial Intelligence (AI). In *Agriculture and Aquaculture Applications of Biosensors and Bioelectronics* (pp. 392-407). IGI Global Scientific Publishing.

Asoronye, G. O., Anthony, O. C., Ogbuikwu, R. I., Ogili, C. O., & Ali, H. U. (2024). SecLM: A Specialized Security Language Model for Advanced Cybersecurity Applications and Threat Mitigation. *EKETE-International Journal Of Advanced Research*, *2*(6), 33–42.

Atoum, M. S., Alarood, A. A., Alsolami, E., Abubakar, A., Hwaitat, A. K. A., & Alsmadi, I. (2025). Cybersecurity Intelligence Through Textual Data Analysis: A Framework Using Machine Learning and Terrorism Datasets. *Future Internet*, *17*(4), 182. DOI: 10.3390/fi17040182

Bahrini, A., Khamoshifar, M., Abbasimehr, H., Riggs, R. J., Esmaeili, M., Majdabadkohne, R. M., & Pasehvar, M. (2023, April). ChatGPT: Applications, opportunities, and threats. In *2023 Systems and Information Engineering Design Symposium (SIEDS)* (pp. 274-279). IEEE. DOI: 10.1109/SIEDS58326.2023.10137850

Baseri, Y., Chouhan, V., & Ghorbani, A. (2024). Cybersecurity in the Quantum Era: Assessing the Impact of Quantum Computing on Infrastructure. *arXiv preprint arXiv:2404.10659*.

Batabyal, G. S. (2024). Ethics, laws on war and artificial intelligence-driven warfare. In *Artificial intelligence, ethics and the future of warfare* (pp. 187–215). Routledge India. DOI: 10.4324/9781003421849-9

Bhagat, N. (2024). Artificial intelligence challenges and its impact on detection and prevention of financial statement fraud: A theoretical study. In *Demystifying the Dark Side of AI in Business* (pp. 60–80). IGI Global Scientific Publishing.

Bhangar, N. A., & Shahriyar, A. K. (2023). Iot and ai for next-generation farming: Opportunities, challenges, and outlook. *International Journal of Sustainable Infrastructure for Cities and Societies*, *8*(2), 14–26.

Bharati, R. K. (2020). Legal and Ethical Considerations in the Use of Digital Forensics by Law Enforcement: A Multi-jurisdictional Study. *Turk. Online J. Qual. Inq*, *11*(4), 10594–10610.

Bhat, S. A., & Huang, N. F. (2021). Big data and ai revolution in precision agriculture: Survey and challenges. *IEEE Access : Practical Innovations, Open Solutions*, *9*, 110209–110222. DOI: 10.1109/ACCESS.2021.3102227

Bhawna, & Mahajan, S. (2024). Artificial Intelligence Perspective on Digital Forensics. *Applying Artificial Intelligence in Cybersecurity Analytics and Cyber Threat Detection*, 33-44.

Bhawna, & Mahajan, S. (2024). Artificial Intelligence Perspective on Digital Forensics. *Applying Artificial Intelligence in Cybersecurity Analytics and Cyber Threat Detection*, 33-44. Chaudhary, P. K. AI, ML, AND LARGE LANGUAGE MODELS IN CYBERSECURITY.

Bishwas, A. K., & Sen, M. (2024). Strategic Roadmap for Quantum-Resistant Security: A Framework for Preparing Industries for the Quantum Threat. *arXiv preprint arXiv:2411.09995.*

Bonfanti, M. E. (2022). *Artificial intelligence and the offence-defence balance in cyber security. Cyber Security: Socio-Technological Uncertainty and Political Fragmentation*. Routledge.

Borta, H. G., Alemu, A., Shute, T., Zewdie, B., Fantaw, D., Shimelis, B., ... & Tamiru, M. T. (2024). Narcotic Drugs and Psychotropic Substances Control System in Ethiopia: A National Survey.

Bousri, M. M. S. (2019). *A comparative analysis of legal and institutional framework for arbitration: Comoros and Uganda* (Doctoral dissertation, School of law).

Bryce, C., Kalousis, A., Leroux, I., Madinier, H., Mermoud, A., Mulder, V., ... & Ruch, P. Trends in Large Language Models: Actors, Applications, and Impact on Cybersecurity.

Bush, S. F., Challener, W. A., & Mantelet, G. (2021). A perspective on industrial quantum networks. *AVS Quantum Science*, *3*(3), 030501. DOI: 10.1116/5.0051881

Butt, J. (2024). Analytical study of the world's first EU Artificial Intelligence (AI) Act. *International Journal of Research Publication and Reviews*, *5*(3), 7343–7364. DOI: 10.55248/gengpi.5.0324.0914

Campus, M. T. (2024). Quantum Machine Learning, Leveraging Al, and. *Integration of AI, Quantum Computing, and Semiconductor Technology*, 57.

Capuano, N., Fenza, G., Loia, V., & Stanzione, C. (2022). Explainable artificial intelligence in cybersecurity: A survey. *IEEE Access : Practical Innovations, Open Solutions*, *10*, 93575–93600. DOI: 10.1109/ACCESS.2022.3204171

Chaudhary, M., & Bansal, D. (2022). Open source intelligence extraction for terrorism-related information: A review. *Wiley Interdisciplinary Reviews. Data Mining and Knowledge Discovery*, *12*(5), e1473. DOI: 10.1002/widm.1473

Chen, T., Lv, L., Wang, D., Zhang, J., Yang, Y., Zhao, Z., & Tao, D. (2024). Empowering agrifood system with artificial intelligence: A survey of the progress, challenges and opportunities. *ACM Computing Surveys*, *57*(2), 1–37.

Chen, Y., Cui, M., Wang, D., Cao, Y., Yang, P., Jiang, B., Lu, Z., & Liu, B. (2024). A survey of large language models for cyber threat detection. *Computers & Security*, *145*, 104016. DOI: 10.1016/j.cose.2024.104016

CHILONGO, L., & KM, A. S. (2024). IMPACT OF ARTIFICIAL INTELLIGENCE ON CYBERSECURITY: A CASE OF INTERNET OF THINGS. *i-Manager's Journal on Digital Forensics & Cyber Security (JDF), 2*(1).

Chowdhury, S. (2024). Towards a Just Climate: Navigating Complexities and Challenges in Climate Change Discourse and Action. *Issue 2 Int'l JL Mgmt. &. Human.*, *7*, 1807.

Cooper, S., & Zell, S. (2023). *Staying on Board: Non-profit housing provider board capacity in a changing context*. Institute of Urban Studies, The University of Winnipeg.

Costantini, S., De Gasperis, G., & Olivieri, R. (2019). Digital forensics and investigations meet artificial intelligence. *Annals of Mathematics and Artificial Intelligence*, *86*(1), 193–229. DOI: 10.1007/s10472-019-09632-y

Daniel, J. (2024). *Environmental Law: Navigating Legal Pathways for a Sustainable Future*. Pencil.

Daraojimba, R. E., Farayola, O. A., Olatoye, F. M. O., Mhlongo, N., & Oke, T. T. L. (2023). Forensic accounting in the digital age: a US perspective: scrutinizing methods and challenges in digital financial fraud prevention. *Finance & Accounting Research Journal*, *5*(11), 342–360. DOI: 10.51594/farj.v5i11.614

Dara, R., Hazrati Fard, S. M., & Kaur, J. (2022). Recommendations for ethical and responsible use of artificial intelligence in digital agriculture. *Frontiers in Artificial Intelligence*, *5*, 884192. DOI: 10.3389/frai.2022.884192

Darvishi, K., Liu, L., & Lim, S. (2022). Navigating the Nexus: Legal and Economic Implications of Emerging Tech-nologies. *Law and Economics*, *16*(3), 172–186. DOI: 10.35335/laweco.v16i3.59

Dembani, R., Karvelas, I., Akbar, N. A., Rizou, S., Tegolo, D., & Fountas, S. (2025). Agricultural data privacy and federated learning: A review of challenges and opportunities. *Computers and Electronics in Agriculture*, *232*, 110048. DOI: 10.1016/j.compag.2025.110048

Denhere, V., & Shao, D. (2024). Artificial Intelligence in Agritourism: Utilitarian Analysis of Opportunities, Challenges, and Ethical Considerations in the African Context. *Agritourism in Africa*, 17-36.

Devare, M., Arnaud, E., Antezana, E., & King, B. (2023). Governing agricultural data: Challenges and recommendations. *Towards Responsible Plant Data Linkage: Data Challenges for Agricultural Research and Development, 201.*

Diaf, A., Korba, A. A., Karabadji, N. E., & Ghamri-Doudane, Y. (2024, April). Beyond detection: Leveraging large language models for cyber attack prediction in iot networks. In *2024 20th International Conference on Distributed Computing in Smart Systems and the Internet of Things (DCOSS-IoT)* (pp. 117-123). IEEE.

Drexl, J., Conde, B., & Kim, D. (2025). Position Statement of the Max Planck Institute for Innovation and Competition of 25 April 2025 in the framework of the revision of the Technology

Đukić, T., Pavlović, M., & Grdinić, V. (2023). Uncovering Financial Fraud: The Vital Role of Forensic Accounting and Auditing in Modern Business Practice. *Economic Themes, 61*(3).

Dunsin, D., Ghanem, M. C., Ouazzane, K., & Vassilev, V. (2024). A comprehensive analysis of the role of artificial intelligence and machine learning in modern digital forensics and incident response. *Forensic Science International Digital Investigation*, *48*, 301675. DOI: 10.1016/j.fsidi.2023.301675

Dunsin, D., Ghanem, M. C., & Quazzane, K. (2022). The use of artificial intelligence in digital forensics and incident response in a constrained environment. *International Journal of Information and Communication Engineering*, *16*(8), 280–285.

Du, X., Hargreaves, C., Sheppard, J., Anda, F., Sayakkara, A., Le-Khac, N. A., & Scanlon, M. (2020, August). SoK: Exploring the state of the art and the future potential of artificial intelligence in digital forensic investigation. In *Proceedings of the 15th international conference on availability, reliability and security* (pp. 1-10). DOI: 10.1145/3407023.3407068

Eisenberg, D. (2024). *Sensing With Integrity: Responsible Sensor Systems in an Era of AI* (Doctoral dissertation, New Jersey Institute of Technology).

Elumilade, O. O., Ogundeji, I. A., Achumie, G. O., Omokhoa, H. E., & Omowole, B. M. (2021). Enhancing fraud detection and forensic auditing through data-driven techniques for financial integrity and security. *Journal of Advanced Education and Sciences, 1*(2), 55–63. DOI: 10.54660/.JAES.2021.1.2.55-63

Emon, M. M. H., Khan, T., Rahman, M. A., Hamid, A. B. A., & Yaakub, N. I. (2025). GreenTech revolution: Navigating challenges and seizing opportunities. In *AI and green technology applications in society* (pp. 63–90). IGI Global Scientific Publishing.

Eswaran, U., & Eswaran, V. (2025). Quantum Machine Learning, Leveraging AI, and Semiconductor Technology. In *Integration of AI, Quantum Computing, and Semiconductor Technology* (pp. 57-78). IGI Global.

Etaywe, A., Macfarlane, K., & Alazab, M. (2024). A cyberterrorist behind the keyboard: An automated text analysis for psycholinguistic profiling and threat assessment. *Journal of Language Aggression and Conflict*.

Faqir, R. S. (2023). Digital Criminal Investigations in the Era of Artificial Intelligence: A Comprehensive Overview. *International Journal of Cyber Criminology, 17*(2), 77–94.

Fenwick, A., Molnar, G., & Frangos, P. (2024). The critical role of HRM in AI-driven digital transformation: A paradigm shift to enable firms to move from AI implementation to human-centric adoption. *Discover Artificial Intelligence, 4*(1), 34. DOI: 10.1007/s44163-024-00125-4

Ferrag, M. A., Ndhlovu, M., Tihanyi, N., Cordeiro, L. C., Debbah, M., & Lestable, T. (2023). Revolutionizing cyber threat detection with large language models. *arXiv preprint arXiv:2306.14263*, 195-202.

Ferrag, M. A., Ndhlovu, M., Tihanyi, N., Cordeiro, L. C., Debbah, M., & Lestable, T. (2023). Revolutionizing cyber threat detection with large language models. arXiv preprint arXiv:2306.14263.

Ferrag, M. A., Alwahedi, F., Battah, A., Cherif, B., Mechri, A., & Tihanyi, N. (2024). Generative ai and large language models for cyber security: All insights you need. *Available at SSRN* 4853709. DOI: 10.2139/ssrn.4853709

Ferrag, M. A., Ndhlovu, M., Tihanyi, N., Cordeiro, L. C., Debbah, M., Lestable, T., & Thandi, N. S. (2024). Revolutionizing cyber threat detection with large language models: A privacy-preserving bert-based lightweight model for iot/iiot devices. *IEEE Access : Practical Innovations, Open Solutions*, *12*, 23733–23750. DOI: 10.1109/ACCESS.2024.3363469

Filetti, S., Fenza, G., & Gallo, A. (2024). Research design and writing of scholarly articles: New artificial intelligence tools available for researchers. *Endocrine*, *85*(3), 1104–1116. DOI: 10.1007/s12020-024-03977-z PMID: 39085566

Flannery, J., Ajayi, S. O., & Oyegoke, A. S. (2021). Alcohol and substance misuse in the construction industry. *International Journal of Occupational Safety and Ergonomics*, *27*(2), 472–487. DOI: 10.1080/10803548.2019.1601376 PMID: 30935301

Ganesh, V. (2017). Artificial intelligence applied to computer forensics. *International Journal (Toronto, Ont.)*, *5*(5).

Gao, M. (2023). The Advance of GPTs and Language Model in Cyber Security. Highlights in Science. *Engineering and Technology*, *57*, 195–202.

Gardezi, M., Joshi, B., Rizzo, D. M., Ryan, M., Prutzer, E., Brugler, S., & Dadkhah, A. (2024). Artificial intelligence in farming: Challenges and opportunities for building trust. *Agronomy Journal*, *116*(3), 1217–1228. DOI: 10.1002/agj2.21353

Gaurav, A., Chui, K. T., Arya, V., Attar, R. W., Bansal, S., Alhomoud, A., & Psannis, K. (2024). Optimized AI-Driven Semantic Web Approach for Enhancing Phishing Detection in E-Commerce Platforms. [IJSWIS]. *International Journal on Semantic Web and Information Systems*, *20*(1), 1–13. DOI: 10.4018/IJSWIS.359767

Gavai, A. K., Bouzembrak, Y., Xhani, D., Sedrakyan, G., Meuwissen, M. P., Souza, R. G. S., ... & van Hillegersberg, J. (2025). Agricultural data Privacy: Emerging platforms & strategies. *Food and Humanity*, 100542.

Gennari, J., Lau, S. H., Perl, S., Parish, J., & Sastry, G. (2024). CONSIDERATIONS FOR EVALUATING LARGE LANGUAGE MODELS FOR CYBERSECURITY TASKS.

Georgescu, T. M. (2020). Natural language processing model for automatic analysis of cybersecurity-related documents. *Symmetry*, *12*(3), 354. DOI: 10.3390/sym12030354

Ghazal, T. M., Janjua, J. I., Abushiba, W., Ahmad, M., Ihsan, A., & Al-Dmour, N. A. (2024, December). Cybersecurity Revolution via Large Language Models and Explainable AI. In *2024 17th International Conference on Security of Information and Networks (SIN)* (pp. 1-6). IEEE. DOI: 10.1109/SIN63213.2024.10871324

Gholami, S., & Omar, M. (2023). Does Synthetic Data Make Large Language Models More Efficient? *arXiv preprint arXiv:2310.07830.*

Gholami, S., & Omar, M. (2024). Can a student large language model perform as well as its teacher? In *Innovations, Securities, and Case Studies Across Healthcare, Business, and Technology* (pp. 122-139). IGI Global. DOI: 10.4018/979-8-3693-1906-2.ch007

Groumpos, P. P. (2023, July). A critical historic overview of artificial intelligence: Issues, challenges, opportunities, and threats. *Artificial Intelligence and Applications (Commerce, Calif.)*, *1*(4), 181–197.

Guastalla, M., Li, Y., Hekmati, A., & Krishnamachari, B. (2023, October). Application of Large Language Models to DDoS Attack Detection. In International Conference on Security and Privacy in Cyber-Physical Systems and Smart Vehicles (pp. 83-99). Cham: Springer Nature Switzerland.

Gupta, B. B., Gaurav, A., & Arya, V. (2024). Navigating the security landscape of large language models in enterprise information systems. *Enterprise Information Systems*, *18*(4), 2310846. DOI: 10.1080/17517575.2024.2310846

Gupta, D. K., Pagani, A., Zamboni, P., & Singh, A. K. (2024). AI-powered revolution in plant sciences: Advancements, applications, and challenges for sustainable agriculture and food security. *Exploration of Foods and Foodomics*, *2*(5), 443–459. DOI: 10.37349/eff.2024.00045

Haddad, H. O. S. S. A. M., Alharasis, E. E., Fraij, J., & Al-Ramahi, N. M. (2024). How do innovative improvements in forensic accounting and its related technologies sweeten fraud investigation and prevention. *WSEAS Transactions on Business and Economics*, *21*, 1115–1141. DOI: 10.37394/23207.2024.21.93

Hadi, M. A., Abdulredha, M. N., & Hasan, E. (2023). Introduction to ChatGPT: A new revolution of artificial intelligence with machine learning algorithms and cybersecurity. *Sci. Arch*, *4*(04), 276. DOI: 10.47587/SA.2023.4406

Hall, S. W., Sakzad, A., & Choo, K. K. R. (2022). Explainable artificial intelligence for digital forensics. *Wiley Interdisciplinary Reviews: Forensic Science*, *4*(2), e1434.

Hamza, Y. A., & Omar, M. D. (2013). Cloud computing security: Abuse and nefarious use of cloud computing. *International Journal of Computer Engineering Research, 3*(6), 22–27.

Happe, A., & Cito, J. (2023, November). Getting pwn'd by ai: Penetration testing with large language models. In *Proceedings of the 31st ACM Joint European Software Engineering Conference and Symposium on the Foundations of Software Engineering* (pp. 2082-2086). DOI: 10.1145/3611643.3613083

Harjuni, J. (2024). The role of forensic accounting in fraud detection and prevention in financial institutions. *Tamansiswa Accounting Journal International, 15*(1), 151–159.

Hasanov, I., Virtanen, S., Hakkala, A., & Isoaho, J. (2024). Application of Large Language Models in Cybersecurity: A Systematic Literature Review. *IEEE Access : Practical Innovations, Open Solutions, 12*, 176751–176778. DOI: 10.1109/ACCESS.2024.3505983

Hassanin, M., & Moustafa, N. (2024). A comprehensive overview of large language models (llms) for cyber defences: Opportunities and directions. *arXiv preprint arXiv:2405.14487.*

Hassan, S. K., & Ibrahim, A. (2023). The role of artificial intelligence in cyber security and incident response. *International Journal for Electronic Crime Investigation, 7*(2).

Hayes, D., & Kyobe, M. (2020, March). The adoption of automation in cyber forensics. In *2020 Conference on Information Communications Technology and Society (ICTAS)* (pp. 1-6). IEEE. DOI: 10.1109/ICTAS47918.2020.233977

He, H., Gray, J., Cangelosi, A., Meng, Q., McGinnity, T. M., & Mehnen, J. (2021). The challenges and opportunities of human-centered AI for trustworthy robots and autonomous systems. *IEEE Transactions on Cognitive and Developmental Systems, 14*(4), 1398–1412. DOI: 10.1109/TCDS.2021.3132282

Ho, C. W. (2023). Implementing the human right to science in the regulatory governance of artificial intelligence in healthcare. *Journal of Law and the Biosciences, 10*(2), lsad026. DOI: 10.1093/jlb/lsad026 PMID: 37854168

Holzinger, A., Weippl, E., Tjoa, A. M., & Kieseberg, P. (2021, August). Digital transformation for sustainable development goals (sdgs)-a security, safety and privacy perspective on ai. In *International cross-domain conference for machine learning and knowledge extraction* (pp. 1-20). Cham: Springer International Publishing.

Huff, A. J., Burrell, D. N., Nobles, C., Richardson, K., Wright, J. B., Burton, S. L., Jones, A. J., Springs, D., Omar, M., & Brown-Jackson, K. L. (2023). Management Practices for Mitigating Cybersecurity Threats to Biotechnology Companies, Laboratories, and Healthcare Research Organizations. In *Applied Research Approaches to Technology, Healthcare, and Business* (pp. 1-12). IGI Global.

Idelhaj, A., Abou El Houda, Z., & Khoukhi, L. (2024). Foundations models in cybersecurity. *Artificial Intelligence for Blockchain and Cybersecurity Powered IoT Applications*, 1.

Iqbal, F., Debbabi, M., Fung, B. C., Iqbal, F., Debbabi, M., & Fung, B. C. (2020). Artificial intelligence and digital forensics. *Machine Learning for Authorship Attribution and Cyber Forensics*, 139-150.

Iqbal, S., & Alharbi, S. A. (2020). Advancing automation in digital forensic investigations using machine learning forensics. *Digital Forensic Science, 3*.

Irons, A., & Lallie, H. S. (2014). Digital forensics to intelligent forensics. *Future Internet*, *6*(3), 584–596. DOI: 10.3390/fi6030584

Iyengar, S. S., Nabavirazavi, S., & Hariprasad, Y. HB, P., & Mohan, C. K. (2025). Privacy-Preserving AI (Federated Learning) for Digital Forensics. In *Artificial Intelligence in Practice: Theory and Application for Cyber Security and Forensics* (pp. 161-176). Cham: Springer Nature Switzerland.

Jafarizadeh, H., Yamini, E., Zolfaghari, S. M., Esmaeilion, F., Assad, M. E. H., & Soltani, M. (2024). Navigating challenges in large-scale renewable energy storage: Barriers, solutions, and innovations. *Energy Reports*, *12*, 2179–2192. DOI: 10.1016/j.egyr.2024.08.019

Jamro, M. Y., & Jamro, F. A. (2023). AI Matters: Chatbot Integration in Holistic STEM Education.

Jarrett, A., & Choo, K. K. R. (2021). The impact of automation and artificial intelligence on digital forensics. *WIREs Forensic Science*, *3*(6), e1418. DOI: 10.1002/wfs2.1418

Jeong, D. (2020). Artificial intelligence security threat, crime, and forensics: Taxonomy and open issues. *IEEE Access : Practical Innovations, Open Solutions*, *8*, 184560–184574. DOI: 10.1109/ACCESS.2020.3029280

Jerhamre, E., Carlberg, C. J. C., & van Zoest, V. (2022). Exploring the susceptibility of smart farming: Identified opportunities and challenges. *Smart Agricultural Technology*, *2*, 2. DOI: 10.1016/j.atech.2021.100026

Jiang, L. (2024). Detecting scams using large language models. arXiv preprint arXiv:2402.03147.

Jin, J., Tang, B., Ma, M., Liu, X., Wang, Y., Lai, Q., . . . Zhou, C. (2024). Crimson: Empowering Strategic Reasoning in Cybersecurity through Large Language Models. arXiv preprint arXiv:2403.00878. DOI: 10.1109/ICCBD-AI65562.2024.00011

Jones, R., Omar, M., Mohammed, D., Nobles, C., & Dawson, M. (2023). Harnessing the Speed and Accuracy of Machine Learning to Advance Cybersecurity. In *2023 Congress in Computer Science, Computer Engineering, & Applied Computing (CSCE)* (pp. 418-421). IEEE. DOI: 10.1109/CSCE60160.2023.00074

Jones, R., & Omar, M. (2024). Revolutionizing Cybersecurity: The GPT-2 Enhanced Attack Detection and Defense (GEADD) Method for Zero-Day Threats. *International Journal of Informatics* [INJIISCOM]. *Information System and Computer Engineering*, *5*(2), 178–191.

Kanyepe, J., Chibaro, M., Morima, M., & Moeti-Lysson, J. (2025). AI-Powered Agricultural Supply Chains: Applications, Challenges, and Opportunities. *Integrating Agriculture, Green Marketing Strategies, and Artificial Intelligence*, 33-64.

Kapoor, P. (2025). Harvesting Ethics: Forging Responsible Paths in AI and ML for the Agri-Food Industry. In *Food and Industry 5.0: Transforming the Food System for a Sustainable Future* (pp. 305–315). Springer Nature Switzerland. DOI: 10.1007/978-3-031-76758-6_19

Karim, R., Galar, D., & Kumar, U. (2023). *AI factory: theories, applications and case studies*. CRC Press. DOI: 10.1201/9781003208686

Karthikeyan, P., Pande, H. M., & Sarveshwaran, V. (Eds.). (2023). *Artificial intelligence and blockchain in digital forensics*. CRC Press.

Kasri, W., Himeur, Y., Alkhazaleh, H. A., Tarapiah, S., Atalla, S., Mansoor, W., & Al-Ahmad, H. (2025). From Vulnerability to Defense: The Role of Large Language Models in Enhancing Cybersecurity. *Computation (Basel, Switzerland)*, *13*(2), 30. DOI: 10.3390/computation13020030

Kaur, R., Gabrijelčič, D., & Klobučar, T. (2023). Artificial intelligence for cybersecurity: Literature review and future research directions. *Information Fusion*, *97*, 101804. DOI: 10.1016/j.inffus.2023.101804

Kaushik, K., Khan, A., Kumari, A., Sharma, I., & Dubey, R. (2024). Ethical considerations in AI-based cybersecurity. In *Next-generation cybersecurity: AI, ML, and Blockchain* (pp. 437–470). Springer Nature Singapore. DOI: 10.1007/978-981-97-1249-6_19

Kelly, L., Sachan, S., Ni, L., Almaghrabi, F., Allmendinger, R., & Chen, Y. (2020). *Explainable artificial intelligence for digital forensics: opportunities, challenges and a drug testing case study*. Digital Forensic Science.

Kereopa-Yorke, B. (2024). Building resilient SMEs: Harnessing large language models for cyber security in Australia. Journal of AI. *Robotics & Workplace Automation, 3*(1), 15–27. DOI: 10.69554/XSQZ3232

Khan, A. A., Akbar, M. A., Ahmad, A., Fahmideh, M., Shameem, M., Lahtinen, V., . . . Mikkonen, T. (2023, July). Agile practices for quantum software development: practitioners' perspectives. In *2023 IEEE international conference on quantum software (QSW)* (pp. 9-20). IEEE.

Kochupillai, M., & Köninger, J. (2023). Creating a digital marketplace for agrobiodiversity and plant genetic sequence data: Legal and ethical considerations of an ai and blockchain based solution. *Towards Responsible Plant Data Linkage: Data Challenges for Agricultural Research and Development*, 223.

Kochupillai, M., Kahl, M., Schmitt, M., Taubenböck, H., & Zhu, X. X. (2022). Earth observation and artificial intelligence: Understanding emerging ethical issues and opportunities. *IEEE Geoscience and Remote Sensing Magazine, 10*(4), 90–124. DOI: 10.1109/MGRS.2022.3208357

Larson, D. B., Harvey, H., Rubin, D. L., Irani, N., Tse, J. R., & Langlotz, C. P. (2021). Regulatory frameworks for development and evaluation of artificial intelligence–based diagnostic imaging algorithms: Summary and recommendations. *Journal of the American College of Radiology, 18*(3), 413–424. DOI: 10.1016/j.jacr.2020.09.060 PMID: 33096088

Lee, S., Mujammami, A. A. H., & Kim, K. (2024). Leveraging Social Networks for Cyber Threat Intelligence: Analyzing Attack Trends and TTPs in the Arab World. *IEEE Access : Practical Innovations, Open Solutions.*

Leong, Y. M., Lim, E. H., Subri, N. F. B., & Jalil, N. B. A. (2023, September). Transforming agriculture: Navigating the challenges and embracing the opportunities of artificial intelligence of things. In *2023 IEEE International Conference on Agrosystem Engineering, Technology & Applications (AGRETA)* (pp. 142-147). IEEE. DOI: 10.1109/AGRETA57740.2023.10262747

Leontidis, G. (2024). Science in the age of ai: How artificial intelligence is changing the nature and method of scientific research.

Liu, Z. (2024, April). A review of advancements and applications of pre-trained language models in cybersecurity. In *2024 12th International Symposium on Digital Forensics and Security (ISDFS)* (pp. 1-10). IEEE. DOI: 10.1109/ISDFS60797.2024.10527236

Lougovski, P., Parekh, O., Broz, J., Byrd, M., Chembo, Y., de Jong, W. A., . . . Svore, K. M. (2023). *Position Papers for the ASCR Workshop on Basic Research Needs in Quantum Computing and Networking*. USDOE Office of Science (SC), Advanced Scientific Computing Research (ASCR).

Luan, H., Perron, B. E., Victor, B. G., Wan, G., Niu, Y., & Xiao, X. (2024). Using artificial intelligence to support scientometric analysis of scholarly literature: A case example of research on mainland China's left-behind children. *Journal of the Society for Social Work and Research, 15*(3), 435–457. DOI: 10.1086/731613

Maennig, W. (2014). Inefficiency of the anti-doping system: Cost reduction proposals. *Substance Use & Misuse, 49*(9), 1201–1205. DOI: 10.3109/10826084.2014.912065 PMID: 24832718

Maguluri, L. P., Arularasan, A. N., & Boopathi, S. (2023). Assessing security concerns for ai-based drones in smart cities. In *Effective AI, Blockchain, and E-Governance Applications for Knowledge Discovery and Management* (pp. 27-47). IGI Global Scientific Publishing. DOI: 10.4018/978-1-6684-9151-5.ch002

Malhotra, K., & Firdaus, M. (2022). Application of artificial intelligence in IoT security for crop yield prediction. *ResearchBerg Review of Science and Technology, 2*(1), 136–157.

Manasa, S., & Kumar, K. P. (2022). Digital forensics investigation for attacks on artificial intelligence. *ECS Transactions, 107*(1), 19639–19645. DOI: 10.1149/10701.19639ecst

Manganelli, A. G. (2019). Reverse payments and risk of bankruptcy under private information. *International Journal of the Economics of Business, 26*(3), 411–429. DOI: 10.1080/13571516.2019.1613146

Manoharan, A., & Sarker, M. (2023). Revolutionizing Cybersecurity: Unleashing the Power of Artificial Intelligence and Machine Learning for Next-Generation Threat Detection. *DOI:* https://www. doi. org/10.56726/IRJMETS32644, *1*.

Mark, R. (2019). Ethics of using AI and big data in agriculture: The case of a large agriculture multinational. *The ORBIT Journal, 2*(2), 1–27. DOI: 10.29297/orbit.v2i2.109

Marshall, J. (2023). What effects do large language models have on cybersecurity.

Matar, D. O. (2023). *Forensic accounting and Cybersecurity examine their interrelation in the detection and Prevention of financial fraud*. American Academic & Scholarly Research Journal.

Mazloum, H., Mazloum, N., & Saleh, A. M. (2025). FORENSIC AUDIT: ENHANCING CERTIFIED PUBLIC ACCOUNTANT USING ARTIFICIAL INTELLIGENCE TECHNIQUES. *BAU Journal-Science and Technology*, *6*(2), 10. DOI: 10.54729/2959-331X.1128

Mendsaikhan, O., Hasegawa, H., Yamaguchi, Y., & Shimada, H. (2019, July). Identification of cybersecurity specific content using the Doc2Vec language model. In 2019 IEEE 43rd annual computer software and applications conference (COMPSAC) (Vol. 1, pp. 396-401). IEEE. DOI: 10.1109/COMPSAC.2019.00064

Mennella, C., Maniscalco, U., De Pietro, G., & Esposito, M. (2024). Ethical and regulatory challenges of AI technologies in healthcare: A narrative review. *Heliyon*, *10*(4), e26297. DOI: 10.1016/j.heliyon.2024.e26297 PMID: 38384518

Metawei, M. A., Eldeeb, H., Nassar, S. M., & Taher, M. (2022). Quantum Computing Meets Artificial Intelligence: Innovations and Challenges. In *Handbook on Artificial Intelligence-Empowered Applied Software Engineering: VOL. 1: Novel Methodologies to Engineering Smart Software Systems* (pp. 303–338). Springer International Publishing. DOI: 10.1007/978-3-031-08202-3_12

Mhia-Alddin, D. A., & Hussein, A. M. (2025). AI-Powered Contract Security: Managing Expiry, Compliance, and Risk Mitigation Through Deep Learning and LLMs. In *Revolutionizing Cybersecurity With Deep Learning and Large Language Models* (pp. 37-64). IGI Global Scientific Publishing.

Mhia-Alddin, D. A., & Hussein, A. M. (2025). Contract Expiry in AI-Driven STM Research: Legal Challenges, Risks, and Regulatory Considerations. In *Ensuring Secure and Ethical STM Research in the AI Era* (pp. 77-110). IGI Global Scientific Publishing.

Mhia-Alddin, D. A. (2025). Legal Implications of Contract Expiry in Modern Commercial Law: Towards a Framework for Post-Expiry Obligations and Risk Management. In Zangana, H., Al-Karaki, J., & Omar, M. (Eds.), *Navigating Law and Policy in STM Enterprises: Ethical Governance, Regulation, and Innovation Strategy* (pp. 139–158). IGI Global Scientific Publishing., DOI: 10.4018/979-8-3373-4862-9.ch006

Mhia-alddin, D. A. (2026). Legal and Regulatory Frameworks for AI in Digital Forensics: Admissibility, Accountability, and Cross-Jurisdictional Challenges. In Zangana, H., & Omar, M. (Eds.), *AI in Digital Forensics and Cybercrime Investigation: Methods, Ethics, and Emerging Technologies* (pp. 31–66). IGI Global Scientific Publishing., DOI: 10.4018/979-8-3373-6536-7.ch002

Mitchell, F. R. (2014). An overview of artificial intelligence based pattern matching in a security and digital forensic context. *Cyberpatterns: Unifying Design Patterns with Security and Attack Patterns*, 215-222.

Mohamed, N., & Ahmed, A. A. (2024, June). AI in Combatting Man-in-the-Middle Attacks: A Comprehensive Review. In *2024 15th International Conference on Computing Communication and Networking Technologies (ICCCNT)* (pp. 1-6). IEEE. DOI: 10.1109/ICCCNT61001.2024.10725789

Mohammed, D., Omar, M., & Nguyen, V. (2018). Wireless sensor network security: Approaches to detecting and avoiding wormhole attacks. *Journal of Research in Business. Economics and Management*, *10*(2), 1860–1864.

Montasari, R. (2023). *Countering cyberterrorism: the confluence of artificial intelligence, cyber forensics and digital policing in US and UK national cybersecurity* (Vol. 101). Springer Nature. DOI: 10.1007/978-3-031-21920-7

Morić, Z., Dakić, V., & Urošev, S. (2025). An AI-Based Decision Support System Utilizing Bayesian Networks for Judicial Decision-Making. *Systems*, *13*(2), 131. DOI: 10.3390/systems13020131

Motlagh, F. N., Hajizadeh, M., Majd, M., Najafi, P., Cheng, F., & Meinel, C. (2024). Large language models in cybersecurity: State-of-the-art. *arXiv preprint arXiv:2402.00891.*

Motlagh, F. N., Hajizadeh, M., Majd, M., Najafi, P., Cheng, F., & Meinel, C. (2024). Large Language Models in Cybersecurity: State-of-the-Art. arXiv preprint arXiv:2402.00891.

Moustafa, N. (2022). *Digital Forensics in the Era of Artificial Intelligence.* CRC Press. DOI: 10.1201/9781003278962

Mubarrat, A. A. (2024). of the Research: Role of Artificial Intelligence and Big Data in Modern Forensic Accountancy. *Available at SSRN* 5078259.

Mughal, A. A. (2019). A comprehensive study of practical techniques and methodologies in incident-based approaches for cyber forensics. *Tensorgate Journal of Sustainable Technology and Infrastructure for Developing Countries*, *2*(1), 1–18.

Murphy, J. P. (2022). *Digital Forensic Investigations and Automated and Artificial Intelligence Technologies* (Master's thesis, Utica University).

Naili, Y. T., Mangkunegara, I. S., Purwono, P., & Baballe, M. A. (2025). Regulatory challenges in ai-based diagnostics: Legal implications of ai use in medical diagnostics. In *BIO Web of Conferences* (Vol. 152, p. 01034). EDP Sciences.

Nair, M. M., Deshmukh, A., & Tyagi, A. K. (2024). Artificial intelligence for cyber security: Current trends and future challenges. *Automated Secure Computing for Next-Generation Systems*, 83-114.

Narayana, S. A., Pati, R. K., & Padhi, S. S. (2019). Market dynamics and reverse logistics for sustainability in the Indian Pharmaceuticals industry. *Journal of Cleaner Production*, *208*, 968–987. DOI: 10.1016/j.jclepro.2018.10.171

Neupane, S., Mitra, S., Fernandez, I. A., Saha, S., Mittal, S., Chen, J., Pillai, N., & Rahimi, S. (2024). Security considerations in ai-robotics: A survey of current methods, challenges, and opportunities. *IEEE Access : Practical Innovations, Open Solutions*, *12*, 22072–22097. DOI: 10.1109/ACCESS.2024.3363657

Nguyen, V., Mohammed, D., Omar, M., & Banisakher, M. (2018). The Effects of the FCC Net Neutrality Repeal on Security and Privacy. [IJHIoT]. *International Journal of Hyperconnectivity and the Internet of Things*, *2*(2), 21–29. DOI: 10.4018/IJHIoT.2018070102

Oduro, P., Uzougbo, N. S., & Ugwu, M. C. (2024). Renewable energy expansion: Legal strategies for overcoming regulatory barriers and promoting innovation. *International Journal of Applied Research in Social Sciences*, *6*(5), 927–944. DOI: 10.51594/ijarss.v6i5.1145

Okonta, C. N., & Nnamdi, C. A. (2025). Forensic Investigation and Fraud Detection in Nigeria: Leveraging on Artificial Intelligence. *Review of Ethics in Sustainable Finance and Accounting*, *1*(1), 31–38. DOI: 10.70865/jiatis.v2i1.80

Omar, M. (2021). New insights into database security: An effective and integrated approach for applying access control mechanisms and cryptographic concepts in Microsoft Access environments.

Omar, M. (2022). *Machine Learning for Cybersecurity: Innovative Deep Learning Solutions*. Springer Brief. https://link.springer.com/book/978303115

Omar, M. (2024). From Attack to Defense: Strengthening DNN Text Classification Against Adversarial Examples. In *Innovations, Securities, and Case Studies Across Healthcare, Business, and Technology* (pp. 174-195). IGI Global.

Omar, M. (2024). Revolutionizing Malware Detection: A Paradigm Shift Through Optimized Convolutional Neural Networks. In *Innovations, Securities, and Case Studies Across Healthcare, Business, and Technology* (pp. 196-220). IGI Global. DOI: 10.4018/979-8-3693-1906-2.ch011

Omar, M., & Zangana, H. (Eds.). (2025). *Digital Forensics in the Age of AI*. IGI Global., DOI: 10.4018/979-8-3373-0857-9

Omar, M., & Zangana, H. M. (Eds.). (2024). *Redefining Security With Cyber AI*. IGI Global., DOI: 10.4018/979-8-3693-6517-5

Omar, M., & Zangana, H. M. (Eds.). (2025). *Application of Large Language Models (LLMs) for Software Vulnerability Detection*. IGI Global., DOI: 10.4018/979-8-3693-9311-6

Otieno, M. (2023). An extensive survey of smart agriculture technologies: Current security posture. *World J. Adv. Res. Rev*, *18*(3), 1207–1231. DOI: 10.30574/wjarr.2023.18.3.1241

Ozkan-Okay, M., Akin, E., Aslan, Ö., Kosunalp, S., Iliev, T., Stoyanov, I., & Beloev, I. (2024). A comprehensive survey: Evaluating the efficiency of artificial intelligence and machine learning techniques on cyber security solutions. *IEEE Access : Practical Innovations, Open Solutions*, *12*, 12229–12256. DOI: 10.1109/ACCESS.2024.3355547

Öztürk, M. S., & Usul, H. (2020). Detection of accounting frauds using the rule-based expert systems within the scope of forensic accounting. In *Contemporary issues in audit management and forensic accounting* (pp. 155–171). Emerald Publishing Limited. DOI: 10.1108/S1569-375920200000102013

Pai, Y. (2018). Patent Injunction Heuristics in India. *Pai, Yogesh, Patent Injunction Heuristics in India in Rafal Sikorski (Ed.) Patent Law Injunctions, Kluwer Law International BV (2019).*

Pandey, D. K., & Mishra, R. (2024). *Towards sustainable agriculture: Harnessing AI for global food security*. Artificial Intelligence in Agriculture.

Patra, S. P. (2025). Navigating the legal landscape of sustainable Industry 4.0. *Industry 4.0 for Manufacturing Systems: Concepts, Technologies, and Applications*, 109.

Pearce, H., Tan, B., Ahmad, B., Karri, R., & Dolan-Gavitt, B. (2023, May). Examining zero-shot vulnerability repair with large language models. In *2023 IEEE Symposium on Security and Privacy (SP)* (pp. 2339-2356). IEEE. DOI: 10.1109/SP46215.2023.10179420

Pedro, F., Subosa, M., Rivas, A., & Valverde, P. (2019). Artificial intelligence in education: Challenges and opportunities for sustainable development.

Perron, J. K., DeLeone, C., Sharif, S., Carter, T., Grossman, J. M., Passante, G., & Sack, J. (2021). Quantum undergraduate education and scientific training. *arXiv preprint arXiv:2109.13850*.

Pesapane, F., Bracchi, D. A., Mulligan, J. F., Linnikov, A., Maslennikov, O., Lanzavecchia, M. B., Tantrige, P., Stasolla, A., Biondetti, P., Giuggioli, P. F., Cassano, E., & Carrafiello, G. (2021). Legal and regulatory framework for AI solutions in healthcare in EU, US, China, and Russia: New scenarios after a pandemic. *Radiation*, *1*(4), 261–276. DOI: 10.3390/radiation1040022

Pesapane, F., Volonté, C., Codari, M., & Sardanelli, F. (2018). Artificial intelligence as a medical device in radiology: Ethical and regulatory issues in Europe and the United States. *Insights Into Imaging*, *9*(5), 745–753. DOI: 10.1007/s13244-018-0645-y PMID: 30112675

Pimpalkar, A. P., Wankhade, N. R., Chole, V., & Golhar, Y. (2024). Women's Empowerment Through AI: Discovering Data Analytics for Predictive Safety Solutions and Future Trends. In *AI Tools and Applications for Women's Safety* (pp. 304-326). IGI Global Scientific Publishing.

Piraianu, A. I., Fulga, A., Musat, C. L., Ciobotaru, O. R., Poalelungi, D. G., Stamate, E., Ciobotaru, O., & Fulga, I. (2023). Enhancing the evidence with algorithms: How artificial intelligence is transforming forensic medicine. *Diagnostics (Basel)*, *13*(18), 2992. DOI: 10.3390/diagnostics13182992

Pleshakova, E., Osipov, A., Gataullin, S., Gataullin, T., & Vasilakos, A. (2024). Next gen cybersecurity paradigm towards artificial general intelligence: Russian market challenges and future global technological trends. *Journal of Computer Virology and Hacking Techniques*, *20*(3), 429–440. DOI: 10.1007/s11416-024-00529-x

Qatawneh, A. M. (2025). The role of artificial intelligence in auditing and fraud detection in accounting information systems: Moderating role of natural language processing. *The International Journal of Organizational Analysis*, *33*(6), 1391–1409. DOI: 10.1108/IJOA-03-2024-4389

Rahul, R., Geetha, S., Priyatharsini, S., Mehata, K., Sundaresan Perumal, T., Ethiraj, N., & Sendilvelan, S. (2024). Cybersecurity Issues and Challenges in Quantum Computing. *Topics in Artificial Intelligence Applied to Industry*, *4*(0), 203–221. DOI: 10.1002/9781394216147.ch11

Rajendran, R. K., & Tulasi, B. (2025). Natural Language Processing (NLP) for Threat Intelligence. In *Analyzing Privacy and Security Difficulties in Social Media: New Challenges and Solutions* (pp. 247-262). IGI Global Scientific Publishing.

Ramachandran, D., Naqi, S. M., Perumal, G., & Abbas, Q. (2023). DLTN-LOSP: A Novel Deep-Linear-Transition-Network-Based Resource Allocation Model with the Logic Overhead Security Protocol for Cloud Systems. *Sensors (Basel)*, *23*(20), 8448. DOI: 10.3390/s23208448

Ramos, J. R. M. (2021). The use of Big Data and Artificial Intelligence: to prevent and detect fraud. *Artificial intelligence in the economic sector: prevention and responsibility*, 85-115.

Ranade, P., Piplai, A., Joshi, A., & Finin, T. (2021, December). Cybert: Contextualized embeddings for the cybersecurity domain. In 2021 IEEE International Conference on Big Data (Big Data) (pp. 3334-3342). IEEE.

Rashid, A. B., & Kausik, A. K. (2024). AI revolutionizing industries worldwide: A comprehensive overview of its diverse applications. *Hybrid Advances*, 100277.

Rawat, R., Oki, O., Chakrawarti, R. K., Adekunle, T. S., Lukose, J. M., & Ajagbe, S. A. (2023). Autonomous artificial intelligence systems for fraud detection and forensics in dark web environments. *Informatica (Vilnius)*, *47*(9).

Read, A., Botha, R., & Jamaloodien, K. (2023). COVID-19 vaccination procurement and contract management in a South African context. *Journal of Strategic Contracting and Negotiation*, *7*(1-2), 33–43. DOI: 10.1177/20555636231198053

Rizvi, S., Scanlon, M., Mcgibney, J., & Sheppard, J. (2022). Application of artificial intelligence to network forensics: Survey, challenges and future directions. *IEEE Access : Practical Innovations, Open Solutions*, *10*, 110362–110384. DOI: 10.1109/ACCESS.2022.3214506

Rodriguez, M. Y., & Storer, H. (2020). A computational social science perspective on qualitative data exploration: Using topic models for the descriptive analysis of social media data. *Journal of Technology in Human Services*, *38*(1), 54–86. DOI: 10.1080/15228835.2019.1616350

Rughani, P. H. (2017). Artificial Intelligence Based Digital Forensics Framework. *International Journal of Advanced Research in Computer Science*, *8*(8), 10–14. DOI: 10.26483/ijarcs.v8i8.4571

Saikia, B. (2024). Ecologically-Informed approaches: International mechanisms for navigating environmental challenges and ensuring sustainability in the oil and gas exploration and production industry. *Proceedings of the International Academy of Ecology and Environmental Sciences*, *14*(2), 60.

Sakapaji, S. C., García Molinos, J., Parilova, V., Gavrilyeva, T., & Yakovleva, N. (2024). Navigating legal and regulatory frameworks to achieve the resilience and sustainability of indigenous socioecological systems. *Resources*, *13*(4), 56. DOI: 10.3390/resources13040056

Samtani, S., Kantarcioglu, M., & Chen, H. (2020). Trailblazing the artificial intelligence for cybersecurity discipline: A multi-disciplinary research roadmap. [TMIS]. *ACM Transactions on Management Information Systems*, *11*(4), 1–19. DOI: 10.1145/3430360

San Biagio, M., Cipolla, M., La Mattina, E., & Morreale, V. (2023, December). A Topic Clustering Method to Identify Online Threats against Soft Targets. In *2023 International Conference on Computational Science and Computational Intelligence (CSCI)* (pp. 727-733). IEEE. DOI: 10.1109/CSCI62032.2023.00124

Sangher, K. S., Singh, A., & Pandey, H. M. (2024). LSTM and BERT based transformers models for cyber threat intelligence for intent identification of social media platforms exploitation from darknet forums. *International Journal of Information Technology : an Official Journal of Bharati Vidyapeeth's Institute of Computer Applications and Management*, *16*(8), 5277–5292. DOI: 10.1007/s41870-024-02077-5

Sangher, K. S., Singh, A., Pandey, H. M., & Kumar, V. (2023). Towards safe cyber practices: Developing a proactive cyber-threat intelligence system for dark web forum content by identifying cybercrimes. *Information (Basel)*, *14*(6), 349. DOI: 10.3390/info14060349

Santos, O., Salam, S., & Dahir, H. (2024). The AI revolution in networking, cybersecurity, and emerging technologies.

Sarker, I. H. (2024). Generative AI and large language modeling in cybersecurity. In *AI-Driven Cybersecurity and Threat Intelligence: Cyber Automation, Intelligent Decision-Making and Explainability* (pp. 79–99). Springer Nature Switzerland. DOI: 10.1007/978-3-031-54497-2_5

Schünemann, C., Johanning, S., Reger, E., Herold, H., & Bruckner, T. (2024). Complex system policy modelling approaches for policy advice–comparing systems thinking, system dynamics and agent-based modelling. *Political Research Exchange : an ECPR Journal*, *6*(1), 2387438. DOI: 10.1080/2474736X.2024.2387438

Senoo, E. E. K., Anggraini, L., Kumi, J. A., Luna, B. K., Akansah, E., Sulyman, H. A., & Aritsugi, M. (2024). IoT solutions with artificial intelligence technologies for precision agriculture: Definitions, applications, challenges, and opportunities. *Electronics (Basel)*, *13*(10), 1894. DOI: 10.3390/electronics13101894

Seskir, Z. C. (2019). *Current state of quantum information technologies in Turkey* (Master's thesis, Middle East Technical University).

Shafik, W. (2024). Data privacy and security safeguarding customer information in ChatGPT systems. In *Revolutionizing the Service Industry Wth OpenAI Models* (pp. 52–86). IGI Global. DOI: 10.4018/979-8-3693-1239-1.ch003

Shafik, W., Tufail, A., De Silva, C. L., Haji, R. A. A., & Apong, M. (2025). The Role, Application, and Impact of Artificial Intelligence in the Agriculture Industry. In *Future Tech Startups and Innovation in the Age of AI* (pp. 36–60). CRC Press.

Sheliemina, N. (2024). The use of artificial intelligence in medical diagnostics: Opportunities, prospects and risks. *Health Economics and Management Review*, *5*(2), 104–124. DOI: 10.61093/hem.2024.2-07

Shukla, R. P., & Taneja, S. (2024). Ethical considerations and data privacy in artificial intelligence. In *Integrating generative AI in education to achieve sustainable development goals* (pp. 86–97). IGI Global. DOI: 10.4018/979-8-3693-2440-0.ch005

Siddiqui, T., Amer, A. Y. A., & Khan, N. A. (2019, November). Criminal activity detection in social network by text mining: comprehensive analysis. In *2019 4th International Conference on Information Systems and Computer Networks (ISCON)* (pp. 224-229). IEEE. DOI: 10.1109/ISCON47742.2019.9036157

Sikos, L. F. (2021). AI in digital forensics: Ontology engineering for cybercrime investigations. *WIREs Forensic Science*, *3*(3), e1394. DOI: 10.1002/wfs2.1394

Simbolon, R., Adriana, N., Rustam, A., Sulistyowati, N. W., & Rewa, K. A. (2024). The Impact of Forensic Accounting on Financial Fraud Prevention: A Comparative Analysis Across Countries. *The Journal of Academic Science*, *1*(8), 1074–1084. DOI: 10.59613/m6jrt421

Singh, B., & Kaunert, C. (2025). Navigating the Terrain of Sustainability Trajectories of Environment: Biodiversity Protection and Legal Landscapes. In *Community Resilience and Climate Change Challenges: Pursuit of Sustainable Development Goals (SDGs)* (pp. 355-374). IGI Global Scientific Publishing.

Sodiya, E. O., Umoga, U. J., Amoo, O. O., & Atadoga, A. (2024). Quantum computing and its potential impact on US cybersecurity: A review: Scrutinizing the challenges and opportunities presented by quantum technologies in safeguarding digital assets. *Global Journal of Engineering and Technology Advances, 18*(2), 049-064.

Sood, A., Sharma, R. K., & Bhardwaj, A. K. (2022). Artificial intelligence research in agriculture: A review. *Online Information Review, 46*(6), 1054–1075. DOI: 10.1108/OIR-10-2020-0448

Soomro, J. A., Suhrab, M., & Abbasi, B. A. (2025). Navigating Green Regulations in the Business Ecosystem: Government Support, Compliance, and Obstacles in the Context of Pakistan. In *Government Influences on Eco-Friendly Practices in Business* (pp. 55-86). IGI Global.

Sparrow, R., & Howard, M. (2021). Robots in agriculture: prospects, impacts, ethics, and policy. *precision agriculture, 22*, 818-833.

Sparrow, R., Howard, M., & Degeling, C. (2021). Managing the risks of artificial intelligence in agriculture. *NJAS: Impact in Agricultural and Life Sciences, 93*(1), 172–196. DOI: 10.1080/27685241.2021.2008777

Stutz, D., de Assis, J. T., Laghari, A. A., Khan, A. A., Andreopoulos, N., Terziev, A., ... & Grata, E. G. (2024). Enhancing Security in Cloud Computing Using Artificial Intelligence (AI). *Applying Artificial Intelligence in Cybersecurity Analytics and Cyber Threat Detection*, 179-220.

Sufi, F. (2023). Novel application of open-source cyber intelligence. *Electronics (Basel), 12*(17), 3610. DOI: 10.3390/electronics12173610

Sufi, F. (2023). Social media analytics on Russia–Ukraine cyber war with natural language processing: Perspectives and challenges. *Information (Basel), 14*(9), 485. DOI: 10.3390/info14090485

Sultana, M., Taylor, A., Li, L., & Majumdar, S. (2023, October). Towards Evaluation and Understanding of Large Language Models for Cyber Operation Automation. In *2023 IEEE Conference on Communications and Network Security (CNS)* (pp. 1-6). IEEE. DOI: 10.1109/CNS59707.2023.10288677

Sun, N., Ding, M., Jiang, J., Xu, W., Mo, X., Tai, Y., & Zhang, J. (2023). Cyber threat intelligence mining for proactive cybersecurity defense: A survey and new perspectives. *IEEE Communications Surveys and Tutorials, 25*(3), 1748–1774. DOI: 10.1109/COMST.2023.3273282

Syed, F. M., & ES, F. K. (2024). AI-Driven Forensic Analysis for Cyber Incidents in Healthcare. *International Journal of Machine Learning Research in Cybersecurity and Artificial Intelligence*, *15*(1), 473–499.

Taghavi, S. M., & Feyzi, F. (2024). Using large language models to better detect and handle software vulnerabilities and cyber security threats.

Tann, W., Liu, Y., Sim, J. H., Seah, C. M., & Chang, E. C. (2023). Using large language models for cybersecurity capture-the-flag challenges and certification questions. arXiv preprint arXiv:2308.10443.

Tao, F., Akhtar, M. S., & Jiayuan, Z. (2021). The future of artificial intelligence in cybersecurity: A comprehensive survey. *EAI Endorsed Transactions on Creative Technologies*, *8*(28), e3–e3. DOI: 10.4108/eai.7-7-2021.170285

Terry, N. (2019). Of regulating healthcare AI and robots. *Yale JL & Tech.*, *21*, 133.

THANDI, N. S. (2024). Revolutionizing Cyber Threat Detection With Large Language Models: A Privacy-Preserving BERT-Based Lightweight Model for IoT/IIoT Devices.

Tihanyi, N., Ferrag, M. A., Jain, R., & Debbah, M. (2024). CyberMetric: A Benchmark Dataset for Evaluating Large Language Models Knowledge in Cybersecurity. arXiv preprint arXiv:2402.07688.

Trotsyuk, A. A., Waeiss, Q., Bhatia, R. T., Aponte, B. J., Heffernan, I. M., Madgavkar, D., Felder, R. M., Lehmann, L. S., Palmer, M. J., Greely, H., Wald, R., Goetz, L., Trengove, M., Vandersluis, R., Lin, H., Cho, M. K., Altman, R. B., Endy, D., Relman, D. A., & Magnus, D. (2024). Toward a framework for risk mitigation of potential misuse of artificial intelligence in biomedical research. *Nature Machine Intelligence*, *6*(12), 1–8. DOI: 10.1038/s42256-024-00926-3 PMID: 40994707

Tuli, F. A., & Thaduri, U. R. (2023). The Integration of Artificial Intelligence in Forensic Accounting: A Game-Changer. *Asian Accounting and Auditing Advancement*, *14*(1), 12–20.

Tyagi, A. K., Kumari, S., & Richa. (2024). Artificial Intelligence-Based Cyber Security and Digital Forensics: A Review. *Artificial Intelligence-Enabled Digital Twin for Smart Manufacturing*, 391-419.

Tzachor, A., Devare, M., King, B., Avin, S., & Ó hÉigeartaigh, S. (2022). Responsible artificial intelligence in agriculture requires systemic understanding of risks and externalities. *Nature Machine Intelligence*, *4*(2), 104–109. DOI: 10.1038/s42256-022-00440-4

Uduehe, E. M., Okoye, E. I., & Amahalu, N. N. (2024). Forensic accounting techniques and fraud management of commercial banks in Awka-South Anambra State. *Journal of Global Accounting, 10*(2), 307–346.

Ukwen, D. O., & Karabatak, M. (2021, June). Review of NLP-based systems in digital forensics and cybersecurity. In *2021 9th International symposium on digital forensics and security (ISDFS)* (pp. 1-9). IEEE. DOI: 10.1109/ISDFS52919.2021.9486354

Uplaonkar, S. S., Veershetty, R., Bahar, Z., & Sangeeta, G. (2024). The role of productive AI: A supporter or challenger in the future of agricultural librarianship. *IJAR, 10*(4), 46–53.

Veluru, C. S. (2024). Responsible Artificial Intelligence on Large Scale Data to Prevent Misuse, Unethical Challenges and Security Breaches. *Journal of Artificial Intelligence & Cloud Computing. SRC/JAICC-349. DOI: doi. org/(3), 331*, 2-6.DOI: 10.47363/JAICC/2024

Verma, A., Rao, K., Eluri, V., & Sharma, Y. (2020). Regulating AI in public health: systems challenges and perspectives. *ORF Occasional Paper, 261.*

Verma, M., & Rohit, K. (2024). Ethical AI Shaping Scholarly Communication: Challenges and Opportunities.

Vijayalakshmi, D., & Jeevan, J. (2024). Forensic Accounting: Uncovering Fraud with Advanced Analytics. *Library of Progress-Library Science, Information Technology & Computer, 44*(3).

Vladescu, C., Dinisor, M. A., Grigorescu, O., Corlatescu, D., Sandescu, C., & Dascalu, M. (2021, December). What are the latest cybersecurity trends? a case study grounded in language models. In 2021 23rd International Symposium on Symbolic and Numeric Algorithms for Scientific Computing (SYNASC) (pp. 140-146). IEEE.

Vyawahare, H., Khandelwal, S., & Rathod, S. (2024). Artificial Intelligence in Detecting and Preventing Online Harassment. In *AI Tools and Applications for Women's Safety* (pp. 14–35). IGI Global Scientific Publishing. DOI: 10.4018/979-8-3693-1435-7.ch002

Wang, F. (2023). Using large language models to mitigate ransomware threats.

Wang, Q. (2024). Maritime law enforcement concerning offshore energy platforms: Navigating international law constraints and challenges. *Marine Policy, 170*, 106370. DOI: 10.1016/j.marpol.2024.106370

Wei, H., Xu, W., Kang, B., Eisner, R., Muleke, A., Rodriguez, D., deVoil, P., Sadras, V., Monjardino, M., & Harrison, M. T. (2024). Irrigation with artificial intelligence: Problems, premises, promises. *Human-Centric Intelligent Systems*, *4*(2), 187–205. DOI: 10.1007/s44230-024-00072-4

Williamson, H. F., Brettschneider, J., Caccamo, M., Davey, R. P., Goble, C., Kersey, P. J., May, S., Morris, R. J., Ostler, R., Pridmore, T., Rawlings, C., Studholme, D., Tsaftaris, S. A., & Leonelli, S. (2023). Data management challenges for artificial intelligence in plant and agricultural research. *F1000 Research*, *10*, 324. DOI: 10.12688/f1000research.52204.2

Wright, J., Dawson, M. E.Jr, & Omar, M. (2012). Cyber security and mobile threats: The need for antivirus applications for smartphones. *Journal of Information Systems Technology and Planning*, *5*(14), 40–60.

Xu, H., Wang, S., Li, N., Wang, K., Zhao, Y., Chen, K., . . . Wang, H. (2024). Large language models for cyber security: A systematic literature review. *arXiv preprint arXiv:2405.04760*.

Xu, J., Stokes, J. W., McDonald, G., Bai, X., Marshall, D., Wang, S., . . . Li, Z. (2024). AutoAttacker: A Large Language Model Guided System to Implement Automatic Cyber-attacks. arXiv preprint arXiv:2403.01038.

Ya'u, M. S., & Mohammed, M. S. (2025). AI-Assisted Writing and Academic Literacy: Investigating the Dual Impact of Language Models on Writing Proficiency and Ethical Concerns in Nigerian Higher Education. *International Journal of Education and Literacy Studies*, *13*(2), 593–604. DOI: 10.7575/aiac.ijels.v.13n.2p.593

Yang, H., Xiang, K., Ge, M., Li, H., Lu, R., & Yu, S. (2024). A comprehensive overview of backdoor attacks in large language models within communication networks. *IEEE Network*, *38*(6), 211–218. DOI: 10.1109/MNET.2024.3367788

Yao, Y., Duan, J., Xu, K., Cai, Y., Sun, Z., & Zhang, Y. (2024). A survey on large language model (llm) security and privacy: The good, the bad, and the ugly. *High-Confidence Computing*, *4*(2), 100211. DOI: 10.1016/j.hcc.2024.100211

Yu, J., Shvetsov, A. V., & Alsamhi, S. H. (2024). Leveraging machine learning for cybersecurity resilience in industry 4.0: Challenges and future directions. *IEEE Access : Practical Innovations, Open Solutions*, *12*, 159579–159596. DOI: 10.1109/ACCESS.2024.3482987

Zangana, H. M. (2024). Exploring Blockchain-Based Timestamping Tools: A Comprehensive Review. *Redefining Security With Cyber AI*, 92-110.

Zangana, H. M. (2024). Exploring the Landscape of Website Vulnerability Scanners: A Comprehensive Review and Comparative Analysis. *Redefining Security With Cyber AI*, 111-129.

Zangana, H. M., Omar, M., Al-Karaki, J. N., & Mohammed, D. (2024). Comprehensive Review and Analysis of Network Firewall Rule Analyzers: Enhancing Security Posture and Efficiency. *Redefining Security With Cyber AI*, 15-36.

Zangana, H. (2025). Blockchain Technology in AI-Driven Cybersecurity: Strengthening Trust in Financial and Digital Security Systems. *Jurnal Ilmiah Computer Science*, *4*(1), 49–49. DOI: 10.58602/jics.v4i1.54

Zangana, H. M., Mohammed, A. K., Sallow, A. B., & Sallow, Z. B. (2024). Cybernetic Deception: Unraveling the Layers of Email Phishing Threats. [INJURATECH]. *International Journal of Research and Applied Technology*, *4*(1), 35–47.

Zangana, H. M., Mohammed, H. S., & Husain, M. M. (2025). Addressing insider threats: The human factor in cybersecurity for financial institutions. *Journal of Innovation Information Technology and Application*, *7*(1), 88–96. DOI: 10.35970/jinita.v7i1.2686

Zangana, H. M., & Mustafa, F. M. (2026). Enhancing Educational Visual Content Through AI-Based Image Denoising Techniques: Implications for Remote Teaching and Digital Resource Development. In Zangana, H., Nobles, C., & Omar, M. (Eds.), *Harnessing AI for Teacher Support and Professional Development* (pp. 101–136). IGI Global Scientific Publishing., DOI: 10.4018/979-8-3373-5951-9.ch004

Zangana, H. M., & Omar, M. (2020). Threats, Attacks, and Mitigations of Smartphone Security. *Academic Journal of Nawroz University*, *9*(4), 324–332. DOI: 10.25007/ajnu.v9n4a989

Zangana, H., Al-Karaki, J., & Omar, M. (Eds.). (2025). *Revolutionizing Cybersecurity With Deep Learning and Large Language Models*. IGI Global., DOI: 10.4018/979-8-3373-3296-3

Zangana, H., Mohammed, H. S., & Husain, M. M. (2025). Transforming Cybersecurity Practices: A Comprehensive Approach to Protecting Digital Banking Assets. *Jurnal Ilmiah Computer Science*, *4*(1), 1–9. DOI: 10.58602/jics.v4i1.51

Zangana, H., & Omar, M. (Eds.). (2025). *Ensuring Secure and Ethical STM Research in the AI Era*. IGI Global., DOI: 10.4018/979-8-3373-4252-8

Zangana, H., & Omar, M. (Eds.). (2025). *Leveraging Large Language Models for Quantum-Aware Cybersecurity*. IGI Global., DOI: 10.4018/979-8-3373-1102-9

Zangana, H., & Yazdeen, A. (2025). A Federated Architecture for Enhancing Security and Scalability in IoT-Cloud Integrated Systems. *Jurnal Ilmiah Computer Science, 4*(1), 50–59. DOI: 10.58602/jics.v4i1.55

Zayed, L. M. M., Nour, M. I., Al Attar, K., Almubaideen, H., & Abdelaziz, G. A. M. (2024). Role of artificial intelligence (AI) in accounting information systems in detecting fraud. In *Artificial Intelligence and Economic Sustainability in the Era of Industrial Revolution 5.0* (pp. 397–409). Springer Nature Switzerland. DOI: 10.1007/978-3-031-56586-1_30

Zeadally, S., Adi, E., Baig, Z., & Khan, I. A. (2020). Harnessing artificial intelligence capabilities to improve cybersecurity. *IEEE Access : Practical Innovations, Open Solutions, 8*, 23817–23837. DOI: 10.1109/ACCESS.2020.2968045

Zheng, W., Tan, Y., Jiang, B., & Wang, J. (2025). Integrating Machine Learning into Financial Forensics for Smarter Fraud Prevention. *Technology and Investment, 16*(3), 79–90. DOI: 10.4236/ti.2025.163006

Zohouri, M., Sabzali, M., & Golmohammadi, A. (2024). Ethical considerations of ChatGPT-assisted article writing. *Synesis (ISSN 1984-6754), 16*(1), 94-113.

Zreik, M. (2024). Harnessing AI for entrepreneurial idea generation: Navigating the new frontier. In *Generating Entrepreneurial Ideas With AI* (pp. 1–18). IGI Global Scientific Publishing. DOI: 10.4018/979-8-3693-3498-0.ch001

About the Contributors

Hewa Majeed Zangana is an Assistant Professor at Duhok Polytechnic University (DPU), Iraq, and a current PhD candidate in Information Technology Management. He has over 15 years of academic and administrative experience, serving in key roles such as Acting Dean of the College of Computer and IT at Nawroz University, Head of the Computer Science Department, Director of the Curriculum Division at DPU, and Manager of the Information Unit at DPU's Research Center. His research expertise spans network systems, cybersecurity, computer vision, intelligent systems, and Information Technology, with a strong focus on integrating classical methods and advanced AI-driven approaches. Dr. Zangana has authored and co-authored numerous peer-reviewed journal articles, conference papers, and more than ten academic books with IGI Global, several indexed in Scopus and Web of Science (Clarivate). His works appear in respected outlets such as IEEE, EAI Endorsed Transactions on AI and Robotics, Sistemasi, BAMJ, and others. In addition to his prolific research output, he actively contributes to the academic community as a reviewer, editorial board member, and scientific committee member. He currently serves on the Editorial Board of EAI Endorsed Transactions on AI and Robotics (Scopus Q2), alongside roles with other international journals and organizations. Dr. Zangana is also an active member of several professional associations, including the European Alliance for Innovation (EAI), International Association of Engineers (IAENG), and the Computer Science Teachers Association (CSTA). Fluent in Kurdish, Arabic, and English, Dr. Zangana continues to contribute to advancing knowledge in AI, cybersecurity, and IT management, while mentoring future generations of scholars and practitioners in Iraq and beyond.

***

Luay Albtosh is a dedicated and accomplished professional currently pursuing a Ph.D. in Cyber Leadership. With a robust academic background and over a decade of industry experience, Luay Albtosh has established a strong foothold in the field of computer science. Luay Albtosh holds a master's degree in computer science, which laid the groundwork for a career marked by continuous learning and impactful contributions to the field. Throughout the years, Luay Albtosh has developed a profound expertise in various aspects of computer science, including cybersecurity, software development, and IT project management. In addition to academic achievements, Luay Albtosh has consistently demonstrated a commitment to excellence in professional endeavors. With more than 10 years of hands-on experience, Luay Albtosh has successfully led numerous projects, drove innovation and ensuring the seamless integration of technology solutions. This extensive experience has provided Luay Albtosh with a deep understanding of both the technical and strategic facets of the industry.

Widi Aribowo as an Assistant Professor in the Department of Electrical Engineering at the Faculty of Vocational Studies, Universitas Negeri Surabaya. Known as a leading researcher, he has made significant contributions in the fields of metaheuristics, optimization, artificial intelligence, power systems and Microgrid. His scientific impact is evident through various publications in leading journals. In addition, Widi Aribowo has demonstrated his expertise as a peer reviewer for several prestigious Q1 journals, demonstrating his commitment to advancing academic discourse in the fields of metaheuristics, optimization, artificial intelligence, power systems and Microgrid.

Sachi Nandan Mohanty, received his Postdoc from IIT Kanpur in the year 2019 and Ph.D. from IIT Kharagpur in the year 2015, with MHRD scholarship from Govt of India. He is currently working as an Associate Professor in the Department of Computer Science & Engineering at ICFAI Foundation for Higher Education Hyderabad. Prof. Mohanty research areas include Data mining, Big Data Analysis, Cognitive Science, Emotional Intellegnce, Fuzzy Decision Making, Brain-Computer Interface, and Computational Intelligence. Prof. S N Mohanty has received 3 Best Paper Awards during his Ph.D at IIT Kharagpur from International Conference at Benjing, China, and the other at International Conference on Soft Computing Applications organized by IIT Rookee in the year 2013. He has published 20 SCI Journals. As a Fellow on Indian Society Technical Education (ISTE), The Institute of Engineering and Technology (IET), Computer Society of India (CSI), Senior Member of Institute of Engineers and IEEE Computer Society, he is actively involved in the activities of the Professional Bodies/Societies.

Firas Mahmood Mustafa holds a Ph.D. in Computer Engineering from Mosul University, Iraq. His academic journey began with a B.Sc. in Electrical Engineering

(Electronics and Communication), graduating in the top quarter of his class. He earned an M.Sc. in Computer Engineering from Mosul University in 2000. Mustafa joined the Computer Science Department at AlHadba University in 2003 and completed his Ph.D. in 2007. From 2013 to 2017, he was with DPU University, and from 2017 to 2020, he chaired the CCE Department at Nawroz University. An active participant in Erasmus+ and IREX programs, he now teaches at DPU University, shaping future computer engineering professionals.

Sharyar Wani completed his Doctorate in Computer Science in 2016 from International Islamic University Malaysia. Following his Post-Doctorate from 2016 – 2017 at the Centre of Cyber Security, National Defence University Malaysia, he was appointed as a Senior Lecturer by the university. Currently, he is an assistant professor at the Department of Computer Science, Kulliyyah of Information & Communication Technology, International Islamic University Malaysia. He is also a fellow in the Computational Intelligence research group and Centre for Cyber Security. His interest interests mainly include artificial intelligence, machine learning, information retrieval, knowledge engineering, data analytics, natural language processing and cybersecurity. He is a lead researcher for several government-funded research projects and serves as a reviewer for multiple international journals. Besides the recent academic appointments, he has several years of industrial experience and has taught in several other universities and institutions in other countries.

Index

A

B

C

D

E

F

I

L

www.ingramcontent.com/pod-product-compliance
Lightning Source LLC
LaVergne TN
LVHW081530300926
849161LV00006B/1368